" No woman of any rank whatsoever is permitted to go in the street without two muslims, one that covers her face all but her eyes and another that hides the whole dress of her head and hangs half way down her back; and their shapes are wholly conceal'd by a thing they call a *Feridge*, which no woman of any sort appears without."

Lady Mary Wortley-Montagu

The thermal baths of Eski Kaplica in Bursa, at the base of the hill of Çerkige, are the oldest baths ever built by the Ottomans in their first capital: "copied from the Thermæ of Diocletian in Rome, although very much smaller" (Penzer, 1540).

The Orthodox Church opened special schools and seminaries for Bulgarian children in Adrianople (Edirne).

These photographs were taken in Istanbul by the photographers Sebah and Joaillier. Their compositions reflect an idealistic vision of the Orient as seen by travelers, orientalist painters and writers. They show tzigane musicians, bashibazouks and a woman with a narghile.

The rococo palace of Küçüksu on the
shores of the Bosphorus was built in
1856–7 by the architect Nikoğos Balyan for
the sultan Abdül Mecit I.

NUMEROUS SPECIALISTS AND ACADEMICS HAVE CONTRIBUTED
TO THIS GUIDE. SPECIAL THANKS TO DEMIR ONGER, PRESIDENT OF THE
CULTURAL CENTER OF ANATOLIA

CONTRIBUTORS
Abidine, Zeynep Avçi, Christophe Bardèche, Murat Belge,
Jean-François Binet, Norbert Boussot, François Brosse,
Augusto Romano Burelli, Henri Daumas, Gérard Degeorges,
Guzine Dino, John Freely, Altan Gokalp, Pierre-Xavier Grézaud,
Ara Güler, Catherine Laussucq, Sophie Lavaux, Marc-Henri Lebrun,
Gérard Georges Lemaire, W.D. Nesteroff, Mme Onger,
Hâluk Özözlü, Edouard de Pazzis, Ersu Pekin,
Jean-François Péneau, Nathalie Phan, Philippe Pradel,
Guido Rossi, Meltem Savçi, Ugur Tanyelli, Arthur Thévenart,
Samuel Tranlé, Stéphane Yérasimos.

WE WOULD ALSO LIKE TO THANK
Pierre de Gigord and Godfrey Goodwin.

PRACTICAL INFORMATION TRANSLATED BY JOHN FERGUSSON.
EDITED AND TYPESET BY BOOK CREATION SERVICES, LONDON.
PRINTED IN ITALY BY EDITORIALE LIBRARIA.

EVERYMAN GUIDES
PUBLISHED BY DAVID CAMPBELL PUBLISHERS LTD, LONDON

© *1993 David Campbell Publishers Ltd*

© *Editions Nouveaux-Loisirs, a subsidiary of Gallimard, Paris*

Endpapers cartography © 1992 Touring Club Italiano, Milan

ISBN 1 85715 815 6

ISTANBUL
AND NORTHWEST
TURKEY

EVERYMAN GUIDES

CONTENTS

EDIRNE

GELIBOLU

ÇANAKKALE

DARDANELLES

AEGEAN SEA

IZMIR

(MILES)	ISTANBUL	EDIRNE	IZNIK	BURSA
ISTANBUL				
EDIRNE	372			
IZNIK	304	676		
BURSA	373	745	114	
ÇANAKKALE	549	367	557	443

BLACK SEA

BOSPHORUS

ISTANBUL

SEA OF MARMARA

IZNIK

BURSA

LAKE MANYAS

ULU DAĞ

How to Use this Guide

The symbols at the top of each page refer to the different parts of the guide.

■ NATURAL ENVIRONMENT

● UNDERSTANDING VENICE

▲ ITINERARIES

◆ PRACTICAL INFORMATION

The itinerary map shows the main points of interest along the way and is intended to help you find your bearings.

The mini-map locates the particu[...] itinerary within the wider area covered by the guide.

★ The star symbol signifies that a particular site has been singled out by the publishers for its special beauty, atmosphere or cultural interest.

● ▲ ■ ◆
The symbols alongside a title or within the text itself provide cross-references to a theme or place dealt with elsewhere in the guide.

At the beginning of each itinerary, the suggested means of transport to be used and the time it will take to cover the area are indicated:

🚢 By boat
🚶 On foot
🚴 By bicycle
🕐 Duration

THE GATEWAY TO VENICE ★

PONTE DELLA LIBERTA. Built by the Austrians 50 years after the Treaty of Campo Formio in 1797 ● 34, to link Venice with Milan. The bridge ended the thousand-year separation from the mainland and shook the city's economy to its roots as Venice, already in the throes of the industrial revolution, saw

🚶 Half a day

BRIDGES TO VENICE

NATURE

Mining Research
and Exploitation
Institute of Turkey.

Anatolia, or Asian Turkey, is composed of a central plateau with an average height of 2,900 ft, bordered by the Pontides and Taurus mountain ranges which reach an altitude of 10,000 ft. This plateau slopes gently from the eastern mountain ranges to the Aegean Sea in the west. Three hundred million years ago the area that is present-day Turkey was part of the supercontinent of Gondwana, which was bordered to the north by the paleo-Tethysian sea, which separated it from the Eurasian continent. Throughout the following ages this area experienced a series of tectonic upheavals, causing the Tethys sea to split and fill with sediments. When it closed up it was squeezed between the two continental blocks, which forced all of its rock formations (sediments, oceanic crust, ophiolites) to the surface. In the early Miocene period (23 million years), Anatolia was a compact continental block situated between the Black Sea and the eastern Mediterranean, and subjected to pressure from the surrounding plates.

Quaternary	Paleogezoic	Triassic	Paleozoic
Neogene	Mesozoic	Mesozoic-Paleozoic	

Anatolia and the Aegean Sea are caught in a vice between the African-Arabian plate, which is moving north, and the Eurasian fixed plate. To the west the collision is absorbed by the plunging of the northern border of the African plate beneath an Aegean Crete-Cyprus arc. This subduction transformed the Aegean Sea into a zone of expansion.

North Anatolian Fault   East Anatolian Fault

Arabian Plate

African Plate

SHALE AND LIMESTONE ROCKS

The shores of the Bosphorus are lined predominantly with shale and limestone, as well as platy limestone (**6**) (**7**) from the Devonian era (410 to 360 million years). Granitic batholiths reach the surface in massifs like the Ulu Dağ near Bursa. Fractures in the granite (**9**) sometimes reveal dendrites (**10**). More recent rocks like clay, marl, sandstone, sand, and volcanic tuffs now fill the ancient sedimentary basins.

PETROGRAPHY

A wide variety of petrographic rocks exist. The ophiolithic series are made up of fragments of ancient oceanic crusts (ophioliths), raised during the paleo-Tethys and neo-Tethys eras. These rocks form the mountains bordering the Anatolian plateau: the Taurus mountains to the south and the Pontides to the north. In cross-section, it is also possible to observe the oceanic crust from the base towards the surface: peridotites (**5**), gabbros (**3**) basalts (**4**), pillow lavas (**8**) and finally cherts (**1**) and bauxites (**2**).

Meanwhile, to the east, the Arabian plate continued its climb, colliding with Anatolia. Caught in a pincer-like movement, the Anatolian block moved (over 11 million years) towards the west and the Aegean Sea, alongside the old sutures of the East and North Anatolian faults. This movement continues, and it is along the North Anatolian fault that the most significant quakes are registered today.

MARBLES, PLAQUES AND PILASTERS

Marble revetments, most of them from the quarries of Anatolia, cover the walls of the basilica of Haghia Sophia. The architects of the Hellenistic period used marble for the supporting elements of the ornamentation. In the mosques there were delicately carved sculptures on the small marble columns and on the pillars that framed doors and windows.

17

Twice a year millions of migratory birds fly over the Straits of the Bosphorus, which is situated beween their nesting sites in Europe and western Asia and their East African winter homes. For most of the birds, this involves a journey of thousands of miles. Birds of prey and other gliders (cranes and storks, for example) are reluctant to fly over the open seas, so instead they cross by the isthmuses and straits. They use thermals over the land to gain altitude, which enables them to then glide over long distances, saving valuable energy

GREY CRANE
Crane flocks migrate primarily in the month of October.

BLACK KITE
These are often seen along the Golden Horn scavenging for dead fish.

WHITE STORK
Approximately 315,000 fly over the Bosphorus each year.

OLIVACEOUS WARBLER
Large numbers of these warblers nest in the hills of Camlica.

RED-BACKED SHRIKE
On their journey to East Africa these birds pause in the bushes in the hills around Istanbul.

- ■ Swallows
- ■ Black kites
- ■ Honey buzzards
- □ Storks
- ■ Lesser spotted eagles
- ■ Sparrowhawks

EGYPTIAN VULTURE
Only 300 to 500 of these birds fly over the Bosphorus each year, primarily during August and September.

LESSER SPOTTED EAGLE
Nearly 18,000 of these birds migrate across the Bosphorus in the fall.

HONEY BUZZARD
25,000 cross in the fall on their way from central and western Europe.

THE BOSPHORUS
The strait is like a river with its abrupt curves, flowing between fairly steep-sided banks, with cultivated and forested hills on either side. The speed of its current varies depending upon the season. The fall migration is more spectacular than that of the spring because it also includes the young birds, which were hatched only a few months earlier.

LAKE MANYAS

CHLIDONIAS HYBRIDA

Lake Manyas – also called Kuş Gölü, "bird lake" – is situated between Bursa and Çanakkale, 50 feet below the level of the Sea of Marmara. It covers an area of approximately 65 square miles, next to the small Kuş Cenneti national park. Its waters are home to a multitude of amphibians (especially frogs) and twenty types of fish.

WHISKERED TERN

Fishing is an important part of the area's economic life. Large reed beds line the banks, and a little willow forest near the mouth of the Sigirci river is a perfect habitat for herons, pelicans, and cormorants, which return to nest there every year. However, this exceptional bird life is under threat from excessive draining, poaching, and industrial pollution, which has already resulted in Lake Iznik, once home to numerous species, being abandoned by most birds.

IBIS FALCON
With its curved beak, it resembles a curlew.

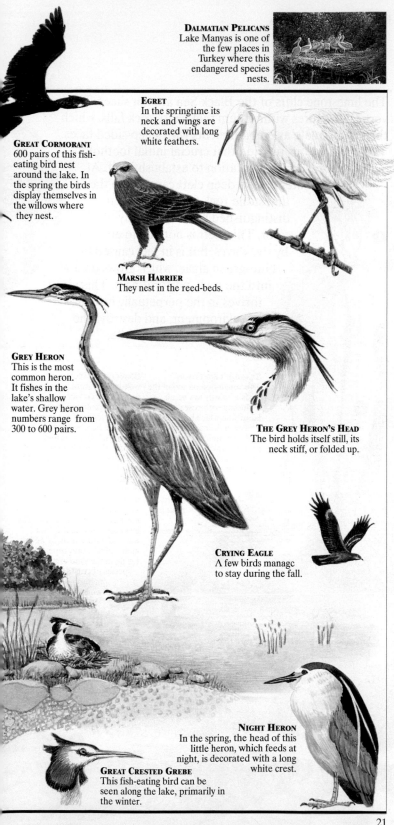

DALMATIAN PELICANS
Lake Manyas is one of the few places in Turkey where this endangered species nests.

GREAT CORMORANT
600 pairs of this fish-eating bird nest around the lake. In the spring the birds display themselves in the willows where they nest.

EGRET
In the springtime its neck and wings are decorated with long white feathers.

MARSH HARRIER
They nest in the reed-beds.

GREY HERON
This is the most common heron. It fishes in the lake's shallow water. Grey heron numbers range from 300 to 600 pairs.

THE GREY HERON'S HEAD
The bird holds itself still, its neck stiff, or folded up.

CRYING EAGLE
A few birds manage to stay during the fall.

NIGHT HERON
In the spring, the head of this little heron, which feeds at night, is decorated with a long white crest.

GREAT CRESTED GREBE
This fish-eating bird can be seen along the lake, primarily in the winter.

■ THE BLACK SEA

The limestone cliffs of the Black Sea are not sheer. There are vertical fractures within them that cause rock falls, which then accumulate as embankments with steep-sided faces. These formations provide that crucial initial foothold for scrub vegetation to establish itself. At water level a deep cleft carved into the limestone rock face can be seen, distinguished by its dark, gray-black color. This cleft is not due to erosion by the waves, but is in fact caused by blue-green algae, which grows on and into the rock, perforating it. This algae thrives in the perpetually humid environment, and destroys the limestone little by little.

SEASIDE VEGETATION
The vegetation on top of the cliffs is mostly low scrub, including rock-roses and laburnum which begin to flower in the early spring and sometimes continue until the fall(1). The sea grasses are singed by seaspray which drenches them in salt. In the spring miniscule romulea flower on the rocks, and wonderfully scented narcissi grow in the crevices. Mesembryanthemums cover large stretches of the coast, along the beaches and on the rocks (3).The plants and animals that live on the rocky coasts between the spring and neap tides are divided among a number of zones. The supralittoral level is the zone where such creatures as acorn shells and limpets are found, as it is rarely under water (4). The laminaria grow in the area where the tides turn, as well as in the infralittoral zone (5). Living in the sand are many species of crustaceans, anemones, and worms.

THE SEA BED
The rocky bottom of the Black Sea makes it easy to explore when diving. There is a wide variety of habitats in the first 30 feet beneath the surface while on the bottom, among the algae, it is possible to find numerous shellfish and invertebrates, and in the sand and silt there are many flatfish.

1. SEA URCHIN
Its shell is green and it clings on to rocks, stones, and algae from the edge of the cliff down to a depth of 100 feet.

2. PEARLY NUCULE
This bivalve lives in the sand at depths of up to 500 feet.

3. ABALONE
The abalone lives among the rocks. The inside of its shell has an opalescent sheen.

4. DRILLER
This mollusk lives on silty and sandy beds.

5. ACORN SHELL
The carapace of this rock-clinging crustacean is made up of six smooth plates.

MENDOLE
Also known as the cackarel, it lives in coastal waters and estuaries.

COMMON MACKEREL
The common mackerel travels in shoals that stay near the coast.

SPANISH MACKEREL

SPRAT This fish lives near the coast and in briny waters.

CHINCHARD Rarely found, this fish lives in the open sea.

The Ulu Dağ national park

The creation of a large skiing area poses a threat to the park's natural beauty and the whole environment.

The road within the park crosses a scrub of lavender and juniper, then runs on through the various types of woodland, past rivers and torrents.

Syrian woodpeckers, warblers, and birds of prey nest in the pine trees.

The boundaries of the national park extend to the southern slopes of the Ulu Dağ massif. The vegetation is divided into four zones, from 1,600 to 8,000 feet in altitude. The first zone is the Mediterranean level, from sea-level to 2,000 feet, where lavender, arbutus, and green oak flourish (1). The second or upper Mediterranean level, from 2,000 to 4,000 feet, is characterized by Byzantine hazel trees, lindens, eastern beech trees, and oaks (2). The mountain level, from 3,000 to 5,900 feet, has firs and pines (3). Above 5,900 feet, in the meadows of the subalpine level, lies the area designated for skiing.

In the scrubland little orchids and sweetly scented hyacinths bloom in springtime.

This thick forest of conifers and deciduous trees harbors a great variety of wildlife. *Cervidae* – red (4) and fallow deer (5) – are found there as well as boar and sometimes bears and wolves.

The Ulu Dağ national park was created to protect this natural site, and to safeguard the animal population, which includes many endangered species.

MOUFFLON
A type of wild mountain sheep, the moufflon is found on the highest summits of the Ulu Dağ.

THE VEGETATION is made up of rock-roses, arborescent briar bushes, mastic trees, pistachio trees, and honeysuckle.

GRASSHOPPERS AND BEES
The national park is home to numerous insects. Many of the species are found only in this part of Turkey and are completely unknown in Europe. The best time to see them is during the summer months.

CREEPING CYCLAMEN
These cyclamen mix with violets and ranunculae in shrubs growing at the highest altitudes in the forest.

APOLLO
This remarkable butterfly is indigenous to the mountain regions and rarely descends below 2,000 feet.

In the 18th and 19th centuries landscape gardeners were charged with creating parks for the sultans' palaces, embassies and yalı by the Bosphorus. For these gardens, they selected a mixture of forest, fruit, and ornamental trees and created arbors from a variety of plants and flowers, which were either transplanted or grown from cuttings. They had to fight against the established tradition of more modest gardens but they won, and the resulting parks and town squares are beautiful creations of great artistry.

JUDAS TREE

JUDAS TREE WITH PODS

JUDAS TREE FLOWERS
These appear in May, before the leaves.

ROSE BUSH FLOWER
Rose bushes with large flowers are used as ornamental shrubs. They are remarkable for their size and for the scent of their flowers.

HOLM-OAK (ILEX)
This oak has long-lasting leaves, and is planted in parks.

EUCALYPTUS
An imported tree, which tends to sterilize the soil.

OLIVE TREE
This tree has silvery leaves and heavily scented flowers.

BALKAN PINE (OR BOSNIAN PINE) This type of pine is cultivated in the gardens of the Bosphorus.

HISTORY AND LANGUAGE

ORIGINS. Turkey, a cradle of civilizations and a crossroads of history, is the meeting place of East and West. The first human settlements date back to 10,000 BC and archeological excavations have shown that, from around this time, communities had been established at Çatal Hüyük and possibly other unexcavated sites in Central Anatolia. Millennia later, the Neolithic site at Hacılar is much less sophisticated. In the early 3rd millennium BC, peoples crossed the straits and settled along the Aegean and on the site of Troy. In the 2nd millennium BC, the Hittites moved into Asia Minor. There were further numerous migrations from the end of the 2nd millennium.

THE NEOLITHIC PERIOD

8000–1200 BC
Anatolia is settled.

THE FIRST CITIES. The oldest known city, Çatal Hüyük, perished in about 5500 BC. Simple agriculture, metallurgy and weaving began in Anatolia before their later development in Europe.

THE BRONZE AGE

4000 BC
Influx of Neolithic people.

3600 BC
Troy I is founded.

2600 BC
Anatolian migrations to Crete.

2100 BC
Troy II is invaded and destroyed.

2000 BC
The Ionians invade Greece.

1400–1200 BC
The Dorians invade Greece.

THE SITE OF TROY. Archeological excavations in Anatolia began in 1870, with Schliemann's work at the site of Troy on the Asian side of the straits, which were known to the Greeks as the Hellespont. The fortified city was founded layer by layer between 3600 and 2500 BC, that is, between the end of the Chalcolithic period and the beginning of the Bronze Age. Throughout the Bronze Age, the city was continuously inhabited and was in contact with the Aegean and Cycladic peoples. Around 2100–2000 BC, Troy was destroyed by people who left no trace of their culture behind. A new civilization appeared around 1800 BC.

THE HATTIANS. Writing was introduced to Anatolia in the Middle Bronze Age (2000–1500 BC) by Assyrian merchants from Hattian cities. The Hattians were a people indigenous to Asia Minor whose civilization produced some very beautiful works of art – such as a golden ewer found at Alaca Hüyük. They dominated the area for over 500 years and, at the beginning of the 2nd millennium BC, were supplanted by the Hittites, a warrior people who seem to have come from southern Russia. The Hittites (2000–1800 BC) conquered Anatolia and founded their capital at Hattusa, now known as Boğazköy. They were the first great fortress builders: the city of Hattusa was surrounded by curtain walls set with towers, and five great temples and a complex with shops have been uncovered.

THE HITTITE KINGDOM. Hattusa was the capital of the Hittite Kingdom (1700–1450 BC) and of the Hittite Empire (1450–1200 BC). During the Late Bronze Age the Hittite rulers rivalled the Egyptians in their power, and in 1286 BC when Ramses II was pharaoh, these great empires fought one another at the famous battle of Kades in Syria. This conflict was settled by the earliest-known peace treaty, signed in 1269 by Hattousil and Ramses II. The clay tablet on which it is recorded is preserved at the Museum of the Ancient Orient in Istanbul.

THE SEA PEOPLE. Around 1200 BC all the great cities of the Late Bronze Age – most notably Troy, Mycenae and Hattusa – were destroyed, perhaps by the warrior race that the Egyptians knew as the Sea People. This was followed by an obscure period in Anatolian history, which lasted several centuries (1180–750 BC) and during which there is little or no evidence of civilization.

THE NEO-HITTITE STATES. Something of the Hittite culture survived in southeastern Anatolia and in Syria in the period c. 1000–700 BC. But in western and central Anatolia the Phrygians dominated the Hittites between 900 and 650 BC. Their kings were named Midas or Gordius and they were conquered by the rich Lydians who ruled until they, in turn, were defeated by the Persians under Cyrus. During the same period, the Urartians took control of the eastern part of the subcontinent.

GRECO-ANATOLIAN CIVILIZATION. From the 14th century BC, the Greeks settled along the Anatolian coast and established important Greek cities like Miletus and Ephesus which in the 7th century BC colonized the Bosphorus and the Black Sea.

ANATOLIA UNDER THE PERSIANS. The former Lydian empire was to remain under Persian rule from 546 to 334 BC, when Alexander the Great crossed the Dardanelles.

1230–25 BC
Fall of Troy and destruction of Mycenae and Hattusa.

753 BC
Foundation of Rome.

600 BC
Foundation of Marseilles.

490 BC
Battle of Marathon.

448–30 BC
Pericles reaches the height of his power at Athens.

FOUNDATION OF BYZANTIUM

According to tradition, Byzantium was founded by the hero Byzas the Megarian, who led an expedition of colonists from Megara and Athens to establish a new city on the Bosphorus. Byzas chose a site on a steep, sharp-topped hill, opposite the Golden Horn and the Bosphorus. At this confluence, the Megarian leader built an acropolis, surrounded with ramparts. This hill town, with its port in a sheltered cove below, was the embryo of a city that would endure until the early 4th century AD.

FROM ALEXANDER THE GREAT TO THE ROMAN EMPIRE

A new era in the history of Anatolia began in 334 BC, when Alexander the Great invaded Asia. He secured his first victory at the battle of the Granicus, then freed from Persian rule all the Greek cities of Asia Minor. His campaign then carried him on deep into Asia and to Babylon, where he died in 323 BC. After his death, his successors, the Diadochi, fought against the Ptolemaic dynasty, the Seleucids in Syria. The Hellenistic period (323–129 BC) saw the emergence of a number of independent kingdoms, the most powerful being that of Pergamum, established when Philetaerus assumed power in 281 BC on the death of Lysimachus and becoming a Roman province in 133 BC. The Greek cities of Asia Minor prospered during the first two centuries of imperial rule, this prosperity reaching its peak with the Emperor Hadrian (117–138), under whose rule temples, theaters and monuments were built.

88–63 BC
The Romans reconquer Asia Minor.

27 BC
Octavian is crowned Emperor.

THE GREAT INVASIONS. From 263 BC, the Goths started to invade western Asia Minor. Descending in successive waves they brought death and destruction and paved the way for other invaders who eventually destroyed all the Greek cities of Asia Minor.

CONSTANTINOPLE, THE SECOND ROME

70 AD
The Romans sack Jerusalem.

253–60
The Franks and Alamns invade Gaul.

260
The Persian Sassanids in Central Anatolia.

324–37
Reign of Constantine the Great.

325
Council of Nicaea and the establishment of the Christian Creed.

340–63
The Persians and Romans fight over northern Mesopotamia.

CONSTANTINE THE GREAT. While the great cities of the Greco-Roman world were suffering destruction, a new empire was taking shape in Constantinople. In 330 Constantine the Great proclaimed the city capital of the Byzantine Empire, and the entire history of this empire was to revolve around Constantinople, the Byzantium of the Greeks.

BYZANTIUM AND RIVAL POWERS. During the six centuries of its existence, Byzantium often fell under the control of more powerful states: first Persia, then Athens and Sparta during the Peloponnesian War, later Alexander and his successors, and then Rome. Byzantium was destroyed and rebuilt several times in the course of its history, notably in 196, when it fell to the Roman emperor Septimius Severus after a two-year siege. The city was then enlarged and the walls around the acropolis were strengthened and extended to embrace an area between the Golden Horn and the Sea of Marmara. In 324, Constantine the Great took Byzantium after his victory over Licinius, which made him the sole ruler of the Roman Empire.

THE CITY OF CONSTANTINE.

Constantine decided to move the capital of the Roman Empire from Rome to Byzantium, and rebuild the old Greek city on a much larger and grander scale in keeping with its new imperial status. The

new capital was dedicated on May 11, 330 as Nova Roma, but popularly it came to be known as Constantinople, the City of Constantine. The new capital, covering an area five times larger than that of the old city of Byzantium, now had ramparts running more than two miles from the Golden Horn to the Sea of Marmara. In the first hundred years of its history, the capital grew rapidly and soon spread beyond the limits defined by its founder. In the 5th century Theodosius replaced Constantine's walls with a new and stronger line of defence walls topped by ninety-six towers. These walls have defined the limits of the old city from that time on, although subsequent expansion took place on the other side of the Golden Horn and along the shores of the Sea of Marmara and the Bosphorus. The area thus enclosed included seven hills, the same as in old Rome, with the acropolis of ancient Byzantium on the First Hill.

FROM THE ROMAN TO THE BYZANTINE EMPIRE.

Great changes in the Roman Empire took place during the two centuries following the reign of Constantine the Great (324–337). After the death of Theodosius I in 395, the Empire was divided between his two sons, Arcadius and Honorius. Arcadius took command of the empire from Constantinople eastwards and Honorius governed from Rome westwards. In the following century, the western part of the Empire was invaded by barbarians and in 476 its last Emperor of the West was deposed, leaving the Emperor of the East in Constantinople sole ruler of what was left of the Roman Empire. Classical Greco-Roman traditions were gradually obliterated as the Empire's Christian and Greek culture took hold. This brought about a profound change in the character of the Empire, which from now on was centered around lands populated largely by Greek-speaking Christians, even though Latin remained the official language of the court until the 6th century. By choosing Byzantium, Constantinople's original name, as the generic name of the Empire, the Emperor declared his intention to break the ties of the Greek Christian state with the old imperial, pagan Rome. Thenceforth the influence that Christianity had on Byzantium was not only religious but also political and economic.

361
Reign of Julian the Apostate and reinstitution of paganism.

379
Theodosius I becomes Emperor at age 16.

391
Christianity becomes the state religion.

395
Death of Theodosius I. Final division of the Western and Eastern Empires.

410
Alaric plunders Rome.

429
The Vandals invade Africa.

431
The Council of Ephesus

441–51
Attila and the Huns overrun the Western Empire.

THE REIGN OF THE EMPEROR JUSTINIAN. The Byzantine Empire reached the pinnacle of its greatness during the reign of Justinian (527–565), who recaptured many of the lost dominions of the Roman Empire. By the end of Justinian's reign, the Empire embraced a large part of the Mediterranean world, reaching as far west as Spain, eastward into Persia, northward as far as the Danube and south into Egypt, an area only slightly less than that of the Roman Empire under Augustus. Capitalizing on the opulence that his vast empire could provide, Justinian built magnificent churches, palaces and public buildings with such zeal that no other city in the world could rival the splendor of Constantinople. It was he who built the Basilica of Haghia Sophia, completed in 537 and dedicated to the Holy Wisdom, a symbol of the universal radiance of the Byzantine Empire.

THE DECLINE OF THE EMPIRE. The Byzantine Empire endured for nearly a thousand years after Justinian, even though on his death decline had already begun. During the Middle Ages, its dominions were reduced to Asia Minor and the southern Balkans, including what is now Greece. The Selçuk Turks inflicted a cruel blow when they routed the Byzantine army at the battle of Mantzikert in 1071. In the same year the Normans took Bari, the last Byzantine possession in Italy.

622
Mahomet flees to Medina (the hegira).

913–59
Reign of Constantine VII Porphyrogenitus,

THE LATIN KINGDOM

1067
The Selçuk Turks occupy Caesarea.

1204–61
The Greek Empire of Nicaea.

1209–12
The Venetians conquer Crete.

1256–1335
Mongol Dynasty in Persia.

THE FOURTH CRUSADE. In 1204 the Byzantine Empire was almost destroyed again when the Venetians joined forces with the knights of the Fourth Crusade, organized by Pope Innocent III to 'come to the aid of' the Holy Land. The French crusaders, under the command of Count Thibaud de Champagne, and the Doge of Venice undertook to join and finance the Crusade; the Venetians suggested that the Crusaders take Constantinople. Having reached the city, even though Pope Innocent III had been banned and excommunicated, the Crusaders placed Alexius IV Angelus on the throne. He was unable to produce the money that the Crusaders demanded and in March 1204 they decided to do away with him and establish a Latin kingdom. By April 13, the Crusaders had torched and taken control of every quarter of

the city. Constantinople was sacked, thousands of Greeks massacred, churches pillaged and relics stolen and sent back to the West. On May 9, 1204, after the spoils had been divided, Baldwin of Flanders was crowned Emperor and Tomaso Morosini patriarch. The victors divided up the land between them and, as Baldwin of Flanders put it, laid their hands on riches both physical and spiritual. This kingdom lasted for more than half a century. However, certain provinces of the empire kept their independence during this period, notably Nicaea in northwestern Asia Minor, the capital of an empire ably ruled by the Lascarid dynasty which began the rebirth of Byzantine power. Finally, under Michael IX Paleologus the Greeks captured the city in 1261. Over two centuries before it finally fell, the Byzantine Empire was gradually disintegrating, suffering repeated attacks from the Osmanlı Turks, known in the West as the Ottomans.

1261
Foundation of the Palaeologus dynasty.

1331
Nicaea taken by the Turks.

THE OSMANLI TURKS

THE FIRST OTTOMAN CONQUESTS. In 1326, the Osmanli captured Prusa (Bursa), which Sultan Orhan Gazi established as the capital of the burgeoning empire. From then on, they were unstoppable. In the mid-14th century they crossed the Dardanelles and took Adrianople (Edirne), where in 1371 Sultan Murat I founded the new capital of the Ottoman Empire. In 1422, Murat II invaded Greece and the Peloponnese, conquering Thessalonika in March 1430. In 1438 the *devşirme* was instituted. This was a system for recruiting young Christian slaves given by their families in payment of tribute due to the sultan. Educated in the palace barracks, they formed the backbone of the powerful Turkish army and were later to make up the famous élite corps known as Janissaries. In 1440, Belgrade, a powerful and well defended city, managed to fend off a six-month siege but Ottoman expansion was only briefly thwarted and Venice intervened.

THE BYZANTINE EMPIRE IS REDUCED TO CONSTANTINOPLE. By the mid-15th century, the Ottomans had conquered most of Asia Minor and reached southern Europe, even though the popes had the Christian princes to raise armies to halt their progress. The Byzantine Empire was reduced to little more than the town of Constantinople and its immediate environs. Pope Nicholas V would only give his support on condition that the Greeks joined the Catholic Church. Emperor John III was forced to accept these terms and on December 12, 1452, Cardinal Isidore, the Pope's envoy, celebrated Roman Catholic mass at Haghia Sophia. However, help from the Christian powers of Europe was not to materialize.

1328
Victory of Orhan Gazi over Andronicus III Palaeologus.

1369–1403.
Mongolian incursions in Asia Minor.

1402
Beyazıt I vanquished by Tamerlane.

1422
First Ottoman siege of Constantinople.

1423
Venice promises to defend Thessalonika, until it falls in 1430.

1453
End of the Hundred Years War.

1456
Ottomans take Athens.

33

February 3, 1451: Mehmet II, born March 30, 1432, succeeded his father to the Ottoman throne.

February 14, 1452: The Venetian senate informed the Byzantine ambassador of unprecedented preparations by the Turks for the siege of Constantinople.

March 26: Mehmet II reached the Bosphorus and started building a fortress, the Rumeli Hisarı, on the western bank to control seaborne traffic. It faced the fortress of Anadolu Hisarı, built by his grandfather Beyazıt I in 1396.

September 3: The construction of the fortress was completed. After inspecting his 50,000 troops, as well as Constantinople's

defenses, the Sultan returned to Edirne, the new capital of the Empire, where he set up his winter quarters and carefully planned the siege.

September 10: Mehmet agreed another peace treaty with Venice.

October 26: Cardinal Isidore of Kiev, sent by the Pope, arrived in Constantinople to seal the union between the Orthodox and Catholic churches. He was accompanied by a troop of 200 men. The city was thus divided into two camps: those who were for and those against the union.

December 12: The union of the churches was solemnly proclaimed in Haghia Sophia by the Emperor Constantine XI and Cardinal Isidore.

January 26, 1453: Seven hundred Genoese mercenaries arrived in Constantinople, led by Giovani Giustiniani. He was put in charge of defending the walls. These were the only Western reinforcements.

February 26: Seven Venetian ships with 700 men aboard secretly sailed out of Constantinople despite a promise given to the emperor that no one would flee the city.

March 1 to 15: The Turkish forces gathered in front of the city.

April 2: Preceded by cannons and siege engines, Mehmet arrived at the city walls.

April 4: The start of the siege. About 17,000 men defended the ramparts. The Turkish

army was estimated to be 250,000 men, and had the most powerful artillery ever amassed.

April 18: The first attack was repulsed.

April 20: Three Genoese merchant ships and a Byzantine ship brought reinforcements to break the blockade of the Ottoman flotilla, prying open the enormous chain that closed the entrance to the Golden Horn and joining the besieged citizens.

April 22: Aiming to enter the harbor and command the Golden Horn, Mehmet had some 50 ships transported overland on wooden rollers from the Bosphorus. His navy thus avoided the Genoese city of Galata and reached the Golden Horn, where it reinforced the troops already attacking Constantinople. He built a bridge.

May 7: The second assault began at four in the morning. The 30,000 attackers were repulsed, with heavy losses.

> «AND THE GREATEST OF ALL THIS, THAT YOU WILL CAPTURE A
> CITY WHOSE RENOWN HAS GONE TO ALL PARTS OF THE WORLD.»
>
> MEHMET II

May 11: Constant bombardments seriously damaged the walls of Constantinople.
May 12: A third assault of 50,000 men was launched at midnight. Serious losses on both sides.
May 16: Galleries dug by Serbian miners

for the Sultan were parried by a system of counter-galleries designed by a German engineer who was working for the Byzantines.
May 19: Mehmet II had a bridge built on the Golden Horn to allow him to attack the sea walls.
May 22: Two other Turkish galleries were

put out of action. A partial eclipse of the moon terrified those under siege.
May 23: A brigatine sent to meet the

Venetian navy returned to report that no reinforcements were in sight.
May 26: Before the city was taken, Mehmet II ordered three days of solemn fast and prayer.
May 28: The final assault was announced for the following day.
May 29: Three hours before daybreak, Mehmet II gave orders for the final assault to begin. At dawn, Saint-Roman Gate (known as Top Kapı today) was destroyed and taken by the infantry which poured into the city. The Western defenders fled back to

their ships. Emperor Constantine died in the battle and, even though the citizens,

exhausted after seven weeks of siege, put up a fight, the Turks poured into the city. The fall of Constantinople, on May 29, 1453, marked the end of the Byzantine Empire.

FROM THE EMIRATE TO THE OTTOMAN EMPIRE

Through his physical appearance and his majestic bearing Süleyman projected an image worthy of such a powerful monarch.

A. GRECIAN

A. EGIPTIA

A. ASSYRIAN

A. ARABIAN

A. PERSIAN

The Anatolian Selçuk kingdom, created after the Turkish conquest two centuries earlier, collapsed at the end of the 13th century under Mongolian pressure. Of the 15-odd tribal principalities set up opposite Byzantium, it was in fact the smallest, founded by Osman, an obscure tribal chief, that was constantly waging war on its neighbors. In 1326 Osman consolidated his conquests by taking Bursa. His son Orhan transferred the Selçuk capital there and, in 1354, took possession of Nicaea (Iznik) and Gallipoli (Gelibolu). Not content with taking over the other principalities, the Ottomans were to establish the last great near-eastern empire, worthy successors to the Romans, the Byzantines and the Arabs. No longer hemmed in by rival powers, the Ottoman emirate contemplated a Byzantine world in crisis and, beyond, the Balkans.

OTTOMAN SULTANS
Osman I (1288–1326)
Orhan Gazi (1326–1362)
Murat I (1362–1389)
Beyazıt I (1389–1413)
Mehmet I (1413–1421)
Murat II (1421–1451)
Mehmet II (1451–1481)
Beyazıt II (1481–1512)
Selim I (1512–1520)
Süleyman I (1520–1566)
Selim II (1566–1574)
Murat III (1574–1595)
Mehmet III (1595–1603)
Ahmet I (1603–1617)
Mustafa I (1617-1618)

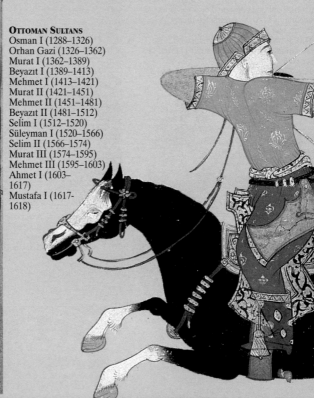

«THE SULTAN OF SULTANS OF THE EAST AND THE WEST, HE WHO LAVISHES CROWNS UPON MONARCHS THROUGHOUT THE LAND, THE SHADOW OF GOD ON EARTH...»

OTTOMAN SULTANS
Osman II (1618–1622)
Mustafa I (1622–1623)
Murat IV (1623–1640)
Ibrahim (1640–1648)
Mehmet IV (1648–1687)
Süleyman II (1687–1691)
Ahmet II (1691–1695)
Mustafa II (1695–1703)
Ahmet III (1703–1730)
Mahmut I (1730–1754)
Osman III (1754–1757)
Mustafa III (1757–1774)
Abdül Hamit I (1774–1789)
Selim III (1789–1807)
Mustafa IV (1807–1808)
Mahmut II (1808–1839)
Abdül Mecit I (1839–1861)
Abdül Aziz (1861–1876)
Murat V (1876, deposed)
Abdül Hamit II (1876–1909)
Mehmet V (1908–1918)
Mehmet VI (1918–1922)
Abdül Mecit II (1922, caliph, abdicated in 1924)

HIS WIFE

HIS WIFE

HIS WIFE

HIS WIFE

HIS WIFE

The age-old rivalry between the Turks and Venice caused seven wars, totalling 71 years of conflict over two and a half centuries – wars that exhausted both states. At the same time the abandonment of the traditional Mediterranean trade routes and the discovery of the new worlds resulted in the rise of the Atlantic powers.

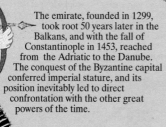

The emirate, founded in 1299, took root 50 years later in the Balkans, and with the fall of Constantinople in 1453, reached from the Adriatic to the Danube. The conquest of the Byzantine capital conferred imperial stature, and its position inevitably led to direct confrontation with the other great powers of the time.

HIS WIFE

37

THE BATTLE OF LEPANTO

Under the reign of Sultan Selim II, son of Süleyman, the empire suffered a number of set-backs, but, between the victory of Preveza (1538) and the defeat at Lepanto (1571), the Ottomans ruled the sea. Their naval supremacy in the Mediterranean put the Christians on the defensive. Pope Pius V called for a Holy War and took the lead of the Holy League (Philip II's Spain, Naples, Genoa, and Venice). The Christian fleet gathered in Messina under the command of Don Juan of Austria. The Ottoman armada, strengthened by a privateer fleet from Algeria and Tripoli, was made up of galleys crewed by Greek sailors under the command of Ali Paşa. After this naval defeat, the Grand Vizier Sokollu set to rebuilding his fleet which would take Tunis in 1574.

THE ROLE OF THE INFANTRY

The fleet blocked the Gulf of Corinth near the city of Lepanto. Just before the engagement began the four Venetian galleys opened fire with their formidable artillery causing considerable losses among the Turkish ranks. Boarding maneuvers and hand-to-hand combat followed. Throughout the afternoon the Italian and Spanish troops fought the Janissaries along the length of both fleets. The Turkish Grand Admiral Müezzinzade Ali Paşa was killed.

THE BATTLE

At dawn on October 7, 1571, the two fleets found themselves face to face. The Christian fleet consisted of 208 galleys; the Ottoman fleet of 260 galleys. In the center, the two flagship galleys; the galley of Ali Paşa and that of Don Juan faced off. In three hours the fleet was destroyed and only 30 ships managed to return to their home port.

MINIATURE OF THE CITY OF LEPANTO
This detailed map of Lepanto was made around 1540. The city and its port were conquered by Sultan Beyazıt II in 1499. Kasim Bey, Süleyman's vizier, then governor of the Moors, built fortifications. The citadel was surrounded by moats and protected by Janissaries. Because of its location, Lepanto controlled the entrance to the Gulf of Corinth.

THE ATLAS OF ALI MACAR RE'IS
The Ottoman seafarers possessed precise maps such as this one of the western Mediterranean made in 1567. It consists of nine maps drawn on parchment. The coastline is marked in blue and islands and important cities are highlighted in green. The names of the ports are written in Turkish.

In the 16th century the Ottomans negotiated the first "capitulations" between Süleyman and François I, then with the English (1580) and the Dutch (1612). At its height the empire included Mesopotamia, Syria, most of the coast of the Arab peninsula, Egypt, and the coast of North Africa. It engaged in a merciless fight against the Hapsburgs, who controlled not only the German empire, but also that of Spain and soon Portugal (1580–1640). The struggle took place on two fronts: Central Europe, with the conquest of Hungary (1526) and the siege of Vienna, and the Mediterranean, where the Ottomans maintained their supremacy from the victory of Preveza (1538) through to their defeat at Lepanto (1571).

At the end of the 16th century the Ottomans had an inadequate army and were at a disadvantage when engaging the Hapsburg army, which used numerous technical innovations paid for by the gold from the recently discovered Americas.

The European Wars of Religion, especially the Thirty Years War (1618–1648), interrupted this struggle. When it began again in the second half of the 17th century the Ottoman Empire had a fragile economy, and was in a weak position.

«THE OVER JOYOUS SOULS IN THESE COUNTRIES ARE LIKE CHILDREN TREATED TO HALVA.»

SÜLEYMAN THE MAGNIFICENT

After the defeat of the Turks outside Vienna (1683) the Hapsburgs began to take back Central Europe. At the same time the Russian Empire showed signs of expanding, which was to lead to a long conflict: there would be nine Russo-Turkish wars between 1683 and 1918. In 1699, the Ottomans signed the Treaty of Karlowitz (the first to be unfavorable to them) and lost important territory. In the 19th century the treaty of San Stefano (1878) pushed Turkey out of Europe. Serbia, Romania, and Bulgaria were given independence, Bosnia and Herzegovina were occupied by the Austrians, and western Anatolia by the Russians.

In 1891 Russia obtained free passage for its commercial ships through the straits.

MAP OF THE OTTOMAN EMPIRE
Turkey and other countries under Ottoman sovereignty in 1626: in Europe, Greece, Albania, Bulgaria, Bosnia, Hungary, Romania, and Bessarabia; in Asia and Africa, Algeria, Tunisia, Libya, and Egypt. At this time the empire experienced several setbacks at the hands of the Iranians in Georgia and in Azerbaijan.

At the turn of the century national movements led to the subdivision of the empire. In addition to the Balkan revolutions there was the National Arab Movement which, along with World War I, brought about the end of the empire. New states were founded upon its remains. The treaty of Lausanne, signed on July 24, 1923, recognized that Turkey's permanent borders included Thrace and the territories under dispute: Smyrna, Cilicia and the Eastern provinces.

TURKEY AND THE TANZIMAT (1839–1878)

This great modernizing movement was pushed forward by the ministers and the sultans. The reforms affected the administration and the state machinery, such as the army, the law, and education. Influenced in its innovations by the great powers (Britain, Germany, and France), Turkey created the first Ottoman Constitution in 1876. The Westernization of the society can be seen in the arts as well: literature, painting, and theater were all inspired by Western models. Newspapers also played an important role. But the 19th-century sultans remained caliphs and took part in traditional ceremonies just as their predecessors did.

THE END OF THE EMPIRE

THE YOUNG TURKS. At the outbreak of World War I, Enver Paşa favored an alliance with Germany. The constitution was then restored and a new parliament elected, but the real power lay in the hands of the Young Turks and the Union and Progress Committee led by the junior officers Cemal and Enver and the future Minister of the Interior Talat. All three were to become paşas. This triumvirate persuaded the Sultan to fight on the German side in the First World War.

THE DARDANELLES. It was this alliance that led to the Allies' expedition to the Dardanelles in 1915, to force a passage through the straits then blocked by German ships. The resistance put up by the Turkish army under the command of Mustafa Kemal, Enver Paşa and the German General Liman von Sanders, together with strategic errors on the part of the Allies, resulted in failure. This was to be the first and last resounding success that the Turkish troops would have during the war, as they were all but wiped out in the bloody campaigns fought on the Russian front and in Palestine. The defeat of Germany and other Axis powers in November 1918 led to the collapse of the Ottoman Empire. The Ottomans lost all their European territories except Istanbul.

August 2, 1914
Secret pact with Germany.

ENVER PAŞA

November 13, 1918
The allied fleet occupies Istanbul.

June 28, 1919
Treaty of Versailles.

August 10, 1919
Treaty of Sèvres.

1920
The first Great National Assembly at Ankara. The war of independence begins.

1922
Smyrna is recaptured.

THE OCCUPATION OF ISTANBUL. Early in 1919 the British and French occupied Istanbul and took control of the Straits and other strategic coastal areas in Turkey, while the Greeks landed in Smyrna (Izmir) and soon afterwards advanced into western Asia Minor. On August 10, 1919, the completely powerless Mehmet VI was forced to sign the Treaty of Sèvres, by which the Ottoman Empire lost almost all

Moustafa Kiemal Pacha

of its territory in Europe and in Asia retained only those parts of Anatolia that were not claimed by the Greeks, Italians and the French.

TURKISH NATIONALISM AND MUSTAFA KEMAL. The great majority of Turks refused to bow to the diktat of the western powers. Nationalist fervor began in Anatolia. Mustafa Kemal, an officer who had distinguished himself in the Dardanelles, mobilized the Anatolian population, which consisted largely of peasants, and embarked on a war of national liberation. On April 23, 1920, Mustafa Kemal, later acclaimed as Atatürk, Father of the Turks, presided over the new National Assembly at Ankara, which formed a government in opposition to the Sultan's postwar puppet regime in Istanbul.

1922–1924
Short reign of the last Ottoman calif, Abdul Mecit.
1922–1923
Exchange of Greek and Turkish nationals.

THE TURKISH REPUBLIC

The Turkish Nationalists then defeated the Greek army in several engagements in Anatolia, forcing them to flee to Greece in September 1922. During the following year more than a million Greeks were forced to leave Asia Minor and resettle in Greece, while about half a million Turks left Crete and Greece. This population exchange was one of the consequences of the Treaty of Versailles, signed in July 1923, which established the boundaries of Turkey essentially as they are today.

July 24, 1923
Treaty of Lausanne.

October 19, 1923
Ankara becomes the capital of Turkey.

MUSTAFA KEMAL ATATÜRK, FIRST PRESIDENT OF THE TURKISH REPUBLIC. The Turkish National Assembly abolished the sultanate on November 1, 1922, and Mehmet II fled Istanbul aboard a warship. His younger brother Abdül Mecit II succeeded him as Caliph. On March 3, 1924, the National Assembly abolished the caliphate, and the Caliph, accompanied by his whole family, was driven to the frontier. On October 29, 1923, the National Assembly created the Republic of Turkey, with Mustafa Kemal as its first president and Ankara as the new capital.

1928
The Latin alphabet is adopted.

TURKEY BETWEEN THE WARS. Kemal Atatürk's political agenda caused far-reaching change in the politics of Turkey as a whole. The new republic was modeled on the Constitution of April 30, 1924. Atatürk pursued a policy of secularization; judicial law replaced the Koran and religious education was banned in schools.

One of the most dramatic changes was the banning of the Arabic alphabet in favor of the Latin alphabet. Istanbul, having been an imperial city for almost 1600 years, became Turkey's cultural capital in 1923. European dress became popular and rather than the fez worn by Ottoman officials, Mustafa Kemal chose the Anatolian peasant's cap. The Ottoman sultans had been wanting to catch up with the West since the 19th century and in the 1930's a similar desire edged republican Turkey towards industrialization. In 1938, on the death of Mustafa Kemal, Ismet Inönü became President of the Republic. Turkey remained neutral during World War II.

October 1939
Aid pact signed with France and Great Britain.

TURKEY TODAY

1938–50
Presidency of Ismet Inönü.

1950–60
Government of Menderes.

1960
General Gürsel's military coup

1961–5
Inönü's coalition government.

From 1947, Turkey benefited from Marshall Plan aid. In the 1950's Menderes' government gave agriculture a boost by introducing mechanization. In 1952 Turkey joined NATO.

INDUSTRIALIZATION. Based on five-year plans, industrial policy until the end of the 1970's was geared to financing food imports. Later, after the liberalization that took place in the 1980's, it was oriented towards exports. Thus, having initially built steelworks and refineries and geared itself to heavy industry, Turkey subsequently turned to producing consumer durables.

AGRICULTURE. Turkey is one of the few countries with a rapidly expanding population which is still able to feed itself. Agricultural mechanization introduced in the 1950's was followed by major irrigation and sanitation projects. One of these is GAP, the ambitious project in southeastern Anatolia to increase the region's agricultural and energy-producing potential by diverting the Euphrates. Agriculture is moving away from tobacco and dried fruits and towards industrial crops such as cotton and oil-producing plants and greenhouse fruit and vegetables grown for export.

1965–71
Demirel's coalition governement.

1974
Turkish troops invade Cyprus.

1974 and 1977–9
Ecevit's coalition governments.

> «THERE IS NO LAND OR CITY THAT IS LIKE
> NO PLACE TO LIVE THAT CAN COMPARE WITH IT.»
>
> NÂBÎ (1642–1712)

ISTANBUL'S DEMOGRAPHIC EXPLOSION. Today Turkey has 52 million inhabitants, five times more than in 1920. The increase has been considerable in Istanbul. In 1920 there were about 500,000 living in Istanbul, half of whom were not Turks. In 1990, a census counted over 7,500,000, of whom only 20,000 to 30,000 were from ethnic minorities (Greek, Armenian or Jewish). Istanbul's demographic explosion has been caused by the continuous influx of people from country areas who have given up agriculture in the hope of improving their quality of life. They settle in hurriedly built areas of Istanbul, and often live in makeshift buildings known as *gecekondu*.

FATIH MEHMET BRIDGE

OPENING UP TOWARDS EUROPE

Opening up towards Europe should lead to the integration of the Turkish economy in the world economy. This is being achieved through deregulation of foreign investments, which has increased since 1980, attracting a large number of private investors and also through the growth and diversification of exports. In the last ten years, exports have risen from 9 to 18 percent of the gross national product. The proportion of exported manufactured goods leaped from 10 percent in 1970 to 67 percent in 1990. Consumers of these products, exclusively Western from the 1960's, and Turkey's Middle Eastern orientation during the Iran-Iraq war is being evened out by the EEC taking the lion's share with 40 percent of exports, the Middle East 20 percent and the United States 10 percent. For over 30 years Turks living in Western Europe and in Arab countries have sent back the foreign currency that is essential for the balance of payments. Finally, opening up is also being achieved through investment abroad. Civil engineering firms have been the pioneers in this sector, exporting capital, skills and technology first to Arab countries then to Russia and Central Asia, which make up important new markets.

THE BREAK-UP OF THE SOVIET UNION. The dramatic upheaval which the Balkans and especially the Caucasus have experienced in recent years are as much a cause of concern as of hope for Turkey, which sees an opportunity of increasing its cultural and political influence in this vast region.

September 12, 1980
Military coup. General Evren becomes head of state.

1983
General election. Turgut Ozal becomes prime minister.

November 24, 1987
General election.

May 14, 1987
An associate member of the European Community since the Ankara agreement of 1963, Turkey applies for full membership, invoking Article 237 of the Treaty of Rome.

June 14, 1993
Mrs Tansu Ciller, President of the DYP party, is elected prime minister.

45

A little

ORIGINS

The so-called Turkish languages of the Ural-Altaic family (Turkic and Mongolic) make up a huge linguistic group of some 120 million speakers (in Siberia, Central Asia, Altai etc.), half of whom live in Turkey. The fact that this young republic was associated with the residual Ottoman Empire gave Turkey's Turkish prestige and a status as the standard

The oldest Turkish map is an extract from the *Divan-ü-Lügat-it turc*. This dictionary was published in the 11th century by Kâşgartlı Mahmut, and is a summary of all of the languages and customs of the Turkish tribes. It was written to be presented to their new allies, the caliphs of Baghdad. This map shows the Caspian Sea to the right.

of reference for other Turkish-speaking communities. A distinction is generally made between contemporary Turkish and historic "Ottoman Turkish", which is hardly spoken at all now.

LINGUISTIC REFORM

Today the Turkish spoken in Turkey is standardized – the product of significant linguistic alterations and planning undertaken during the Atatürk reforms from 1928 onwards.

From me to you

Come towards me

Go away

The reforms took into consideration the recommendations of various contemporary linguists and philologists who worked together to define the *yeni türkçe* (new Turkish), or *öz türkçe* (purified Turkish). The policy of reform adopted by Atatürk had two aims: to break completely with the Ottoman system, notably by abandoning the Arabic alphabet and replacing it with the Latin equivalent, and to give a noble written form to the popular Turkish dialect which was the living heritage of the ancient Central-Asian pre-Islamic Turkish languages.

RETURN TO OTTOMAN ORIGINS. The results of the linguistic reform are impressive: in July 1932, 35 percent of the Turkish vocabulary was of Turkish origin; by 1946 it was 46 percent, and today it has reached 80 percent. The one thousand Turkish words most used today were "born" following the 1932 reform.

THE STRUCTURE OF THE LANGUAGE

Turkish is an agglutinative language. Its basic structure is made up of verbal or nominative roots of two or three syllables. To these are attached some 200 suffixes, with various grammatical functions, ranging from declension suffixes, to those for plurals, conjugations, adverbs, etc. All suffixes are added according to a rule of concatenation which is structured according to vocal harmony. Vowels are divided into two groups: those pronounced at the back of the mouth (e, i, ö, ü), and those pronounced at the front (a, ı, o, u). Other criteria also come into play, such as open/closed and high/low. This phonology also governs consonants.

CONSEQUENCES OF THE REFORM

The abrupt linguistic break, along with the banning of the Arab alphabet, had disastrous consequences. The teaching of the Ottoman language and literature in the Arabic alphabet could have formed the basis of learning about a great culture, just as does Latin or Ancient Greek. Though steeped in an architectural and historic environment rich in inscriptions – there are more than 55 million in the Ottoman archives – the children of the Republic cannot even decipher the inscription on their grandfathers' tombstones.

CONTEMPORARY TURKISH LITTERATURE
The new Turkish literature, recognized both nationally and internationally and including for example the poems of Nazım Hikmet and novels of Yaşar Kemal, has given modern Turkey its literary prestige.

THE RUNES OF THE FUNERARY STELAE
The funerary stelae of Central Asia were carved in the 6th century. They relate the heroic deeds of the Turkish chiefs of the region – such as government and political councils – and were commissioned by the deceased during their lifetime.These funerary stelae constitute a written history of a nation of nomadic pastoralists. The vocabulary and syntax of this language is very close to that of Anatolian Turkish: drawing on archaic scources *öz türkçe* was inspired by the language of these runic inscriptions.

THE TURKISH LANGUAGE

PHONETICS

Turkish has few sounds that are difficult for an English-speaker. It is usually pronounced as it is written. There are 29 letters in the Turkish alphabet. Below are listed only those letters that are additional to or are pronounced differently from English. The letters Q, W, and X do not exist: their equivalents are K, V and KS.

CONSONANTS	PRONOUNCIATION	VOWELS	PRONOUNCIATION
c	'j'	e	'e' as in bed
ç	'ch' as in chair	ı	'i' in flirt
g	'g' as in gift	ö	'u' as in furniture
ğ	silent	u	'u' as in you
s	'z'	ü	the French 'u'
ş	'sh' or 's' in sugar		

Head tilted back: no

Movement of the head up and down: yes

Movement of the head from left to right: expresses doubt

Hand over the heart: thank you

To ward off bad luck you pinch the lobe of your right ear with your right hand, and whistle, then knock wood three times.

ARTS, CRAFTS AND TRADITIONS

The Dolmabahçe Sarayı was built for Sultan Abdül Mecit between 1842 and 1856. It was designed by the Armenian architect Balyan, and is surrounded by a large tree-filled park, interspersed with beds of scented flowers and shrubs which are reflected in a pond with a fountain. Abdül Aziz succeeded his brother and had Balyan construct a palace for him at Beylerbeyi, on the opposite side of the river. The park is planted with rare trees arranged in terraces on the hillside. His successor, Abdül Hamit II, established himself in the Yıldız palace where he built many summer-houses in landscaped grounds among tree-lined rivers and lakes.

A SUMMER-HOUSE BY THE BOSPHORUS
The strait is the site of many yalı and summer houses. In the 19th century several new palaces were built there for the sultans.

PALACE BY THE SEA AND HOUSES ALONG THE RIVER
Two miniatures and a medallion by Abdullah Buhari, 1729.

THE PRINCES' ISLANDS
An engraving by Thomas Allom. These mountainous islands remained relatively isolated until the arrival of the first steamships at the end of the 19th century. From then on people from Istanbul began building yalı among the pine forests and on the coasts.

SUMMER-HOUSE WITH FAIENCE FAÇADE Painting by Gedikpaşalı, 1889.

YILDIZ PALACE AND GARDEN Painting by Şevki, 1891.

KAĞITHANE MOSQUE Painting by Mustafa, 19th century.

SUMMER-HOUSES AND GARDENS Mural painting, 1789–1807.

The style of mural painting inaugurated in the Topkapı Sarayı at the end of the 18th century was imitated in numerous yalı and *konak*: whether the paintings represent houses surrounded by gardens or open countryside, water is always part of the picture.

The yellow salon in the ceremonial wing of the Yıldız palace is famous for the landscapes painted on the ceiling.

The Turkish concept of the ideal house has hardly changed since Mehmet II's palace and gardens were constructed on a promontory overlooking the Golden Horn on one side and the Sea of Marmara on the other. The summer-houses within the parks and the yalı on the shoreline are constructed following the same basic principles: they are built in wood and can be thrown wide open to the outdoors, where the water and greenery create a fresh and beautiful backdrop.

The most splendid Ottoman costumes were made of precious fabrics such as brocades, silk velvets, and marbled organdy. The Bursa workshops span raw silk which was imported from Iran, doubled, milled, and dipped in baths of vegetable dye before being woven or used for embroidery. The printed or embroidered patterns and weaves were especially intricate on womens' costumes. They tended to be very detailed, showing primarily flowers (such as eglantine, hyacinths, carnations, roses, tulips, and cherry or pomegranate tree blossoms) which were either lifelike or stylized in arabesques, palmettes, or foliage. Collections of Istanbul's most beautiful costumes are shown at the Topkapı and Sadberk Hanem museums.

FUNCTIONARIES AND JANISSARIES
Their leader wore a "bonnet of crimson velvet, in the shape of a brimless cap, lined with cotton, and around which they wrap a turban. The turban is made up of a fabric or silk scarf which is several yards long, and as wide as the fabric bolt: they wrap it around a number of times [...]; there are several ways to wrap it. You can identify the condition and quality of a man by the way he wears his turban."
J. Thévenot, *Voyage au Levant*

KISLAR AĞASI
The chief eunuch and leading dignitary of the seraglio, painted by J.B. Van Mour (1671–1737), is dressed in a *ferace* of green and white silk, and a red silk robe clasped with a decorated buckle. On his head is a red muslin turban.

In the 17th century the Turks wore a sort of fabric dolman, made of taffeta, satin, or cotton, beneath their shirts. This dolman was knotted at the waist by a wide fabric or leather belt with a gold or silver buckle. One or two daggers were tucked into the belt, along with handkerchiefs and a tobacco pouch. They then donned a *ferace*, a large floor-length coat with very long sleeves. In the 19th century, with the arrival of the Reform era, the Turks adopted a Western-style costume characterized by a long redingote in a dark color called stambouline. The turban was eventually abandoned in favor of the fez, a stiff red cap. In the 20th century, with the end of the Ottoman Empire, the wearing of the fez was abolished by Atatürk.

WOMEN'S COSTUMES IN THE 18TH CENTURY

They wore a long coat which was usually green, and an ankle-length *ferace* made out of satin or tafetta with such long sleeves that their fingers could not be seen. The embroidered brocade dress was open and covered wide pants, known as shalvar, which were knotted at the ankles. The long-sleeved silk smocks, (*bürümcek*) were embroidered with skill. A wide embroidered velvet, satin, leather, or cashmere belt was worn around the waist. In the winter the *ferace* was lined with fur. The hem of the fabric was sewn onto yellow or red leather slippers (*mest*) over which they pulled babouches.

WOMEN'S COSTUME IN THE 19TH CENTURY

These women adopted the Western style, but their head was covered with a veil, a *mahrem*, which consisted of two pieces of muslin: the first covered the face up to the nose, the second was wrapped around the head and neck and knotted.

ISTANBUL MERCHANT AND HIS WIFE

He wore the traditional costume, while his wife was dressed in an *entari*, a long jacket with a train and wide pants.

YOUNG GROOM, COUNTRY PEASANT

The groom was clothed in a *yelek*, a jacket made of a rich fabric with blue and black stripes, embroidered in wool and silk.

MUSLIM WOMAN

The woman's dress was held together by a silver belt decorated with gold and silver buckels.

● MUSIC

Classical Turkish music draws its inspiration
from various Islamic cultures, and was further
enriched during the Ottoman era by influences
from conquered lands. In the 8th century traditional
songs and poetry recitals were accompanied by
instruments such as the *def* (drum), the *tanbûr* (lute), and
the *ney* (flute). The repertoire, as well as the variety of
instruments, increased during the 13th century, a period in
which some very important music was written, during which
the great poet Mevlâna composed a number of works. The
apogee of Ottoman music coincided with the brilliant reign of
Süleyman the Magnificent (1520–66). Along with vocal music
(*fasil*), instrumental music was also developed, notably that
played by the Janissaries
(*mehter*).

**PERCUSSION
INSTRUMENTS IN A
JANISSARY REGIMENTAL
BAND** The *kös*, large
copper kettledrums, are
predominant in the
mehter, with their sound
resembling thunder. The
davul is the most
common drum: players
wear it hung from their
necks, and beat it with a
drumstick.

ÇANK
harp.

TANBUR lute.

KEMENÇE
A long-necked lute
and bow.

THE SANTUR
Of Persian origin, this 72-chord zither is played with drumsticks and is very popular in Turkey.

THE SAZ
There is evidence that this instrument has been in use since the 12th century, and it is still played in some traditional Turkish music. This type of lute can be easily recognized by its long neck which is bent backwards, and by its pear-shaped drum.

In the 18th century, Gluck integrated Turkish kettledrums into his *Iphigénie en Tauride* and Mozart was inspired by the music of the Janissaries in his opera *Escape From the Seraglio*.

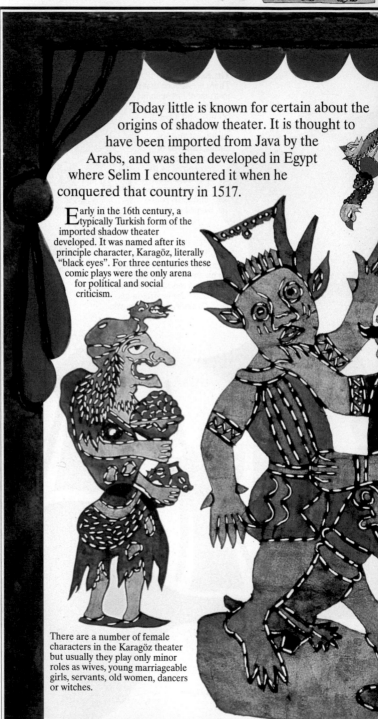

Today little is known for certain about the origins of shadow theater. It is thought to have been imported from Java by the Arabs, and was then developed in Egypt where Selim I encountered it when he conquered that country in 1517.

Early in the 16th century, a typically Turkish form of the imported shadow theater developed. It was named after its principle character, Karagöz, literally "black eyes". For three centuries these comic plays were the only arena for political and social criticism.

There are a number of female characters in the Karagöz theater but usually they play only minor roles as wives, young marriageable girls, servants, old women, dancers or witches.

The puppeteer moves the figures about in front of a fabric screen which is strongly lit from behind. The jointed marionettes are made of camel skin and painted with bright colors, and they are moved around by means of a stick attached to them.

Some of the plots are taken from ancient myths or traditional folk tales. They can involve fantastical characters, demons from the underworld or mythical animals.

Karagöz and his accomplice Hacıvat are at the center of all the plots and intrigues. The comic element is reinforced by figures called Taklits who are caricatures of merchants, the middle classes, country-dwellers, and foreigners.

The Ottoman conquerers retained much more of Byzantium's heritage than one might imagine, including the institution of public baths. The baths both surprised and impressed most of the Western travelers who discovered them. In the 18th century, Jean Thévenot described them minutely in his *Voyage au Levant*: "I will describe the one at Tophana, next to a superb mosque, since it is one of the most beautiful that I have seen. You enter by a large square room, about 20 feet long, with a very high ceiling. This room is lined with stone benches built against the surrounding wall. They are as wide as the wall, and half as high, and all are covered with matting." The Turkish hammams retain the structure of Roman baths, with the tepidarium, the frigidarium and the caldarium; where there were thermal springs, the baths are called kaplıcas.

THE STEAM ROOM OF YENI KAPLICA
This gives access to the private bathrooms which were originally reserved for dignitaries.

1. Entrance hall.
2. Intermediate room.
3. The old private entrance.
4. Private bathrooms.
5. Steam room.

PLAN OF THE YENI KAPLICA, IN BURSA
These public baths were founded in 1550 by the Grand Vizier Rüstem Paşa. They include an entrance hall, often with a decorative fountain, and a cloakroom; an intermediate room to allow you to get used to the heat; and an octagonal steam room with a great circular pool in the middle and baths in alcoves round the sides. The wash-basins provided hot and cold water.

Some kaplıcas had a pool in the center of the steam room where the clientèle could bathe after being washed.

Western imagination has transformed the hammam and the harem into erotic fantasies which are reinforced by the works of the French and Italian painters who visited Istanbul. Lady Mary Wortley-Montagu's visits to the Turkish baths in Edirne and later in Istanbul, and her admiration for the beauty of Turkish women's bodies, provided the inspiration for a painting by Ingres (shown left): *The Turkish Bath* (1862). Lady Mary noted that the hammam was for women what the café was for men – a chance to socialize.

"Turkish women, following an ancient Asian and Greek custom, go to the baths in all weathers, less for their health than to beautify themselves. The other, and main, reason is because it gives them an excuse to get out of their houses.**"**

Nicholas de Nicolay

There were separate hammams for men and women except in small towns, where they bathed at different times. Young boys bathed with the women until puberty.

CARPETS AND KILIMS

The origins of kilim decorations go back to prehistoric times, with motifs symbolizing goddesses.

The importance of carpets in Turkish life is a result of the lifestyles of the Turkish people. Carpets or kilims were essential for providing shade from the sun and lining the insides of tents, thus giving protection from the rigors of the climate. When the nomadic tribes of Anatolia converted to Islam, carpets acquired a new function as prayer mats. The different types range from knotted carpets woven of wool or silk to tapestry weave kilims. *Cicims* were embroidered kilims.

ÇUVAL
Carpet bag from Malatya.

KILIMS
In nomadic tribes and in villages, kilims were kept for domestic use. The techniques and motifs of each tribe and region were passed on from one generation of women to the next. Therefore the styles were not altered by commercial pressures until this century.

THE STITCHING OF KILIMS
The diversity of styles results from the different techniques developed from one tribe to the next.

CARPET WORKSHOPS
The carpets which decorated the palaces of sultans and dignitaries came from great workshops which, from the 16th century, exported examples to Europe. The workshops of Uşak, Kumkapı and Hereke were among the better known.

Elibelinde   Burdock   Rose

PRAYER RUG FROM ERZERUM
The central image is an alcove in a mosque
pointing in the direction of Mecca, which is known
in Turkish as *Mirhab*.

UŞAK CARPET (16TH CENTURY)
The geometric Turkish patterns are
influenced by the Persian safavid
style.

**A COURT CARPET OF HEREKE STYLE
(LATE 16TH CENTURY).** In the symbolic
mihrab niche is a tree of life – here an
almond tree with birds perching on it
– surrounded by a floral border.

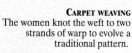

CARPET WEAVING
The women knot the weft to two
strands of warp to evolve a
traditional pattern.

The method of knotting differs
from place to place. The double
or Ghiordes knot, also used in
Europe, made the carpets

strong. The Persian, Sehna
knot resulted in more intricate
patterns and gave a beautiful
finish.

Panels of tiles in a mosque.

In the middle of the 11th century the khans of the Oğuz Turks of central Asia adopted Islam in order to control the silk route, in alliance with their former enemies the Arabs. It was an entirely political conversion, and was only a matter of convenience. Until the mid 16th century the epics of the time celebrate the ancient divinities of the Turkish religion, while affirming the strength of their Muslim faith in opposition to the Christians. The Ottoman version of Turkish Islam is primarily political: the sultan is the swordsman of Islam and Allah's shadow on earth. With the coming of the Republic in 1923, Mustafa Kemal Atatürk pursued a policy of secularization, because religion had become synonymous with attachment to the past.

Some of the finest examples of Ottoman art are found in the decoration of the mosques and the ornamentation of religious objects, such as sumptuously illuminated copies of the Koran, with leather covers embossed with gold, silver, or sometimes precious stones, or Koran stands made of ebony inlaid with mother-of-pearl and bone. The religious manuscript shown here, and its rich tabernacle, are remarkable for the fineness of the calligraphic writing as well as for their pastel-toned floral decoration.

With the revival of the Islamic religion over the past few years, Koranic schools and places of worship are proliferating. Here a *softa* or older student is reading the Koran in the Bursa Ulu Cami.

WOMEN AND ISLAM
The Turkish state, deeply secularized since the Kemalist reforms of forced secularization, have multiplied measures in favor of the equality of the sexes. The 1926 civil code defines the rights of women in marriage, divorce, inheritance, and education. The right to vote was granted in 1935, well before many European countries.

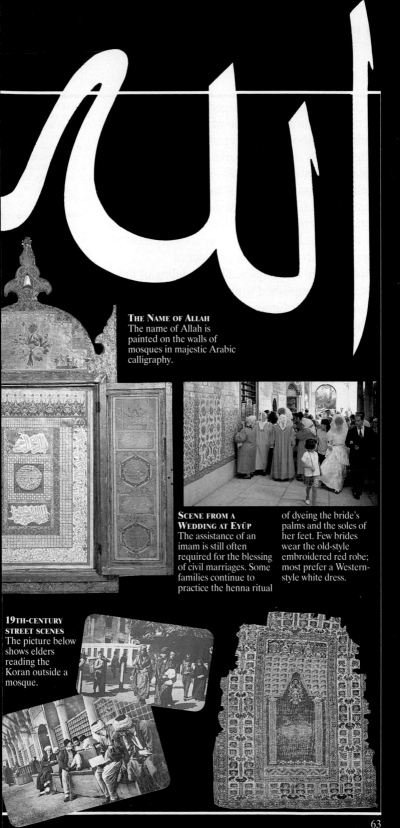

THE NAME OF ALLAH
The name of Allah is
painted on the walls of
mosques in majestic Arabic
calligraphy.

**SCENE FROM A
WEDDING AT EYÜP**
The assistance of an
imam is still often
required for the blessing
of civil marriages. Some
families continue to
practice the henna ritual
of dyeing the bride's
palms and the soles of
her feet. Few brides
wear the old-style
embroidered red robe;
most prefer a Western-
style white dress.

**19TH-CENTURY
STREET SCENES**
The picture below
shows elders
reading the
Koran outside a
mosque.

BYZANTINE ART

A characteristic style emerged at the beginning of the 6th century: a fusion of classical realism with the symbolic figurativeness of Roman art. The majority of known works date from after the iconoclastic period (726–843). The fresco technique was developed sometime in the 10th century, but it was not considered to be a serious alternative to the more expensive mosaics. The latter are the true masterpieces of Byzantine art and are the product of sophisticated techniques. The modeling of the faces is accomplished with graded colors of stone, and their luminous appearance is achieved by varying the position of the tiles, so the light is caught at different angles.

CHRIST IN MAJESTY, A 9TH- TO EARLY 10TH-CENTURY MOSAIC
This mosaic (right) decorates the tympanum of the Imperial Gate and the entrance to the nave of Haghia Sophia basilica.

A 14TH-CENTURY FRESCO
One of the angels surrounding the Virgin and Child in the funerary chapel in the old Saint-Savior-in-Chora church (Kariye Cami'i).

From the 9th century onwards the positioning of the tableaux and the hierarchy of the characters represented in Byzantine churches were obliged to follow an official schema, probably decreed by Michael III. Christ Pantocrator, or Master of the Universe, always had to be placed in the center of the main cupola.

BYZANTINE IVORIES

In the center of this fine example of a Byzantine ivory (left), which dates from the 6th century, is the emperor Justinian (527–65), along with the symbolic figures of Victory and Earth. In the bottom section it portrays the conquered people of India, who are presenting offerings, including an elephant tusk, to the emperor.

ICON OF SAINT EUDOXIA

This 11th-century icon represents the Empress Eudoxia, wife of Theodosius II (408–450). Her dress and her crown are incrusted with precious stones. Imperial dignity was considered to be synonymous with divine selection, and Byzantine monarchs and their spouses were frequently portrayed wearing halos.

A 14TH-CENTURY FRESCO OF THE ANASTASIS OR HARROWING OF HELL.

This fresco dominates the Pareeclesion of the Church of Saint Savior-in-Chora. Christ rescues Adam and Eve from their tombs.

The locks of the gates of Hell surround Satan bound at his feet. Other figures are St John the Baptist, David, Solomon and Abel.

A 14TH-CENTURY MOSAIC OF THE GENEALOGY OF CHRIST

Christ, in the center, is surrounded by his ancestors, from Adam to Ersom Japhet and the eleven sons of Jacob. This mosaic (left) decorates the southern dome of the inner narthex of Saint Savior-in-Chora.

● FOUNTAINS

Istanbul has many fountains. Their sites were chosen according to the needs of the city's residents and travelers, as well as for aesthetic reasons. There were two types of public fountain: the *çeşme* or public fawcet for filling jugs and the *sebil* where drinking water was given to passers-by from behind a grille.

The grandest fountains combined most functions. The *şadırvan*, or ablution fountain had an almost sacred status; at the Eyüp mosque the faithful would leave the fountain fawcets open so that the water – the symbol of their destiny – could flow freely. Behind high walls were the ornamental fountains of private mansions and the yalıs of the Bosphorus.

HOLY FOUNTAINS
Building a fountain was a good deed, a philanthropic act according to the teachings of Islam. Accordingly the sultans, princes, ladies of the seraglio, and dignitaries vied with each other to endow them.

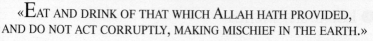

«EAT AND DRINK OF THAT WHICH ALLAH HATH PROVIDED,
AND DO NOT ACT CORRUPTLY, MAKING MISCHIEF IN THE EARTH.»

THE KORAN

THE FOUNTAIN OF SULTAN AHMET III

This Baroque-style fountain, built in 1728, is the most famous of all. A basin flanked with niches in the shape of a mihrab occupies the center of each of its four faces. The *sebil* of the angles are closed by bronze gates.

PRECIOUS MARBLE

The Baroque style was used to great effect on many of the pediments and façades of fountains. These often have fanciful complicated forms, such as delicate drapery and marble carved to represent flowing water.

ENGRAVED PEDIMENTS

Fountains are often engraved with calligraphy. The most common inscription of all is a verse from the Koran: "By water all things have life."

ÇEŞME, STREET FOUNTAINS

The citizens of Istanbul carried water in earthenware jugs. Watersellers carried it in porous skins which kept the water at a refreshingly cool temperature.

MONUMENTAL FOUNTAINS

Antoine-Ignace Melling (1763–1831) painted *Procession in Honour of a Turkish Wedding* (below). It shows the traditional order of the people who took part in the procession, as well as the bride's chariot, in great detail. The crowd of characters gathered around the fountain is carefully portrayed, all of them dressed in costumes and turbans in a myriad of colors.

One visit to the Grand Bazaar is enough to convince you of the diversity and richness of the Turkish craft industry. First, of course, are the rugs (*halı*) and kilims, but you might also be tempted by the leather and suede goods. Equally famous is the golden jewelry decorated with precious stones, as well as the traditionally shaped pieces in silver. There are also copper objects and onyx trinkets, as well as pottery and ceramics from Iznik and Izmir. Smokers will appreciate the meerschaum pipes and the hookahs, while gourmets will prefer the canned stuffed vegetables or the spices and dried fruits that can be bought in bulk at the Egyptian or Spice Bazaar.

The pistachios that are served as snacks all day long are also a common ingredient in Turkish cuisine, as are dried apricots and raisins from Smyrna (Izmir).

PASTIRMA Spiced meat dried with fenugreek.

SOME SPICES Pul biber, a flaked pepper (1), aniseed (2), fenugreek (3) and sumak (4). An aromatic infusion prepared from mint and lemon (5) is a drink to aid digestion.

ZEYTINYAĞLI DOLMALAR These are vegetables stuffed with onions, rice, and olive oil: stuffed peppers (Biber Dolması), stuffed vine leaves (Yaprak Dolması) and stuffed eggplant (Patlıcan Dolması).

BAKLAVA Puff pastry layered with walnuts or pistachios.

TURKISH PASTRIES Often very sugary and rich in butter. They combine almonds, hazelnuts, sesame seeds, and, as here, pistachios.

The famous "Bebek" – squares of pistachio-flavored almond paste.

KELIM This kilim in shades of blue, red and unbleached wool, is an example of those currently made in Uşak.

SMOKING ACCESSORIES
A pipe with a meerschaum bowl carved in the shape of a head is a typical product made by Turkish craftworkers.

TURKISH JEWELRY
The jewelers draw their inspiration from many sources: traditional motifs, reinterpretation of Ottoman and Byzantine designs (see the earring, right), and variations on the romantic style, as with this hair ornament in silver filigree (below).

THE TURKISH DAILY PRESS
The large-circulation daily papers are *Cumhuriyet* (*The Republican*), *Milliyet* (*The Nation*), *Tercüman* (*The Interpreter*), and *Hürriyet* (*The Independence*).

SWEETS
Rose jelly (*Gül Reçeli*), fig jam (*Incir Reçeli*) and dried rose petals are used to flavor tea, desserts and narghile, or hookah, water.

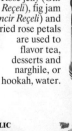

ALCOHOLIC BEVERAGES
Those include Buzbağ, a Turkish red wine produced in the Elazığ vineyards, and Rakı, an aperitif made from grapes and aniseed.

CHICKEN WITH APRICOTS AND ALMONDS

In the 16th century the Ottoman Empire dominated the Mediterranean, uniting diverse lands and cultures. The influence of Turkish cuisine spread to Greece, North Africa, and the Middle East. A refined court cuisine, partly inherited from the Byzantine imperial court, was developed in Istanbul, in the sumptuous palaces of the sultans and in the *konaks*.

INGREDIENTS FOR 4 TO 6 PERSONS
1 free-range chicken (3 lb), 1 large onion, 1 tablespoon honey, 1 cup dried apricots, ½ cup almonds, 3 tablespoons Izmir raisins, 5 tablespoons of butter, 2 cups of rice, salt and pepper.

1. Cut the chicken into 8 parts and finely chop the onion.

2. In a thick-bottomed skillet melt 3 tablespoons of butter, then brown the chicken pieces all over.

3. Add the chopped onion and allow to brown for several minutes.

> «... DINNER CAME IN, WHICH WAS SERVED ONE DISH AT A TIME...
> THEIR SAUCES ARE VERY RICH, ALL THE ROASTING VERY WELL
> DONE. THEY USE A GREAT DEAL OF SPICE.»
>
> LADY MARY WORTLEY-MONTAGU

4. While the onions brown, mix the apricots, raisins, honey, salt and pepper.

5. Add this mixture to the skillet and moisten with ½ cup of water.

6. Cover and simmer over a low heat for 30 minutes.

7. Soak the rice in warm, salted water.

8. After 30 minutes rinse and drain the rice. Pour the rice over the chicken and add 2 cups of water.

9. Cover and simmer for a further 10 to 15 minutes, over a low heat.

10. While the chicken cooks melt the remaining butter in a skillet and brown the almonds in it.

11. Arrange the chicken in a serving dish and sprinkle with the almonds. Serve hot.

● THE CAFÉS

Coffee was first drunk in the 9th century and was for a long time very rare and expensive, available only to the powerful of Arabia. At the beginning of the 16th century it was still served with great pomp in the court of Süleyman. It became more popular and widely available in 1555 when two Syrian traders, Hakim and Shams, opened the first coffee shop in Istanbul. It was an enormous success and they soon opened many more establishments. Coffee was nicknamed "milk of chess players and thinkers" and became the favorite drink of intellectuals. The coffee shops were places for discussion and relaxation where one came to smoke a chibouk or a hookah. Soon they would offer their clientèle a range of entertainments: musicians and dancers would perform, and crowds would gather to hear the storyteller or *meddah*, or to watch the shadow theater, the Karagöz.

Pierre Loti particularly loved to go to a small Eyüp café that looks over the Golden Horn. Today the café is named after him and this has helped to keep it in business.

During the 19th century, some cafés became specialized. The *kiraathane* were reading rooms that provided newspapers, magazines, and sometimes the latest literary creations. The *çalgili kahveleri*, or "instrumental cafés", were reserved for music. In the *asık kahveleri*, "cafés of love", poetry readings were held, sometimes accompanied by a soloist or small group of musicians.

TURKISH CAFÉ IN THE 18TH CENTURY
Engraving by A. I. Melling.

REAR FAÇADE OF THE CHURCH OF ST JOHN STUDION. A classic example of a basilica erected around 450 but now in ruins.

Although Istanbul contains some magnificent examples of Byzantine architecture, very little from that period remains, scarcely enough to provide even a representative selection of an architecture that spread across three continents and eleven centuries. Apart from Haghia Sophia and a few land walls, there is almost no civil architecture, and barely thirty churches are still in existence today.

HAGHIA SOPHIA
Built in five years (532-537), from foundations to completion, Haghia Sophia is a unique structure in both conception and size, without precedent and unrivaled until the building of the Ottoman mosques. The dome, with a diameter of more than 100 feet and a height of more than 180 feet, borders on the miraculous, given the technology that was available. Subsequent generations actually believed Haghia Sophia to be the product of supernatural intervention.

THE CHURCH OF STS SERGIUS AND BACCHUS Erected by Justinian between 527 and 536 to an octagonal plan inscribed within a circle. A foretaste of Haghia Sophia – hence its present Turkish name, Küçük Ayasofya ("Small Haghia Sophia") – the church was converted into a mosque at the end of the 15th century. Its elegance makes Sts Sergius and Bacchus one of the best examples of Byzantine architecture from this period.

BYZANTINE CAPITALS
Three examples, from the Theotokas Pammakaristos (Fethiye Cami'i) (**1**), Haghia Sophia (**2**), and Haghia Irene (**3**).

The Ottomans added four corner minarets to Haghia Sophia and reinforced the structure with buttresses, all of which considerably altered its exterior appearance.

KALENDERHANE CAMI'I
Probably built in the 9th century, it was radically restored during the period of the Paleologos renaissance. It may possibly have been the church of St Savior Akataleptos. After the conquest, Mehmet II gave it to the order of the Kalenderi dervishes, hence its present name.

TEKFUR SARAYI
The most important surviving example of Byzantine civil architecture, the imperial palace known in Turkish as Tekfur Sarayı, or "Palace of the Porphyrogenitus", dates from the 13th century. Situated near the land walls, it was occupied until the Turkish conquest.

● AQUATIC ARCHITECTURE

The largest of the Byzantine covered cisterns is known in Turkish as Yerebatan Sarayı ("Underground Palace"). It measures 360 by 230 feet.

Istanbul needed a steady, reliable source of fresh water for it was built on an arid peninsula and at several points in its history the population reached as many as several hundred thousand inhabitants. So the Byzantines, who were under almost constant threat of siege, constructed a system of aqueducts together with a vast array of cisterns, the latter both covered and also open to the sky. The interlinked dams and aqueducts culminated in a network of fountains which were spread throughout greater Istanbul.

CORINTHIAN CAPITAL
One of the 5th-century capitals which crown the majority of the 336 columns in the Justinian cistern of Yerebatan Sarayı. They were of many designs and clearly job lots because not intended to be seen.

TURKISH BATHS
A standard feature of the Ottoman city, the public baths could be quite magnificent buildings, particularly if founded by a member of the imperial family or the high administration.

The chambers are surmounted by cupolas which are pierced with bell-shaped glass lights.

MAĞLOVA AQUEDUCT
Built in the 1560's by Sinan, at the behest of Süleyman, this water-supply system is the most impressive of the four aqueducts in the Istanbul network.

FOUNTAIN AT A YALI

In the 18th century, ahead of the city's expansion, a system of aqueducts was created for the quarter situated on the Asian bank opposite the Golden Horn. The new water supply would primarily serve the houses of the wealthy.

AHMET III FOUNTAIN

The public fountain was the charitable gesture par excellence for the rich or powerful Ottoman eager to perpetuate his good name by means of a dedicatory inscription. The imperial fountains are very grand, like this one erected in front of Topkapı Palace.

FOUNTAIN IN THE LIBRARY OF AHMET III (1719)

The fountain seen here was built in 1578 by the architect Sinan in front of the library in the third court of Topkapı Palace. It is decorated with Iznik faience in floral motifs.

BÜYÜK ÇEKMEÇE

This 28-arch bridge, constructed by Sinan in 1565-67, spans Lake Büyük Çekmeçe, at the point where it flows into the sea, on the Edirne road some 25 miles from Istanbul.

● OTTOMAN ARCHITECTURE

For their classic religious and funerary architecture, the Ottomans adopted forms already established in Arabia and Persia and brought to Anatolia by the Selçuk Turks. From the end of the 13th century, the architectural structures became more elaborate and in this area, the Ottoman builders benefitted from Byzantine expertise. Many religious works were built: mosques, *medreses* (colleges), and *türbes* (mausoleums). In the 14th century Ottoman architects began to use local techniques and materials.

THE GREEN MOSQUE
Built in 1378 in Iznik, this is a classic example of a square-plan mosque with a single dome.

PORTICO OF THE MOSQUE OF BEYAZIT I
This is one of the earliest of the porticos that would become so characteristic of the imperial mosques; it was built in Bursa, 1379–1402.

THE GREEN MOSQUE
Built by Mehmet I (1413–21) it is, by virtue of its size and the beauty of its decor, one of the most important works in Bursa. Here, two cupolas succeed one another within a rectangular plan, the first crowned by a 19th-century lantern.

PLAN OF THE GREEN MOSQUE
In Bursa, the designs for the first mosques with paired successive domes, to cover court and then prayer halls, evolved towards a single cupola. The earliest of this type, which had a flanking half-dome, appeared in the Mosque of Mehmet II (Fatih) (**1**), now lost, and the Mosque of Atık Ali Paşa, erected in 1496 (**2**).

Ottoman "stalactite" capitals, with wood used for those of the first period based directly on Selçuk models (**1**), and stone for those in the 15th-century Green Mosque in Iznik (**2**) and the 16th-century Süleymaniye in Istanbul (**3**).

TÜRBE. The architecture of these Ottoman mausoleums is derived from that of tombs in Iran and Central Asia, as well

as Armenian and Georgian architecture.

Niğde, central Anatolia. The center image represents the Green Mausoleum of Mehmet I at Bursa, decorated with turquoise ceramics. On the right is the Mausoleum of

Süleyman in Istanbul, one of the most elaborate structures of its kind; an octagonal building encircled by a gallery and capped by a double cupola, its interior is ornamented with ceramic panels.

Originally intended to house the tombs of the reigning family, *türbe* became more widespread in the 15th century when high state officials began to build them. Illustrated on the left is the octagonal Selçuk mausoleum of Princess Hüdavend Hatun at

THE COMPLEX (KÜLLIYE) OF BEYAZIT II AT EDIRNE. Constructed in 1484–88, this is one of the supreme works of Ottoman architecture. The complex comprises a mosque in the center, a public soup kitchen (*imaret*) on the left, a medical college on the extreme right, and a hospital for the mentally ill with a magnificent octagonal hall.

PLAN OF THE ATIK ALI PAŞA MOSQUE BUILT IN 1496

THE BEYAZIT II MOSQUE IN ISTANBUL Shown here in cross-section with its grand forecourt, this mosque dates from 1500–5. It is a typical mosque with its design of a single dome on two half-domes modeled on the Haghia Sophia.

THE SELIMIYE, IMPERIAL MOSQUE

The mosque at Edirne, built by Sinan between 1568 and 1574 for Sultan Selim I, was considered by the architect himself, by contemporaries, and also by posterity, as his masterpiece and as the finest example of Ottoman architecture ever built. The building is admired for its originality and renowned for a dome with a diameter of 90 feet and a height of 160 feet, identical to that of Haghia Sophia.

STRUCTURE
The huge cupola, set on eight piers surmounted by eight segments of a circle, appears almost to float on air. Meanwhile, the absence of bearing walls made it possible to pierce windows at every level, thereby flooding the mosque with natural light.

GENERAL PLAN
While reducing the need for external buttressing, numerous side aisles and galleries also create isolated or private spaces, reserved for prayer or the recitation of the Koran, as well as for the superb imperial loggia decorated with the most beautiful Ottoman tiles. The great variety of the spaces within is reflected on the exterior, with its wonderful mix of façades. The four minarets mark the cardinal points.

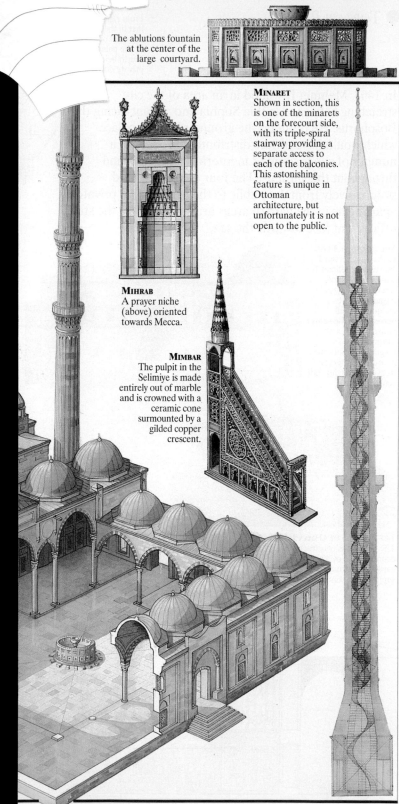

The ablutions fountain at the center of the large courtyard.

MINARET
Shown in section, this is one of the minarets on the forecourt side, with its triple-spiral stairway providing a separate access to each of the balconies. This astonishing feature is unique in Ottoman architecture, but unfortunately it is not open to the public.

MIHRAB
A prayer niche (above) oriented towards Mecca.

MIMBAR
The pulpit in the Selimiye is made entirely out of marble and is crowned with a ceramic cone surmounted by a gilded copper crescent.

● TOPKAPI PALACE

From right to left: the council met in the second courtyard, the third one was surrounded by the palace school, and the fourth belonged to the private domain of the sultan.

In 1463, Mehmet II walled in an area of the city stretching between Haghia Sophia and a point facing the Bosphorus. He outlined the ground plan of a palace which would have offices distributed throughout a number of wings situated in interior courtyards and throughout the gardens. The four courtyards lead progressively from the public to the private. The private apartments in the garden areas are connected to the state offices that face towards the sea.

THE HOUSE OF FATIH
In the palace's third courtyard, Mehmet II built a pavilion of freestone on massive foundations. It includes a small belvedere in the center and, on the Sea of Marmara side, a loggia. The vaults have housed the imperial treasure since the 16th century.

THE PAVILION OF OSMAN III (1754–57)
The pavilion is constructed of wood as an economy and overhangs one of the palace gardens. A curved wooden console supports the central chamber.

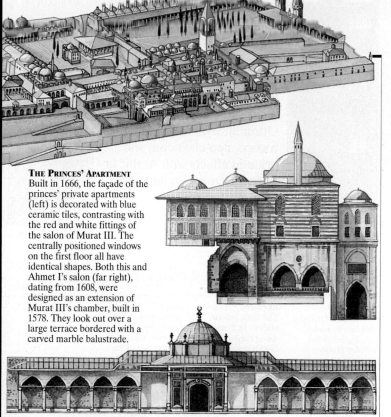

THE PRINCES' APARTMENT
Built in 1666, the façade of the princes' private apartments (left) is decorated with blue ceramic tiles, contrasting with the red and white fittings of the salon of Murat III. The centrally positioned windows on the first floor all have identical shapes. Both this and Ahmet I's salon (far right), dating from 1608, were designed as an extension of Murat III's chamber, built in 1578. They look out over a large terrace bordered with a carved marble balustrade.

THE GATE OF FELICITY OR OF THE WHITE EUNUCHS
This passage, between the second and third courtyards, leads to the Throne Room.

The arcaded entranceway is surmounted by cupolas, and was used only by dignitaries and ambassadors.

BAGHDAD PAVILION
Murat IV constructed this house in 1635, over-looking the Golden Horn to mark the taking of Baghdad. Its cross-shaped layout is inscribed in an octagon and covered with a cupola.

The walls are covered with blue ceramic from Iznik, and the interior decoration of the cupola is painted. The house is illuminated by the light that comes through the stained-glass windows, and is encircled by an exterior gallery.

CHAMBER OF MURAT III
This was the state room of the sultan. Symmetrical cabinets and alcoves with low sofas and a fireplace mark the center. The walls are decorated with ceramic panels. A splendid wall with a superb central çeşme is an outstanding feature.

● BAROQUE ARCHITECTURE IN THE 19TH CENTURY

At the end of the 18th century, the influence of western architecture was overturning the rules of Ottoman civil and religious architecture. Thus was born the Baroque Ottoman style which mixed rococo, neo-classicism and oriental effects with Arabic or Indian elements reimported from the west. The development was due to Ahmet III in the early 18th century.

BAS-RELIEFS FROM THE KÜÇÜKSU HOUSE
Sculpture decorated windows, doors, palace façades and public fountains with rococo motifs.

HOUSE IN ARNAVUTKÖY
The eclectic Ottoman style can be seen in the façades of this wooden house.

KÜÇÜKSU
This little palace, built in 1870 on the Asian bank of the Bosphorus, reflects the influence of the École des Beaux-Arts at this period. Two bowed balconies on consoles add to the elaboration of the façade.

PORTAL OF THE DOLMABAHÇE PALACE A marble wharf runs along the Bosphorus side of the palace. On the land side the palace is protected by very high walls. The monumental portal, in the Beaux-Arts style, is the work of the architect Karabet Balyan.

ORTAKÖY MOSQUE Sultan Abdül Mecit built the Ortaköy Mosque by the Bosphorus in 1855. It retains the characteristics of earlier 16th- and 17th-century mosques, but shows a Beaux-Arts influence in its decoration.

The traditional Ottoman house was usually built of wood on a stone ground floor. It first appeared in its present form in the middle of the 17th century. A characteristic feature of such a house is its corbeled construction: each floor is supported by a corbeled wooden platform. It has many windows which provide good ventilation, and a stairway which leads to an open gallery (*hayat*). The painted façades are decorated with carved wood. This type of house is found in the cities as well as in the country.

CORBELED CONSTRUCTION
The wooden floor of an Ottoman house is built on a stone or adobe wall, and overhangs the front of the house.

Plan illustrating the evolution of the *hayat* into a *sofa*.

A TRADITIONAL HOUSE IN BURSA
The floor plan of an Ottoman house often has to allow for an irregularly shaped plot and twisting roads, and through the use of complicated corbeling on the upper floors ensure that the rooms on the upper floors are rectangular.

MAIN ROOM with cabinets and alcoves.

HOUSE FLOOR PLAN
The central space (*sofa*) is surrounded by four corner bedrooms (*oda*).

HAYAT

The oldest example of an Ottoman house has a first-floor gallery, called a *hayat*. It is reached by exterior stairs from the courtyard, which all the rooms open onto. These rooms were originally entirely lit from the courtyard side, while the street side of the house was filled in. The raised parts of the *hayat* are used as the main living space in summer. This form did not necessarily originate in the country, but it has survived for a long time in rural areas.

HALF-TIMBERED OTTOMAN HOUSE

This house is built around a wooden framework which is then filled in with rubble or scrap material, and covered with an ochre-, brick-, or indigo-colored roughcast. In Istanbul, from the mid-19th century, horizontal wooden slats were added.

SOFA HOUSE

During the 19th century, and especially in the cities, it became increasingly inconvenient to use the *hayat*. These open galleries were enclosed by glass or by rooms added on piecemeal. On the courtyard side the room would become an interior antechamber, or *sofa*. Houses with a *sofa* were composed of a central space and four corner rooms often projecting on corbels.

87

The yalı are summer residences built of wood and situated along the banks of the Bosphorus (the word *yalı* also means shore). Their symmetrical design was influenced by being on the seafront, and includes two entrances – one facing the sea, the other the land. The main rooms jut out from the front of the house and have wide bay windows which open onto the sea.

INTERIOR OF A YALI
This view shows the low *sedir* (divan) which runs along the painted wood partitions.

CLASSIC YALI WITH INTERIOR "SOFA"
The *sofa*, or central room, is framed by four corner rooms (*oda*) built out from the façade. There was also a family or harem wing.

THE AMCAZADE HÜSEYIN PAŞA YALISI
The yalı of the celebrated Köprülü family, shown below, dates from the end of the 17th century. It is the oldest example of an Ottoman house in existence. The row of openings protected by horizontally opening shutters was a typical feature of the yalı by the sea.

Yalı are luxurious houses which belonged to the great dignitaries of the Empire. Along the Bosphorus more modest wooden houses can also be found, for example at Arnavutköy and Yeniköy on the European side.

The ground floor of the yalı sometimes includes a shelter for caiques or skiffs.

ISTANBUL
AS SEEN BY PAINTERS

« THE MOST MAJESTIC, MOST VARIED, MOST MAGNIFICENT, AND
MOST UNTAMED SITE THAT A PAINTER COULD HOPE TO FIND.»
LAMARTINE

In the 18th century in an attempt to save the empire from its successive defeats, the Ottoman élite adopted the most efficient Western military and civil systems. Thanks to this opening up towards Europe, a number of orientalist painters moved to Istanbul. When their paintings were displayed in the Seraglio they were admired, and little by little they began to change the perceptions about art of those who saw them. J.-E. Liotard, known as the "Turkish painter" (1702–89), is the creator of the *Portrait of Richard Pococke* (1), an archeologist and English traveler. The background of the portrait shows a view over Seraglio Point and the Bosphorus, the blues of which are in harmony with those of the sky and the turquoise of the oriental costume. Jean-Baptiste Hilair's blue-toned *The Point of the Seraglio as seen from Galata* (2) is seen from the eye-level of the people in the foreground. To the left, the Sepetçiler Köşkü, to the right Haghia Sophia, Haghia Irene, and the smokestacks of the Topkapı Sarayı. In the background is a ship with its sails unfurled. Fabius Brest, who painted the *View of the Bosphorus* (3), lived in Istanbul during the 19th century.

	2
1	3

Devrim Erbil,
General View of Istanbul,
1986.

Cihat Burak was born in Istanbul in 1915. He was an architect and a gifted, original writer, whose taste for realism did not preclude either the strange or the humorous. His *Interior View of the Süleymaniye* (1), painted in 1975, gives an idea of the splendid displays during the investiture ceremonies of the Ottoman sultans. Fikret Muallâ (1904–69), who was born in Turkey but died in France, has admirers in both countries. The portrait of his friend Avni Arbaş (4) was painted in 1948. Despite a life full of misery and drama, his work is pure exaltation, full of the charm and color of everyday city life, as in his *Countryside* (3) painted in 1945. Istanbul and Paris were his two great passions. Namik Ismail (1890–1935) excelled in a number of genres, especially that of female portraiture. In 1925 he painted the lyrical work, *Full Moon over Istanbul* (5).

2		
		3
1		
	5	4

In his early works Bedri Rahmi (1913–75) was greatly influenced by Turkish popular art. He created his own lively and colorful language in order to celebrate his Anatolian home, although he did not neglect the charm and colors of Istanbul, as in the façade of his *Kahriye cami'i* (1). Hüseyin Avni Lifij (1889–1927) was a

student of the great painter Osman Hamdi. Avni did his studies at the Paris École des Beaux-Arts. His canvases are imbued with a nostalgic fervor, and celebrate the light of Istanbul like no other painter before him. His landscapes are interspersed with an intense interior life. He touches upon allegorical themes that appeal to Ottoman taste, as in this Zeyrek landscape, *Zeyrekten Görünü* (2). The watercolors of Mustafa Pilevneli, a contemporary of Lifij, are inspired by the Ottoman miniaturists of the 18th century. Pilevneli's favorite subject was the depiction of scenes from the daily life of the city.

3

2

1

Abidine Dino, born in 1913, adopted the city of Istanbul as his subject, finding in it both reality and mystery. He was the founder of the first Turkish avant-garde group, the D group (1933) as well as the "Port" group (1939). Abstraction, figurative work, sculpture, writing, and film-making all influenced him at different periods in his quest for uncompromising plastic purity. Shown here are *Seraglio Point* (1), *I dreamt of Istanbul* (2), and *Portrait of Nazim Hikmet* (3). Abidine

has exhibited regularly in Paris and other European capitals as well as in his own country.

1

2

3

Istanbul
AS SEEN BY WRITERS

Ralph Waldo Emerson's statement, "A city lives by remembering", has a great deal of truth in it. Today's Istanbul has a memory that spans twenty-seven centuries. The city reverberates with the whispers of history and the murmurs of human drama. It is full of songs of joy, elegies and paeans from all of its centuries. Authors from many cultures listen to Istanbul and give new echoes to it. The city lives by remembering and listening.

IMPERIAL CONSTANTINOPLE

VIEW FROM THE SERAGLIO

Pierre Gilles (Petrus Gyllius, 1490–1555) spent several years in the Ottoman capital between 1544 and 1550. His extensive work on the history and topography of the city was published posthumously: "Three Books on the Thracian Bosphorus" and "Four Books on the Topography of Constantinople and on its Antiquities".

❝ Though all the hills of Constantinople afford a very pleasing prospect, there is none that entertains you with such peculiar delight as the first hill, where the Sultan lives in a licentious and luxurious manner. He has before him, whether he is walking in his gardens or in his chambers of the Seraglio, a full view of the Bosphorus and both its shores, which are green and flourishing with woods belonging to the neighboring farms. On the right hand he beholds a spacious field of Chalcedon covered with his own gardens; he sees the Propontis, islands without number, and the woody mountains of Asia. If he looks an immense distance behind him he beholds Mount Olympus always clothed in snow. If he takes a shorter prospect he views before him the wonders of his own city, the Church of Saint-Sophia and the Hippodrome. If he casts his eyes to the left, he beholds the seven hills on which the city is seated, and more remotely he looks around the immeasurable, spacious fields of Thrace. If he extends his prospect over the seas, he views a moving scene of ships passing and repassing before him; some sailing from the Hellespont or the Black Sea, others again coming into his port from all the coasts of the Propontis; while at the same time other vessels are sailing up and down the Bay of Ceras, where there is also an abundance of ferries and small boats always rowing from side to side. And if he looks below him, he has the agreeable pleasure of beholding the three sides of the first hill, dressed with trees, flowers, and plants of all kinds. He not only has a fine prospect from the palace but is entertained with several delightful vistas from the top of the gardens rising on the hills. If he has an inclination to take a view of his Seraglio from the point of land that projects so far into the sea and that, as I observed, divided the Bosphorus, here he beholds it in all its glory, strengthened with large pillars of marble and fanned with gentle, refreshing breezes. Here he often sits with small osier lattices before him, so that, like another Gyges, he discerns all that sail near him, though he himself is visible to none. And if at any time he is weary of the company of his domestics, he can divert himself with the ridiculous drollery of the watermen fixing their oars and boat-poles to the shore as they tug against the violent stream of the Bosphorus, which is much more rapid than the Rhone. **❞**

PIERRE GILLES, *FOUR BOOKS ON THE TOPOGRAPHY*
OF CONSTANTINOPLE AND ON ITS ANTIQUITIES, LONDON 1729,
TRANSLATED BY JOHN BALL

HUNDREDS OF PALACES

Lady Mary Wortley-Montagu (1689–1762) was in the Ottoman imperial capital in 1718 as the period later named "The Tulip Age" was about to start. She was the wife of the British consul. Her letters describing life in the city and its environs are remarkable for their observations, style, and understanding of Ottoman culture.

❝ To Lady Bristol – Pera of Constantinople, 10 April 1718

The pleasure of going in a barge to Chelsea is not comparable to that of rowing upon the canal of the sea here, where for twenty miles together down the Bosphorus the most beautiful variety of prospects present themselves. The Asian side is covered with fruit trees, villages and the most delightful landscapes in nature. On the European side stands Constantinople, situated on seven hills. The unequal heights make it seem as large again as it is (though one of the largest cities in the world), showing an agreeable mixture of gardens, pine and cypress trees, palaces, mosques and public buildings, raised one above another with as much beauty and appearance of symmetry as your ladyship ever saw in a cabinet adorned by the most skilful hands, jars showing themselves above jars, mixed with canisters, babies and candlesticks. This is a very odd comparison, but it gives me an exact image of the thing. ... I have taken care to see as much of the Seraglio as is to be seen. It is on a point of land running into the sea: a palace of prodigious extent, but very irregular; the gardens a large compass of ground full of high cypress trees, which is all I know of them; the buildings all of white stone, leaded on top, with guilded turrets and spires, which look very magnificent, and indeed I believe there is no Christian king's palace half so large. There are six large courts in it all built round and set with trees, having galleries of stone: one of these for the guard, another for the stables, the fifth for the divan, the sixth for the apartment destined for audiences. On the ladies' side there is at least as many more, with distinct courts belonging to their eunuchs and attendants, their kitchens, etc.[...]Nothing can be pleasanter than the Canal, and the Turks are so well acquainted with its beauties, all their pleasure-seats are built on its banks, where they have at the same time the most beautiful prospects in Europe and Asia. There are near one another some hundreds of magnificent palaces ... I was yesterday to see that of the late Grand Vizier ... The extent of it is prodigious; the guardian assured me there is eight hundred rooms in it ... The garden is suitable to the house, where arbors, fountains, and walks are thrown together in an agreeable confusion. **❞**

LETTERS OF THE RIGHT HONOURABLE
LADY MARY WORTLEY-MONTAGU,
LONDON, 1763

About the Bosphorus
Lord Byron (1788–1824), traveled extensively in the western parts of the Ottoman Empire and visited Istanbul. He was active in support of the Greek independence movement against the Turks and lost his life during that struggle. He wrote both acerbic and admiring verses about Ottoman Turkey.

III
The European with the Asian shore
Sprinkled with palaces; the ocean stream
Here and there studded with a seventy-four;
Sophia's cupola with golden gleam;
The cypress groves; Olympus high and hoar:
The twelve isles, and the more than I could dream,
Far less describe, present the very view
Which charm'd the charming Mary Montagu.

V
The wind swept down the Euxine, and the wave
Broke foaming o'er the blue Symplegades;
'Tis a grand sight from off "the Giant's Grave"
To watch the progress of those rolling seas
Between the Bosphorus, as they lash and lave
European and Asia, you being quite at ease:
There's not a sea the passenger e'er pukes in,
Turns up more dangerous breakers than the Euxine.

Lord Byron, *Don Juan*, Canto V, 1819–24

The fall of Byzantium
Joseph von Hammer-Purgstall (1774–1856) served as an Austrian diplomat in Constantinople. He was renowned for his academic studies of oriental languages, and for his magnum opus, "The History of the Ottoman Empire".

❝No miracle was to save the Empire. The gates were hacked down by axes; the Turks flooded the streets; looting started, a looting which nothing was to stop, neither weeping women and girls, nor cries of the children nor the oaths of the wounded. No restraint could curb soldiers intoxicated with victory. The only criteria that affected the fate of the trembling creatures were those of youth, beauty and fortune. Without any distinction of rank or sex, prisoners were tied two by two with their belts or veils. Next it was the turn of the churches: pictures of saints were torn from their walls and cut up; sacred vessels were destroyed; vestments were turned into coverings; the crucifix, capped by a Janissary's bonnet, was carried around the streets; altars were profaned and used as dining-tables, or as beds to violate girls and boys, or as stalls for horses. 'Aya Sophia,' says Phranzes, 'God's sanctuary, the throne of His glory, the marvel of the earth, was transformed into a place of horrors and abominations.' Thus antique Byzantium fell, 1125 years after having been built by Constantine. The siege, which had lasted fifty-three days, ended on 29 May 1453; it was the 29th it had undergone since its foundation.❞

Ritter J. von Hammer-Purgstall,
The History of the Ottoman Empire, Paris, 1835,
translated by Marie Noële Kelly and Lawrence Kelly

SULTAN MURAD III

Evliya Çelebi (1611–1682) was the premier travel writer of the Ottoman Empire. In 1630 he had a dream which urged him to travel: first he toured all over Istanbul, then the far-flung territories of the empire.

❝Murad III never himself took the field, but the conquests of the empire were multiplied every year by his generals. He was buried beneath a separate cupola with his children, in the harem (court-yard) of Aya Soifiyah. He was the first Ottoman sovereign who lived and died at Constantinople without having once left it. Being much given to women and pleasure he had an immense number of male and female children, altogether three hundred and twenty-six. It is stated that in one single night fifty five of his women were lying in. At his death nineteen princes were killed according to the bloody code of the Ottoman empire. One of them, a very young boy, was eating chestnuts at the moment the executioner came in, to whom he said, 'Let me eat my chesnuts, and strangle me afterwards.' A request with which the executioner did not comply. Another was torn from his mother's breast and put to death, emitting at the same time his mother's milk by the nose, and his soul by his mouth. Twenty six daughters, some of them married to vezírs, survived their father. They all now lie buried in his sepulchre. God's mercy upon them!❞

EVLIYA ÇELEBI EFENDI, *NARRATIVE OF TRAVELS IN EUROPE,*
ASIA, AND AFRICA IN THE SEVENTEENTH CENTURY,
LONDON 1834, TRANSLATED BY RITTER J. VON HAMMER-PURGSTALL

THE SULEYMANIYE

❝Then he heard his Royal Chief Architect's impatient voice cry out from the top of the scaffolding surrounding one of the gigantic granite monoliths, to say something like this: 'No! No! That's not the way to cut stalactites. Here, give me that mallet and chisel. I'll show you how to carve the capital.

Then, standing at the base of the pillar, the Sultan had to put up his hand to shield his eyes as the chips flew and the marble dust rained down. He may then have smiled. I doubt that he interrupted Sinan as he cut the geometrical crystalline stalactites in the round to come out right.

Sinan finished the Süleymaniye in 1557. It is an enormous space, full of light by day, once lit by twenty-two thousand flames by night. In the seventeenth century, when the mosque was not a century old, Evliya Çelebi saw ten 'Frankish infidels skillful in geometry and architecture' take off their shoes and put on slippers to enter the southwestern portal. He followed them to watch the great spaces of the Süleymaniye take their effect. Heads back, the ten men shuffled along in their baboushes; they walked on thick carpets woven to Sinan's patterns at Ushak instead of on the rush matting and scatter rugs of today. ... Each of the ten Frankish infidels raised his right hand and laid his forefinger across his open mouth. 'They tossed up their hats and cried out ... "Mother of God!" ' ...

(Sinan) was a robust man of sixty-eight when he climbed up onto the dome to put the burnished finial in place. According to legend, when he got down again, he said to the Sultan, 'I have built thee, O Padishah, a mosque which will remain on the face of the earth till the day of judgement, and when Hallaj Mansur comes and rends Mount Demavend from its foundations, he will play tennis with it and the dome of this mosque!'❞

ARTHUR STRATTON, *SINAN,*
LONDON, 1972

101

THE HAREM

Ottaviano Bon (1551–1622) was a diplomat at the Sublime Porte, the court of the Ottoman sultans, between 1604 and 1607.

66 If he should require one of them for his pleasure or to watch them at play or hear their music, he makes known his desire to the Head Kadin, who immediately sends for the girls who seem to her to be the most beautiful in every respect and arranges them in a line from one end of the room to the other. She then brings in the King, who passes before them once or twice, and according to his pleasure fixes his eyes on the one who attracts him most, and as he leaves throws one of his handkerchiefs into her hand, expressing the desire to sleep the night with her. She, having this good fortune, makes up as well as she can and, coached and perfumed by the Kadin, sleeps the night with the King in the Royal chamber in the women's apartments, which is always kept ready for such an event. And while they are sleeping the night the Kadin arranges for some old Moorish women ... to stay in the room ... There are always two torches burning there, one at the door of the room, where one of the old women is, and the other at the foot of the bed ... On rising in the morning the King changes all his clothes, leaving the girl those he was wearing with all the money that was in the purses: then, going to his other rooms, he sends her a present of clothes, jewels, and money in accordance with the satisfaction and pleasure recieved. The same procedure holds good for all the others who take his fancy, lasting longer with one than with another according to the pleasure and affection he feels for her. And she who becomes pregnant is at once called Cassachi Sultan – that is to say, Queen Sultana – and if she bears a son its arrival is heralded with the greatest festivities. 99

OTTAVIANO BON, *PURCHAS HIS PILGRIMS*, LONDON 1625

EUNUCHS

Thomas Dallam (fl. 1599–1615) was an English organ-maker who traveled to Constantinople in 1599 to take a gift of an organ to Sultan Mehmed III from Queen Elizabeth I. While there, he looked into the Harem at Topkapi through a wall grating, one of the few people ever to do so and live to tell the tale.

❝ When he (a black eunuch) had showed me many other thinges which I wondered at, than crossinge throughe a litle squar courte paved with marble, he poynted me to goo to a graite in a wale, but made me a sine that he myghte not goo thether him selfe. When I came to the grait the wale was verrie thicke, and graited on bothe the sides with iron verrie strongly; but through that graite I did se thirtie of the Grand Sinyor's Concubines that weare playinge with a bale in another courte. At the firste sighte of them I thoughte they had bene yonge men, but when I saw the hare of theiir heades hange doone on their backes, platted together with a tasle of smale pearle hanginge in the lower end of it, and by other plaine tokens, I did know them to be women, and verrie prettie onew in deede.

Theie wore upon theire heades nothinge bute a little capp of clothe of goulde, which did but cover the crowne of her heade; no bandes a boute their neckes, nor anythinge but faire cheans of pearle and a juell hanginge on their breste, and juels in their ears; their coats weare like a souldier's mandilyon (cloak), some of reed sattan and som of blew, and som of other collors, and grded like a lace of contraire collor; they wore britchis of scamatie, a fine clothe made of coton woll, as whyte as snow and as fine as lane (muslin); for I could desarne the skin of their thies throughe it. These britchis cam doone to their mydlege; som of them did weare fine cordevan buskins, and som had their leges nakcd, with a goulde ringe on the smale of her legg; on her foute a velvett panttoble (high shoe) 4 or 5 inches hie. I stood so longe loukinge upon them that he which had showed me all this kindnes began to be verrie angrie with me. He made a wrye mouthe, and stamped with his foute to make me give over looking; the which I was verrie lothe to dow, for that sighte did please me wondrous well. ❞

THOMAS DALLAM, *DIARY, 1599–1600*, IN *EARLY VOYAGES AND TRAVELS IN THE LEVANT*; ED. J.T. BENT, HAKLUYT SOCIETY 1ST SERIES, VOL. 87, 1893

A CITY OF THE SENSES

A DIFFERENT ISTANBUL

Sait Faik (Abasıyanık, 1906-1954), one of Turkey's best-loved short story writers, used the vivid scenes and colorful characters of Istanbul in most of his fiction. His selected stories are available in translation in books published in France, Spain and the United States.

❝ I have realized that the Istanbul of our dreams is more beautiful than the real city. Or is it, really? Are we happier beside a mean Galata Bridge, an ugly Beyazıt Tower, a mighty dome of the Mosque of Süleyman, or St Sophia the amiable giant?… Could it be that the Istanbul we miss, even when we are just an hour's distance away from it, is the Istanbul of our visions, dreams and memories?

I feel joyous when I create an Istanbul lovelier than Istanbul on three feet of snow… Actually, I used to get sad thinking that I could not create Istanbul within Istanbul. There is an Istanbul more beautiful than Istanbul. You ought to know that. This Istanbul is a different one that we construct, through our imagination, at all sorts of places — the plain through which a train hurtles at a hundred kilometres per hour, the sea through which a ship goes swishing, or a mountain covered with knee-deep snow. ❞

SAIT FAIK, *ESSAY*, 1930,
TRANSLATED BY TALAT SAIT HALMAN

SAILING TO BYZANTIUM

William Butler Yeats (1865–1939), Irish poet and dramatist, won the Nobel Prize for Literature in 1923. "Sailing to Byzantium" is considered one of the masterpieces of the English language.

That is no country for old men. The young
In one another's arms, birds in the trees
— Those dying generations — at their song,
The salmon-falls, the mackerel-crowded seas,
Fish, flesh, or fowl, commend all summer long
Whatever is begotten, born, and dies.
Caught in that sensual music all neglect
Monuments of unageing intellect.

An aged man is but a paltry thing,
A tattered coat upon a stick, unless
Soul clap its hands and sing, and louder sing
For every tatter in its mortal dress,
Nor is there singing school but studying
Monuments of its own magnificence;
And therefore I have sailed the seas and come
To the holy city of Byzantium.

O sages standing in God's holy fire
As in the gold mosaic of a wall,
Come from the holy fire, perne in a gyre,
And be the singing-masters of my soul.
Consume my heart away; sick with desire
And fastened to a dying animal
It knows not what it is; and gather me
Into the artifice of eternity.

Once out of nature I shall never take
My bodily form from any natural thing,
But such a form as Grecian goldsmiths make
Of hammered gold and gold enamelling
To keep a drowsy Emperor awake;
Or set upon a golden bough to sing
To lords and ladies of Byzantium
Of what is past, or passing, or to come.

WILLIAM BUTLER YEATS, *SAILING TO BYZANTIUM*, 1926

DELIGHT IN SEEING

Abidine Dino was born in 1913 in Istanbul. Painter and writer, journalist, cineast and sculptor, he is a founder of the Avant-Garde Turkish group D of painters (1933). In the following excerpt, he writes of his feelings about his country.

❝Whenever I am asked about my country, Turkey, I am always haunted by a feeling that no one has ever really seen it, neither I nor anyone else. Its essence always seems to escape me. A land and a people steeped in tragedy, coulours turning in a flash from drabness to moving intensity, frenzied agitation beneath outward calm, the wild anger of nature and of men that suddenly fades away, the antagonism of man and of dispro-portionate space, doldrums and seismic shocks, silences so thick one can touch them, but occasionally torn by the endless screeching of an ox cart or a son howled as wildly as if the singer were on the rack. But there is gentleness, too. The eyes of women, the hair of camels, the fields of narcissus, and spreading tectonic movement – as the geographers say. Zones of weakness, broken topography, slumped ridges...Then the lakes, salty and turquoise, the phenomenal waterfalls of Pamukkale "Cotton Fortress" and their terraced basins so dazzlingly white that Marx Ernst might have signed them. No, I could never finish this list of "delights to be seen." Every summer the Turks placidly watch foreign migrations flowing into their country, those same Turks who had at one time practised, and admittedly more belligerent form of migration. But the old motive is still there: a delight in seeing the world. Today the verb "see" is gaining ground: one learns to see, one is able to see, one occasionally loses all hope of seeing. We try to see with paintings, photography, films and television, with the eyes of others and with our own. Nothing is ever totally satisfying. I still remember one morning in 1953 at Vallauris, where Picasso said, with a note of sadness: "A man sees only once or twice in a lifetime." It is true, but also shattering. How does one approach this Turkey? Should you forget about seeing and instead, taste grilled swordfish or Bosphorus strawberries?Or the contraband alcohol known as bogma "stangler" or lamb grilled over vine shoots?To glimpse Turkey would it be better to prance dead drunk to the beat of an enormous drum on the roofs of a village in round dances of another era? Or is the answer to sit at the bow of a Bosphorus boat under the finger of light piercing a snow storm at night?Perhaps one could guide a plough behind a bony ox or suffocate from dust on a road while jeeps race by.Or would it be better to go to Bergama, ancient Pergamum, with its temple to Aesculapius the healer and spend a night there to cure an imaginary ailment? But what can one do to see this Turkey since crayons and brushes have been of no help to me? Turkish miniaturists were not able to grasp much of it either, even though the Matrakis and the Levnis and others are magnificent. Perhaps only Sıyah Kalem saw things clearly. Then there is the music of Dede Effendi but it represents only Istanbul. Are the songs of Anatolia enough in themselves? As a last resort, if one is in Uskudar, one can still visit a friend who is an expert in preparing colours for illuminated manuscripts.One can also draw spirals with a quill facing Leander's tower, unless one races to the other end of the country to sketch the day labourers at Adana bridge. One can sail for Trebizond, wander in Kayseri, try to board Noah's Ark if it is ever found on Mount Ararat, drop in at Raman to watch the oil wells, come back to Istanbul to look at the city from the top of the Hilton or, even better, take the measure of Galata Tower from a rowboat. 〞

> ABIDINE DINO,
> *UNPUBLISHED EXCERPT*, 1993

THREE CIVILIZATIONS

A LAND AND WATER CITY

Lord Kinross (1905–1976) traveled extensively in Turkey and wrote several memorable books about its history and cultural landscapes. His biography of Atatürk is regarded as perhaps the best in any language and his one-volume "The Ottoman Centuries: The Rise and Fall of the Turkish Empire" is one of the most readable accounts of Ottoman history.

“ The land-and-water city which I now explored was a world in itself, on three neighbouring seas: the deep Bosphorus linking the Black Sea, with its dark Russian storms, to the Sea of Marmara, as pellucid and calm as an enclosed Mediterranean. It was a world of two seasons. When the wind blew from the South, we could stay in the cool of the Bosphorus, braced by its sparkling waters. When it blew from the North, we would seek relaxation and shelter on the beaches and in the shallows of the pine-clad islands of the Marmara.

The city itself, looking out to these seas over the remains of its medieval walls, is a world of three civilisations — the Byzantine, the Ottoman, the Western European. In essence the skyline is still Byzantine, the flat, sixth-century dome of St Sophia matched a thousand years later — the art of building on such a scale having lapsed meanwhile — by the more rounded domes of the great mosques of the incomparable Ottoman architect, Sinan. But now, giving to the city of the Greeks an oriental character, there were minarets, tall and slender as pencils, to punctuate the array of domes, much as in a landscape cypresses punctuate the dome-shaped trees beneath them. Minarets, domes of all sizes whether of mosques or tombs or baths, courtyards colonnaded, cooled by fountains, flanked by the libraries and schools and hospitals and workhouses of the medieval Welfare State — such, architecturally, is Istanbul.

But there is some of it still, besides St Sophia, that is wholly Byzantine. There are the Kahriye and the Fethiye Mosques (St Saviour in Chora and St Mary Pammakaristos), still yielding to the restorer lost masterpieces of fresco and mosaic. There are some two dozen other churches, one, St Sergius and St Bacchus, a miniature replica of St Sophia, by the sea, others hidden away amid the slums, the Phanar and in the outskirts of the city. There are the Byzantine "Golden Gate", through the city walls, and just within them the ruins of the monastery of St. John the Baptist, which grew from a Greek basilica.

Thus does Christian Constantinople dovetail into Muslim Stamboul. Opposite, the modern quarter of Péra, now Beyoğlu, climbs vertiginously upwards beyond the Golden Horn, while the ornate nineteenth-century palaces of the Sultans decorate, like triumphs of confectionery, the shores of the Bosphorus beyond.

If, in their architecture, the Turks learnt from the Greeks in the West, in their decorative arts they learnt from the Persians in the East. For a century before venturing, in 1453, to besiege Byzantium and thus assume control of the remainder of its

Empire, the Ottoman Sultans reigned in Brussa, a city burgeoning amid gardens on the lower and more fertile slopes of the snow-capped Mount Olympus. Here they absorbed, by observing the Greeks, the art of good administration, meanwhile enriching their city with the arts of decoration which they had absorbed on their progress through Persia. Persians were employed to build their mosques and to embellish them with a wealth of tile work and copper work, of carpets and textiles, of wood-carving and stone-carving. The geometric motifs of their earlier Seljuk forbears, austere as some fugue by Bach, had sprouted, as the centuries went on, into tendrils and leaves and flowers as naturalistic as those of the Persian garden. Whith these, after the conquest, they adorned the mosques and the palaces of Istanbul, reaching an apotheosis of elegance in the Grand Seraglio, its palatial precincts disposed around gardens on a point commanding the Bosphorus, the Marmara and the Golden Horn. Here in Istanbul, between East and West, is the flavour of Ottoman Turkey. **"**

LORD KINROSS, INTRODUCTION TO *TURKEY*,
ED. BY ROBERT MANTRAN, 1959

THE SPIRIT OF THREE CITIES
Michel Butor, born in 1926, is a leading proponent of the nouveau roman, and he also enjoys fame as a poet, critic, and travel writer. He taught at Manchester, Geneva, and Thessalonika in the 1950s. This passage is from a chapter entitled "Istanbul" in his "Le Génie du lieu".

" It was lucky for me there was rain and fog the first time I crossed the floating bridge of Galata, which breathes gently under your feet every time a tugboat goes by. The bridge is in fact both a bridge and a railway station with two levels, with many iron stairways, flanked by loading quays with landing steps, for the Bosphorus, the Princes' Islands or Eyüp; with ticket windows, waiting rooms, shops and cafés, congested with a crowd of fishermen dropping their lines, leaning on the railings or crouching on the edges, and with travellers carrying their baskets, or people walking by, dressed in European style…

The coast of Asia was barely visible… large caiques with sails, long strings of black barges, to the left the big ships that ran to Smyrna and Alexandria, to the right the cranes, the smoke from the trains, the trees of Gulhane Park, and, above the roofs of the Seraglio with its odd bell tower like a French church, the cupola of Saint Irené, then the Sophia looking as though it were floating, as though it were being borne away in a very slow, imperturbable flight by its four enormous buttresses.

It may be that I never again felt so profoundly the effect of this immense and solemn spectacle, this animated maritime crossroads, this unfolding ceremony… as I watched it I was delighted by the pearl and amber light that was so wonderfully diffused, reflected, set in motion by the shimmer of the omnipresent water, I was delighted by all the minarets on the hills like the tent poles of some sumptuous camp, or like reeds in an angel's pool; then, in the evening, everything becoming transfigured in the contagion of the sky's dripping gold, flashing back from that immense luminous horn that plunges into the interior of Europe, dyeing the domes and the depots, dyeing the eyes of men, entering their blood, entering my blood, entering my hands…The Spirit of Three cities are superimposed on one another, and as one wanders one unravels them, three cities born of profoundly different structure, three cities born of three invasions. **"**

MICHEL BUTOR, *THE SPIRIT OF MEDITERRANEAN PLACES*, 1986,
TRANSLATED BY LYDIA DAVIS

● ISTANBUL AS SEEN BY WRITERS

NATURAL BEAUTY

MISTRESS OF THE WORLD

Augier Ghislain de Busbecq (1522–1592) was born in Flanders. He served as the Habsburg Ambassador at the Court of Süleyman the Magnificent in the mid-1550s. He stayed for seven years in Constantinople. His letters, written in Latin, contain great insights into the Ottoman life of the time, government, and culture.

66 As for the situation of the City itself, it seemed to me, to be naturally placed as fit to the Mistress of the World; it stands in Europe, and hath Asia in view, and on its right, hath Egypt and Africa, which though Countries not adjacent to it, yet by reason of frequent intercourse and naval commerce, they seem as it were, contiguous: on its left hand is the Euxin Sea, and the Palus Maeotis, whose banks are inhabited round about by many Nations, and so many navigable Rivers have influx into them, that there is no thing that grows in any of the Countries there about, fit for man's use, but there is a great conveniency of transporting it by sea to Constantinople. 99

AUGIER GHISLAIN DE BUSBECQ,
TRAVELS INTO TURKEY, 1744

THE BOSPHORUS

Julia Pardoe (1806–1862), a British poet, went to Istanbul with her father in 1835 and, in the following year, published her enchanting book entitled "The City of the Sultan and the Domestic Manner of the Turks". Later she wrote "The Romance of the Harem" and "The Thousand and One Days".

66 To be seen in all its beauty, the Bosphorus should be looked upon by moonlight. Then it is that the occupants of the spacious mansions which are mirrored in its waters, enjoy to the fullest perfection the magnificence of the scene around them. The glare of noonday reveals too broadly the features of the locality; while the deep, blue, star-studded sky, the pure moonlight, and the holy quiet of evening, lend to it, on the contrary, a mysterious indistinctness which doubles its attraction. The inhabitants of the capital are conscious of this fact; and during the summer months, when they occupy their marine mansions, one of their greatest recreations is to seat themselves upon the seaward terraces, to watch the sparkling of the ripple, and to listen to the evening hymn of the seamen on board the Greek and Italian vessels; amused at intervals by a huge shoal of

porpoises rolling past, gambolling in the moonlight, and plunging amid the waves with a sound like thunder: while afar off are the dark mountains of Asia casting their long dusky shadows far across the water, and the quivering summits of the tall trees on the edge of the channel sparkling like silver, and lending the last touch of loveliness to a landscape perhaps unparalleled in the world.

Shakespeare must have had a vision of the Bosphorus, when he wrote the garden scene in Romeo and Juliet!

All the Orientals idolize flowers. Every good house upon the border of the channel has a parterre, terraced off from the sea, of which you obtain glimpses through the latticed windows; and where the rose trees are trained into a thousand shapes of beauty sometimes a line of arches risen all bloom and freshness above a favourite walk – sometimes the plants are stretched round vases of red clay of the most classical formation, of which they preserve the shape – ranges of carnations, clumps of acacias, and bosquets of seringa, are common; and the effect of these fair flowers, half shielded from observation, and overhung with forest trees, which are in profusion in every garden, is extremely agreeable.**"**

JULIA PARDOE, *THE CITY OF THE SULTAN,*
LONDON, 1837

A CITY UNDER SNOW

"I shall never forget my first impression of Constantinople. It has been my good fortune since then, to see it again and again, at every time of year, and under every possible aspect, but no subsequent picture has had either the vividness or the beauty of the first. I remember that it was in February and we steamed up the Sea of Marmora to the entrance of the Bosphorus in a heavy snow-storm. The flakes fell so thick and fast that scarcely a single building was distinctly visible. Then, suddenly, just when we were opposite St. Sophia, the snow ceased to fall, the clouds parted in a bright blue rent, and the clear morning sun, rising behind us, shone full upon Stamboul. It was a marvellous sight. Every dome and minaret and tower was frosted with thick silver. It was as though the whole beautiful city were moulded in precious metal finely chiselled and richly chased. The slender minarets shot up like rays of light, the dark cypresses were changed to silver plumes, even the Seven Towers, far on the western wall, were as white as Parian marble. Only the sea had colour. A moment earlier it had been grey and dull as weather-beaten lead, but under the touch of the Eastern sun it flashed all at once to a deep opaque blue, more like lapis lazuli than sapphire.

The glory of the scene was beyond description, and, in its way, surpasses anything I have witnessed in any part of the world. A few minutes later it was gone, the wintry clouds rolled together, the light went out, snow fell again, then rain, and then more snow, and my second impression was of dismal, slushy, filthy streets, dripping eaves, marrow-biting air, and an intense longing for a comfortable room and a good fire. Perhaps the contrast has served in memory's gallery to throw the first picture into unreasonable prominence, but remembrance may have exaggerations which one does not regret.**"**

F. MARION CRAWFORD,
CONSTANTINOPLE, 1895

BUILDINGS OF THE CITY

THE FAIREST SHOW

Edward Lithgoz, the intrepid British traveler, visited Constantinople in the early years of the 17th century and wrote extensively about the city and the life of its inhabitants, in his "Rare Adventures and Painefull Peregrinations".

66 I beheld (...) the Prospect of that little World, the great City of Constantinople; which indeed yeeldeth such an outward splendor to the amazed beholder, of goodly Churches, stately Towers, gallant Steeples, and other such things, whereof now the World make so great accompt, that the whole earth cannot equal it. For indeed outwardly it hath the fairest show, and inwardly in the streets being narrow, and most part covered, the filthiest & deformed buildings in the world; the reason of its beauty, is, because being situate on moderate prospective heights, the universal textures, a farre off, yeeld a delectable show, the covertures being erected like the backe of a Coach after the Italian fashion with gutterd tyle. But being entred within, there is nothing but a striking deformity, and a loathsome contrived place; without either internal domesticke furniture, or externall decorements of fabricks palatiatly extended. Notwithstanding that for its situation, the delicious wines, & fruits, the temperate climat, the fertile circumjacent fields, and for the Sea Hellespont, and pleasant Asia on the other side: it may truely be called the Paradice of the earth. 99

EDWARD LITHGOZ, *RARE ADVENTURES AND PAINEFULL PEREGRINATIONS*, LONDON, 1640

THE GREAT WALLS OF STAMBOUL

Pierre Loti, born Louis Marie Julien Viaud (1850–1923), achieved wide-spread popularity with his novels and travel writing about exotic places. His name became virtually synonymous with "Ottoman romance". His "Les Désenchantées" and "Aziyadé", set in Istanbul, are touching romantic novels.

66 It was a bright winter afternoon and we were out wandering together, she and I, rejoicing like a couple of children to be out in the sun for once, and roaming the countryside. But we had chosen a cheerless region for our walk. We were strolling along by the great wall of Stamboul, the most solitary spot in the world, where nothing seems to have stirred, since the days of the last Byzantine Emperors. ... The ancient ramparts are steeped in a silence, such as broods over the approach to a necropolis. Here and there a gate has been built in the thickness of these walls, but to no purpose, for never a soul goes in or out. These queer, little, low doors have an air of mystery, and above the lintels are gilded inscriptions and curious decorations. Between the inhabited quarters of the town and the fortifications, lie great tracts of waste land, dotted with suspicious-looking hovels, and with crumbling ruins, dating from every epoch of history. There is nothing from without to break the eternal monotony of these walls, save here and there the white shaft of a minaret, rising in the distance. Always the same battlements, the same turrets, the same dark hues, laid on by the hand of time, the same regular lines, running straight and dreary, till they are lost on the far horizon. 99

PIERRE LOTI, *CONSTANTINOPLE (AZIYADÉ)*, TRANSLATED BY MARJORIE LAWRIE, 1927

ARRIVING BY SEA

Rose Macaulay (1881-1958), the prolific British novelist and essayist, is perhaps best known for her novel entitled "The Towers of Trebizond", which contains vivid scenes from various parts of Turkey and long descriptions of Istanbul and its streets, shops and cafés.

66 ... Before dark Istanbul could be seen ahead, and it is true that it must look more splendid than any other city one comes to by sea. Even Father Chantry-Pigg, who did not think that Constantine's city and the Byzantine capital ought to have had all those mosque-domes and minarets built on to its old Byzantine shape, of which he had engravings in a book, even he thought the famous outline climbing above the Bosphorus and the Sea of Marmara, with all its domes and minarets poised against the evening sky, was very stupendous. ... I saw Istanbul, the mosques and palaces and the Seraglio and the cisterns and the Turkish cemetery and the walls and the Bazaar, and the excavations going on in Justinian's palace... and one day I went up the Bosphorus and saw the castles and palaces and mosques and old wooden houses and villages on the shores. But in the evenings I wandered about old Stambul, down by the quays and among the narrow streets and cafés and old shops, and watched the ships in the harbour and the people. 99

ROSE MACAULAY, *THE TOWERS OF TREBIZOND*, 1956

THE GARBAGE HILLS

Latife Tekin was born in 1957 in Karacafenk, in the Turkish province of Kayseri. Her first book "Dear Cheeky Death", ("Sevgili Arsız Ölün"), was published in 1983. John Berger wrote that "In Berji Kristin, a shanty-town community becomes the center of the world, holding the stage and addressing the sky."

66 One winter night, on a hill where the huge refuse bins came daily and dumped the city's waste, eight shelters were set up by lantern-light near the garbage heaps. In the morning the first snow of the year fell, and the earliest scavengers saw these eight huts pieced together from materials bought on credit – sheets of pitchpaper, wood from building sites, and breezeblocks brought from the brickyards by horse and cart. Not even stopping to drop the sacks and baskets from their backs, they all ran to the huts nd began a lively exchange with the squatters who were keeping watch. A harsh and powerful wind kept cutting short their words and at one point almost swept the huts away. The scavengers pointed out that the ramshackle walls and makeshift roofs would never stand up to the wind, so the squatters decided to rope down the roofs and nail supports to the walls.

When the garbage trucks had come and gone, the simit-sellers on the way to the garbage heard that eight huts had been built on the slopes and spread the news throught the neighbouring warehouses, workshops and coffee houses. By noon people had begun to descend on the hillside like snow. Janitors, pedlars and simit-sellers all arrived with pickaxes, closely followed by people who had left their villages to move in with their families in the city, and by others roaming the hills behind the city in the hope of building a hut. Men and women, young and old, spread in all directions. Kneeling and rising they measured with feet and outstretched arms. Then with their spades they scratched crooked plans in the earth. By evening Rubbish Road had become a road of bricks and blocks and pitchpaper.

That night in snowfall and lantern-light a hundred more huts were erected in the snow.

Next morning, by the garbage heaps – downhill from the factories which manufactured lightbulbs and chemicals, and facing the china factory – a complete neighbourhood was fathered by mud and chemical waste, with roofs of plastic basins, doors from old rugs, oilcloth windows and walls of wet breezeblocks.

Throughout the day bits and pieces arrived to furnish the houses, and remaining women and children, with sacks on their backs and babies in arms, entered their homes. Mattresses were unrolled and kilim-rugs spread on the earthen floors. The damp walls were hung with faded pictures and brushes with their blue bead goodluck charms and cradles were slung from the roofs and a chimmey pipe was knocked through the side wall of every hut. **99**

LATIFE TEKIN, *BERJI KRISTIN, TALES FROM THE GARBAGE HILLS*, 1993

THE BUSTLING MASSES

KAGITHANE

Evliya Çelebi Efendi, the Ottoman travel writer, collected his vivid impressions of his journeys in his ten-volume "Seyahatname" ("Book of Travels"). His monumental work is a treasure-house of geographic data, anthropological knowledge, oral history and personal observation.

66 While my humble self was lodging with Melek Ahmed Pasha at Topçular (Artillery) Palace, every evening we used to watch thousands of firecrackers reach the sky and hear the report of thousands of guns and rifles. Later, when I enquired of a fellow man-of-pleasure about this feast, he said 'Woe to the hopeless fool who has dissipated his wits, wisdom and yielded to sorrow and despair… Why is it that you are so aggrieved as not to know about Kâğıthane? Ever since this Great Ottoman Empire has existed, never has there been a gayer and more joyful feast than Kâğıthane. Anyone who has not seen this place has seen nothing'.

I then immediately went and got the Pasha's permission to go to Kâgıthane. I spent 40 gold bullions to buy two *kayım*, food and drinks and, together with five or six Agas, pitched our tents in the shadow of the great oak trees along the Kâgıthane river; thus settling, we started our feast of reason and the flow of soul to continue day and night.

During the two months from the beginning of the month of Recep until the holy crescent of Ramazan appears in the sky there has been such amusements and pleasures on these green fields that no words can fully describe. All gentry, noblemen and prodigal sons of the plutocrats of Istanbul adorned the valley with more than three thousand tents. Every night these tents were illuminated with thousands of candles, oil lamps and lanterns. In the evening, the leading groups were entertained by musicians, singers, minstrels and performers like the Ahmed group, Cevahir group, Nazlı group, Garibanu group, Ahide group, Zümrüt group, Postalcı group, Batakoglu group, Hasena group, Samur-ka group, who played many tunes on their 'Ceng-ür Rebab' 'Santur', tambour and 'Ud-u Kanun' until sunrise while a hundred thousand fireworks adorned the sky with lightnings, stars, butterflies, etc., and the entire Kâgıthane was bathed in this radiant splendour. Guns were fired from dawn to dusk. Besides these tents, scattered along the two banks of the Kâgıthane river, were more than two thousand shops vending not only foods and drinks but also myriad valuables. Every day the clowns, jesters, magicians, weight lifters, ropedancers, acrobats, jugglers, jongleurs, bear, monkey, donkey and dog trainers, puppet shows, birdmen, and swordeaters, about three hundred and sixty entertainers performed and made great profit. Four Janissary platoons were assigned by the palace to maintain order in this area. Most of these Janissaries used to swim in the Kâgıthane river. Never in history there has been such union of gentlemen and scholars. **99**

EVLIYA ÇELEBI EFENDI, *SEYAHATNAME (BOOK OF TRAVELS)*
(EXCERPT FROM A SMALL COLLECTION OF PASSAGES PUBLISHED IN THE 1960'S
BY THE TURKISH MINISTRY OF TOURISM AND INFORMATION)

● ISTANBUL AS SEEN BY WRITERS

CAPITAL OF THE WORLD

Gustave Flaubert (1821–80)), the French novelist, is perhaps most famous for "Madame Bovary" (1857). Certain passages were deemed to be offensive to public morals and so Flaubert was tried in the courts but subsequently acquitted. At the age of twenty-nine, he decided to visit Istanbul and the Middle East and compare the reality with the various descriptions he had read in books. He wrote about his impressions to several intimate friends.

❝ About Constantinople, where I arrived yesterday morning, I'll tell you nothing today, except to say that I have been struck by Fourier's idea that some time in the future it will be the capital of the world. It is really fantastic as a human anthill. That feeling of being crushed and overwhelmed you had on your first visit to Paris;: here one is penetrated by it, elbowing as one does so many unknown men, from the Persian and the Indian to the American and the Englishman, so many separate individualities which in their frightening total humble one's own. And then, the city is immense. One gets lost in the streets, which seem to have no beginning or end. The cemeteries are forests in the midst of the city. From the top of the tower at Galata, looking out over all the houses and all the mosques (beside and between the Bosphorous and the Golden Horn, both full of ships), the houses too seem like ships – a motionless fleet, with the minarets as masts. (A rather tortuous sentence – skip it.) We walked through (no more that that) the street of

the male brothels. I saw bardashes buying sugared almonds, doubtless with bugger-money – the anus thus about to provision the stomach instead of the usual other way round. I heard the sound of a scratchy violin coming from ground-floor rooms: they were dancing a Greek dance. These young boys are usually Greeks. They wear their hair long. ❞

GUSTAVE FLAUBERT,
LETTER, 1850

THE GREAT BAZAAR

Edmondo De Amicis (1846–1908), an officer in the Italian army, published "Vita militare" in 1868. He was one of the most perceptive as well as colorful of the 19th-century European observers of Ottoman Istanbul and also an unqualified admirer of the city. The passage below is from his book "Constantinople".

❝ The Great Bazaar has nothing on the exterior to attract the eye, or give an idea of its contents. It is an immense stone edifice, of Byzantine architecture, and irregular form, surrounded by high grey walls, and surmounted by hundreds of little cupolas, covered with lead, and perforated with holes to give light to the interior. The principal entrance is an arched doorway without architectural character; no noise from without penetrates it; at four paces from the door you can still believe that within those fortress walls there is nothing but silence and solitude. But once inside you stand bewildered. It is not an edifice, but a labyrinth of arcaded streets flanked by sculptured columns and pilasters; a real city, with its mosques, fountains, crossways and squares, dimly lighted like a thick wood into which no ray of sunlight penetrates; and filled by a dense throng of people. Every street is a bazaar, almost all leading out of one main street, with an arched roof of black and white stone, and decored with arabesques like the nave of a mosque. In this dimly lighted thoroughfare, carriages, horsemen, and camels are constantly passing, making a deafening noise. The visitor is apostrophized on all sides with words and signs. The Greek merchants call out in loud voices and use imperious gestures. The Armenian, quite as cunning, but more humble in manner, solicits obsequiously; the Jew whispers his offers in your ear; the silent Turk, seated cross-legged upon his carpet at the entrance of his shop, invites only with his eye, and resigns himself to destiny. Ten voices at once address you; Monsieur! Captain! Caballero! Signore! Eccellenza! Kyrie! My Lord! At every turn, by the side doors, are seen perspectives of arches and pilasters, long corridors, narrow alleys, a long confused perspect of bazaar, and everywhere shops, merchandise piled up or hanging from wall and ceiling, busy merchants, loaded porters, groups of veiled women, coming and going, a perpetual noise of people and things enough to make one dizzy…You may linger a whole day in one bazaar, unconscious of the flight of time; for example, the bazaar of stuffs, and clothing. It is an emporium of beauty and riches enough to ruin your eyes, your brains, and your pocket; and you must be on your guard for a caprice might bring upon you the consequence of sending for help by telegraph. You walk in the midst of towering heaps of brocades from Bagdad, carpets from Caramania, silks from Broussa, linens from Hindustan, muslins from Bengal, shawls from Madras, cachemeres from India and Persia, many tinted tissues from Cairo; cushions arabesqued in gold, silken veils woven with silver stripes, scarfs of gauze in blue and crimson, so light and transparent that they seem like sunset clouds; stuffs of every kind and every design, in which red, blue, green, yellow colors the most rebellious to sympathetic combination, are brought together and interwoven, with a happy audacity and harmony, that makes one stand in open-mouthed wonder; table covers of all sizes, with red or white grounds embroidered all over with arabesques, flowers, verses from the Koran, and imperial ciphers, worthy of being admired for hours, like the walls of the Alhambra. 99

EDMONDO DE AMICIS, *CONSTANTINOPLE*, 1878
TRANSLATED BY CAROLINE TILTONM

A BARBARIC POPULATION

Virginia Woolf (1882–1941) visited Istanbul on two brief occasions in 1905 and 1910. At one point, she outlined a novel to take place in Galata but did not continue with it. She wrote briefly of her impressions of Istanbul in "Orlando".

66 Orlando's day was passed, it would seem, somewhat in this fashion. About seven, he would rise, wrap himself in a long Turkish cloak, light a cheroot, and lean his elbows on the parapet. Thus he would stand, gazing at the city beneath him, apparently entranced. At this hour the mist would lie so thick that the domes of Santa Sofia and the rest would seem to be afloat; gradually the mist would uncover them; the bubbles would be seen to be firmly fixed; there would be the river; there the Galata Bridge; there the green turbanned pilgrims without eyes or noses, begging alms; there the pariah dogs picking up offal; there the shawled women; there the innumerable donkeys; there men on horses carrying long poles.

Soon, the whole town would be astir with the cracking of whips, the beating of gongs, cryings to prayer, lashing of mules, and rattle of brass-bound wheels, while sour odours, made from bread fermenting and incense, and spice, rose even to the heights of Pera itself and seemed the very breath of the strident and multicoloured and barbaric population. **99**

VIRGINIA WOOLF, *ORLANDO*, 1928

LIVING IN ISTANBUL

TURKISH LAW

Lady Mary Wortley-Montagu returned to England in 1718, bringing back several lessons learned in the Turkish capital. One of these was the practice of innoculation against smallpox, an illness by which she had been badly marked herself in 1715. She was also very impressed by Turkish ideas of crime and punishment but fortunately did manage to have them introduced in England.

66 The climate is delightful in the extremest degree. I am now sitting, this present fourth of January, with the windows open, enjoying the warm shine of the sun, while you are freezing over a sad sea-coal fire; and my chamber set out with carnations, roses, and jonquils, fresh from my garden. I am also charmed with many points of the Turkish law, to our shame be it spoken, better designed and better executed than ours; Particularly, the punishment of convicted liars (triumphant criminals in our country, God knows): They are burned in the forehead with a hot iron, being proved the authors of any notorious falsehood. How many white foreheads should we see disfigured, how many gentlemen would be forced to wear their wigs as low as their eyebrows, were this law in practice with us! I should go on to tell you many other parts of justice, but I must send for my midwife. **99**

LADY MARY WORTLEY-MONTAGU,
LETTER, 1763

THE VEGETABLE VENDOR

66 But to go back to the vegetable vendor and his bedecked and beflowered animal and bulging baskets. As he ambles slowly through the streets, most of which are paved with cobblestones, the doors of the houses are flung open and the housewife or the cook appears, tray in hand. Even the well-to-do families buy from these ambulant merchants. And what a variety of vegetables they carry in the spring and summer! Purple eggplants, smaller and slimmer than yours, tomatoes, green peppers, green squash and a kind called *asma kabak* which measures several feet in length. The men also sell ochra and artichokes, the hearts of which are as big as saucers but sweet and tender to eat. Other vegetables sold are horse bean (the pods are eaten while tender and the beans inside when big and mealy), several varieties of green beans, shell beans and peas, lettuce and radishes, not to mention those indispensable herbs to a Turkish cook – parsley, dill, fresh mint and scallions.
June is the month of strawberries and they are sold in small round wicker baskets. A sweet and fragrant kind grows on the hills behind the villages along the Bosphorus. No sugar is needed to sweeten them. The berries are picked late in the

evening. They are carefully packed in the round baskets, the largest resting on the top. Some twenty baskets are hung on a thick pole which a man then balances over his shoulders. Every evening, while the strawberries are in season, one can see these men, trousers rolled up to their knees, feet and head bare, bringing their heavy loads to the city markets after having walked for miles to get there. As they pass by, the delicious fragrance of fresh strawberries tempts the appetite of all the passers-by.

I should also mention the nut vendors who are seen frequently in the summer. The Turkish people are very fond of fresh walnuts, almonds and hazelnuts and eat a great many of them. The walnut man, his

hands black from shelling the nuts, carries his wares in a glass jar filled with water; the almond man, in a flat basket where the nuts rest on fresh leaves or cakes of ice. The outer green shells are carefully removed and the white milky nuts inside, covered with their thin yellow skins, are sold in the streets.

In the fall, the chestnut man and his small brazier appear in the city. He has a special brazier, small, round and with a wide cover in which are many holes. Charcoal is burned in this implement. When the coal turns into red-hot embers and the cover is piping hot, the chestnuts are put on top to roast. Autumn is always connected with the smell of roasting nuts and one can see the merchant and his brazier in almost every street of the city. **99**

SELMA EKREM, *TURKEY OLD AND NEW*, 1967

SMOKING HOOKAHS
Pierre Loti writes here about one of the best-known Turkish pastimes.

66 As he felt deeply Turkish on this warm, clear evening, when the full moon would soon shine blue on the Sea of Marmara, he returned to Stamboul at nightfall, and climbed up to the heart of the Muslim quarter, to go and sit on the familiar esplanade in front of Sultan-Fatih's mosque. He wanted to dream there, in the pure cool of the evening, and in sweet Oriental peace, smoking hookahs while surrounded by dying splendour, decay, religious silence and prayer.

When he arrived at the square, all the little cafés had lit their modest lamps; lanterns hanging in the trees – old oil lanterns – also cast a discreet light; and everywhere, on benches, on stools, turbanned dreamers smoked, talking little and in low voices, hundreds of hookahs made a curious whispering sound — water bubbling in the flask as the smoker takes a long, deep breath. They brought him one, with small, live embers on leaves of Persian tobacco, and soon like all around him, he felt a gentle semi-intoxication, harmless and thought-inducing. He sat under the trees, where the hanging lanterns cast barely any light, facing the mosque on the far side of the esplanade. The square was empty and full of shadows, with uneven paving stones, dirt and holes; the wall of the mosque filled the entire far side, tall, huge, imposing, severe, like a rampart with only one opening : the thirty-foot-high archway leading to the holy court. **99**

PIERRE LOTI, *LES DÉSENCHANTÉES*, 1906, TRANSLATED BY MARINA BERRY

TURKISH BATHS

William Makepeace Thackeray (1811–1863) began his career as a journalist. His first major novel, "Vanity Fair", did not appear until 1847. He died suddenly and this account of his trip "from Cornhill to Grand Cairo" was published posthumously.

❝The spacious hall has a large fountain in the midst, a painted gallery running round it; and many ropes stretched from one gallery to another, ornamented with profuse draperies of towels and blue cloths, for the use of the frequenters of the place. All round the room and the galleries were matted enclosures, fitted with numerous neat beds and cushions for reposing on, where lay a dozen of true believers smoking, or sleeping, or in the happy half-dozing state. I was led up to one of these beds to a rather retired corner, in consideration of my modesty; and to the next bed presently came a dancing dervish, who forthwith began to prepare for the bath.

When the dancing dervish had taken off his yellow sugar-loaf cap, his gown, shawl, etc., he was arrayed in two large blue cloths; a white one being thrown over his shoulders, and another in the shape of a turban plaited neatly round his head; the garments of which he divested himself were folded up in another linen, and neatly put by. I beg leave to state I was treated in precisely the same manner as the dancing dervish.

The reverend gentleman then put on a pair of wooden pattens, which elevated him about six inches from the ground; and walked down the stairs, and paddled across the moist marble floor of the hall, and in at a little door ...But I had none of the professional ability of the dancing dervish; I staggered about very ludicrously upon the high wooden pattens; and should have been down on my nose several times, had not the dragoman and the master of the bath supported me down the stairs and across the hall. ...

The dark room was the tepidarium, a moist oozing arched den, with a light faintly streaming from an orifice in the domed ceiling. Yells of frantic laughter and song came booming and clanging through the echoing arches, the doors clapped to with loud reverberations. ...

When you get into the Sudarium, or hot room, your first sensations only occur about half a minute after entrance, when you feel that you are choking. I found myself in that state, seated on a marble slab; the bath man was gone; he had taken away the cotton turban and shoulder shawl: I saw I was in a narrow room of marble, with a vaulted roof, and a fountain of warm and cold water; the atmosphere was in a steam, the choking sensation went off, and I felt a sort of pleasure presently in a soft boiling simmer, which, no doubt, potatoes feel when they are steaming. You are left in this state for about ten minutes; it is warm certainly, but odd and pleasant, and disposes the mind to reverie.

But let any delicate mind fancy my horror, when, on looking up out of this reverie, I saw a great brown wretch extended before me, only half dressed, standing on pattens, and exaggerated by them and the steam until he looked like an ogre ... This grinning man belabours the patient violently with the horse brush. When he has completed the horse-hair part, and you lie expiring under a squirting fountain of warm water, and fancying all is done, he reappears with a large brass basin containing a quantity of lather, in the midst of which is something like old Miss MacWhirter's flaxen wig that she is so proud of, and that we have all laughed at. Just as you are going to remonstrate, the thing like a wig is dashed into your face and eyes, covered over with soap, and for five minutes you are drowned in lather; you can't see, the suds are frothing over your eyeballs; you can't hear, the soap is whizzing into your ears; you can't gasp for breath ... You little knew what saponacity was till you entered a Turkish bath.

When the whole operation is concluded, you are led – with what heartfelt joy I need not say – softly back to the cooling room, having been robed in shawls and turbans as before. You are laid gently on the reposing bed; somebody brings a narghile, which tastes as tobacco must taste in Mahomet's Paradise; a cool sweet dreamy langour takes possession of the purified frame; and half an hour of such delicious laziness is spent over the pipe as is unknown in Europe, where vulgar prejudice has most shamefully maligned indolence, calls it foul names, such as the father of all evil, and the like; in fact, does not know how to educate idleness as those honest Turks do, and the fruit which, when properly cultivated, it bears. **"**

W.M. THACKERAY, *NOTES OF A JOURNEY FROM CORNHILL TO GRAND CAIRO*, 1865

TERRIBLE CONFLAGRATIONS

Edward Lear (1812–1888), artist, traveler and writer is remembered chiefly for his watercolors and for his nonsense verse, including "The Owl and the Pussy-cat". He traveled widely throughout Europe and north Africa and published accounts of many of his trips. The following passage is from a letter to his elder sister, Ann Lear.

❝I must now devote a word to conflagration general & especial. You know that nearly all the houses in Constantinople are of wood – & you may have heard of the frequency of the fires, & their extent, but you will yet be surprised to hear that since I came – (Aug 1st) there have been 8 dreadful burnings – the least of which destroyed 60, & the largest 5,000 houses – & reduced hundreds and thousands to wretchedness. If I had not seen these things, I could not have believed them. ... And now I come to the night of Wed, the 6th – when about 12 everybody was awakened by the waiters (throughout the hotel) with the news that a tremendous fire was raging in Pera, & advancing to the inn. But Misseri said there was no danger - as there was a stone house, & a church (Greek) between him and them, where the flames would stop, & as I guessed from his coolness – he was in the right. However, I packed up, & then joined everybody else on the house top – where wet carpets, & water were all the fashion. A most horrible sight it was. ... The flames were tremendous – & all the city light as day. The houses fell crash, crash, crash, as the fire swept on nearer & nearer – & by 4 o'clock after midnight, it reached within 2 houses of the hotel – but there it stopped ... As it was, only 300 houses were burnt! – no lives lost; they very seldom are – & all the property is carried through the streets by innumerable porters to the cemeteries etc. – & there the poor people live till another wooden suburb arises in less than a year's time. Such is life in Constantinople.!!!❞

EDWARD LEAR, *LETTER*, 9 SEPTEMBER 1848

NIGHTLIFE

Graham Greene (1904–92) was a master of many forms of writing from thrillers to travel writing and reportage, and short stories to detective novels and children's books. "Stamboul Train" was his first commercially successful novel.

❝It was easy to talk hard all through dinner and to put his arm round her as they walked from the Pera Palace to the Petits Champs near the British Embassy. The night was warm, for the wind had dropped, and the tables in the garden were crowded. ... On the stage a Frenchwoman in a dinner jacket pranced up and down with a cane under her arm, singing a song about 'Ma Tante', which Spinelli had made popular in Paris more than five years before. The Turkish gentlemen, drinking coffee, laughed and chattered and shook their small dark feathery heads like noisy domestic birds, but their wives, so lately freed from the veil, sat silent and stared at the singer, their faces pasty and expressionless. Myatt and Janet Pardoe walked along the garden's edge, looking for a table, while the Frenchwoman screeched and laughed and pranced, flinging her desperate indecencies towards the inattentive and the unamused. Pera fell steeply away below them, the lights of fishing boats in the Golden Horn flashed like pocket torches, and the waiters went round serving coffee. 'I don't believe there's a table. We shall have to go in to the theatre.' A fat man waved his hand at them and grinned. ... 'There's an empty one.' Under the table their legs touched. The Frenchwoman disappeared, swinging her hips, and a man flung cartwheels on to the stage from the wings. He got to his feet, took off his hat, and said something in Turkish which made everyone laugh.
'What did he say?'
'I couldn't hear,' Myatt said. ❞

GRAHAM GREENE, *STAMBOUL TRAIN*, 1932

ITINERARIES

▲ Beyoğlu

Istanbul from Saray Burnu to the Beyazıdiye▼

▲ The Süleymaniye Mosque

▲ Topkapı Sarayı

Yedikule ▼

▲ The Blue Mosque and Haghia Sophia   The Grand Bazaar ▼

▲ Fields in Bithynia

▲ Harvesting in Thrace

Shepherds near Bursa▼

ISTANBUL

MAP OF THE CITY
A red and silver miniature painted by Seyyid Loqman depicting the districts of Stamboul, Galata, and Pera in 1584, from the *Hunarmana Manuscript* in the Topkapı Museum. The protective shield of walls which completely enclosed the Ottoman capital has been painted in a light, pale color. The green area is the gardens at Topkapı Sarayı.

THE CRADLE OF ISTANBUL

According to legend, it was on the Seraglio Point, called *Saray Burnu* in Turkish, that Byzas the Megarian landed around 660 BC and founded the city of Byzantium ● *29*. The two illustrious capitals that would succeed it, Byzantine Constantinople and Turkish Istanbul, created the heart of the present-day metropolis. Here the waters of the Bosphorus and the Golden Horn meet and then flow on into the Sea of Marmara. Over the centuries this stretch of land and sea has been the site of many epic events, and it is here also that the most spectacular buildings are situated: the Basilica of Haghia Sophia ● *74* ▲ *138*, the temple of the New Rome; and the Topkapı Palace ● *82* ▲ *150*, the center of Ottoman power. The Galata, Üsküdar, and Stamboul quarters sit astride the crossroads between Europe and Asia, facing one another across the water as they have for centuries, and today they remain the heart of the city, whose suburbs stretch along the shores of both strait and sea. At the extreme edge of the promontory, a quiet park has replaced the sultans' gardens, while the great Ottoman palace and its kiosks now open their doors to the public, who come in droves to appreciate the treasures of the imperial past.

«No city has eaten the fruits of the garden of art
so richly as the city of Istanbul,
birthplace and school of famous men,
the nursery of many nations.» Nabi (1642-1712)

The great basilica of Haghia Sophia is now admired primarily for the beauty of its architecture, after a millennium as the cathedral of Byzantium and a further 500 years as a mosque. In 1923, the basilica became a museum, thanks to Mustafa Kemal Atatürk, the father of modern Turkey ● 42, whose bronze statue stands on the far edge of the Saray Burnu. Fifty years later, the Boğaziçi Köprüsü bridge over the Bosphorus was inaugurated to commemorate the birth of the New Turkey.

The Saray Burnu

Gülhane Park. This park occupies the lower part of the former gardens of Topkapı Sarayı. In the Ottoman period many wooden pavilions were built in the cypress groves, where the court took up residence in summer, but a fire destroyed them in 1863.

The Goths' Column. Tucked away on the park's wooded slopes is one of the oldest monuments in Istanbul, the *Gotlar Sütunu* or Goths' Column, a 50-foot high granite monolith capped by a Corinthian capital. The column takes its name from the Latin inscription on its base: *Fortunae reduci ob devictos Gothos* ("To the prosperity that returned with the defeat of the Goths"). The monument is attributed either to Claudius II the Goth (268–270) or to Constantine the Great (324–337), both of whom had victories over the Goths. According to a Byzantine historian, it was once surmounted by a statue of Byzas the Megarian ● 29.

The Kiosk of the Basket-Weavers. From Saray Burnu, proceed towards the Galata Bridge, on the near side of which spreads the Eminönü quarter. Along the shore railway tracks run past the docks. En route, you pass the Sepetçiler Köşkü – the Basket-Weavers' kiosk – a seaside pavilion presented in 1643 to Sultan Ibrahim the Mad (1640–48) by the eponymous guild. Today it serves as an International Press Center.

Sirkeci station. After the Sepetçiler Köşkü, you come to Sirkeci İstasyon, a station built in 1889 for the first of the great luxury trains: the Orient Express. This celebrated but now slightly less glamorous train still makes a regular trip between Paris and Istanbul. Further along is the main pier for the ferries calling along the Bosphorus, the Golden Horn, the suburbs of Üsküdar and Kadıköy, and the Princes' Islands ● 271.

The Galata Bridge
This 18th-century painting (below left) shows the Third Hill from the Golden Horn with the Mosque of Süleyman the Magnificent in the background. On the right can be seen the wooden bridge that once linked Stamboul to the free quarters of Galata and Pera. Built in 1845, on the orders of Sultan Abdül Mecit, it was replaced at the beginning of the 20th century by an iron bridge. Seriously damaged by a fire in 1992, this structure has now been replaced by a new one, which opened to traffic on June 18, 1992. The present Galata Bridge spans the Golden Horn slightly upstream from the site of the old one.

The gardens of the seraglio
The once-private gardens of the sultans, here seen in an engraving by Thomas Allom, are now a public park. It is much favored by the people of Istanbul who, in good weather, come here for family picnics. There is a small café near the Goth's Column. Offshore, motorized ferries ply waters once sailed by wind-powered caiques.

129

RÜSTEM PAŞA CAMI'I · SPICE BAZAAR · YENI CAMI · ALAY KÖŞKÜ

✄ Four hours

THE EMINÖNÜ QUARTER

THE GALATA BRIDGE. Spanning the Golden Horn between Eminönü and Galata, this bridge is the main artery of Istanbul. Every day vast numbers of people cross it or pass under its arches in the many ferries that ply the lower Golden Horn. From the western side it is reached by way of an enormous square, the EMINÖNÜ MEYDANI, at the edge of which looms Yeni Cami, the New Mosque.

YENI CAMI

Officially known as the Yeni Valide Sultan Cami'i, or the New Mosque of the Valide Sultan, Yeni Cami was commissioned around 1600 by the Dowager Sultana Safiye, the widow of Murat III (1574–95) and mother of Mehmet III (1595–1603). However, the death of Mehmet in 1603 brought construction to a halt. The half-finished building hovered like a ghost on the Saray Burnu until 1660, when Turhan Hadice, the mother of Mehmet IV (1648–87) ordered Mustafa Ağa, the Sultan's chief architect, to resume work on the abandoned mosque, which, with its complex, would be completed in 1663 and dedicated on November 6 of that year.

THE STRUCTURE OF THE MOSQUE. As in all Ottoman mosques, there is a vast walled-in and porticoed forecourt in front of Yeni Cami, to the west, called an *avlu*. The ceremonial entrance is at the western end of the courtyard, where a broad flight of steps leads to a richly ornamented gateway. Inside there is a space bordered all around by a portico of six columns on each side. At the center stands a pretty octagonal *şadırvan*, an ablution fountain that, like so many old things today, serves primarily as decoration, since the faithful now use the water taps along the south side of the building. From the corner where the *avlu* and the mosque join, the slender shafts of two minarets shoot up, their three *şerefe* (balconies) carried on stalactite

TÜRKIYE CUMHURIYETI POSTALARI
ISTANBULUN FETHI 1453–1953
30 KURUŞ

SOĞUK ÇEŞME SOKAĞI

GOTH'S COLUMN

Other than Eyüp Cami'i, Yeni Cami is the most important mosque among those built on the banks of the Golden Horn. It is easily identified by the two minarets rising from the corners of the *avlu*. Situated near the Galata Bridge as well as next to a major

parapets. At the northeast corner of the mosque is the royal pavilion – the *hünkar kasrı* – with its great central gateway through which a street runs. The entrance to the pavilion is by way of a ramp alongside the mosque, after which a corridor leads to the imperial loge located in the upper gallery. The sultan and his family used the pavilion whenever they came to pray in Yeni Cami, making themselves at home in a suite composed of a salon, bedchamber, toilet, and kitchen.

THE MOSQUE INTERIOR. The central area of the mosque's interior – measuring 135 feet on each side – is defined by four corner pillars that support the central dome through four great arches, with squinches making the transition from square to circle. At the east end of the nave is the mihrab, the niche that indicates the direction of Mecca, and to its right is the mimbar, or pulpit, from which the imam delivers the sermon at the Friday noon prayer. The royal loge is at the northeast corner of the gallery, screened by a gilded grille.

THE COMPLEX ● 80. Turhan Hadice's *külliye* (complex) originally included a *medrese* (Koranic school), *darü'ş-şifa* (hospital), *mektep* (primary school), *türbe* (mausoleum), and both *çeşme* and *sebil* (fountains), as well as a hammam and a *çarşı* (bazaar). The last two were built to provide income to support the rest. Everything, save the hospital, hammam, and primary school, survive, but only the mosque and bazaar are open to the public.

pier, Yeni Cami has long been surrounded by the clamor of heavy traffic, with cars, buses, and ferries all intersecting at the very foot of the great basilica.

THE EGYPTIAN OR SPICE MARKET
"If you follow the little streets that wind their way from the Yeni Djami leading to the Mosque of Sultan

Bayezid, you will arrive at the Egyptian Bazaar – the Drug Market – an immense hall crossed from end to end by a lane reserved for the movement of both merchandise and consumers. Immediately one is struck – indeed intoxicated – by a penetrating odor composed of scents from all the exotic products. Displayed on every side, in heaps or open sacks, are henna, sandalwood, cinnamon, benzoin, pistachios, ambergris, mastic, ginger, nutmeg, opium, hashish – all watched over by merchants nonchalantly sitting on crossed legs as if they were benumbed from the sheer weight of an atmosphere so steeped in aroma."
       Théophile Gautier
       Constantinople, 1851

THE SPICE BAZAAR ★

This covered market is the attractive L-shaped building to the southwest of the Yeni Cami. The bazaar is called the *Misir Çarşısı* or Egyptian Market because it once received income from the tax levied on Egypt. Its English name survives from

the time when the market specialized in the sale of spices and herbs, as well as medicinal plants and drugs. The heavy aroma of the Orient that captivated 19th-century travelers has now lost some of its power. Only six shops of the original eighty-eight are still devoted to the traditional products. Inside these the shelves are laden with great, bulging sacks of multicolored spices and jars filled with precious foodstuffs and essential oils. One enters the market through a monumental gatehouse, in the upper story of which there is an excellent restaurant called Pandeli. Two gateways open out at the angle of the bazaar's L shape. The one on the right leads to Hasırcılar Caddesi – the Avenue of the Mat-Makers – which runs parallel with the Golden Horn. Some 200 yards along this avenue on the right is the

Rüstem Paşa Cami'i. A vaulted stairway then brings you to the porticoed forecourt of the mosque, built on a terrace overlooking shops and warehouses.

RÜSTEM PAŞA CAMI'I ★

Rüstem Paşa Cami'i is one of the most beautiful of the vizierial mosques built by the great Sinan ▲ *314*, Chief Imperial Architect under Süleyman the Magnificent (1520–66) and his two successors, Selim II (1566–74) and Murat III (1574–95). Sinan built the mosque for Rüstem Paşa, Grand Vizier to Süleyman and the husband of Princess Mihrimah, the Sultan's only daughter. The mosque is entered through a rather curious double porch; the inner porch is composed of a portico with five domed bays, and the outer part has a deep, low-slung penthouse roof supported at its extremity by a colonnade. The plan is an octagon inscribed within a rectangle. At the corners, four half-domes flank the main cupola, which rests upon four arches rising from four octagonal columns, two to the north and two to the south, as well as on four pillars projecting from the east and west walls. Alternating pillars of stone and small marble columns support the galleries on the north and south sides.

THE INTERIOR DECORATION. The Rüstem Paşa Cami'i is renowned for the gorgeous tiles that cover most surfaces, not only inside but also on the front of the porch. Possibly even more remarkable is the faience on the gallery level, revealing a different style. As with all great ceramics, those of Rüstem Paşa Cami'i came from Iznik ● *292*, ancient Nicea, where the ceramic art attained its apogee in the years 1555–1620 – the golden age of Ottoman architecture. Here the beauty of the floral and geometric motifs spreads radiance over walls, mihrab, mimbar, and even the columns, making a harmonic whole that sets the mosque apart as one of the most spectacular in Istanbul.

THE MAUSOLEUM OF ABDÜL HAMIT

Returning to Yeni Cami, walk eastward between the mosque and the Spice Bazaar, then continue along Hamidiye Caddesi. The first turning on the right brings us to the *türbe* of Abdül Hamit (1774–89), which survives from a small *külliye* ● *79* that originally included a *sebil* and a *medrese*. The *medrese* is still there, but the *sebil* has been removed. Buried alongside Abdül Hamit is his son, the mad and murderous Mustafa IV, who was deposed on July 28, 1808 and executed three months later. At the end of Hamidiye Caddesi we turn right on Ankara Caddesi, a busy avenue leading up from the Golden Horn to the ridge between the First and Second Hills. On the left side of the avenue we pass the Vilayet, the headquarters of the governor of the Istanbul province.

THE CAĞALOĞLU HAMMAM

One block beyond the Vilayet turn left, and then proceed for about a hundred yards until, on the left, you see one of the entrances to the magnificent and justly famous Cağaloğlu Baths. Built for Mahmut I they are double baths, one part reserved for men and the other for women. Remarkably,

VERTICAL SECTION OF THE CENTRAL AXIS OF THE RÜSTEM PAŞA MOSQUE
The axis cuts through the multicolored mirhab and the monumental entrance way which points towards Mecca.

133

THE STEAM ROOM OF THE HAMMAM
The ritual of a Turkish bath is an enjoyable way to escape the clamor of the city. It involves a massage before bathing, followed by a relaxing drink of tea. Engraving by Thomas Allom, 1834.

AFFAIR OF THE SOFA
One day in 1677 the Marquis de Nointel entered the Audience Chamber only to discover that his stool was placed not upon the *sofa*, but on the floor below. Furious, the diplomat seized the stool and carried it onto the *sofa* and sat down. And so began the famous "Affair of the Sofa", which was to have diplomatic consequences.

the hammam has remained in operation since it opened in 1741. Mahmut I had the Cağaloğlu built in order to generate income for the library he had established at Haghia Sophia. Istanbul boasts over a hundred Ottoman hammams ● *58*, most of them still frequented by people who do not have baths at home. No Muslim may attend Friday prayers without having first washed from head to toe. In the Cağaloğlu Hammam the most interesting chamber is the *hararet* or steam room, which is cruciform and surmounted by a central dome supported by a circle of columns. The four lateral arms of the chamber are also dome-vaulted. One of the most beautiful public baths, the Cağaloğlu remains almost exactly as it was in Ottoman times.

THE COMPLEX OF BEŞIR AĞA

At the first intersection beyond the hammam turn left onto Alay Köşkü Caddesi, and then take the first turning on the left which places you before a small mosque set upon a platform. The mosque and its *külliye* were built in 1745 on the orders of Beşir Ağa, Chief Black Eunuch in the Topkapı Harem during the reign of Mahmut I. When it was finished the complex also included a *medrese*, a *tekke* (Dervish monastery), and shops installed under the vaults. The monastery was closed in the early days of the Turkish Republic because the dervish orders were disbanded. Both the *tekke* and the *medrese* house a cultural center for the Turks of Western Thrace, now part of Greece.

THE SUBLIME PORTE

At the next intersection Alay Köşkü Caddesi crosses Alemdar Caddesi, running next to the wall of the Topkapı Sarayı and on to the top of the First Hill. On the left is a large gateway decorated in the Turkish rococo style. This is the famous Sublime Porte, or Bab-i-Ali. During the late 16th century it led to the offices of the Grand Vizier, where most of the empire's business was dealt with. It therefore came to symbolize the Ottoman government itself, with the result that ambassadors were accredited to the Sublime Porte (just as in the UK they are to the Court of St. James). The present gateway dates from 1843 and leads to the Vilayet, the administrative department of Istanbul.

THE ALAY KÖŞKÜ

Opposite the Sublime Porte, in a corner of the outer defense wall of Topkapı Sarayı, there is a large polygonal gazebo in the Turkish Baroque style. This is the Alay Köşkü, or Review

Pavilion, first built in c. 1565 and then reconstructed in 1819 by Mahmut II (1808–39). From here the Sultan would observe the life of the city, keep an eye on the activities of his Grand Vizier at the Sublime Porte, and attend both civil and military parades. The trade guilds of Istanbul took part in several grand processions in the Ottoman era. The last such event occurred in 1769 during the reign of Mustafa III (1757–74). They were held for various reasons: to mark the circumcision of a young prince; to celebrate a

great victory won by the Ottoman army; or even to take a census. In 1638, for instance, Murat IV (1623–40) used the march-past to determine the health of the capital's trade and commerce on the eve of his campaign in Iraq. A contemporary witness, Evilya Çelebi, describes the procession in his *Seyahatname* (*Book of Travels*). It was organized into 57 sections and included 1,001 corporations, though Çelebi describes only 735. Representatives of the guilds filed by in their characteristic garb, pulling floats dedicated to their various trades, while also competing to amuse and amaze the Sultan, who, with his court, looked on from the latticed Alay Köşkü. Sometimes the parade turned into a festival that went on for an entire month. The sheer color and variety of these affairs attracted many painters, as we know from the collection of miniatures in the Topkapı Sarayı Museum. Now restored, the pavilion is used to exhibit the Kenan Özbel collection of Turkish embroideries and carpets. Its suite of rooms can be reached by a ramp from just inside the gate of Gülhane Park, a short distance up Alemdar Caddesi.

SÜLEYMAN THE MAGNIFICENT
Woodcut,
Venice, c. 1550.

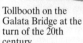

Tollbooth on the Galata Bridge at the turn of the 20th century.

THE FISH MARKET
The cuisine of Istanbul is renowned for the variety of the fish it uses – *kefal*, *lüfer* and *barbugna*, for example – all readily available from markets and restaurants. Along the quays of the Golden Horn itinerant vendors offer grilled fish fresh from the sea. The Galatasaray fish market is one of the most famous in Istanbul. It is depicted in the painting on the right by the contemporary Turkish artist Nedim Günsür, a member of the Group of Six who first exhibited their work in 1947.

ZEYNEP SULTAN CAMI'I

Following Alemdar Caddesi to the top of the first hill and then to the right, away from the outer walls of Topkapı, you arrive at a small Baroque mosque, commissioned by Princess Zeynep, daughter of Ahmet III. Its architect, Mehmut Tahir Ağa, completed the mosque and its complex in 1749. The complex included an elementary school, which still exists in the corner of the street just below the mosque, and a small cemetery, where the Princess and members of both her family and her household are buried. At the gate of the graveyard there is a rococo fountain ● *66*, also designed by Mehmet Tahir Ağa in 1778 but for the *külliye* of Abdül Hamit, whence it was relocated to the Zeynep Sultan Cami'i in 1950.

SOĞUK ÇEŞME SOKAĞI

A bit further along on the opposite side of Alemdar Caddesi stands the Soğuk Çeşme Sokağı Medrese, a handsome school building erected in the outer precincts of Haghia Sophia soon after the Conquest and recently restored. It is named for the street where the entrance is situated – the Street of the Cold Fountain – which climbs the first hill from Gülhane Park to the defensive walls surrounding Topkapı Sarayı.
OTTOMAN HOUSES. The elegant old Ottoman dwellings that border Soğuk Çeşme Sokağı are the result of a major renovation launched in 1986 by the TTOK (Turkish Touring and Automobile Club). By this time the long-abandoned houses had so deteriorated that their demolition seemed inevitable. It required two years of work to complete the restoration, at which time most of the houses were integrated into a luxury hotel, the AYASOFYA PANSIYONLARI ◆ *367*. With their fronts freshly painted in pastel or bright colors the houses bring great charm to the old cobblestone street as it gently winds its way down towards the sea. The excavations at the lower end of the street uncovered a cistern whose brick vaults rest on six blocks of marble. This remnant of late Roman architecture now houses a deluxe restaurant, the SARNIÇ LOKANTASI, also managed by the TTOK.

THE ISTANBUL LIBRARY. The largest of the old houses on Soğuk Çeşme Sokağı is a wooden *konak* (mansion) built at the beginning of the 19th century. Today it houses a part of the Çelik Gülersoy Foundation, the Istanbul Library and its rich collection of books and prints related to the history of the city.

THE SOĞUK ÇEŞME MEDRESE

Continuing on Soğuk Çeşme Sokağı as far as Caferiye Sokağı, turn right and make your way down the blind alley on the right, where a gateway at the end leads into the Soğuk Çeşme Medrese. This theological school was founded by Cafer Ağa, Chief White Eunuch during the reign of Süleyman the Magnificent. Cafer Ağa died in 1557 while construction was still underway, but Sinan finished it in 1559–60. Owing to the steepness of the land, the architect had first to construct a vaulted substructure under the west end of the complex, along today's Alemdar Caddesi, providing space for four large shops. The domed *dershane*, or lecture hall, occupies the south side of the courtyard, with the student cells (*hücre*) placed around the periphery of the cloister.

BAZAAR OF OTTOMAN ARTS AND CRAFTS ★. Today the *medrese* serves as a bazaar of Ottoman crafts; each specialty – embroidery, bookbinding, paper-marbling – has been given one of the stalls opening onto the court. Two stalls in the right corner have been made into a café, a perfect place to pause after a walk from Saray Burnu, before continuing along Caferiye Sokağı. A left turn at the end leads into Aya Sofya Meydanı, the huge square before Haghia Sophia at the top of the First Hill.

THE SOĞUK ÇEŞME SOKAĞI
Above left is an unrestored house in the midst of a cluster of renovated buildings. The Ayasofya Pansiyonları (above right), on the "Street of the Cold Fountain," is open to visitors interested in knowing more about traditional Ottoman architecture.

THE GOLDEN HORN
A photograph taken in the 1960's of the old tramway crossing the Galata Bridge. Behind the trams looms the massive Yeni Cami.

✗   Two hours

A VIEW OF HAGHIA SOPHIA
In a detail from his panorama of 1557, the Danish painter Melchior Lorichs shows the basilica from the Asian shore.

Haghia Sophia and the old Ottoman houses after the restoration work by the Fossatis in 1852.

THE HISTORY OF THE BASILICA

Haghia Sophia was built at the command of Emperor Justinian in the years 532 to 537. The present basilica is the third church called Haghia Sophia to stand upon this site. The first, known as the Great Church, was finished on February 15, 360, and on that day Emperor Constantius (337–361), Constantine the Great's son and successor, dedicated it to Haghia Sophia, or "Divine Wisdom," an attribute of Christ. This building was destroyed by fire on June 9, 404, during a riot by supporters of John Chrysostomos, the sainted Patriarch of Constantinople who had been deposed by Empress Eudoxia, wife of the Emperor Arcadius (395–408). By 415 a new church had been constructed on the site, and was dedicated on October 10 by Theodosius II (408–450), Constantius' son and successor. Known to archeologists as the Theodosian Church, this building also burned down, during the Nika Revolt of January 15, 532. The insurrection almost cost Justinian his throne, which he retained only through the steadfastness of his Empress, Theodora.

JUSTINIAN'S HAGHIA SOPHIA. Shortly after the revolt was crushed, Justinian set about rebuilding the church on an even grander scale, bringing in workers and artisans from all over the Byzantine Empire. Provincial governors were asked to send the most beautiful parts of ancient monuments found in their regions for incorporation into the new basilica. In this way Justinian gathered the finest materials as well as columns and ornaments from pagan temples as far away as Ephesus, Athens, Delphi, Delos, and even Egypt. The Emperor appointed Anthemius of Tralles, the greatest mathematical physicist of late antiquity, as the principal

architect and for an assistant builder he employed Isidorus of Miletus, a renowned geometrician who had been director of the Platonic Academy in Athens. Anthemius died during the first months of the project, whereupon Isidorus took charge, completing the building within five years. The new church was formally opened on December 26, 537, St Stephen's Day, when Justinian and Theodora rededicated it to Haghia Sophia. Two decades later a series of earthquakes severely damaged the basilica, causing the collapse of the eastern part of the great dome along with the arch and half-dome on that side of the building. Because Isidorus of Miletus had died, Justinian entrusted the task of reconstruction to the architect's nephew, Isidorus the Younger, who accomplished it in five years. The building was rededicated on Christmas Eve 563, by an 81-year-old Justinian, less than two years before his death. Haghia Sophia would then serve as the Greek Orthodox cathedral of Constantinople throughout the remainder of Byzantine history, except for the Latin interregnum of 1204 to 1261, when it was a Roman Catholic church administered by the Venetian clergy. After the Ottoman Conquest of Constantinople in 1453, Haghia Sophia was converted into a mosque by Sultan Mehmet II, and it then became known as Aya Sofya Cami'i.

HAGHIA SOPHIA
MUSEUM ★

Haghia Sophia continued to serve as a mosque until 1932, when it was closed and converted into a

N

PLAN
1. Narthex
2. Imperial door
3. Nave
4. North tympanum
5. Tribunes (Ottoman)
6, 7. South and north galleries, linked by the Emperor's gallery (2)
8. Baptistery

CHRIST BLESSING
In this detail from the mosaic Deisis (Christ flanked by the Virgin and the Baptist) the Son of Man is presented in a hieratically posed half-figure. However, though the iconic face is haloed in other-worldly gold, it suggests kindness and sympathy rather than the stern, judgmental Pantocrator. Cleared of whitewash in 1932, the mosaic is in the southeast gallery on the right.

THE LARGEST DOME IN THE ANTIQUE WORLD
The interior surface of the main dome – approximately 100 feet in diameter – is constructed of 40 stone ribs, all decorated with geometric motifs. Around the circumference, a diadem of 40 windows contributes to the sense of this immense cupola floating in airy lightness above the prayer hall below. Gold calligraphy on a black background encircles the emblematic sun at the center.

THE INTERIOR OF THE UPPER GALLERY
The basilica underwent major restoration in the 19th century, between 1847 and 1849. Louis Haghe produced the lithograph (right) from drawings by Gaspare Fossati, one of the architects responsible for the renovation. It gives a clear picture of the way Haghia Sophia looked at that time, far better than any verbal description or photograph from the period.

museum, which opened two years later. The entrance to the museum is in the garden to the west of Haghia Sophia, an area that was once the *avlu*, or outer courtyard, of the church. The west side and rear of the garden are filled with ancient columns and other architectural fragments, all of which were unearthed in various excavations around the city, most of them on the first hill. Approaching the entrance to the museum, it is possible to see the excavated remains of the Theodosian Church, discovered in 1935 by the German archaeologist Alfons Maria Schneider. The remaining fragments of the Theodosian basilica show that this was a building of monumental proportions, comparable in size and grandeur to Justinian's church.

THE STRUCTURE OF THE GREAT CHURCH ● 74.
Before entering the museum, visitors should pause to examine the structure of the building, which the Greeks called *Megale Ekklesia*, the "Great Church." The main ground plan of Haghia Sophia is that of a basilica, which is a rectangle, and measures some 230 by 250 feet. At the center of the east wall there is a projecting apse, semicircular within and three-sided on the exterior, while to the west, in front of the church, is an inner and an outer vestibule, known in Greek as the *narthex* and the *exonarthex*. The central part of the rectangular nave is surmounted by the great dome, one of the great wonders of architecture, as well as by smaller half-domes on the east and west, and by conch vaults over both the semicircular apse at the eastern end and the semicircular exedrae at all four corners. These spherical surfaces cover the central area of the

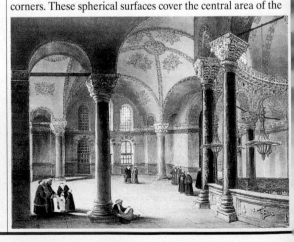

nave, which is flanked by side aisles, while upper galleries extend around the sides of the church and also the narthex. This was the basic form of Justinian's church, but engineering problems which developed in the course of construction and damage caused by earthquakes made it necessary to add buttresses all around the building.

AYA SOFYA CAMI'I

Haghia Sophia gained four corner minarets after the Ottomans converted the church into a mosque. The precincts also acquired a number of structures, some of them introduced by the Byzantines and others by the Ottomans. The additions included the baptistery and the imperial Turkish tombs on the south side. The conversion also involved some minor modifications of the interior, principally the construction of a mihrab and mimbar ● 81. All of the Ottoman sultans continued to keep Haghia Sophia in good repair, for it would always hold pride of place among the imperial mosques.

THE FOSSATIS' RESTORATION OF HAGHIA SOPHIA. The last and most important restoration in the Ottoman era came at the instigation of Sultan Abdül Mecit (1839–61), who commissioned the Swiss architects Gaspare and Giuseppe Fossati to carry out the work, which was begun in 1847 and completed in 1849. In addition to structural work the Fossatis cleared the figurative mosaics, surviving from Christian times, of the whitewash and plaster that had covered them since the adaptation of the building to Muslim worship. Then, having completed their restoration, the architects re-covered the mosaics for safekeeping. In April 1932, Thomas Whittemore, of the Byzantine Institute of America, began once more to uncover and restore the mosaics, a number of which had disappeared since the Fossatis' time. Whittemore's renovation work continued until 1964, when the galleries of Haghia Sophia were opened to the public for the first time.

THE BYZANTINE MOSAIC DÉCOR ● 64

The present entrance to the church is through the central door of the exonarthex, which is flanked by the two middle buttresses on the west side of the building. You will pass through the exonarthex into the narthex, from which nine large doors open into the nave. Pausing in the narthex, you can see, glittering on the vaults above, some of the original mosaic

THE INSCRIPTION ON THE CENTRAL DOME
The enormous inscription on the intrados of the great dome is by the calligrapher Mustafa Izzet Efendi. Executed between 1847 and 1849 at the time of the Fossati restoration, it preserves the text that had been there before: "Allah is the Light of the heavens and the earth. The similitude of His light is a niche wherein is a lamp. The lamp in glass. The glass is as it were a shining star."
Koran XXIV:35

THE PAINTED WOODEN PLAQUES
The six enormous *levhas* (inscribed plaques) hanging from the corner pillars at the gallery level were introduced by the Fossatis.

Mustafa Izzet Efendi executed the calligraphy, a golden Arabic script evoking the sacred names of Islam: Allah, the Prophet Mohammed, and the first four Caliphs: Abu Bakir, Umar, Othman, founder of the Ottoman dynasty, and Ali.

THE EMPEROR ALEXANDER
Alexander came to the throne in May 912, succeeding his elder brother Leo VI. His portrait, the last mosaic uncovered during the restoration work begun in 1932, dates from the brief period of his reign, 912–13. The Emperor is shown full length, clad in the sumptuous ceremonial garb of the Byzantine sovereigns. In his left hand he holds a skull, symbol of the vanity of life on earth.

decoration that survives from Justinian's church. The great dome, the half-domes, the north and south tympana, and the vaults of the narthex, aisles, and gallery – a total of more than four acres – were originally sheathed in gold tesserae. It is clear from the descriptions given by Procopius and other sources that the mosaics in Justinian's church depicted no figurative images, and none would have been permitted during the Iconoclastic period (730–843), when icons were banned throughout the Byzantine Empire. Thus the representational mosaics still extant in Haghia Sophia date from after the end of the Iconoclastic era. Most of the mosaics from Justinian's time survive on the vaults of the narthex and the side aisles, as well as on the thirteen ribs of the original dome. They consist of large fields of gold around architectural forms, articulated by bands of geometric or floral design in various colors. Outline crosses appear again and again on the crowns of the vaults and the soffits of arches, creating a remarkably simple but brilliant décor that must have been quite dazzling.

THE PORTAL OF THE IMPERIAL DOOR. Among the depictive mosaics still in place, one of the most impressive fills the lunette above the huge central door leading from the narthex into the nave, a portal known as the Imperial Door (**2**) and once reserved for the Emperor and his entourage. Here Christ is shown seated upon a jeweled throne, his feet resting upon a stool. He raises his right hand in a gesture of blessing, while in his left hand he holds a book with this inscription in Greek: "Peace be with you, I am the Light of the World." At the left a crowned figure prostrates himself before the throne, his hands upraised in supplication. Above, on either side of the throne, there are two roundels, the one on the left containing a bust of the Blessed Virgin and the other an angel with a staff. The Imperial figure is thought to portray Leo VI, which dates the mosaics to his reign: 886–912.

THE NAVE. You now pass through the Imperial Door into the nave, an immense space shot through with slanting shafts of sunlight falling from the diadem of forty windows at the base of the fabled dome. The central area is defined by four colossal pillars some 100 feet in height. Four great arches rise from these pillars, connected by four corner pendentives to make a continuous base for the circular, slightly elliptical, dome hovering above the square structure below. From this base rises the majestic, fairly shallow dome, with its crown soaring over 180 feet above the floor (about the height of a fifteen-story building). Pairs of subsidiary pillars to the east and west support the main half-domes. These give the nave its great length, about 260 feet, and, from the entrance, allow one to view the whole vast interior as well as the huge cupola – a massive structure that nonetheless creates the uncanny illusion of simply floating overhead. The tympana

between the central arches on the north and south are pierced
by twelve windows, a row of seven underneath a row of five,
where the three central openings form a kind of arcade.
Between the pillars on the north and south, there are four
huge columns of verd antique which support the upper
galleries, and above these columns are a further six columns
of the same marble supporting the tympanum. At the four
corners of the square nave, semicircular exedrae extend the
space, carried by two massive columns of porphyry below and
six of verd antique above, on which rest smaller half-domes or
conch vaults. The capitals of the columns ● *74* and pillars
are remarkable – among the greatest glories of Haghia
Sophia. Each of them is unique, but all are alike in their
acanthus-leaf and palm-foliage décor, as well as in their
carving, which is so deeply undercut in places that it
creates a snowflake lightness and complexity on a dark
background. Most of the capitals are bowl-shaped,
and those in the nave and gallery arcades boast
abacuses, Ionic volutes, and the imperial
monograms of Justinian and Theodora. Viewed
overall, the central area of the nave, with its
flanking, two-tiered colonnades of columns, becomes
a rhythmic procession which Procopius likened to "a
line of dancers in a chorus." To the east, beyond the
secondary pillars, a semicircular apse with conch
vaulting juts out from the main wall.

Motifs used in
carpets also appear
often in ceramics

THE MOSAIC ON THE TYMPANUM OVER THE NARTHEX DOOR
Here, the Blessed Virgin is depicted enthroned in a hieratic pose with the Christ Child on her lap. She is flanked by two haloed figures. On the left, Justinian – the "illustrious Emperor," according to the inscription – makes a symbolic offering of Haghia Sophia, while on the right, Constantine I – the "great Emperor among the saints" – presents a model of Constantinople itself. The mosaic, probably commissioned by Emperor Basil II (976–1024), dates from around the end of the 10th century.

ST GREGORY THE MIRACLE-WORKER. Legend has it that St Gregory the Miracle-worker imbued one of the aisle pillars with his healing power. To save the stone it was encased in brass; even so, credulous pilgrims have punctured the metal and worn a hole into the pillar itself, believing the moisture collected in the hollow to be a cure for eye diseases and beneficial for fertility.

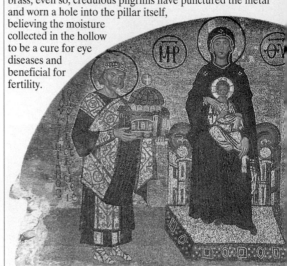

THE MARBLE FACING. A great variety of rare and beautiful marbles, from all over Justinian's Empire, were used for the splendid cladding of both pillars and walls. The elaborate, symmetrical pattern of each panel was obtained by sawing thin blocks of marble in two, sometimes in four, and opening them out like a book so that the natural veining of the stone would be duplicated in a mirror image. Among other rare marbles found in the church, the large square of the *opus Alexandrinum* pavement at the southeast end of the nave has always attracted particular attention. It consists mainly of circles of granite, red and green porphyry, and verd antique. According to Antony, Archbishop of Novgorod, who visited the church in 1200, the Emperor's throne stood upon this square, surrounded by a bronze enclosure.

THE MAUSOLEUM OF SELIM II
In the garden around Haghia Sophia stands the tomb of Sultan Selim II (1566–74), built by the great

Sinan. Completed in 1577, it is one of the most beautiful examples of Ottoman funerary architecture. Iznik tiles clad the interior walls and the façade on either side of the entrance. Above the doors calligraphic inscriptions of Ottoman verse evoke the beauties of Paradise.

THE INTERIOR OF THE MOSQUE. Haghia Sophia, or Aya Sofya, contains a number of structures added after the church was adapted into a mosque, most notably the mihrab and mimbar and the royal loge against the northeast pillar, all of which date from the Fossatis' restorations of 1847 to 1849. Other objects dating from the Ottoman period were given by various sultans, and some of these gifts are described by Evliya Çelebi, a muezzin in Aya Sofya Cami'i during the reign of Murat IV (1623–40): "Murat III brought from the island of Marmara two princely basins of white marble, each resembling the cupola of a bath. They stand inside the mosque, full of fresh water for all the congregation to perform their ablutions and quench their thirst. The same sultan caused the walls of the mosque to be cleaned and smoothed; he increased the number of lamps and built four raised stone platforms for the readers of the Koran, and a lofty pulpit on slender columns for the muezzins. Sultan Murat IV, the Conqueror of Baghdad, raised upon four marble columns a marble throne for the preacher. Sultan Murat, who took great delight in this incomparable mosque, erected a wooden enclosure within it near the southern door, and when he went to prayer on Friday he had his attendants hang there cages containing a great number of singing birds, particularly nightingales, so that their sweet notes, mingled with those of the muezzins' voices, filled the mosque with a harmony approaching to that of paradise." Other than the wooden cages for nightingales, all of these objects can still be seen in the nave of Haghia Sophia, along with the gifts of later sultans. The two lustration urns that Evliya mentions stand in the western exedrae. They are late Hellenistic or early Byzantine vases with Turkish lids. An English traveler in the 17th century noted that the vessels were kept full of water "to cool the Mohammedans overheated by their pious gesticulations." The "lofty pulpit" survives in the north arcade. It is made of marble, as are the "raised platforms" for the readers of the Koran, which stand against the four main pillars.

THE OTTOMAN LIBRARY. The finest of the later Ottoman additions is the elegant library that Mahmut I installed beyond the south aisle in 1739.

Invested by the Sultan with revenue from the Cağaloğlu Baths, the library consists of several domed rooms enclosed with metal grilles. These rooms, housing some five thousand Ottoman books and manuscripts, are clad in superb Iznik tiles, all found stored in Topkapı Sarayı.

THE NAVE MOSAICS. Little now remains of the mosaics (**3**) that once adorned the nave of Haghia Sophia. The largest and most beautiful of those that survive lines the conch vault over the apse. This mosaic depicts the Mother of God with the Christ Child on her knees, an image unveiled by Patriarch Photius on Easter Sunday 867. At the bottom of the arch framing the apse there is a colossal representation of the Archangel Gabriel. Despite the loss of the upper left side and the tops of his wings, the Archangel makes a fine and striking figure. Opposite him, on the north side of the arch, are only a few surviving fragments of the great wings from a mosaic of the Archangel Michael.

THE MOSAICS ON THE NORTH TYMPANUM WALL. Three other mosaic portraits (**4**) decorate the niches at the base of the north tympanum wall, every one of them visible from the nave. In the first niche on the left appears St Ignatius the Younger, who served as Patriarch of Constantinople from 847 to 858 and again from 867 to 877. In the central niche is St John Chrysostomos, Patriarch from 398 to 404, and St Ignatius Theophoros of Antioch is portrayed in the fifth niche.

DANDOLO, DOGE OF VENICE
In the pavement opposite the Deisis mosaic is a stone sarcophagus lid inscribed in Latin with the name of Henricus Dandolo, Doge of Venice. Though almost 90 years old, Dandolo led the Venetian contingent of the Fourth Crusade that stormed and sacked Constantinople in 1204. Chevalier Villehardouin, in his chronicle *Histoire de la conquête de Constantinople*, describes Dandolo at the height of the assault: "The Doge of Venice, despite his great age and his total blindness, stood erect on his galley, the banner of Saint Mark unfurled before him."

Thereafter, until his death in 1205, Dandolo served as the self-styled "Despot" of the Venetian quarter, which included Haghia Sophia. The Venetian clergy buried him in the gallery of the basilica, but the Turks, after the Conquest of 1453, violated the tomb and threw the bones to the dogs. Mehmet II allowed the Italian painter Gentile Bellini, who had come to Istanbul to paint the Sultan's portrait, to take the Doge's armor back to Venice.

145

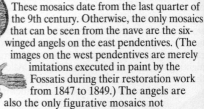

THE MOSAIC ON THE TYMPANUM OF THE IMPERIAL DOOR
This detail, of a Byzantine emperor in supplication before Christ, is thought by most experts to portray Leo VI, which dates the mosaic to the years 886 to 912.

THE IMPERIAL KIOSK
This painting from 1904 by Zeikâi Paşa depicts the Imperial Kiosk of the Haghia Sophia Mosque. The kiosk was an addition conceived by the Venetian architect Gaspare Fossati for the Sultan Abdül Mecit I (1839–61). The decorative style blends oriental traditions with the European Baroque, still fashionable in the 19th century. Polygonal in shape, the kiosk is crowned by a dome supported on small columns. The enclosing elements, which shelter the interior from the curious, echo the balustrades of the upper galleries in Haghia Sophia, though in a more elaborate manner.

These mosaics date from the last quarter of the 9th century. Otherwise, the only mosaics that can be seen from the nave are the six-winged angels on the east pendentives. (The images on the west pendentives are merely imitations executed in paint by the Fossatis during their restoration work from 1847 to 1849.) The angels are also the only figurative mosaics not whitewashed by the Ottomans. However, the Fossatis, after restoring the images, covered their faces with gold-starred medallions, which are still in place today. The angel mosaics date from the mid-14th century, when the east pendentives were rebuilt following a partial collapse of the dome in 1346.

THE GYNACAEUM. There are other figurative mosaics in the galleries, which are reached by a corridor leading up from the northern end of the narthex. According to Byzantine sources the galleries were reserved for the *gynacaeum*, or women's quarters, although the two eastern bays of the south gallery seem to have been used by the royal family and, on occasion, by synods of the Greek Orthodox Church. The empress sat upon a throne behind a balustrade at the center of the west gallery, the spot marked by a circle of green Thessalian marble and a pair of double columns of the same material.

THE MOSAICS OF THE SOUTH AISLE. Three of the four surviving mosaics in the galleries are situated at the extreme end of the south aisle. Here the gallery is set apart by a pair of false doors, both richly carved marble screens symbolizing the Gates of Heaven and Hell. The actual doorway lies between them, surmounted by a slab of translucent Phrygian marble. Still higher, a wooden beam, relief-carved with floral designs, forms a cornice stretching across and unifying the entire gateway. Well after Justinian's time, the gateway seems to have been added to close off the end of the gallery for use as a royal enclosure or as a meeting place for church synods.

THE DEISIS ★.
Turning to the right once inside this portal, one sees the most magnificent of all the surviving mosaics in Haghia Sophia, the Deisis (**5**), which is located past the last pillar on the east wall. This is an iconographic type of mosaic, in which Christ appears flanked by the Blessed Virgin and St John the Baptist (who in Greek is known as *Prodromus*, or the Forerunner). Here John stands to the

right and the Virgin to the left, reversing the usual order in Deisis compositions. They lean towards Christ in suppliant attitudes, pleading, so the iconographers tell us, for the salvation of humankind. Christ, holding up his right hand in a gesture of benediction, looks off into space with an expression of sadness, as if his nature were more human than divine – despite the teaching of medieval theology. Although two-thirds of the mosaic has gone, the features of the three figures are miraculously intact, making the Deisis a work of great power and beauty. This mosaic dates from the second half of the 13th century, when Byzantium experienced a renaissance under the Palaeologus dynasty, the last to rule the Empire.

THE MOSAICS OF THE SOUTH GALLERY. The two other mosaics in the south gallery (**6**), both of them Imperial portraits, are on the east wall of the building at the far end of the last bay, flanking a window beside the apse. The mosaic adjacent to the window depicts a royal couple kneeling on either side of Christ enthroned. On the right is the notorious Empress Zoe, one of the few women ever to rule Byzantium in her own right, reigning together with her sister Theodora in 1042. The mosaic to the right of the window shows a royal couple presenting gifts to the Virgin and Christ Child, a composition that continues on the narrow panel of the side wall, where young Prince Alexius has been portrayed together with his parents, John II Comnenus (1118–43) and Empress Eirene, daughter of King Ladislaus of Hungary. The Emperor was known in his time as Kalo Yanis, or John the Good, and Nicetas Choniates wrote of him: "He was the best of all the emperors, from the family of the Comneni, who ever sat upon the Roman throne."

THE MOSAICS OF THE NORTH GALLERY. Another imperial portrait survives in the main bay of the north gallery (**7**), high on

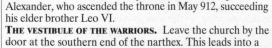

The Fountain of Ahmet III
with Haghia Sophia
in the background.

THE FRENCH
PAINTER AND TRAVELER
G.J. GRELOT
When he entered
Haghia Sophia in
1672, Grelot was the
first "infidel" to do so
since the basilica's
conversion into a
mosque. He had to
disguise himself as a
Turk, and once inside
he was able to make
several sketches and
even draw a plan of
the structure.
"Foreseeing that I
would need a light
meal and not having
decided to observe
Ramadan, the Turkish
fast, I had taken with

me a Bologna
sausage, a bottle of
wine, and some
bread. The first day
that I spent thus
prepared in the
gallery went off quite
well and without
anyone taking notice
of me. However, the
next day did not
prove so uneventful.
Indeed, after a while,
I saw a man
approaching the
position I had taken
up. Now, an infidel
drawing figures,
eating pork, and
drinking wine in a
Turkish Holy of
Holies was
committing a crime
for which neither a
firing squad nor the
stake would have
been sufficient
expiation."

the east face of the northwest pillar. It is of the Emperor
Alexander, who ascended the throne in May 912, succeeding
his elder brother Leo VI.

THE VESTIBULE OF THE WARRIORS. Leave the church by the
door at the southern end of the narthex. This leads into a
hallway known in the Byzantine period as the Vestibule of the
Warriors, for it was here that the troops of the imperial guard
waited while the emperor attended services in the church.

THE COMPLEX OF HAGHIA SOPHIA

The courtyard of Haghia Sophia harbors a number of minor
but fascinating Ottoman structures, all of them part of the
külliye of Aya Sofya Cami'i. In the center of the courtyard
stands the ablution fountain built in the Turkish rococo style
for Mahmut I around 1740. The building on the right of the
gateway to Ayasofya Meydanı (Place) is the *mektep*, a
primary school for the children of the mosque's staff. The little
domed structure to the left of the gate is the *muvakithane*, the
house and workshop of the mosque astronomer, whose
sundial can still be seen on the front of Haghia Sophia
near the southwest corner of the building.

THE IMPERIAL OTTOMAN TOMBS. The four domed
buildings in the garden just to the south of Haghia
Sophia are all imperial Ottoman tombs. The oldest of
them is the one on the left as you leave the south end of
the narthex. As the form – a domed octagon – would
suggest, this was the baptistery of Haghia Sophia. The
Ottomans then converted it into a mausoleum for the
mad Sultan Mustafa I. A quarter of a century later the
Sultan Ibrahim was also interred here, on September
10, 1648, after he had been deposed and executed, on
the orders of his own mother.

THREE IMPERIAL TOMBS. These are in the east end of the
garden, all of them attractive structures with superb Iznik
tile cladding. The oldest tomb is the one in the center.
Designed by the great Sinan for Selim II (1566–74), it ranks
among the finest Ottoman tombs in the city. The
westernmost of the three tombs houses the remains of
Murat III (1574–95). This *türbe* was finished in 1599 by
Davut Ağa, who succeeded Sinan as Chief of the Imperial
Architects. The tomb at the eastern end of the garden is that
of Mehmet III (1595–1603), completed in 1603 by Dalgic
Ahmet Ağa, Davut Ağa's successor as chief architect.

THE FOUNTAIN OF AHMET III. Walk around the south and
east sides of Haghia Sophia to approach the Imperial Gate of
Topkapı Sarayı. This brings you, on your right, to the grandest
of all Istanbul's Ottoman street fountains. Built in 1728 for
Ahmet III (1703–30), the Tulip King, it is a particularly fine
example of Turkish rococo architecture. Topped by five small
domes and a projecting roof, the fountain is gaily decorated
with red and white marble, floral reliefs, elegant columns, and
bright calligraphy.

THE TREASURY. Diagonally opposite the
Imperial Gate at the upper end of Soğuk
Çeşme Sokağı, a large Ottoman
gateway, in the rococo style, leads to the
northeast corner of Haghia Sophia's
precincts. The domed structure inside the

« THE MOST PERFECT, THE RICHEST, AND
THE MOST SUMPTUOUS OF TEMPLES, NOT ONLY IN THE ORIENT
BUT ALSO IN THE WORLD.»

NICOLAS DE NICOLAY

THE BYZANTINE CAPITAL
Byzantine architects reinforced the column capital with a crowning impost block or "cushion" formed like a truncated, upside-down pyramid. To overcome the instability of this structure, builders fused the two parts and created the impost-capital, which developed from an undecorated, massive state into the lavishly ornamented "bowls" at Haghia Sophia. Other than the acanthus, decorative themes, such as beasts' heads, were possibly derived from oriental textiles and mosaics, as were many of the techniques. This left the capital deprived of classical plasticity but rich in all-over, filigreed, chiaroscuro pattern, sometimes so delicately as well as intricately carved as to appear chased. However, the relief could also be deep enough to resemble open work. Drawing on the strong, malleable marble from the nearby quarries at Preconnese, the builders and sculptors of Constantinople exported the new impost-capital and consequently spread their influence throughout the Mediterranean world.

gate was part of the church built by Justinian and served as its *skeuphylakion*, or treasury. It housed all of the precious objects used in the liturgies of Haghia Sophia, as well as such sacred relics as the Crown of Thorns from Christ's Passion and fragments of the True Cross, which Constantine's mother, the Empress Helena, had brought back from her pilgrimage to Jerusalem. All of these treasures were looted when the knights of the Fourth Crusade and their Venetian convoy sacked Constantinople in 1204. The Director of the Haghia Sophia Museum now makes his office in the Treasury, which is therefore closed to the public. Here you might pause to look back on Haghia Sophia, for this is one of the best vantage points for viewing the Great Church, before which travelers have stood in awe for more than fourteen centuries. Some thousand years ago an envoy of Prince Vladimir of Kiev reported after his pilgrimage to Haghia Sophia: "We know not whether we were in heaven or on earth. For on earth there is no such splendor or such beauty, and we are at a loss how to describe it. We only know that God dwells there among men, and their service is fairer than the ceremonies of other nations. For we cannot forget that beauty."

149

▲ Topkapi Sarayi

1. First Court
2. Orta Kapı
   (Middle Gate)
3. Second Court
4. Divan
5. Inner Treasury
   (Arms and armor)
6. Carriage Gate
7. Gate of the Dead
   (Meyyit Kapısı)
8. Imperial Stables
9. Kitchens
10. Gate of Felicity
    (Bab-üs Saadet)
11. Throne Room
    (Arz Odası)
12. Third Court
13. Library of
    Ahmet III
14. Mosque of the Ağa
    (Ağalar Cami'i)
15. Campaign Hall
16. Apartment of
    Felicity
    (Hirka-ı Saadet
    Dairesi), relics of
    the Prophet
17. Imperial Treasury

18. Fourth Court
19. Rivan Köşkü
20. Circumcision
    Room
    (Sünnet Odası)
21. Terrace
22. Baghdad Pavilion
    (Baghdad Köşkü)
23. Sofa Köşkü
24. Abdül Mecit
    Pavilion
    (Mecidiye Köşkü)
    Konyalı Restaurant
25. Golden Way
    (Altın Yolu)
26. Harem
27. Aviary Gate
    (Kuşhane
    Kapısı)

28. Courtyard of the
    Valide Sultan
29. Imperial Chamber
    (Hünkar Odası)
30. Chamber of
    Murat III
31. Apartments of the
    crown princes and
    Terrace of the
    Favorites
    (Gözdeler
    Taşlığı)

THE FIRST COURT OF THE PALACE

Also known as the Courtyard of the Janissaries, the First Court was the mustering place for the Ottoman Army's élite corps while it was on duty at the palace. During the reign of Süleyman the Magnificent there were almost 12,000 Janissaries, and they were described as "the nerve center and the mightiest force in the service of the great Turk". Rank in the corps was identified by the degree of richness and magnificence of the clothing and headgear. There is a collection of Ottoman costumes on display in the Imperial Costume Collection at Topkapı Palace.

HAGHIA EIRENE

This Byzantine church – "Holy Peace" – was once closely linked to Haghia Sophia – "Divine Wisdom." As the administration buildings of Topkapı Palace were built all around the square, the church was eventually isolated within the walled enclosure of the imperial palace grounds.

THE GREAT PALACE OF THE OTTOMAN SULTANS

In 1461 or 1462, less than ten years after the Conquest ● *34*, Fatih Mehmet ordered the construction of Topkapı Sarayı ● *82*, a palace that would be known as Dar-üs-Saadet, the

"House of Felicity." Having found the Great Palace of Byzantium so ruined as to be uninhabitable, Fatih decided to build a new imperial residence at a different site, on the northern side of the first hill overlooking the Bosphorus where it joins the Golden Horn and the Sea of Marmara. Topkapı Sayarı remained the seat of the Ottoman Sultans until 1853, when Abdül Mecit moved into Dolmabahçe, his new residence on the shores of the Bosphorus ● *85*. More or less abandoned, the old palace would not reopen its doors until 1924, the year that Mustafa Kemal Atatürk inaugurated it as a museum ● *44*.

THE IMPERIAL GATE. Dating from 1478, Bab-ı Hümayün – the Imperial Gate – served as the main entryway to the palace complex. It once had a second story, which was demolished in 1867 when Abdül Aziz had the structure faced in marble. Garrisoned in the gate were some fifty guards – the Kapıcı – who kept watch night and day.

Topkapı Sarayı in 1590

THE FIRST COURT OF THE SARAY

The Imperial Gate opens into the First Court, or the SQUARE
OF CEREMONIES (**1**), where a number of service buildings
once stood: a bakery, housing for its staff, an infirmary, and a
warehouse for firewood. Here too was the
DARPHANE, the Imperial Mint, which is
still there today, though the structure
dates from a period later than that of
Mehmet II. The vast courtyard was also
used by the Janissaries as a mustering
point, and ceremonies were held there
before the commencement of a military
campaign. The gate next to it leads down
to GÜLHANE PARK and the museums on
the western terrace (details of which will
be given after a tour of the Inner Palace).
In Ottoman times, this gateway was
known as the Kız Bekçiler Kapısı – the
Gate of the Watchman of the Girls – for
the sentries were stationed there to secure
the Harem and prevent intruders from
entering.

GRAND VIZIER

HAGHIA EIRENE. While crossing the
courtyard, you should take note of the
Byzantine Church of Haghia Eirene,
dedicated to "Divine Peace," an attribute
of Christ, and one of the most beautiful of surviving
Byzantine churches. Justinian had it built in 537, at the same
time as Haghia Sophia, to replace a church destroyed during
the Nika Revolt of 532. Shortly after the conquest of
Constantinople, the Janissaries took over the building and
made it their arsenal. In 1826, the Sultan Mehmet II decided
to suppress this élite branch of the armed services, whose
power had long been a threat to political stability. The arsenal
was later converted into a military and archeological museum.
Since its restoration in the 1970's the building has been used
as a concert hall during the Istanbul Music Festival, which is
held in the summer.

PALACE OFFICIALS

THE MIDDLE GATE. Continuing along the right, to the bottom
of the First Court,
we arrive at the
Orta Kap (**2**), or
the Middle Gate,
which is also called
Bab-üs Selam – the
Gate of Salutations.
Dating from the
reign of Süleyman
the Magnificent,
this monumental gateway takes us into the Inner Palace of
Topkapı Sarayı. No one except the sovereign was permitted to
ride a horse past its flanking pair of towers, cone-capped and
linked by an upper walkway concealed behind crenellations.
The suite of rooms to the right of the gate was originally
occupied by the head of the palace guard. The watchmen
under his command lived in rooms on the left, where a small
suite of chambers was also set aside for the chief executioner,
an official who was also employed as principal gardener.

HEAD GARDENERS

Created in 1850, the
Imperial Costume
Collection began with
an exhibition of 140
figures representing
the former Janissaries.
Théophile Gautier
described it thus:
"Here are assembled,
like specimens of
antedeluvian animals
in the Museum of
Natural History, the
very people suppressed
by Mahmoud's coup
d'état. Here brought
back from the dead is
that fantastic and
fanciful Turkey of the
pastry-mold turbans,
of dolmans trimmed
in cat fur – the Turkey
of comic opera and
fairy tales."

THE SECOND COURT

Once beyond the Middle Gate, we enter a vast court, approximately 430 feet long and 330 feet wide. This is the Second Court, also known as the COURT OF THE DIVAN (**3**) because up until the 18th century ● *40* the Imperial Council – the Divan – met in the domed chambers in the left corner of the courtyard. Here the Grand Vizier and the chief administrators of the empire met during the first four days of every week to deal with ongoing affairs of state. In the early years after the Conquest, Fatih Mehmet himself presided over all the sessions. Subsequently, he came to prefer following the discussions from an adjacent loge, through a grilled window installed above the Grand Vizier's seat, a practice that his successors would also adopt. On the days the Divan met, the courtyard teemed with officials, Janissaries, and other palace guards, making a colorful, noisy crowd of some 5,000 people, and twice that many on special occasions. From the Middle Gate, five paths fan out towards various points in the courtyard. The second path from the left leads to the Divan and its attendant chambers, the whole crowned by the tall, cone-topped towers that make Topkapı Sarayı so easy to distinguish against the swarming panorama of Istanbul when viewed from the Golden Horn. Essentially, the architecture of the complex remains that of Fatih's time, though admittedly there have been many alterations over the centuries.

THE DIVAN ● *83*. The Divan (**4**) is composed of a suite of three dome-vaulted rooms, surrounded by a deep, colonnaded portico with wide, overhanging eves. The first room on the left is the council chamber, around three sides of which there is a low carpet-covered couch, the divan that gave the Council its name. Its lower walls are clad in the finest tiles. The room at the center was the Public Records Office, and that on the right

«THE PALACE OF SARAY BURNU WITH ITS CHINESE ROOFS,
ITS WHITE CRENELLATED WALLS, ITS LATTICED KIOSKS, ITS GARDENS
OF CYPRESSES, UMBRELLA PINES, AND SYCAMORES....»

THÉOPHILE GAUTIER

the Office of the Grand Vizier. Today the Public Records Office houses a good part of the Topkapı clock and watch collection.

Next to these three rooms is the Treasury or Inner Treasury (**5**), a long hall vaulted with four pairs of domes supported upon three massive pillars. It dates from the end of the 15th century or the beginning of the 16th. In here were deposited the tax receipts and tribute monies collected from all over the Ottoman Empire. This revenue was used to defray the cost of government until quarterly pay days, after which all remaining funds went to the Imperial Treasury in the Third Court. Today, the collection of arms and armor, much of it booty, together with other personal objects once owned by the sultans, is housed where once there was the ring and jingle of money being counted. At the corner of the Divan, south of the tower, is the main door to the Harem, also known as the Carriage Gate (**6**).

THE GATE OF THE DEAD. On the west side of the Second Court is a long portico at the far end of which is the Meyyit Kapısı – the Gate of the Dead (**7**). Funeral processions passed through this gate on their way to the cemeteries. The gate also leads down to the Imperial Stables, where the sultans' carriages and harnesses are now exhibited (**8**).

THE KITCHENS. The right side of the Second Court is mostly taken up by the kitchens (**9**) as well as the living quarters of those in service at the palace. The kitchens themselves are a suite of ten large chambers which are situated along the eastern wall of the Inner Palace; their lofty domes and tall, thin chimneys make them conspicuous landmarks when seen from the Sea of Marmara. The two southernmost domes date back to Fatih's time and the other eight to that of Beyazıt II (1481–1512). As for the chimneys in front, Sinan added them when he rebuilt much of the area following its destruction by fire in 1574. At present, the kitchens house an important collection of Chinese porcelain, celadon and silver, as well as kitchen utensils, notably the great cauldrons known as *kazans*.

THE TREASURY OF MINIATURES
Two buildings form a right angle at the north end of the Pavilion of Fatih. The one on the left – beyond a passage leading to the Fourth Court – is the former dormitory of the senior students of the Palace School. Today it houses one of the great treasures of Topkapı Sarayı: the manuscripts of calligraphy and Persian as well as Turkish miniatures. A unique collection of 13,000 works, most of them are kept in albums and therefore only part of the collection is on view at any one time. Generally, the miniatures illustrate texts recounting the lives of great men and important historical events. Plans and maps were used for documentary or even strategic purposes.

THE GATE OF FELICITY
Also called Akağalar Kapısı, or the Gate of the White Eunuchs, this fortified gate leading to the Inner Palace dates mainly from the reign of Selim I (1512–20). The decoration dates from the 19th century. On either side are apartments once occupied by the head gatekeeper and the White Eunuchs.

155

16TH-CENTURY IZNIK CERAMIC PLATES

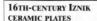

THE GATE OF FELICITY ● *83.* At the bottom of the Second Court, the Bab-üs-Saadet (**10**), or Gate of Felicity, opens into the Third Court, the sultan's own private residential quarters and the heart of the Inner Palace – the House of Felicity. The great gateway, which has stood since the time of Fatih, was reconstructed in the 16th century and redecorated in the rococo style in the 18th. It was here that the Sultan received his subjects and heard their complaints on the eve of two important Muslim holidays: Şeker Bayramı, the Festival of Sugar, and Kurban Bayramı, the Festival of Sacrifice, commemorating the sacrifice of Abraham. Just inside the Gate of Felicity stands the Arz Odası, the Throne Room (**11**), a handsome pavilion with massive, projecting eves carried upon an arcade of ancient marble columns. It was here that the Sultan received ambassadors from abroad, as well as, and far more often, the Grand Vizier and other members of the Divan who came to report on their most recent decisions and to seek the sultan's consent. Here too, each newly installed sultan mounted the throne for the first time and accepted the homage of the empire's civil and religious dignitaries, beginning with the descendants of the Prophet Mohammed.

Several thrones are on display in the Treasury. The most sumptuous of them is surely the one the Ottomans brought back from their victory over the Persians at Çaldiran, which is fashioned in red and green enamel on gold leaf and encrusted with 25,000 pearls and precious stones. Although based on a plan designed during Fatih's reign, most of the structure dates from the time of Selim I (1512–20). Moreover, inscriptions on the building cite renovations carried out under Ahmet III, Mahmut II (1808–39), and in 1856, the last following a fire that destroyed much of the furniture and decorations. Only the magnificent canopy over the throne, erected in 1596, and the bronze-gilt *ocak* (chimneypiece) escaped the flames. The building consists of a small antechamber on the right and, on the left, the audience hall itself.

THE THIRD COURT

THE PALACE SCHOOL AND IMPERIAL TREASURY. The buildings of the school for the pages were situated around the Third Court or ENDERUN (**12**). The purpose of this institution was to prepare the future civil, religious, and military leaders of the empire. The pupils entered the school at the age of twelve and left at eighteen; most of them were Christians taken from their families in the annual *devşirme* (levy) throughout the empire. Also in the Third Court were the quarters for the White Eunuchs and the *ağa*, the teachers responsible for administration and discipline

THE AĞALAR CAMI'I
Situated in the Third Court, the Ağalar Mosque now houses the museum's new library. A great many Turkish and Persian manuscripts from various parts of the palace have been assembled in its collection. At the center of the Third Court stands the library of Ahmet III (**13**), founded in 1719.

at the school. The large building positioned diagonally in the northwest corner of the Third Court is the Ağalar Cami'ı, the Mosque of the Ağa (**14**), where pages, pupils, teachers, and the White Eunuchs all attended services. Today, it shelters the New Library of the Museum. On the right is the former Campaign Hall (**15**), where the pages chosen to accompany the sultan on his campaigns were trained. It is entered through a dome-vaulted colonnade constructed from

splendid Byzantine columns of verd antique. The building now serves as an exhibition hall for the Imperial Wardrobe, a collection of the sultans' ceremonial kaftans, masterpieces of weaving and decorative design.

THE APARTMENT OF FELICITY. In the far left corner of the Third Court is the Hırka-ı Saadet Dairesi (**16**), which contains the relics of the Prophet Mohammed: his banner, saber, and,

most sacred of all, his mantle. They were brought from Egypt by Selim I after he had captured Cairo in 1517 and made himself Caliph, a title that would also be taken by his successors. The pavilion comprises four domed rooms that together form a square. Its foundation and plan were established under Fatih Mehmet, but Murat III rebuilt and refurnished a good part of the structure.

THE EVERYDAY LUXURY OF THE SULTANS
Several parts of the Topkapı Museum are devoted to precious objects used regularly at the Ottoman court, among them the glass and ceramic pieces displayed in the former kitchens. Especially noteworthy are the dishes produced at the Iznik workshops. Together they reveal the entire evolution of the classic decorative style created by the Iznik artisans, from simple arabesques in blue and white, through floral motifs in five colors, to the brilliant polychromy of late works. Ewers and pitchers could be transformed into masterpieces of the silversmith's art, especially when inlaid with precious stones. The most important pieces, however, have been assigned to the Treasury, which is in the Third Court.

A TIGHTROPE SHOW FOR AHMET III
In 1720 Sultan Ahmet III commissioned a glorious illuminated manuscript to commemorate the circumcision of his four sons, which was celebrated by a two-week festival involving continuous entertainments arranged by the city's guilds. The shows involved magicians, acrobats, tightrope walkers, and dancers and musicians, who performed on the Okmeydanı and by the seaside pavilions.

THE FOURTH COURT

The next destination on the tour is the Fourth Court (**18**),
also called the TULIP GARDEN with its terraces dotted with
pavilions or kiosks. On the highest level, in the southwest
corner, a flight of stairs leads to the L-shaped PORTICO OF
COLUMNS, which was built as an extension to the PAVILION OF
THE SACRED MANTLE. Here, in the axis of the angle, we find a
marble pool. On one side stands the Rivan Köşkü
(**19**), a kiosk erected by Murat IV in 1636 to
commemorate the taking of Rivan in the
Caucasus (present-day Yerevan). The
cruciform room is completely clad in
beautiful Iznik tiles and the exterior
faced in rare, variously colored marbles.
THE CIRCUMCISION ROOM. On the other
side of the pool is the sünnet Odası, the
Circumcision Room (**20**) commissioned
by the Sultan Ibrahim in 1642 to
celebrate the circumcision rites of his
first son, the future Mehmet IV. This rectangular building is
also generously clad in Iznik faience, both inside and out
▲ *292*. It stands on the edge of a wide terrace paved in
marble, bordered on the west by a curving, white-marble
balustrade with a view over the gardens below and the
Golden Horn beyond. Inserted at the center of the
balustrade is a delightful little balcony with a domed,
bronze-gilt canopy held aloft by four, thin bronze pillars. An
inscription on the domed canopy gives the date of
construction as 1640, the first year in the reign of Ibrahim I.
It also names the balcony Iftariye, after Ibrahim's practice of
taking Iftar on the balcony – that is, the festive meal
consumed just after sunset during the holy month of
Ramadan. Several miniatures in the Saray collection depict
the scene. One of them portrays the Sultan watching his
children at play on the terrace.
THE BAGHDAD KÖŞKÜ ● *83*. At the northern end of the
terrace stands another pavilion, the cruciform Baghdad
Köşkü (**22**) built by Murat IV in 1638 to mark his capture of
Baghdad in the same year. Its broad-eaved roof, a
masterpiece of the genre, is carried on an arcade of slender
columns with lotus capitals and serrated voussoirs of
alternating white and colored marble. Inside
and out, the walls are clad in blue and
white ceramic tiles. The
sumptuously furnished interior
includes a magnificent bronze
fireplace, two tiers of
stained-glass windows on
one wall, carved tables and
cabinets inlaid with
mother-of-pearl, window
recesses fitted with
embroidered divans, and a
domed canopy made of
leather decorated with
arabesques painted on a
crimson ground. This
pavilion also provides a

spectacular view over the lower Bosphorus.

THE SOFA KÖŞKÜ. The charming kiosk at the center of the garden, on the main terrace of the Fourth Court, is the SOFA KÖŞKÜ (**23**). Built at the beginning of the 18th century for Ahmet III, it was probably used as a private gallery for observing the famous Tulip Festival staged by the sultan in these gardens. In 1752, Mahmut I had the kiosk restyled in the rococo manner.

THE MECIDIYE KÖŞKÜ. At the bottom of the courtyard, on the right, we find a European-style pavilion upon a marble terrace. This is the MECIDIYE KÖŞKÜ (**24**), built in 1840 during the reign of Abdül Mecit. An excellent restaurant, the

THE "DINING ROOM" OF AHMET III (1705–06) A superbly decorated room, distinguished by a revived interest in still-life motifs from Europe's Renaissance. The main theme – simple trompe l'oeil bouquets in niches – is enhanced by the Oriental passion for geometry.

KONYALI ◆ *366*, now occupies the building. It is situated on the northwest extremity of the Saray and its hill, so there is a superb view looking out over the Bosphorus.

THE HAREM

To reach the entrance of the Harem (**26**), return to the northwest corner of the Second Court. This brings us to the CARRIAGE GATE (**6**), which was built in 1588 but had to be almost completely rebuilt after a fire in 1665. The Harem is open to visitors but it is necessary to make an appointment in advance.

THE GOLDEN WAY. From the gateway we enter a vestibule that opens into a guardroom clad in faience. The Black Eunuchs guarded this entranceway to prevent intruders from gaining

great detail. Thanks to this writer, we have a description of Süleyman the Magnificent: ". . . a handsome round face, with knitted brows, blue eyes, the nose of a ram, a body like that of a graceful lion, a full beard, a long neck and great height, a fine-looking man with a broad chest and square shoulders, long fingers, strong arms and feet, a sovereign without fear or fault and glorious. . . ."

access to the Altın Yolu, the Golden Way (**25**), a passage paved with pebble mosaics that runs along the eastern side of the Harem. The Golden Way begins on the left, with a portico of ten columns crowned by lotus capitals and hung with wrought-iron lamps, which, in the days of the sultans, lighted the way to the Carriage Gate.

THE EUNUCHS' QUARTERS. Built in 1668 to 1669, the tile-clad building behind the portico was once used as the dormitory of the Black Eunuchs. A passageway leads into the central courtyard of the dormitory, around which there are a dozen cells on each side of the building's three stories. Here the hundreds of eunuchs must have slept in relays, according to their round-the-clock watches. Elderly ones were

Murat III's ceremonial throne of pure gold studded with emeralds.

«O Sultan, let your friends be joyful and happy
and your enemies be full of woe.»
Cufic inscription, *Çesmeli Oda* (AD 1665-66)

The Imperial Treasury
The second building on the right in the Third Court is the Pavilion of Fatih or the Imperial Treasury (**17**). Mehmet the Conqueror had it built as the *selamlık*, a suite of reception rooms reserved for the sultan, his sons, and the court pages, together with two domed rooms for the Treasury. Soon after the apartments became a repository for precious objects and the *selamlık* was transferred to another part of the palace. Recently restored, the Treasury now displays a unique collection of valuable works that once belonged to the Sultan.

in charge of the "inner services," under a chief known as Kizlar Ağası, "Lord of the Women." He lived apart, in the building on the left of the Golden Way which commanded the approach to the Cümle Kapısı, the main entrance to the Harem proper. Beyond this entrance is another guardroom, strategically located at the principal intersection of the Harem, which was designed as a veritable gilded prison.

The women's quarters. The corridor on the right leads to the Kuşhane Kapısı – the Aviary Gate (**27**) – which leads to a third courtyard. On the left, a long and narrow passageway descends towards the courtyard of the *cariyeler*, the female servants of the Harem. From there, straight ahead, a gateway opens onto the large courtyard of the Valide Sultan (**28**) on the western side of the Golden Way. The apartments of the dowager sultana take up most of the two floors on the west side of the courtyard, while those on the north side were occupied by the first and second kadin, the highest ranking of the sultan's four hasekis. The mounting block in the northwest corner was used by the sultan when he arrived or departed on horseback.

The Room with a Hearth. Behind the mounting block, the Throne Door leads into the Ucaklı Oda, the magnificent "Room with a Hearth" completely clad in faience and dominated by a bronze fireplace. The door on the right leads to the apartments of the *kadın*, and the one on the left to a smaller chamber, the Çeşmelı Oda or "Fountain Room" named after its wall fountain ● *66* dating from 1665. These two rooms, like the next one, served as antechambers between the Harem and the sultan's own suite.

The chambers of the Valide Sultan. In the southwest corner of the courtyard a passageway leads into the salon of the dowager sultana. The Valide's chambers also included an adjoining reception room, an interior courtyard, a sitting room, a prayer room, and a small suite upstairs. Leaving the Valide's salon, we now make our way past the sultan's and Valide's baths into the largest chamber of the Inner Palace.

The roofs of the Topkapı Harem, beyond which rises a structure known as the Tower of Justice, situated in a corner of the Divaıı.

▲ Topkapi Sarayi

The "Alexander Sarcophagus" (6th century BC).

THE SARCOPHAGUS OF AN IMPORTANT PERSON
This gentleman (right) is reclining on a couch, with his wife seated at its head. A serving boy prepares a rhyton of wine. The dog, sparrowhawk and helmet suggest he was a military hero.

EURIPIDES
The subject (right, below) brings the mask of tragedy towards his face. Although there are oriental elements, the style of this relief sculpture adheres closely to that of classical Greek art, in particular the way the figures are posed and the rendering of the folds of their clothing.

THE KIOSK OF FAIENCES
This is a distinctly characteristic example of Turkish architecture from Central Asia, in its structure as well as in its décor of tiles displaying calligraphy on a blue ground.

THE IMPERIAL CHAMBER. The HÜNKAR ODASI (**29**) is divided by an arch into two unequal parts. The larger part is dome-vaulted and the smaller, slightly raised one has a balcony for musicians. This splendid salon must have been built during the reign of Murat III, which would make it the work of Sinan. The dome, pendentives, and arches have been restored to their original state, but the lower sections still display the Baroque décor installed by Osman III (1754–7). The small chamber off the southwest corner of the Hünkar Odası functioned as a private sitting room for the sultan. A door in the northeast corner opens into the Room with a Hearth, which you cross in order to enter a small but sumptuously tiled antechamber, also probably by Sinan.

THE SALON OF MURAT III.
Although a bit smaller than the Hünkar Odası, this splendid chamber is more authentic since it retains the whole of its original décor. In addition to the gorgeous Iznik tiles covering the walls, an exquisite panel depicting plum blossoms surrounds the

elegant bronze fireplace, and graceful calligraphy forms a frieze all around the room. Opposite the fireplace there is a lovely three-tiered *selşebil*, or cascade fountain, carved of polychrome marble. The sheer perfection of the room's décor and proportions identify it as the work of Sinan.

THE LIBRARY OF AHMET I. Opening off the west side of the Salon of Murat III is the small chamber that Ahmet I had converted into a library and sitting room in 1608. It is one of the most charming chambers in the whole palace, a room of marble shelves, exquisite cabinets inlaid with ivory and tortoiseshell, and walls faced in beautiful green and blue

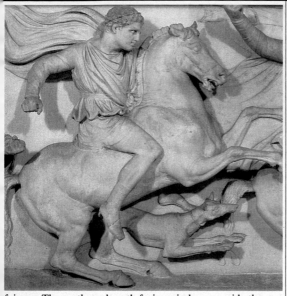

faience. The north- and south-facing windows provide the
library with light as well as stunning views across the Sea of
Marmara, the Bosphorus, and the Golden Horn.

THE "DINING ROOM" OF AHMET III. A door in the south
wall of the library leads into another wonderful chamber, the
Dining Room of Ahmet III, also called the Yemi Odası, the
"Fruit Room". As this name would suggest, the décor features
bowls of fruit and vases filled with flowers, painted in
sparkling colors on laquered wood. This oriental
interpretation of a European style is characteristic of the
"Tulip Period" – Lâle Devri – which emerged in the first half
of the 18th century.

THE APARTMENTS OF THE PRINCES. Returning through the
Salon of Murat III and its anteroom, you now come to this
stunning pair of chambers. The ceramic tiles decorating the
Princes' Apartments are examples from the Iznik workshops
in their prime, which dates the rooms to the end of the 16th
century or the beginning of the 17th. The dome over the first
room is decorated with a painting on canvas, as is the ceiling
of the inner room with a bronze-gilt fireplace, flanked by
some of the most beautiful tiles ever made. Until recently, the

ROMAN HEADS 2nd
century, Pergamon.

**SARCOPHAGUS
OF THE WEEPERS**
Formed like an Ionic
temple, this stone
coffin from the 4th
century BC was one of
the first of its kind.
The marble retains
traces of the original
bright colors.

The Archeological Museum in the First Court of Topkapı Palace.

A Phrygian perfume bottle, from the end of the 7th century BC
This small bottle was found in a tumulus at Gordion, the famous capital of Phrygia, about 60 miles from Ankara. The excavations there uncovered fortifications and houses as well as royal residences.

chambers were thought to have been the infamous *kafes*, in which the younger brothers of the sultan were interned to keep them from challenging the succession. The "cages" are now understood to be a cluster of dark cells situated beyond the Princes' Apartments along a corridor known as the "Consultation Place of the Jinns."
THE TERRACE OF THE FAVORITES. The Consultation Place of the Jinns also leads to the GÖZDELER TAŞLIĞI (**31**), a large courtyard overlooking the lower gardens of the palace. Here, on the eastern edge stands a long, two-story dormitory in which the sovereign's favorite women lived. On the ground floor the Sultan maintained a suite of rooms for his personal use.

THE MUSEUMS OF THE FIRST COURT

Leaving the Inner Palace, return to the First Court, pass through the Kız Bekçiler Kapısı, and go to the terrace below the Saray. On the left is the MUSEUM OF THE ANCIENT ORIENT, on the right, the Archeological Museum, and, farther along on the left, the Çinili Köşkü.
THE ÇINILI KÖŞKÜ. Called the "Tiled Pavilion" in English, the Çinili Köşkü is one of the buildings that survive from the original Topkapı. It is also a masterpiece of Ottoman architecture, both its design and décor showing Persian influences. The façade is decorated with blue and white calligraphy, and turquoise ceramic tiles similar to those on the famous Green Mosque of Bursa. The pavilion was built in 1472 at the command of Fatih Mehmet, who used it as a hunting lodge, as well as a place from which to watch his pages play *cirit*, an early form of polo. From 1874 to 1891 it served as a repository for antiquities, which were subsequently transferred to the Archeological Museum. Restored in the 1950's, the Çinili Köşkü now houses the Museum of Turkish Tiles. This is a remarkable collection, which includes faiences from Iznik and Çanakkale, a mirhab from the Mosque of Ibrahim Bey from the pre-classical period, and a beautiful 19th-century Ottoman-Baroque ablution fountain.
THE ARCHEOLOGICAL MUSEUM. This institution was founded in 1881 by Hamdi Bey, Turkey's first archeologist of international status. In 1991, on the occasion of the one-hundreth anniversary of the museum's opening, a new wing was inaugurated at the southwest end of the old building. Here, pride of place in the collection

is taken by the so-called "Alexander Sarcophagus," one of the funerary monuments discovered in 1887 by Hamdi Bey in the royal necropolis at Sidon in Syria. Because of its decorative bas-reliefs, depicting Alexander in battle and hunting scenes, the sarcophagus was long believed to have come from the tomb of the emperor himself. However, it has now been dated to the 4th century BC and identified as belonging to a sovereign of the Seleucid dynasty. Also among the important sepulchral monuments in the collection are the "Sarcophagus of the Mourners" and the sarcophagi of Meleager, Phaedra and Hippolytus, Sidamara, a Satrap, and, finally, Tabnit. In addition, the museum owns a superb collection of Greek and Roman sculptures, the two most celebrated of which are the Ephebos of Tralles and a head of Alexander, the latter copied after the famous original by Lysippus.

Both date from the 3rd century BC. Also on display is a superbly sculpted late-Roman head of the Emperor Arcadius, dated AD c. 400. Also not to be missed is the colossal statue of Bes, the Cypriot Heracles, a monstrous figure holding a decapitated lioness by her hind legs. In the new wing the floors are installed thematically, beginning with the ground floor devoted to classical sculpture found in Anatolia. In the vestibule there is also a scale model of the Temple of Athena in Assos. On the next floor up, we find "Istanbul through the Ages," an exhibition ranging from prehistoric times through the ancient Greek, Roman, Byzantine, Latin, and Ottoman periods. Above, on the third floor, the theme is "Neighboring Cultures of Anatolia": Cyprus, Syria, and Palestine. The great variety of exhibits and the quality of their presentation ranks the Archeological Museum among the best institutions of its kind.

THE MUSEUM OF THE ANCIENT ORIENT. Two great Hittite lions flank the door of this museum, which shelters an important collection of antiquities from all over Anatolia and the Middle Eastern dominions of the Ottoman Empire. The collection includes Egyptian, Sumerian, Akkadian, Babylonian, Hittite (see especially the "Treaty of Kadesh," the oldest known peace treaty, signed on clay tablets by Hittites and Egyptians ● 29), Urartian, and Assyrian artefacts, as well as unique objects from pre-Islamic Arabia and Nabatea. A visit here gives a complete picture of the archeological and artistic heritage of Turkey, heir to all the treasures of the ancient world acquired by the Ottomans when they conquered Byzantium and the Middle East.

165

THE ORIGINS OF OTTOMAN MINIATURES

For centuries the representation of the human form, either in sculpture or in painting, was forbidden in Islamic countries. Turkish artists, therefore, developed other areas of creativity, principally architecture but also various branches of the decorative arts. The degree of skill and sophistication that were attained in these arts deserves worldwide recognition and appreciation. The origins of the miniature go back to the Anatolian Selçuk period (11th to 13th centuries) and beyond to the pre-Islamic, central Asian Turko-Uygur period, but it is only with the reign of Mehmet II that new schools would develop in Istanbul. The Sultan surrounded himself with miniaturist painters, the most talented of whom was the portraitist Sinan of Bursa; his style shows the influence of the visits of Italian painters, like Gentile Bellini, who were invited to the seraglio by the Sultan.

ISTANBUL AND GALATA
Matrâki, 1536–37. Somewhere between a geographical map and a landscape, Matrâki's prints have a unique charm. Matrâki – warrior, wise man, and topographical painter – produced a series of pictures that show the cities conquered or visited by the sovereign, his armies, and his fleet.

«FROM NOW ON PAINTING, PORTRAITURE, CALLIGRAPHY,
AND MINIATURES WILL MEET WITH SUCCESS AND FINERY
IN ISTANBUL.»

BÂKI

The celebration of the sultan himself, his military campaigns, and the feasts and parties of the palace, would constitute the principal inspiration of the Ottoman miniaturists. Their number, while modest under Mehmet II, would rise to 29 masters under Süleyman the Magnificent, reaching the respectable number of 1000 artists working in 100 studios in the 17th century. Despite a certain uniformity of style, a number of strong personalities would emerge in each reign. Under Beyazıt II, for example, there was Ahmet of Bursa, student of the painter Sinan, as well as Baba Mustafa. The painters recruited by the sultans were mostly of Turkish origin, but there were also many of Iranian or Balkan origin, and this merging of cultures created a style which can be appropriately called Ottoman. Among the host of artists of the reign of Murat III, it was undoubtedly the master Osman who was the most talented. His skill is shown at its best in a collection of exquisite images called *The Book of Accomplishments*, which describes the life of the seraglio and the military campaigns in a decorative light. Whether clean-shaven or bearded, the faces are almost all alike. The particular beauty of the two-dimensional images is due to his technique of using flat colors of equal density.

169

The prohibition of figurative art was not adhered to by the sovereigns, who appreciated and encouraged the art of the miniature, and even, as was the case during the reign of Mehmet II, portraiture. This art was expressed almost entirely in princely books of calligraphy. Turkish miniatures depict men and women in a formulaic, standardized manner, and as part of an erudite composition. The artists are not interested in capturing the personality of the subjects. In a social structure where the land and people are all part of the imperial domain, the quest for an artistic definition of the individual was unnecessary: the people are the servants of the sultan and are inter-changeable. The landscapes of the miniatures do not obey the constraints of perspective, with no distinction made between near and far, flattening the world as though it were all within reach of the great lord. This was an aesthetic bias that, by a curious twist, was often adopted by modern, especially abstract painters. On the left is shown the *devşirme*, or collection of the young Christian children in the *Süleymanahme*, commissioned by Süleyman in 1517. To the right, science is glorified in this representation of *Astronomers in their Observatory in Galatasaray*, an extract from *Sehinsehname*, 1581.

SIYAH QUALEM

The Selçuk Turks and the Ottomans, who came from the depths of Central Asia and converted late to Islam, remained faithful to their pre-Islamic heritage. The work of Siyah Qualem shows traces of Chinese painting and its development in Central Asia. The influence of the Uigur Turks, who had opted for the Manichean religion, was crucial, as iconography occupied a fundamental place in their religion.

Among the masterpieces of this Central-Asian period, the mysterious work of Siyah Qualem can be attributed to this pre-Islamic tradition.

The heros of the Central Asian epics are generally the chiefs of nomadic tribes who perform heroic deeds and do battle with demons from the underworld.

> «YOU COULD NOT CROSS THE LAND OF KARAMAN.
> THERE ARE NO BRIDGES: YOU WOULD NOT MAKE IT
> ACROSS THE TORRENTS.»
>
> YUNUS EMRE

THE ALBUM OF FATIH
In the art collections of Mehmet II (1451–81) there are some superb and unusual works of art from Siyah Qualem. These paintings, of wandering dervishes, warriors and mythic giants, constitute the most vivid and passionate account of this nomadic world which, wave after wave, came down from Central Asia to Asia Minor.

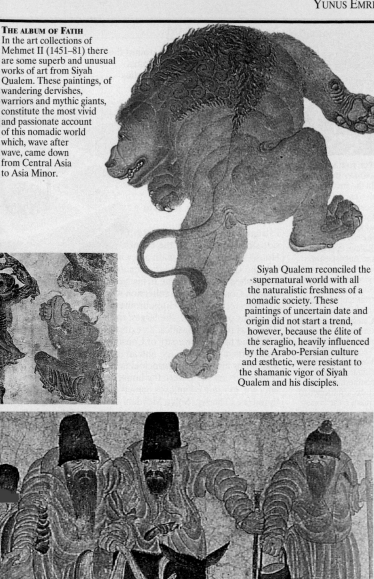

Siyah Qualem reconciled the supernatural world with all the naturalistic freshness of a nomadic society. These paintings of uncertain date and origin did not start a trend, however, because the élite of the seraglio, heavily influenced by the Arabo-Persian culture and æsthetic, were resistant to the shamanic vigor of Siyah Qualem and his disciples.

KÜÇÜK AYA SOFYA

SOKOLLU MEHMET PAŞA CAMI'I

AYA SOFYA MEYDANI

This itinerary will take you around the First Hill, beginning in AYA SOFYA MEYDANI, the great square that lies between Haghia Sophia and Sultan Ahmet Cami'i, the "Blue Mosque." Aya Sofya Meydanı occupies the site of the Augustaeum, which was the focal point of public and cultural life in Constantinople as well as the forecourt to the Great Palace of Byzantium. On the northern side, it gave access to Haghia Sophia and the Patriarchal Palace. On the eastern side stood the Chalke – the Bronze House – which was the main gateway into the Great Palace and the Senate (re-established by Constantine in his New Rome). Completing this collection were, on the southwestern side, the Hippodrome and, on the south, the Baths of Zeuxippe, the largest in the city. In addition, there was the Stoa Basilica, an extension of the Augustaeum which led to the University of Constantinople, the imperial law courts, a public library, and an outdoor book market. It was in this area that the principal avenues of the capital converged and there were the houses of rich Byzantines and later the mosque complexes named after their Ottoman founders. (The Aya Sofya Meydanı is still the site of the university, the law courts, and an important book market).

THE HAMMAM OF ROXELANA. The "Hasseki Hüssem" is also situated in the square ● 58, on the northwest side between Haghia Sophia and Sultan Ahmet (the Blue Mosque). Süleyman commissioned Sinan to build it in honor of his wife. Completed in 1556, this splendid twin-domed structure lies outside the Haghia Sophia precincts. It has recently been restored as a hall for the display and sale of Turkish rugs and kilims ● 60.

THE FORUMS OF ANCIENT BYZANTIUM

In the 5th century, the new capital could boast several major forums or squares, which together gave the city a decidedly Roman appearance: the Augustaeum, whose site is now occupied by Haghia Sophia; the Forum Constantini, situated in what became the Çemberlitaş quarter; the Forum Tauri, later renamed the Forum of Theodosius I; the Forum Amastrianum, situated at the southern end of today's Şehzadebaşi quarter; the Forum Bovis, today covered by Aksaray Square; and the Forum of Arcadius which was south of the Millet Caddesi, where a massive base survives as the sole remnant of the 5th-century Column of Arcadius.

HIPPODROME SEA WALLS BLUE MOSQUE HAMMAM OF ROXELANA HAGHIA SOPHIA

BLUE MOSQUE

Its magnificent series of domes and semi-domes, its six slender minarets sprouting from the corners of the mosque, its spacious courtyard, and its grandiose yet elegant proportions,

make Sultan Ahmet Cami'i (also known as the Blue Mosque) one of the architectural marvels of the world. Mehmet Ağa built it on the orders of Sultan Ahmet I (1603–17), hence its official name. The courtyard in front of it is on a scale equal to that of the enormous mosque itself. It can be entered through one of the large gateways located on each of the three sides. Within there is a peristyle with 26 columns forming a portico surmounted by a series of 30 small cupolas. A handsome octagonal *şadırvan* ● 66 stands in the center.

No other mosque in Istanbul has ever had six minarets. The four at the corners of the building have balconies. The cascade of domes begins with the vast main dome and continues with the four flanking semi-domes, each quite large and abutted by smaller semi-domes, which are further echoed in the smaller cupolas reinforced on either side by round turrets at the corners of the building. Adding to this symphony of spherical forms are the little cupolas atop the tall octagonal turrets

🏛 Four hours

BYZANTINE IVORY WORK
The finest pieces made by the capital's ivory carvers date from the late 5th century. A precious material, ivory was reserved for images of the emperor, who gave them to notables who had supported his bid for the throne.

Interior and mihrab of the Blue Mosque.

**RACES IN
THE HIPPODROME**
A race generally
involved four chariots
running seven laps
around the track, a
distance of some 2,700
yards. Each chariot
driver wore the colors
of one of
Constantinople's
socio-political
factions, which was
sponsoring him
financially. The White
and Blue parties
consisted of aristocrats
and landowners, all
allied with the throne.

that extend the height of the four structural pillars under the
main dome. Along the north and south fronts are two floors of
porticoed galleries, and the form is continued
in the arcades around the walls of the
courtyard below.

THE INTERIOR. Measuring 174 by
167 feet, the prayer hall is almost
square, and above it rises the
immense dome, reaching a height of
77 feet above the pavement and with
a diameter of 141 feet. This heavenly
vault rests upon the cubic base thanks
to a circular rim or cornice formed by four
ogival arches joined at the corners by four smooth pendentives.
But the main support for the superstructure comes from four
colossal pillars – 16 feet in diameter – banded at the waist and
ribbed with convex fluting. Light floods into the building
through 260 windows, which, alas, are modern imitations
of the original ones installed in the 17th century. The
painted tiles that sheath the great dome as well as the
upper walls were also recently installed, and account for
the mosque's popular name. However, the tiles on the
lower walls and the galleries merit close attention.
Indeed, they are from the Iznik workshops and are
decorated with superb floral motifs in an exquisite blue-
green palette. The

white marble mirhab
and mimbar are fine
examples of 17th-
century Ottoman
sculpture. No less

The Red and Green
parties drew their
members primarily
from the artisan and
merchant classes. The
victor emerged as a
great public hero;
thus, Emperor
Anastasius (451–518)
had two bronze
statues erected in
honor of Porphyrus,
one of the most
famous of the
Hippodrome stars.
Members of the
imperial court
watched the races
from a private
enclosure, the
kathisma, which was
probably situated on
the east side of the
arena, where it could
be entered through
the wall of the Great
Palace, now vanished.
Between races,
clowns, dwarves,
acrobats, and wild
animals performed for
the assembled crowd.

remarkable are the bronze
gateways in the forecourt
and, within the mosque, the
doors and window shutters
made of wood inlaid with
ivory, mother-of-pearl, and
tortoiseshell. On the ceiling
under the Sultan's loge,
found in the upper gallery
to the left of the mihrab,
there is a rare example of
the first Ottoman style, an
array of painted floral and
geometric motifs. An
exterior ramp on the
mosque's northwest corner
leads to the *hünkar kasrı*,
the imperial pavilion,
connected to the imperial
loge by an internal corridor.
The *hünkar kasrı* houses
the KILIM MUSEUM ● *60*.
At the east end of the
mosque, the vaulted,
subterranean storerooms
and stables have now been
restored to house the
CARPET MUSEUM.

THE COMPLEX OF THE BLUE MOSQUE. The mosque and its forecourt were in turn surrounded by an outer precinct wall, of which only the northern section remains. This rampart isolated the mosque from the other buildings within the complex: the *medrese*, *türbe*, hospital, caravanserai, primary school, and *imaret*. All of these structures still exist today except the hostel and the hospital. The *medrese* lies outside the walls on the northeast side, near the large square *türbe* or mausoleum, which has now been renovated and opened to the public. Here lie the remains of Ahmet I, his wife Kösem, and three of his sons, Osman II (1618–22), Murat IV, and Prince Beyazıt.

THE HIPPODROME. The AT MEYDANI, the vast, tree-shaded esplanade spread out before the Blue Mosque is on the site of the ancient Roman Hippodrome. The street encircling it corresponds to the course of the original racetrack. Built in AD 198 by the Emperor Septimius Severus, the Hippodrome was reconstructed on a much grander scale by Constantine the Great once he had decided to make Byzantium his new capital. Thereafter, the Hippodrome became the scene of many a Byzantine drama, beginning with the official birth of the New Rome on May 11, 330. It was here the court and public acclaimed victorious emperors and generals; some were also executed here, as were several heretical patriarchs. It was also to the Hippodrome that the people came to vent their frustrations, as when the Nika Revolt broke out on January 13,

THE EGYPTIAN OBELISK
First erected by Pharaoh Tutmosis III (16th c. BC), this obelisk once stood 195 feet tall. It broke apart while being unloaded in Constantinople,

leaving only the top third to be mounted on the spine of the Hippodrome by Theodosius the Great in 390.

177

SOKOLLU MEHMET PAŞA
One of the most capable bureaucrats in the whole of Ottoman history, Sokollu Mehmet entered the Janissary Corps at a very early age and was educated in the Palace School at Topkapı Sarayı. By 1565 he had become Grand Vizier under Süleyman the Magnificent, a post he continued to hold during the reign of Selim II, whose daughter, Princess Esma, he married.

He built the mosque that bears his name in her honor. After the death of the drunken Selim in 1574, Sokollu Mehmet Paşa became Grand Vizier to Murat III; he was assassinated in 1579 by a demented soldier in the Divan.

532 ● *32*, only to be crushed five days later by General Belisarius, who ordered Justinian's troops to block the exits and massacre the 30,000 insurgents trapped inside the arena. During the Roman occupation of Constantinople (1204–61) the Hippodrome was plundered, and by the time the Turks arrived in 1453, it had fallen into ruins.

From 1609 to 1616 the once-glorious Hippodrome served as a quarry for the construction of the Blue Mosque. The site then became known as At Meydanı (Place of Horses), for the game of *cirit*, a forerunner of polo, that the Topkapı pages played. In 1890, the French architect Bouvier drew up plans for converting the square into a park.

THE EGYPTIAN OBELISK. The Obelisk of Theodosius – Dikilitaş in Turkish – is mounted on four bronze cubes set upon a marble base, which is decorated with bas-reliefs portraying Theodosius and his family in their enclosure at the Hippodrome. On the southern face, the Emperor observes the races depicted in the lower part of the relief; on the east, he places a laurel crown on the head of the winning charioteer; on the north, he oversees the erection of the obelisk; and on the west, he receives the homage of his vanquished enemies.

THE SERPENT COLUMN. The central feature of the square is the Serpent Column (Yılanlı Sütun in Turkish), a twisting shaft of three entwined snakes, which once served as a base for the trophy of thanksgiving offered by thirty-one Greek cities whose conscripts had helped defeat the Persians at Platea in 479 BC. Constantine the Great had it brought from the Temple of Apollo at Delphi. The beasts' heads disappeared following the Conquest, although the upper part of one head was found in

1847 and is now exhibited in the Archaeological Museum.

THE COLUMN OF CONSTANTINE. Örme Sütun, as the Turks call the third column which stands on what was the spine of the Hippodrome, is situated at the southwest extremity of At Meydanı. Petrus Gillius referred to it as the "Colossus," but most modern commentators speak, incorrectly, of the "Column of Constantine Porphyrogenitus." Both names derive from Greek inscription on the base, which compare it to the Colossus of Rhodes, and also indicate that the column had been badly damaged but then repaired and clad in bronze by Emperor Constantine VII Porphyrogenitus (913–59). The original column dates from a much earlier period, perhaps that of Constantine the Great.

THE PALACE OF IBRAHIM PAŞA. On the west side of At Meydanı is the Ibrahim Paşa Sarayı, built by Ibrahim Paşa in 1523 shortly after Süleyman named him Grand Vizier. The restored structure now houses the MUSEUM OF TURKISH AND ISLAMIC ARTS, which has a fine collection. Part of the lower floor in the northern wing has been turned into an old-fashioned Istanbul coffee house, a perfect place to relax after visiting the museum. On the right, a stone lion from the Selçuk period guards the stairway to the upper floor of the north wing, where the exhibition begins.

The brilliant polychromy of the finest Iznik tiles decorating the Sokollu Mehmet Paşa Cami'i is accentuated by the stained-glass windows.

THE MUSEUM OF TURKISH AND ISLAMIC ART ★. Objects dating from the 7th to the 19th century are exhibited in the nineteen cells of the north and east wings. They represent every period of Turkish and Islamic art: Ummayid, Abbasid, Mameluk, Selçuk, Beylik, and Ottoman. The superbly organized displays embrace everything from kilims, manuscripts, calligraphy, miniatures, carved wood, ironwork, and stone sculpture to faience, stained glass, and folk art. In the south wing, on the garden level, we find the Ethnological Collection, devoted mainly to the Yürük, the nomads of Anatolia, whose way of life has scarcely changed since the first Türkmen swept across Asia Minor following their victory over the Byzantines at Manzikert in 1071. The objects on display, in black tents made of lamb skins, are still used by the wandering tribes.

THE BYZANTINE PALACE
Constantinople had few links with the ancient Byzantium that preceded it. In place of the old city's unity arose several diverse quarters. The 11th-century miniature seen here depicts a Byzantine palace encircled by a wall, set within a garden, whose fountain fed cistern water through a complex network of pipes ● 76. In the areas around these aristocratic dwellings were comfortable houses of up to three stories tall, or more modest houses containing artisan workshops.

179

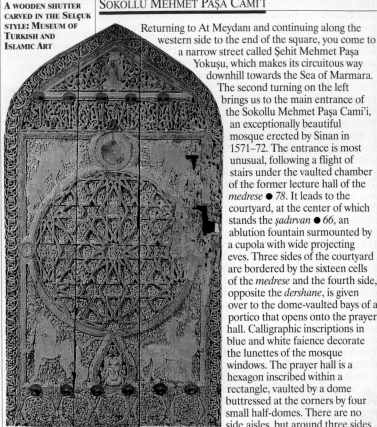

SOKOLLU MEHMET PAŞA CAMI'I

Returning to At Meydanı and continuing along the western side to the end of the square, you come to a narrow street called Şehit Mehmet Paşa Yokuşu, which makes its circuitous way downhill towards the Sea of Marmara. The second turning on the left brings us to the main entrance of the Sokollu Mehmet Paşa Cami'i, an exceptionally beautiful mosque erected by Sinan in 1571–72. The entrance is most unusual, following a flight of stairs under the vaulted chamber of the former lecture hall of the *medrese* ● 78. It leads to the courtyard, at the center of which stands the *şadırvan* ● 66, an ablution fountain surmounted by a cupola with wide projecting eves. Three sides of the courtyard are bordered by the sixteen cells of the *medrese* and the fourth side, opposite the *dershane*, is given over to the dome-vaulted bays of a portico that opens onto the prayer hall. Calligraphic inscriptions in blue and white faience decorate the lunettes of the mosque windows. The prayer hall is a hexagon inscribed within a rectangle, vaulted by a dome buttressed at the corners by four small half-domes. There are no side aisles, but around three sides runs a lower gallery supported by marble columns with lozenge capitals – a typical feature of Ottoman architecture. Characteristic of the period is the vivid color of the ogival arches, with their alternating green and red marble voussoirs.

This wood relief comes from the imaret of Karaman Ibrahim Bey at Konya. It constitutes a rare example of a Beylik work in which figurative elements are used. The central medallion is composed of six- or twelve-pointed stars and twelve-sided polygons. Winged lions and a pair of griffins occupy the corners, while an interlace of palmettes and leaves frames the entire shutter. A calligraphic inscription fills the headband, leaving the octagons of the lower band to be embellished with spirals and palmettes.

TILES AND STAINED-GLASS WINDOWS. The décor of the Sokollu Mehmet Paşa Cami'i is especially refined; the sober walls are brightened only by tiles sheathing the pendentives, a floral frieze, and the beautiful frame around the mihrab on the east wall. This frame is made of faience glazed with turquoise vine and flower motifs on a pale green ground, interspersed with white calligraphy on a deep blue field. The mimbar, finely carved from white marble, is capped by a tall conical hood with the same turquoise tiles as those surrounding the mihrab. There are two tiers of stained-glass windows in the wall above the mihrab. Above the entrance door,

one can still see a fragment of the painted decorations that
originally covered the wall in elaborate multicolored designs.
A fragment of black basaltic stone from the Kaaba in Mecca
survives over the door, and there are other pieces of sacred
stone set in the mimbar and mihrab.

STS SERGIUS AND BACCHUS. Leaving the Sokollu Mehmet
Paşa Cami'i, proceed through one of the most picturesque
parts of the city, towards the Sea of Marmara as far as Küçük
Ayasofya Caddesi. On the right stands the Küçük Aya Sofya
Cami'i, the Little Mosque of Haghia Sophia, so called
because it resembles the famous basilica. In fact, it was
originally the church of Sts Sergius and Bacchus ● 74, one of
the most beautiful in Constantinople and one of the most
important churches in the history of the capital. Justinian
commissioned the building in 527, the first year of his reign,
and it remained a place of Christian worship for almost a
thousand years. Early in the 17th century, the church was
converted into a mosque by
the head of the black
eunuchs under Sultan
Beyazıt II, Hüseyin Ağa,
whose remains lie in a *türbe*
north of the apse. The shape
of the building is an irregular
octagon within an
even more irregular
rectangle. The
transition from the
rectangular to the
circular has been
accomplished in the most astonishing manner, with the dome
divided into sixteen alternating flat and concave sections so
that the latter end precisely at the corners. The dome is
supported by eight polygonal pillars, one on either side of
the four interior angles, separated by pairs of alternate
red and green marble columns which follow the curve
of the exedra at each corner. The space between
this colorful, vibrant screen and the exterior
walls becomes a walkway below and a
capacious gallery above, the latter
reached by a stairway at the southern
end of the narthex. The column
capitals and the classic
entablatures, with their
intricate, deeply undercut
carving, exemplify the
lapidary style of
the 6th century.
The arcaded
epistyle or
architrave
would become
more or less
standard in later
Byzantine
architecture, most
notably in Haghia Sophia.
However, the trabeated
rather than arcuated

**LITTLE
HAGHIA SOPHIA**
This was the first of
many churches
founded by Justinian
which were dedicated
to Saints Sergius and
Bacchus. Martyred
for their faith, they
were the patron
saints of Christian
centurions in the
Roman army.

entablature on the ground floor, with its architrave, frieze, and cornice, remains essentially classical. A dozen hexameters engraved upon the frieze pay tribute to Justinian, Theodora, and St Sergius. As in Haghia Sophia, the interior walls have been clad in variegated marble revetments. The south doors open onto a narrow, winding street that runs under a railway and on to the shore of the Marmara.

THE SEA WALLS

Originally, the walls that Constantine the Great had constructed along the Sea of Marmara coastline extended as far as Samatya, where his land walls descended to the shore below the Seventh Hill. In the following century they were extended still further, all the way to the Theodosian walls, which had just been completed. Four hundred years later, the ramparts would be almost entirely rebuilt by the Emperor Theophilus (829–842), eager to reinforce the capital's defenses against Arab attacks. Theophilus' name can still be made out among the inscriptions on the gigantic towers. Altogether, the sea walls constituted a continuous line of defense 40 to 50 feet high, with 13 gateways and 88 towers at regular intervals. These fortifications extended for some 5 miles, beginning at Saray Burnu, where they intersected those along the Golden Horn, and continuing to the Marble Towers, where they connected with the old Theodosian walls. Constantinople was thus completely surrounded and protected by a barrier of ramparts some 15 miles long. Although a good part of the sea walls, together with their towers and gates, were destroyed in the 19th century, the sections that remain show how formidable they were, particularly the walls at the foot of the First Hill.

THE PALACE OF BUCOLEON. Not far away are the ruins of a very grand Byzantine gateway, which the Turks call Çatladı Kapı, meaning "Cracked Gate." The marble arch and its supporting posts are decorated with bas-reliefs of acanthus leaves and a large monogram of Justinian ● *32*. It is very likely that this was the Imperial Marine Gate, one of the entrances to the Bucoleon port, an exclusive harbor serving the Great Palace. The Bucoleon, or Palace of the Bull and the Lion, took its name from a sculpture of a lion overcoming a bull, which has long since disappeared. Anyone arriving at the port entered the palace by a stairway in the massive tower just beyond the Çatladı Kapı, where all that remains of the Bucoleon can be seen – a loggia with three marble-framed windows opening onto a vaulted hall.

THE GREAT PALACE OF BYZANTIUM. The fragments described above are all that survive from the Great Palace of Byzantium whose pavilions, gardens, and courtyards once spread over the slopes of the First Hill facing the Sea of Marmara. Constantine the Great commissioned the first buildings, which suffered grave damage during the Nika Revolt of 532. Justinian had them reconstructed and enlarged. Later, other emperors, especially Basil I of Macedonia, renovated, expanded, and decorated them. The wonder of the medieval world, the Great Palace remained the imperial residence until the sack of Constantinople by the Venetians and Crusaders in 1204 ● *32*. However, after the restoration of the empire in 1261, the immense, sprawling palace had decayed into such a state that the Palaeologus emperors preferred to live in the Palace of the Blachernae which was in the northwest of the capital overlooking the Golden Horn.

THE STABLE GATE. The next tower in the defensive walls beyond the Bucoleon was used as Constantinople's *pharos* or lighthouse. A little further along we come to the Ahir Kapı or "Stable Gate," the only sea-wall gateway still standing on the shores of the Marmara. During the Ottoman period, it opened into the sultan's stables, which accounts for its popular name. Close by is a modest but excellent restaurant named *Karisma Sen*, which in Turkish means: "Mind your own business."

THE GREAT PALACE The imperial residence in Constantinople was actually a collection of different structures: the Sacred Palace and the Palace of Daphne, both near the present site of the Blue Mosque; the Chalke Palace, or the House of Bronze, abutting the south side of the Forum Augustaeum; the Palaces of Magnaura and Mangana, on the slope of the First Hill facing the Sea of Marmara, slightly to the east of the present Topkapı Palace; and the seaside Palace of Bucoleon. Here stood the famous Pavilion of the Porphyrogenitus, the *gynaeceum,* or women's quarters, reigned over by the empresses; its walls were covered with splendid purple marbles brought from Rome by the first emperors. This décor is behind the saying "born to the purple," which is the meaning of *Porphyrogenitus.* By the time the Turks occupied the city, the Great Palace was little more than ruins. Shortly after the Conquest, Mehmet II surveyed the wasted halls and found them so depressing that he recited a sorrowful distich by the Persian poet Saadi: "The spider weaves the curtains of the Palace of the Caesars. The owl hoots its nocturnal call on the Tower of Aphrasiab."

A striking feature of
the city is the number
and diversity of the
small trades that
figure so prominently
in everyday life.
Strung out along the
streets are tiny
refreshment stalls
stands selling döner
kebab, barber shops,
and public
scribes. Also at
work in the
open are
bootblacks and
itinerant
vendors of such
items as
cigarettes and
newspapers,
indeed
everything
that can be consumed
on the run or can
satisfy a sudden need.
The first drop of rain
brings out a rush of
umbrella peddlers,
only to be replaced by
peddlers of dark
glasses and cool
drinks as soon as the
sun reappears.

THE WHITE MUSTACHE QUARTER

Pass through the Ahir Kapı, turn left onto Ahir Kapı Sokağı
and then right into Heresteci Hakki Sokağı, and you will soon
come to Ak Bıyık Meydanı, the Square of the
White Mustache, which lies at the heart of Ak
Bıyık, one of Istanbul's oldest and most
picturesque quarters. It is a veritable maze of
alleyways with such colorful names as Street of the
Bushy Beard, of the Sweating Whiskers, and of the
Shame-Faced. In the center of the Square of the
White Mustache there are two Ottoman fountains.
The old city boasts more than 400 Ottoman *çeşme*
● 66, ranging from simple wall fountains to great
domed and arcaded street fountains. Formerly, these
facilities provided the citizens with their
only source of drinking water,
and they remain indispensable,
particularly in older quarters.

THE MOSAIC MUSEUM

From Ak Bıyık Sokağı, turn right into
Mimar Mehmet Ağa Caddesi, and then left into Torun Sokağı
or the Street of the Little Child. In this street is the main
entrance to the Mosaic Museum, the repository for fragments
of columns, antique marble capitals, and various other remains
of the Great Palace of Byzantium. Most important of all, the
museum exhibits mosaics salvaged from the Great Palace, all
restored and mounted on panels. On this very site, they once
adorned the Mosaic Peristyle, a colonnaded passage
thought to have led to the *kathisma*, the imperial
enclosure in the Hippodrome. The subjects
depicted in the mosaics include pastoral
landscapes, scenes of hunting and
animal combat, and various events
in the Hippodrome, some of
which are very amusing, for
example the efforts of two
inebriated spectators to
play horse and
charioteer. The

> «A BLUE LIGHT SPREAD MORE AND MORE;
> GRADUALLY IT BATHED THE WISE, DEVOUT SMOKERS,
> BUT THE DESERTED SQUARE REMAINED IN THE SHADOW
> OF THE MASSIVE SACRED WALLS.»   PIERRE LOTI

mosaics date from the first half of the 6th century and must have been installed when Justinian rebuilt the Great Palace.

THE STREET OF THE BUSHY BEARD. From the upper doorway of the Mosaic Museum, turn right into Kaba Sakal Sokağı – the Street of the Bushy Beard – which passes behind the Blue Mosque. This traditional *arasta*, or bazaar street, underwent reconstruction in the 1970's. Since then its arcaded shops have catered largely to the tourist trade. At the end of the street on the right there is an entrance to the Carpet Museum housed in the Blue Mosque. Continuing uphill towards the left, we pass the HAMMAM OF ROXELANA. On the east side of Kaba Sakal Sokağı there are two old buildings, the first of which is the MEHMET EFENDI MEDRESESI, built in the 17th century and restored by the TTOK. This one-time educational building

now shelters the Istanbul Fine Arts Market, and its workshops occupy the little stalls bordering the courtyard, each of them dedicated to one of the old Ottoman crafts, such as bookbinding, paper marbling, embroidery, miniature painting, engraving, and doll-making. The other structure, a fine old *konak* (mansion) has also been restored by the TTOK. Called the Yeşil Ev, or Green House, it is now a deluxe hotel and restaurant, and in good weather tables are set outside in the very attractive courtyard ◆ *367*. This is a perfect place to stop for lunch after a stroll about the First Hill.

THE MUSEUM OF RUGS AND KILIMS
In the 13th century, Marco Polo extolled the beauty of Turkish carpets. The thousand-year-old craft is the fruit of several ancient traditions: those of the Anatolian nomads on the one hand and those of the Türkmen tribes of Central Asia on the other, both of whom passed their skills to the Selçuks.

THE KAISER'S FOUNTAIN
At the northeast extremity of the Hippodrome stands the fountain given by Kaiser Wilhelm II to Sultan Abdül Hamit II. At the end of the 19th century the Ottoman Empire represented a key piece on the geopolitical chessboard of Europe. In the midst of Franco-German and Austro-Russian tensions stood the Balkans, strategically located at the gates to Asia and the eastern Mediterranean. The Balkan wars proved to be a prelude to world conflict. In November 1914 the Ottoman Empire entered World War One on the side of Germany and Austro-Hungary.

▲ THE GRAND BAZAAR

ŞEHZADE CAMİ'İ

BEYAZIT CAMİ'İ

SÜLEYMANIYE

🔆 One day

EXIT FROM THE GRAND BAZAAR
Customers leaving the Grand Bazaar near the Nuruosmaniye Mosque (below). The houses on the ground floor have been converted into grocery shops and stalls for a wide variety of craftsmen.

DIVAN YOLU

Byzantine Constantinople's main thoroughfare was the Mese, or Middle Way, which ran from the Forum Augustaeum to the Adrianople Gate on the Sixth Hill. The first stretch of the Mese followed the same course as today's avenue, which connects the summits of the First and Third Hills. Between the summits of the First and Second Hills the route is known as Divan Yolu, the Road of the Divan, and the section to the top of the Third Hill as Yeni Çeriler Caddesi, the Avenue of the Janissaries. Both names derive from Ottoman times, when the Janissaries paraded along here for the thrice-weekly meetings of the Divan. On these occasions they marched between their barracks near the Şehzade Cami'i and Topkapı Palace.

THE MILION

At the beginning of Divan Yolu on the right we see an Ottoman *suterazi*, or water-control tower, one of the very few that survive. The ancient marble stele at its base has been identified as the Milion, a triumphal archway of the late Roman period crowning the route between the Forum Augustaeum and the Mese. Modeled on the Miliarium Aureum erected in Rome by Augustus as the reference point for all road distances in the empire, the Milion served a similar purpose – the zero point for the milestones on the roads between Byzantium and the Adriatic. According to Petrus Gillius (1545), the Milion was surmounted by statues of Constantine the Great and his mother, Helena, together holding a large cross. The first street on the right leads to the entrance to the Yerebatan Sarayı.

YEREBATAN SARAYI

The so-called Underground Palace is better known to foreigners as the Basilica Cistern ● 76. Until the 1980's only a small part of the vast subterranean reservoir could be viewed, from the landing at the bottom of the stairs. In 1987, however, the Yerebatan Sarayı was reopened to the public after years of restoration. The water level had scarcely fallen and walkways were built throughout its labyrinthine expanse. The Basilica Cistern is by far the largest and grandest of the ancient Byzantine reservoirs in the city. It gets its English name because it was built directly under the Stoa Basilica, or Imperial Portico, on the west side of the Forum Augustaeum. The Stoa Basilica, probably commissioned by Constantine the Great, was destroyed by fire in c. 475. Justinian rebuilt it after the Nika Revolt of 532 and at the same time reconstructed the cistern below, using material from older buildings. The Basilica Cistern provided the main

YEREBATAN SARAYI
Since the Byzantine era, the abundant springs in the Belgrade Forest near the Black Sea have been tapped and their waters stored in reservoirs called *bent*.

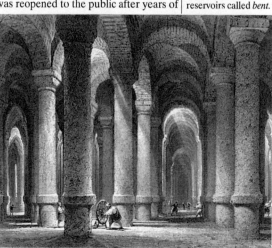

Formerly, the waters flowed into the city's cisterns by means of pipes and a number of monumental aqueducts.

187

Binbirdirek
Sarnıcı, the Cistern
of a Thousand-
and-One Columns

THE MEDUSA HEAD
After dismantling the
walls of Chalcedon,
the city on the Asian
side of the Bosphorus
overlooking the
entrance to the
Euxine Sea, or Black
Sea, Justinian had
much of the building
material brought to
Constantinople and
re-used in the
aqueducts (among
them the Valens
Aqueduct) and the
covered cisterns.
Therefore, it is quite
likely that the
splendid Gorgon's
head turned on its
side and employed as
a column base in the
Basilica Cistern came
originally from the
city of Chalcedon.

source of water for the First Hill throughout the Byzantine
era and on into Ottoman times, when every street corner and
square in Istanbul had its own fountain, or *sebil,* making water
freely available to all who passed. It arrived through porcelain
conduits from sources such as the Yerabatan Sarayı.
Originally, the cistern comprised 336 26-feet columns set at
intervals of 13 feet in 12 rows of 218 each. However, 90 of
them have now disappeared behind a wall built at the end of
the 19th century. Most of the columns are capped by
Byzantine Corinthian capitals, whose impost blocks support
small domes of brick structured herring-bone fashion. In the
far left corner of the cistern there seems to have been a
nymphaion, or ornamental fountain. When first installed, it
would have been accessible from the Stoa Basilica.

FIRUZ AĞA CAMI'I

This little mosque was erected in 1491 for Firuz Ağa, Chief
Treasurer in the reign of Sultan Beyazıt II. It constitutes one
of the few examples in Istanbul of a pre-classical mosque ● 78
– that is, a mosque built before 1500. Austerely elegant in its
simplicity, the building belongs to the "single-unit" type, and
consisted merely of a square domed room entered through a
small, three-bay porch with a minaret placed, atypically, on
the left.

THE REMAINS OF TWO ROMAN PALACES. Beyond the Firuz
Ağa Cami'i there is an archeological site which was first
excavated in the 1960's. The incomplete ruins that were
uncovered are thought to be of two small palaces which were
owned by two patricians of the late Roman period named
Antiochus and Lausus. The somewhat grander palace
belonged to Antiochus and was a hexagonal structure
constructed with paired, semicircular apses which alternated
with circular rooms. Early in the 7th century the palace was
converted into a martyry dedicated to St Euphemia, who had
died for her faith in Chalcedon in AD 303. In the 13th century
it was decorated with frescoes, but these have been moved in
order to preserve them and are kept in a shelter situated next
to the Law Courts.

« YOU MAY LINGER A WHOLE DAY IN ONE BAZAAR.
YOU WALK IN THE MIDST OF TOWERING HEAPS OF BROCADES FROM
BAGHDAD, SILKS FROM BURSA...»

EDMONDO DE AMICIS

THE CISTERN OF A THOUSAND-AND-ONE COLUMNS

At the first corner of Divan Yolu turn left onto Işık Sokaği, which leads uphill to a small park. At the south end of this park there is a shed which is the entrance to Binbirdirek Sarnıcı, the Cistern of a Thousand-and-One Columns. The cistern has not been restored, but the caretaker, if available, will admit visitors in exchange for a modest gratuity. Binbirdirek is the second largest of the city's ancient cisterns, though only a third the size

of Yerebatan Sarayı. Though rather muddy it is worth exploring. The cistern was originally about 60 feet high, from the floor to the crown of the small brick vaults built in a herring-bone pattern, but it is now reduced in size because of a 15-foot layer of mud. The structure is supported on 224 two-tiered columns bound together by stone rings and arranged in 16 rows of 14, though 12 of the columns have long been walled up. The impost capitals are plain except for monograms inscribed by the stone masons. It was traditionally believed that Philoxenus, a Roman senator who accompanied Constantine in his move to Byzantium, commissioned Binbirdirek, but investigations have shown that it was probably built in either the 5th or 6th century.

THE TÜRBE OF MAHMUT II. On returning to Divan Yolu you will see on your right the domed *türbe* (mausoleum) of Mahmut II, a large tomb built in the French Empire style and completed in 1839, the year of Mahmut's death. Buried with him are his son Abdül Aziz and his grandson Abdül Hamit II.

THE KÖPRÜLÜ KÜLLIYE

On the left side of Divan Yolu stands a handsome little brick-and-stone structure housing an Ottoman library which is still used as a research center. The building, with its colonnaded portico and domed reading room, forms part of the Köprülü Cami'i, constructed between 1659 and 1660 by Mehmet Paşa and his son Fazil Ahmet Paşa, two members of the distinguished Köprülü family who both served as Grand Vizier. Along the same side of the avenue there are two other buildings of the Köprülü complex, the open *türbe* of Mehmet Paşa and the mosque of the foundation, the latter, a few steps beyond the tomb, jutting onto the sidewalk of the avenue. This building once served as the lecture hall of the *medrese*.

THE ÇEMBERLITAŞ HAMMAM. The Turkish bath on the opposite side of Divan Yolu is one of the finest examples of the classical period. Founded in 1583 by Valide Sultan Nur Banu, the widow of Selim II and the mother of Murat III, it was originally used by both women and men, but only the men's section survived after the avenue

THE COLUMN OF CONSTANTINE

Also known as Çemberlitaş, the "hooped" Column of Constantine stands in Divan Yolu next to the baths of the same name. It has stood there since May 11, 330, the day the Emperor renamed the city Constantinople and simultaneously inaugurated this monument. It is also called the "Burnt Column" for the damage wrought during a fire of 1779. When new, the column had a square, five-step pedestal and a porphyry plinth, above which rose the seven cylinders of the shaft. Shaken by an earthquake in 416, the column was reinforced with iron hoops, now replaced by steel rings. At first it was crowned by a Corinthian capital supporting a colossal statue of Constantine, and then, after c. 1150, an immense cross resting upon a marble block and brick courses. The cross disappeared after the Conquest. Following the fire, Sultan Abdül Hamit I had encased the base in masonry up to the top of the first porphyry cylinder.

▲ THE GRAND BAZAAR

Birds-eye view of the
Grand Bazaar.

The Grand Bazaar consists of a vast network of covered streets and buildings. At its center rises the Old Bedestan – the secure place for valuable goods – with its little domes.

THE CISTERN OF YEREBATAN
19th-century engraving by Thomas Allom.

was widened in modern times. The plan, like the rest, is paradigmatic, consisting as it does of a large domed *camekan*, or reception room, which leads into a small triple-domed *soğukluk* (chamber of moderate temperature), which in turn leads to a square *hararet* (steam room).

NURUOSMANIYE CAMI'I

From the Column of Constantine, Vezir Hanı Caddesi leads to the Nuruosmaniye Cami'i, the Mosque of the Sacred Light (*Nur*) of Osman. The *külliye*, or complex, which includes a *medrese*, library, *türbe*, and *sebil*, was commissioned in 1748 by Mahmut I and completed in 1755 under his successor, Osman III. Like most mosques influenced by the European Baroque, this one is essentially a cubic prayer hall with an arch in each of the four sides, which all support a large domed vault. The arches are round-headed, rather than ogival or pointed as in classical Ottoman architecture, and are dramatically accentuated, particularly on the exterior.

MAHMUT PAŞA CAMI'I

Early in the 20th century, when the photograph below was produced, the Grand Bazaar had just been restored after an earthquake. Looming high above the scene is Nuruosmaniye Cami'i, its style clearly influenced by the European Baroque which held sway over Turkish art during the second half of the 18th century.

The Mosque of Mahmut Paşa is situated a short distance along the same street. It was constructed in 1462 and is the oldest vizierial mosque in Istanbul. Mahmut Paşa, who commissioned it, was born into the Byzantine nobility, but before the Conquest he converted to Islam and rose in Ottoman service to become Grand Vizier under Fatih Mehmet. However, he fell from grace and was dismissed from his post and in 1474 was decapitated. The prayer hall of the mosque is a long rectangle divided at the center by an arch, which creates two square chambers each vaulted by a dome of the same size. A barrel-vaulted passage, on either side of the prayer hall, provides access to a suite of three small rooms as well as to the body of the mosque. The entrance to the building is through a porch and a narthex, or vestibule, both with five bays that run the width of the building. **THE MAUSOLEUM OF MAHMUT PAŞA.** Mahmut Paşa lies at rest in his *türbe* situated in the mosque garden. A tall octagonal structure, it is illuminated by two tiers of windows but capped by a blind dome. The upper façades are decorated with mosaics of blue and turquoise faience tiles set in wheel patterns.

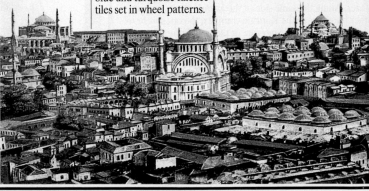

« WE HAVE DRUNK THE LORD'S SHERBET, GLORY TO THE LORD
WE HAVE CROSSED THE SEA OF MIGHT, GLORY TO THE LORD.»

YUNUS EMRE

**A MOSQUE DOOR,
IN A PAINTING
BY ŞEVRET DAĞ**
A pupil of Osman
Hamdi, who had
studied in the Paris
atelier of Gustave
Boulanger, Şevret
Dağ (1876–1944) is
best known for his
pictures of the
interiors of mosques.
Arguably the most
famous of these
works is the one seen
here, painted in 1911.
It shows one of the
heavy leather door-
curtains that, when
rolled down for a
religious service,
insulate the interior
from outside noise
and also prevent
unwelcome intrusions
which may disturb the
prayers within. These
curtains also
symbolize the
invisible frontier
separating the outer,
profane world from
the sacred, exclusive
world accessible only
to the faithful. In
appearance,
moreover, they
resemble the
sumptuous tapestries
of gold-embroidered
velvet that may be
hung from the portico
of the mimbar.

THE COMPLEXES OF THE YENI ÇERILER CADDESI

THE ATIK ALI PAŞA CAMI'I. The Mosque of Atik Ali Paşa
occupies a corner of the Yeni Çeriler Caddesi slightly beyond
the Column of Constantine. Built in 1496 for Hadim Atik Ali
Paşa, eunuch and then Grand Vizier to Beyazıt II, the mosque
presents a vast basilican hall oddly divided into two unequal
parts. The larger western section is dome-vaulted and flanked
on either side by a pair of small rooms capped by cupolas.
The smaller eastern section, with its semi-dome, becomes an
apsidal space terminating in the mihrab. As in most of the
early Ottoman mosques, the corner pendentives supporting
the semidome and the four little cupolas are embellished with
stone-carved stalactites ● 78.

THE KÜLLIYE OF KOCA SINAN PAŞA. A short distance beyond
the Atik Ali Paşa Mosque are the marble wall and iron grilles
enclosing the complex of Koca Sinan Paşa, Grand Vizier
under both Murat III and Mehmet III. This beautiful
Ottoman *külliye*, with its *medrese*, *sebil*, and *türbe*, was
completed in 1593 by Davut Ağa, who succeeded the great
Sinan as Chief Architect of the Empire. The most interesting
building is the polygonal mausoleum, its sixteen sides built of
white- and rose-colored stones surmounted by an exuberant

A street of shops
in the Spice Bazaar.

AN EMBROIDERED OTTOMAN CAFTAN
The museum in Topkapı Palace owns a fine collection of Ottoman fabrics and clothing. The most splendid examples date from the 15th to 17th centuries. During this period, the city of Bursa was the main center of production for brocade, taffeta, silk, and velvets. Silk interwoven with gold and silver thread, and velvets embroidered with similar precious materials were reserved for the making of caftans.

stalactite cornice and pierced by windows with elegant moldings. From an entrance through a gate in the side alley, the *medrese* opens onto an enchanting courtyard with a portico in the form of an ogival arcade. The equally handsome *sebil*, or public fountain, boasts bronze grilles which alternate with small columns and has a deeply overhung roof.

THE KÜLLIYE OF ÇORLULU ALI PAŞA. Across the alleyway from the Koca Sinan Paşa fountain is the Çorlulu Ali Paşa complex, which is also surrounded by a marble wall. Built in 1708 the little mosque and the *medrese* are largely classical in style, though the capitals of the porch colonnade already show the influence of the European Baroque. In 1711, Ali Paşa, the son-in-law of Mustafa II, was beheaded at Mytilene on the orders of Ahmet III, for whom he had been Grand Vizier.

THE KÜLLIYE OF KARA MUSTAFA PAŞA. Opposite Yeni Çeriler Caddesi is the complex of Kara Mustafa Paşa of Merzifon. Its construction had barely begun in 1663 when it came to a halt because of the execution of its patron the Grand Vizier to Mehmet IV, following his failure to take Vienna despite the long Turkish siege ● *36*. The son of the executed vizier oversaw the completion of the complex in 1690, after which he buried Kara Mustafa Paşa's remains in the mosque's cemetery. Stylistically its architecture is transitional, from the classical to the Baroque, and the complex is mainly of interest because of its octagonal mosque, a shape rarely used for such a building. Today the *medrese* houses a research institute dedicated to the poet Yahya Kemal (1884–1958).

«THE GREAT BAZAAR HAS NOTHING ON THE EXTERIOR TO
ATTRACT THE EYE, OR GIVE AN IDEA OF ITS CONTENTS. IT IS AN
IMMENSE STONE EDIFICE OF BYZANTINE ARCHITECTURE,
SURROUNDED BY GRAY WALLS.» EDMONDO DE AMICIS

THE GRAND BAZAAR

On returning to Yeni Çeriler Caddesi, cross the avenue and continue straight ahead on Çarşıkapı Sokağı, the Street of the Market Gate. This takes its name from the Kapalı Çarşı or Covered Bazaar – more commonly known in English as the Grand Bazaar – one of the most famous markets in the world, the entrance to which is at the end of Çarşıkapı Sokağı.

HISTORY. The Grand Bazaar was built at the command of Fatih Mehmet shortly after the Conquest. At first, it consisted merely of two *bedesten* (warehouses); merchants began setting up stores and workshops around it, thereby creating a whole warren of lanes sheltered under canvas. Dignitaries built *hans,* or caravanserais, at its edges and through them riches from all over the empire were imported. After the installation of gates and doors the bazaar became a medieval city within a city, securely locked up each night. In the course of time, the makeshift arrangements were replaced by the ogive-vaulted arcades that we know today. Gradually, the network of galleries expanded until it incorporated the two *bedesten* at the center of an immense labyrinth. From the 16th century until the 19th, the Grand Bazaar was restored and rebuilt on several occasions following earthquakes and numerous fires that ravaged that area of the city.

THE STRUCTURE OF THE GRAND BAZAAR. A census made in 1880 reveals the Kapalı Çarşı to have contained 4,399 shops, 2,195 workshops, 497 stalls, 20 *hans*, 12 storehouses, 18 fountains, a primary school, a tomb, and a *mescit*, or small mosque. Among the 1,742 businesses counted in 1976, there were 472 jewelers, 181 shoemakers, 154 tailors or dressmakers, 131 tourist shops, 129 dealers in furniture and decorations, 116 rug merchants, and 56 restaurants, cafés, and tearooms, of which HAVUZLU LOKANTA was the most famous of them all. Also present are public toilets, two banks, and a tourist information office. On first entering, the great market resembles a bewildering maze, but closer acquaintance

THE WOMEN OF THE GRAND BAZAAR, IN A WATERCOLOR BY A. PREZIOSI (1816–82)
In the 19th century the Grand Bazaar was still one of the very few places where women appeared in public; certainly it was a place they frequented often and with enthusiasm. Invariably they would be accompanied by a servant or a eunuch, and they would always be fully veiled, with only their eyes exposed to view, and their hair hidden under heavy gauze. Théophile Gautier wrote that "their apple-green or sky-blue feredges, their dense and carefully closed yashmaks, their little boots of soft yellow morocco shod in street clogs of the same color have Muslem written all over them in whatever language. . . . The merchant, resting on an elbow, responds with a phlegmatic air to a thousand questions from the young women who rummage through the merchandise and leave his display tumbled in complete disorder."

193

BOOTBLACKS' BOXES
These boxes, made of wood covered with sheets of engraved brass and often embellished with photographs, hold shoe polishes of every color. In Istanbul, bootblacks show up almost everywhere, especially in or around hotels and the Grand Bazaar.

Evliya Çelebi dates the beginning of the gem market to the period of Mehmet the Conqueror. "The Old Bedesten," he wrote, in the mid-17th century,

"held the entire wealth of the Ottomans, and the assets of the high and mighty of the Empire were hoarded there. In its basement were hundreds of storerooms with iron gates." The Old Bedesten had been constructed to house goldsmiths and jewelers. The goldsmiths worked in silver as well as gold, while the jewelers cut and sold emeralds, brilliants, diamonds, rubies, and other precious stones.

reveals it to be a fairly orderly, gridlike arrangement of streets and squares. Traditionally, shopkeepers clustered together according to the kind of goods or services they offered, and the names of the Bazaar's arcades – such as the Street of the Turban-Makers and the Street of the Sword-Cutlers – bear this out, even when the colorful trades they evoke have vanished. Today jewelers, silversmiths, shoemakers, and ironmongers, among others, still occupy the arcades named for them.

THE OLD AND THE NEW BEDESTEN

The Iç Bedesten, which is also known as the Jewelers' Bedesten, or Cevahir Bedesteni, constitutes the very heart of the Grand Bazaar. It is made up of 15 dome-vaulted halls arranged in rows of 3 units each, supported by 8 fat pillars called "elephants' feet." Intended for the sale of the most valuable merchandise, its shops and warehouses were from the beginning fitted with heavy iron gates that could be locked at night, when 70 soldiers stood watch. During the period witnessed by Evliya Çelebi (mid-17th century), the Old Bedesten housed merchants of luxurious fabrics such as silks and velvets, turban-makers, armorers, booksellers, jewelers specializing in precious stones, money changers, and rug merchants. Today the Old Bedesten is dominated by antiquarians dealing in old coins and brass or copper trays and utensils, weaponry and other valuable items from the Ottoman era. Of course, rug dealers also proliferate, as do tourist shops offering a range of objects handcrafted from copper or pewter. The four gates to the Old Bedesten (one on each side) bear the names of the businesses operating there and in neighboring galleries. Over the Gate of the Goldsmiths appears a bas-relief representing the imperial eagle of the Comnenus dynasty that ruled Byzantium in the 11th and 12th centuries. (The Palaeologus dynasty, who held power during the last two centuries of the Byzantine Empire took the two-headed eagle as their emblem ● *32*). Since the Old Bedesten was very likely commissioned by Fatih himself, the Byzantine sculpture must have been salvaged from some other monument and set into the Ottoman structure, a common occurrence in Istanbul.
THE NEW BEDESTEN. Called Sandal Bedesteni in Turkish, after a fabric with a particular motif woven in Bursa, the New Bedesten is situated in the southeast corner of the

«I AM A WELL-STOCKED PEDLAR, I SELL
TO ALL THOSE WHO'LL BUY FROM MY MART.»

YUNUS EMRE

Grand Bazaar. Fatih Mehmet had it constructed towards the end of his reign, as the rapid expansion of Ottoman commerce outstripped the capacity of the Old Bedesten. The immense roof of this building comprises 20 brick domes resting on 12 massive pillars arranged in 3 rows of 4 each. In Ottoman times, the New Bedesten was the center of the silk business, and it eventually accepted commerce in other fabrics, in mirrors, and, as in the Old Bedesten, in arms embellished with precious stones. The principal activity of this Bedesten suffered from the profound changes that occurred in textile manufacture after the Industrial Revolution, which caused one stall and shop after another to close. In 1913, the municipality created in their place a variety of public services, as well as an auction hall, which is particularly lively on Monday and Thursday afternoons, the times reserved for the sale of carpets.

The stores in the Grand Bazaar are owned and operated by individuals, but the New or Sandal Bedesten belongs to the municipality of Istanbul which restored the structure, taking great care to keep its traditional seats and cupboards. Auctions are held twice a week.

SHOPPING IN THE GRAND BAZAAR

CARPETS AND KILIMS. Those eager to take home a Turkish carpet ● *60* will be able to choose from a huge variety in the many carpet shops of the Grand Bazaar, particularly in Sahaflar Caddesi, the first arcade north of the Old Bedesten. Buying a carpet involves a certain amount of ritual, and given the length of the negotiations it is considered poor taste to begin them if the interest in buying is only half-hearted. Indeed, the ritual of taking tea signifies that one is dealing in good faith.

JEWELRY. Jewelers own the greatest number of shops in the Grand Bazaar. In addition to gold jewelry set with precious stones, they also sell handcrafted pieces in silver based on traditional designs.

COPPER AND LEATHER. In Turkey, leather work has always been an important craft, and today it is an industry. The Grand Bazaar offers leather garments in the latest fashion as well as pelisses of the Mongol type made of pigskin.

PIPES AND NARGHILES. Pipe-smoking is rare in Turkey, even though the country is

ÇAY ! ÇAY !...
Every week the merchants of the Grand Bazaar purchase tokens at a stall that only sells tea. Around ten merchants are linked to this shop by telephone; they place their orders and the shop delivers tea to their stalls, where they in turn serve it to their clients.

Seals of the Ottoman
Sultans

In the mid-19th century, Théophile Gautier wrote of the Grand Bazaar: "There are jewelers whose gemstones are put away in safes or in glass cases placed beyond the reach of thieves. In these dark boutiques, rather like cobbler's workshops, riches of the most incredible sort abound." Today the treasures of the Ottoman Empire are in the Topkapı Museum, and the Grand Bazaar no longer yields up superb 16th-century Korans transcribed by calligraphers, bound in guilloched leather, decoratively engraved, and bound.

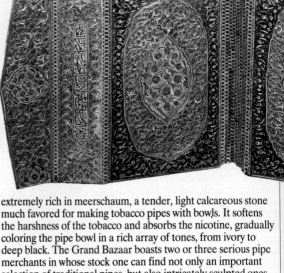

THE GRAND BAZAAR TODAY
Since the devastating fire of 1954, the Bazaar has been modernized, the lighting of its walls, arcades, and cupolas improved and glass showcases added. Some of the names still indicate the kind of merchandise offered there: The Street of the Jewelers, of Carpets, of Leather, even of Jeans! They all remain busy throughout the day.

extremely rich in meerschaum, a tender, light calcareous stone much favored for making tobacco pipes with bowls. It softens the harshness of the tobacco and absorbs the nicotine, gradually coloring the pipe bowl in a rich array of tones, from ivory to deep black. The Grand Bazaar boasts two or three serious pipe merchants in whose stock one can find not only an important selection of traditional pipes, but also intricately sculpted ones, representing everything from the head of a bearded, beturbanned Turk to an eagle's claw and a sleigh drawn by reindeer. In the Egyptian Bazaar, the prices are lower, but so is the quality of both the work and the meerschaum. For centuries the Turks have made an art of smoking, especially in their use of the narghile. However, the time has long passed when young harem women indulged themselves with precious objects of engraved crystal covered with rose petals. Today, the cigarette has become a tough competitor to the elaborate narghile, an impressive instrument that can be as high as 4 feet, not to mention the 6-feet-long copper tube through which the smoke is drawn after being cooled in the water. Nevertheless, there are still two or three public places in Istanbul where one can smoke the water pipe using flavorsome *tömkı*, a tobacco grown on the shores of the Black Sea. Dry and rough-cut, the substance releases its powerful aroma once it has been humidified, rolled into a compact ball, placed in a small terra-cotta bowl, and then burned under a hot coal. The Nargileci on Çorlulu Pasajı is an excellent place to experiment with the narghile. Almost invisible from the street, this café occupies the courtyard of a former *medrese*. After taking a seat at one of the wrought-iron table, you can smoke, talk, and play *tavla* while drinking Rize tea from little balloon-shaped glasses, or *elma çay* ("apple tea") made from a chemical powder, which the people of Istanbul are especially partial to.

The Caravanserais

The Grand Bazaar was once surrounded on all four sides, even in adjacent neighborhoods, by some thirty *hans*, or warehouses, in which merchants and craftsmen stored their goods. Following the earthquake of 1894, which destroyed much of the area, many of the warehouses were moved farther away, with the result that only thirteen remain next to the Grand Bazaar. A number of these continue to serve their original purpose, while the rest house a wide range of workshops and stores. Among the latter, the finest may be the ZINCIRLI HAN, situated near the northeast corner of the Grand Bazaar, which houses carpet merchants and antique dealers. Many of the *hans* outside the Grand Bazaar line the streets leading from the Bazaar to the Golden Horn. Two of them worth special notice are the Valide Han, built in 1651 by the dowager Sultana Kösem, and the Büyük Yeni Han, commissioned by Mustafa III in 1764.

THE HANS
A number of traditional *hans*, or warehouses, cluster all about the Grand Bazaar. It is in their shops that many of the goods sold in the Grand Bazaar are made. Thus, at the Kalcılar Han which specializes in silver, the craftsmen are busily at work upstairs. The Büyük Yeni Han is entered on the third floor, and there, near the entrance, one can buy the little bird houses that the people of Istanbul like to place on their balconies.

Around the Grand Bazaar

A gate in the northeast corner of the market opens onto the Mahmut Paşa Yokuşu.

THE HAMMAM OF MAHMUT PAŞA. About a hundred yards down the street is an imposing hammam within the Mahmut Paşa complex. Completed in 1476, two years after the death of Mahmut Paşa, this bathhouse is the oldest in Istanbul after that of Gedik Ahmet Paşa. Like most of the large Ottoman public baths, this one originally served both women and men. However, the women's section was demolished to make way for the *han* next door.

THE ÇUHACILAR HANI QUARTER. Turning back on Mahmut Paşa Yokuşu and then left along Çuhacılar Hanı Sokağı, you will encounter the gateway to the *han* from which the street takes its name, at the edge of a quarter whose labyrinthine lanes date from the 18th century. As Çuhacılar Hanı Sokağı becomes Çarşıkapı Nuruosmaniye Caddesi, the street runs along the east flank of the Grand Bazaar. On the left we come to Nuruosmaniye Cami'i, entering it through the courtyard just opposite the main gateway to the Grand Bazaar. At

THE BOOK MARKET

From the Nuruosmaniye gate, Kalpakçılar Caddesi runs across the Grand Bazaar to the Bayazıt gate, where, turning to the right and crossing Çardırçılar

Caddesi, is the entrance to the Sahaflar Çarşısı, the ancient and still busy book market of Istanbul. Once built of wood, the shops and stalls that line the charming old square were reconstructed in the 1960's. On display are a vast number of secondhand books in every language, rare Korans, works of history, and cheap, recently published paperbacks. Refreshment is available at the tree-shaded Çay Bahçesi, a tea and coffee house popular with students from the university nearby.

the next corner we turn right onto Kalpakçılar Başı Caddesi, the main artery through the Bazaar that continues along the south side of the market to the upper end, concluding at the gateway in the southwest corner. Turning right at the exit, go along Çadırçılar Caddesi a little way and then make a left turn through Hakkaklar Kapısı, an ancient stone gateway known in English as the "Gate of the Engravers".

THE SAHAFLAR ÇARŞISI

A flight of steps leads us to an ancient vine-shaded courtyard. This is the Sahaflar Çarşısı, a picturesque and noisy market in whose shops bibliophiles can find not only secondhand books but also new editions. One of the oldest markets in Istanbul, the Sahaflar Çarşısı occupies the site of the Chartoprateia, which was the book and paper market of Byzantium. Following the Conquest, turban-makers and metal-engravers set up shop there, the latter trade accounting for the name of the stone portal leading to the market: Hakkaklar Kapısı. Not until the 18th century did booksellers begin to abandon the Covered or Grand Bazaar (where a street is still named after them) and make their headquarters in the courtyard. Shortly thereafter, the legislation controlling printing and publishing allowed the trade to expand its activity enormously, and thus take over the entire market, henceforth known as the Sahaflar Çarşısı. Throughout the 19th century and into the 20th it would dominate the sale and distribution of books in the Ottoman Empire. During the last fifty years, however, the Sahaflar Çarşısı has suffered from the spread of

modern bookshops and libraries elsewhere in the city.
However, it still takes pride of place as the world's oldest
market for publications on Turkey. A bust of Ibrahim
Mütererrika, the first printer of books in the Turkish language
(1732), has recently been installed in the garden at the center
of the square.

BEYAZIT MEYDANI

Passing through Sahaflar Çarşısı brings
you into the outer courtyard of the *külliye*
of the Beyazıt Mosque. This complex
virtually dominates the vast and
somewhat irregular square that sprawls
over the Third Hill. A delightful open-air
café provides a good place to have lunch.
Originally, this was a coffeehouse
frequented by the Janissaries – that
formidable élite corps of the Imperial
Army – who had their main barracks in
this district. The old coffeehouse survived
until the 1960's, shaded by an enormous
çınar or plane tree – the "tree of
idleness" as the poet said – under which
intellectuals loved to while away their
time. Since the construction of the
Beyazıt *külliye* in the early 16th century
the complex has been the favorite
outdoor market among the people of
Istanbul. Recently the throngs of noisy
local pedlars and hawkers have been
joined by similar groups of tradesmen
from Eastern Europe.

THE MOSQUE OF THE BEYAZIT COMPLEX. This *külliye* has
scarcely changed since Evliya Çelebi, writing in
the mid-17th century, described it in his
Book of Travels: "The inner and outer
courts of the Beyazıt Cami'i are ringed
about by stalls offering every kind of
goods or service. There is also a public
kitchen, a refectory, and a hostel for
travelers, as well as a school for
instruction in the Koran. The courtyard,
which can be entered through six different
gateways, is planted with majestic trees in
whose shade thousands of people earn their livelihood by
selling merchandise of the greatest variety."

THE HAMMAM OF GEDIK PAŞA. On the other side of Yeni
Çeriler Caddesi, in the Gedik Paşa Caddesi, stands the oldest
hammam in Istanbul, dating from 1475. The man whose
name it bears, Gedik Ahmet Paşa, was Chief Vizier under
Süleyman the Magnificent. He was also commander of the
fleet that captured Azov, the Greek island of Lefkada, and
the Italian port of Otranto. The *soğukluk* of this hammam –
which is a monumental dome-vaulted space flanked by
alcoves and cubicles – is considerably larger than most.
A feature worth special attention is the alcove on the right,
which has an elaborate vault with numerous carved-stone
stalactites.

**THE GRAND BAZAAR IN
THE 19TH CENTURY**
In Julia Pardoe's
*Beauties of the
Bosphorus*, published
in the 19th century,
the Bazaar was
illustrated with the
above engraving by
W.H. Bartlett.

**THE ARCADED
STREETS OF THE
BAZAAR**
Along every lane of
the Grand Bazaar,
tourists are assailed
from all sides in an
array of languages
babbled by zealous
vendors touting every
conceivable sort of
merchandise. Scores
of shops display
jumbled masses of
junk jewelry next to
fine gems, piles of
rugs, sumptuous
fabrics, and gleaming
copper objects.

THE BEYAZIDIYE

The Beyazıdiye Cami'i was built in 1501–6 by the architect Yakub-şah bin Sultan; his only other known work is the caravanserai at Bursa. The Beyazıdiye marks the beginning of the classical period of Ottoman architecture, which would continue for more than two centuries. Two minarets decorated with geometric motifs are off-center on the outer corners, reinforcing the originality and architectural power of this mosque. In front of the mosque is an attractive courtyard, with magnificent entrances on three sides. A peristyle of twenty ancient columns – porphyry, verd antique, and Syenitic granite – forms an arcade picked out by alternating red-and-white or black-and-white voussoirs and a portico covered by twenty-four small domes. At the center stands a beautifully ornamented ablution fountain. Stalactite moldings bring drama to the capitals, cornices, and niches. The harmonious proportions, the wealth of restrained decoration, and the brilliance of the variegated marbles combine to give the

The Beyazıdiye was founded by Sultan Beyazıt II, Mehmet the Conqueror's son and successor, and the mosque complex was the second of its kind to be built in Istanbul. The first *külliye*, constructed by Sultan Mehmet II shortly after the capture of Byzantine Constantinople, was destroyed by an earthquake in 1766, and the mosque that took its place dates from 1771. The Beyazıt Cami'i is therefore Istanbul's oldest imperial mosque still in existence.

«HE WHOSE FEET HAVE BEEN COVERED WITH DUST
FROM THE PATHS OF THE LORD WILL BE SAVED BY HIM
FROM THE FIRES OF HELL.»

BEYAZIT II

courtyard a charm unlike anything else in Istanbul.

THE INTERIOR.
There is a grandiose entrance to the prayer hall. The basic plan of its interior is a smaller, simplified version of the one already seen at Haghia Sophia ● *74*. As in the basilica, the central dome of the Beyazıdiye (55 feet in diameter) and its two flanking semi-domes on the east and west define the space of the nave, the latter supplemented by side aisles on the south and north. Free of upper galleries, the aisles open directly onto the central space, the division between them marked only by the four corner pillars supporting the great cupola. The sultan's loge, raiscd upon columns of rare, precious marbles, is atypically placed on the right of the mimbar rather than on the left. Along the west side of the interior runs a broad corridor divided into bays that, even while domeless, project from the mass of the building to form a kind of narthex. At the southern end of the corridor there is a small library, which was an 18th-century addition by Seyh-ül Islam Veliyüttin Efendi.

THE BEYAZIDIYE COMPLEX

In addition to the mosque, the *külliye* includes a *medrese*, an *imaret*, a hammam, an elementary school, and several mausoleums ● *80*.

THE MAUSOLEUM OF BEYAZIT II. The cemetery lies behind the mosque, and here the remains of Beyazıt II rest in a simple, well-proportioned *türbe* constructed of limestone accented in verd antique. The nearby tomb of Selçuk Hatun, the Sultan's daughter, is even simpler, particularly by comparison with the French Empire structure erected not far away for Koca Mustafa Reşit Paşa, the Grand Vizier to Abdül Mecit and Tanzimat reform leader who died in 1858 ● *41*. Sinan's long-demolished shopping arcade, installed below the cemetery, has now been reconstructed precisely in keeping with the original plan.

Embedded in the base of the wall bordering Ordu Caddesi are ancient bas-reliefs from the late Roman period, one of which is upside down and carved with a series of centurions. These remains are all that survive from a Roman column that once stood in the Forum

Theodosius, which extended to the top of the Third Hill. Traces of it can be found more or less everywhere along Ordu Caddesi on the far west side of Beyazıt Meydanı.

THE MEKTEP. Behind the bazaar is the double *sibyan mektebi*, or primary school, a building with two domes and a porch that is the oldest Koran school in Istanbul.

THE IMARET. The Beyazıdiye *imaret*, a public kitchen that also included a caravanserai, still stands in the outer courtyard facing the northern minaret. Restored in 1852, at the command of Abdül Hamit II, the Beyazıt *imaret* now houses a research library for journalists.

BEYAZIT SQUARE. The main entrance to the University of Istanbul can be found on the northern edge of Beyazıt or Hürriyet Meydanı, where the institution has been situated since the early years of the Turkish Republic. Dominating the university courtyard is a 100-feet-high tower, erected by Mahmut II as a lookout tower for fires. It remained in service until the 1960's. Some thirty years ago one could still climb to the summit and enjoy the breathtaking panoramic view of Istanbul. Today the tower is closed to the public.

THE CALLIGRAPHY MUSEUM ▲ 206. The Beyazıdiye *medrese* occupies the western edge of the square. Here, as in all classical *medrese*, the students' cubby-holes completely line the four sides of the courtyard, while the *dershane*, or lecture hall, stands directly opposite the main entrance. Now restored, the building shelters the municipal library and the Calligraphy Museum. In one of the cells a calligraphy workshop has been reconstructed, complete with wax figures representing a master teaching his pupils this profoundly Islamic art.

THE THIRD HILL

The Beyazıdiye hammam lies a little farther along the main avenue, here called Ordu Caddesi. Directly opposite the hammam are two Ottoman *hans*. The one on the left, built during the reign of Fatih Mehmet, is the newly rebuilt Şimkeş Hanı – Han of the Silver-Thread Spinners – while that on the right, dating from c. 1740, was commissioned by Seyyit Hasan Paşa, Grand Vizier to Mahmut I. A further 350 yards or so along Ordu Caddesi is the *külliye* of Ragip Paşa, Grand Vizier under

Mustafa III (1757–74). Erected in 1762, this small complex is probably the work of the architect Mehmet Tahir Ağa. Its main building is a lending library. There is a *mektep* over the gates. Two blocks farther along Ordu Caddesi you come to the Lâleli Cami'i – the Tulip Mosque – which is arguably the most beautiful Baroque mosque in Istanbul.

THE TULIP MOSQUE

The Lâleli Cami'i – popularly known as the Tulip or Lily Mosque – was built between 1759 and 1763 at the command of Mustafa III. The architect, Mehmet Tahi Ağa, built it on a high terrace overlooking a maze of small shops and serpentine lanes. In the middle of the complex there is a large hall with a fountain at the center and four enormous piers. The plan of the mosque itself is an octagon inscribed within a rectangle. The walls are load-bearing, except on the west side, where columns support a gallery. On this side as well, the wall is decorated with *opus sectile* medallions made of rare marbles and such semi-precious stones as onyx, jasper, and lapis lazuli.

CALLIGRAPHY
Handwriting is considered to be one of the major art forms of Ottoman and Islamic cultures, intimately linked as it is with the copying of the Koran. Moreover, Arabic script lends itself quite naturally to a number of stylistic variations. ▲ *206*.

Itinerant pedlars proliferate along the main streets and squares of Istanbul, among them watermelon vendors like the one here.

Galata port at the end of the 19th century.

▲ THE BEYAZIDIYE AND THE SÜLEYMANIYE

A lid from a box of Turkish delight.

AHMET III, THE TULIP KING
By the time Ahmet III ascended the throne in 1703, the empire was already in decline. Tired of war, the new Sultan very quickly became known as an aesthete dedicated to a pursuit of the finer pleasures. Ahmet III sponsored many fêtes, and patronized art, music, poetry, and literature. During his reign, five libraries were founded, as well as Turkey's first printing house, established in 1724. The Sultan's infatuation with tulips went to such extremes that the second half of his reign, beginning in 1717, has come to be known as Lâle Devri, meaning the "Tulip Period." The craze for this flower, which was traded like gold, had started a century earlier in the Netherlands, where the first tulips had been imported from Anatolia in 1559. The Janissaries forced Ahmet III to abdicate in 1730, because they were fed up with his Western tastes and his weakness in military matters. His son, Sultan Mustafa III, who ascended the throne in 1757, commissioned the Tulip Mosque.

Elsewhere, extravagantly colored, variegated marbles clad every wall with vibrant effect. The *külliye* includes a *medrese*, an *imaret*, a *han*, and a hammam, as well as a *türbe* in which Mustafa II and his son Selim III (1789–1807) are buried.

THE MOSQUE OF THE PRINCE

Fethiye Bey Caddesi opens into Fevziye Caddesi, which in turn leads to Şehzade Başı Caddesi, where, on the right is the monument that gives the avenue its name: the Şehzade Cami'i, or the Mosque of the Prince. This great complex was commissioned by Süleyman the Magnificent in memory of his eldest son, Prince Mehmet, who died of smallpox in 1543 at the age of twenty-one. The commission went to Sinan ▲ *314*, who completed it in 1548. It was the first of his large-scale, imperial *külliye*.

The mosque is entered through an elegant *avlu* with a portico running entirely around the four sides and, naturally, a *şadırvan* at the center. The forecourt ranks among Sinan's greatest triumphs, and incorporates a brilliant innovation by the architect: colonnaded galleries the full length of the north and south façades in order to conceal the buttressing.

THE INTERIOR. All but unique among imperial mosques, the Şehzade Cami'i has a vast and empty prayer hall, with neither columns nor galleries. Sinan was determined to centralize the plan, and so took the bold step of extending the enclosed space not with two half-domes, as at Haghia Sophia, but instead with four. However, the resulting symmetry along both axes produces a somewhat bland, uninspiring effect. Moreover, the four pillars supporting the dome look a bit stranded in the middle of such an enormous empty space, and their inevitable monumentality appears rather out of place. However, the austere simplicity of the interior is in its own way impressive.

THE TÜRBE GARDEN. In the walled garden behind the mosque there are half a dozen tombs, the largest of which is the sumptuous monument to Prince Mehmet, built by Sinan in 1543 to 1544. The interior is remarkably beautiful, even by Istanbul standards. However, it is not always open to the public, and neither are the other mausoleums in the garden, two of which merit close attention: that of Süleyman's son-in-law, the Grand Vizier Rüstem Paşa, built by Sinan in 1561, and the other in 1603 by Dalgiç Ahmet, for Ibrahim Paşa,

> «THIS TEMPLE HAS BEEN CONSTRUCTED FOR TRUE BELIEVERS BY
> THE GLORIOUS DEPUTY OF ALLAH, THE TENTH OF THE OTTOMAN
> EMPERORS, IN ACCORDANCE WITH THE SACRED LAWS
> OF THE KORAN.» TOMB OF SÜLEYMAN

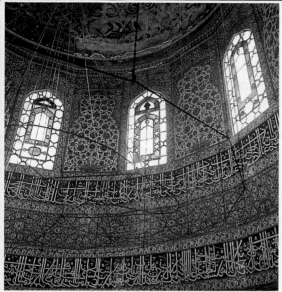

Murat III's son-in-law and Grand Vizier. Both are embellished with superb Iznik tiles. The complex's *medrese* is situated in the northwest corner of the *avlu*. The *imaret* and *mektep* are found in Dede Efendi Sokağı, the street leading off Şehzade Başı Caddesi just beyond the *türbe* garden.

THE MEDRESE OF DAMAT IBRAHIM PAŞA.
Opposite the garden of the Prince's Mosque, at the intersection of Dede Efendi Sokağı and Şehzade Başı Caddesi, is a *medrese* with a charming *sebil* at the corner. The elegant complex was constructed in 1720 at the command of Nevsehirli Damat Ibrahim Paşa, son-in-law of Ahmet III and Grand Vizier (1718–30) during the golden era of Lâle Devri – "the Tulip Period."

THE KALENDERHANE CAMI'I

In the 1970's, the Dumbarton Oaks Society, under the directorship of C. Lee Striker, established that the building now known as the Kalenderhane Mosque was originally the Church of Theotokos Kyriotissa – Our Lady, Mother of God – a structure dating from the 12th century ● 75. Its conversion into an Islamic place of worhip took place shortly after the Conquest ● 34, when it was assigned to an order of dervishes, which gave it the present Turkish name.

THE MARKET OF ADDICTS. A vaulted passage alongside the Kalenderhane Cami'i runs under the Valens Aqueduct. From there turn right and then left into Süleymaniye Caddesi. At the end of this street looms the mighty Süleymaniye Cami'i.

THE ŞEHZADE CAMI'I
The interior of the Mosque of the Prince is decorated with white calligraphy on a blue background.

POETRY AND GEOMETRY
The two minarets rising from the two western corners of the Şehzade Cami'i are justly famous for their bas-reliefs carved with geometric motifs, and for their *şerefe,* or balconies, whose complex fretwork is inlaid here and there with terra-cotta. As a symbol of Islam, the minaret was seen as competing with the bell towers of churches, particularly in a city like Istanbul, where mosques appeared at the same time as a new empire. This explains the concern for their

embellishment. The most beautiful of them reflect the high-art status of geometry in Islam. This aesthetic is a profoundly original one in which the very logic of the forms lends itself to infinite variation according to the principles of geometric symmetry. The crowning cupolas and semi-domes, with their accentuated ribs and openwork cornices, cascade through a series of contrasts and repetitions that is breathtaking in its virtuosity.

The development of oriental calligraphy is closely linked to the celebration of the verses of the Koran and the word (*hadis* in Turkish) of the prophet Mohammed. The calligraphers Ibn Mukle in the 10th century, Ibn Bervah in the 11th century, and Yakut in the 13th century are the main reference sources for sacred writing. In Turkey it is only under Beyazıt II that an innovative master appeared in the person of Sheik Hamdullah (1429–1520). He would later be considered the founder of Ottoman calligraphy. Hamdullah was a great master of the *nesih* style. The writing presented, *sülüs-nesih*, interprets an aphorism of Ali, the son-in-law of the prophet: "It is through uprightness that man gains access to the richness of the great men."

AHMET KARAHISARI
Originally from the Anatolian city of Afyo-Kara-Hisar (The Black Opium Fortress), Ahmet Karahısarı (who died in 1556) was soon nicknamed "Light of Writing" for the perfection of his compositions. The greatness of Karahısarı is due to the epic audacity of his large, alluring horizontal and vertical strokes. In the style exercise presented here, the author has added in the margin: "Each letter is like another ocean, each line like another wave, and each punctuation mark like another pearl."

ANONYMOUS CALLIGRAPHY FROM THE 19TH CENTURY

207

Among the many different styles, which encourage reflection and thought, the anthropomorphic writing developed at the

Bektachis school is perhaps the most interesting. The aim of their skilled calligraphers is to celebrate the divine nature of the human body through their style and the interlacing of letters, in the name of Ali and his martyred sons. Ali, the son-in-law of the prophet, symbolizes the martyr for many Muslim congregations because he was murdered along with his two sons in the city of Karbelâ.

CALLIGRAPHY FROM THE 16TH CENTURY

PORTRAIT OF A PAINTER (c. 1480)
Painters, calligraphers, and illuminators worked in the *Nakkashane* (imperial workshop) created by Mehmet II after the Conquest.

NECMEDDIN OKYAY (1883–1976)
Of the contemporary calligraphers, Okyay and Tugrakes Hakki are among the last exponents of the Istanbul school. Like Hamdullah, his 15th-century predecessor, Okyay excels in writing techniques. He has cultivated 400 varieties of roses which are as dear to him as his writing.

NECMEDDIN OKYAY
BISMILLAHI'R-
RAHMANI'R-RAHÎM

MÜSENNA CALLIGRAPHY OF THE 19TH CENTURY
Hurufism lived on in handwriting. Braving the orthodox ban on the figurative representation of human beings, a distinct calligraphic art was born in the hurufi drawings which combine letters to produce drawings of human faces or sacred animals. A game of mirrors in which images are multiplied, results in a knotting together of Man, God, and the Word.

The calligrapher sits cross-legged and uses his left hand as a support, holding a felt pad on which he places his paper, while in his right hand he uses a reed dipped in a traditional ink well, the *divit*. The writing action involves a double movement of the hands, requiring the calligrapher to control his breathing so as not to upset the line. Success depends upon the perfect co-ordination of all of these factors at the same time. The calligrapher keeps his hands in shape like a musician, with hours of repeated exercises. The accuracy of each piece of work is checked against a drafting system consisting of a lozenge shape traced using the inked reed in order to calculate vertically or horizontally the size of each of the letters.

Sultan Ahmet III (1673–1736) was a renowned calligrapher who became a master in the art of *tugra*. Sultans practiced this art from a very young age, and it was considered to be a written emanation of their power. Learned calligraphers were on good terms with the sultans, and they held a privileged position in the seraglio hierarchy.

The manufacture of black or colored inks, both dense and smooth, involves a fairly complicated process using tallow, grenadine blossoms, vine sap, and various other ingredients, heated and mixed in the correct proportions. The quality of the ink is tested by dipping a hedgehog spine into it. Of the fourteen types of paper used, that from Samarkand is the best. If the calligrapher so desires, he might dye his chosen paper with mixtures prepared from ingredients such as linden, tea, saffron, tobacco, straw, onion skins, and bitter pomegranate skin. The perfect sheen of the ink on the paper is due to egg, as well as different types of polishing materials, such as marble, shells, glass, and ivory.

YAZILI ABRÛ
Calligraphy on marbled paper (*abrû*) by Necmeddin Okyay (1883–1976).

«MUHAMET IS A MAN, BUT AS DIFFERENT FROM HIS PEERS, AS THE RUBY IS DIFFERENT FROM THE STONES.»
CALLIGRAPHY BY MEHMET CELALEDDIN

Calligraphers use a range of shades of color, from light to dark, in their compositions. The masterpieces of calligraphy are more than equal to the magnificent settings they may decorate, whether palaces, mosques, tombs and fountains, or whether they are incorporated into paintings or sculpture. Calligraphy is a distinct art form, with its own masters and fervent admirers. In the past as today the most famous works fetched considerable prices.

ABIDINE Two contemporary calligraphies (1992)

TUĞRA Calligraphy by the Sultan Ahmet III (1673–1736)

Mosques and Türbe

The Ottoman calligraphers used their superb writing to decorate the beautiful blue faïence of the mosques and the *türbe* of the princes or viziers. In the 19th and 20th centuries the calligraphers made signs on wood or calligraphic paintings on slabs of glass which decorated the walls of houses and occasionally the windows of shops and cafés.

BEKTACHI CALLIGRAPHY
This inscription of Bektachi inspiration unites the names of the prophet Mohammed and Ali, his son-in-law. They are superimposed here to form a visual and spiritual unity which constitutes an act of faith.

In the Ottoman Empire a popular type of imagery, often based on the letters of the alphabet, developed parallel to the work of the calligraphic scholar, which was destined for an élite or for the requirements of a monumental art. This imagery allows for all types of caprice and charm. In this way prayers can be transformed into mosques, ewers, lions, or swans, or sometimes into a sacred character. This tradition has not completely disappeared today and one can still find inexpensive examples of the style in the Istanbul markets, in the form of paintings on glass or lithographic reproductions.

Because of the adaptablity of its shape, writing composed in a circular fashion was used to decorate swords, ceramics, and talismans.

AH! LOVE According to a popular tradition, the union of the Arab letters "A" and "H" form the exclamation "Ah!" These two letters express pain or regret and are almost always accompanied by the word "love". In the two cells of the letter "H" nest eyes that cry over their disappointments in love.

The image of the headgear of a brotherhood master is pictured on a ceremonial stool. The turbans and the various ways of covering the head define the hierarchies and functions in Ottoman society, and accompany each person to the grave, which is itself "hatted" according to the rank and function of the deceased.

THE ANCIENT CHURCH OF THEOTOKOS KYRIOTISSA
Excavations carried out in the Kalenderhane Cami'i have brought to light a series of frescoes on the life of St Francis of Assisi, painted in the small chapel to the right of the nave. The full-length portrait of the Saint and the ten related scenes were executed around 1250, during the Latin occupation of Constantinople.

THE CITY AND ITS INHABITANTS
The reign of Süleyman saw the construction of numerous mosques throughout the new quarters. The city was organized so that each quarter had its own mosque and market square. Several quarters together made up a municipality. With the arrival of the Muslims, many churches were converted into mosques. The population of Stamboul grew steadily throughout the 16th century. In 1554, there were 40,000 Christians, 4,000 Jews, and 60,000 Turks, with 10,000 more Turks in the suburbs.

Entering on the south side of the Süleymaniye Cami'i, you proceed through the Tiryaki Çarşısı – the Street of the Addicts. And indeed it appears that in Ottoman times the tea shops of the *medrese*, on the sidewalk to the left, dispensed not only tea, coffee, and tobacco but also opium.

THE MOSQUE OF SÜLEYMAN THE MAGNIFICENT

The complex of the Süleymaniye Cami'i was the fourth imperial *külliye* constructed in Istanbul. Although not as vast as Sultan Mehmet Fatih's complex, it surpasses all three of its precedessors in splendor and majesty. Indeed, the Süleymaniye is without question one of the greatest works of its architect, Sinan. Begun in 1550, the mosque was completed in 1557, with two more years required in order to finish the entire *külliye*. The mosque itself is surrounded by a vast precinct, enclosed by a wall. Arranged around it, in neighboring streets, are the other parts of the complex. Four slender minarets stand like sentinels at the corners of the forecourt. The two taller ones, abutting the mosque, are furnished with three *şerefe* each, while the two shorter ones have only two balconies each. The magnificent dome is flanked on the east and west by two semi-domes and, on the north and south, by arches with tympana pierced by windows. Within the mosque, the central cupola is borne by four gigantic pillars reinforced by thick buttresses, which Sinan cleverly embedded in the north and south walls so that they project equally both inside and out. To mask this projection he constructed an arcaded gallery between the buttresses. The gallery has two tiers on both the outside and inside, with twice as many columns on the upper level. All in all, the design of the building was distinctly innovative and quite magnificent.

THE INTERIOR. The prayer hall, a 230 by 200-feet rectangle, is vaulted by a central dome

«MAY THERE BE ONE GOD IN HEAVEN AND ONE ALL-POWERFUL EMPEROR ON EARTH.»

SÜLEYMAN THE MAGNIFICENT

THE AVLU OF THE SÜLEYMANIYE
The Süleymaniye is approached through the usual colonnaded forecourt, or *avlu*; this particular one is exceptionally grand, with columns of porphyry, marble and granite. At the center is an ablution fountain.

with a diameter of 86 feet and its keystone is 162 feet above the floor. Semi-domes and corner exedrae extend the central space along its main axis, while five domed spaces flanked by galleries extend its width. The only elements separating the nave from the side aisles are the four structural piers under the heroic dome and the two pairs of porphyry columns supporting the tympanum walls pierced by three tiers of arcaded windows. Two other pairs of porphyry monoliths, north and south of those between the pillars, support the intermediate dome-vaulted spaces on either side, with the columns linked together as well as to the engaged buttresses by the gallery arcades. The discreetly decorative tiles from Iznik ▲ 292 are among the finest ever produced, reflecting the new techniques pioneered in the mid-16th century by the Iznik craftsmen. They depict flowers and foliage and are fired in turquoise, sapphire, and red on a pure white ground. The white-marble mimbar and mihrab are sumptuous but simple, as are the doors, shutters, and *kuran kürsü* inlaid with ivory and mother-of-pearl. The inscriptions, which are everywhere in the building,

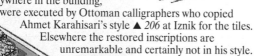

were executed by Ottoman calligraphers who copied Ahmet Karahisari's style ▲ 206 at Iznik for the tiles. Elsewhere the restored inscriptions are unremarkable and certainly not in his style.

THE MAUSOLEUMS OF SÜLEYMAN AND ROXELANA. The great Sultan and his wife lie at rest in their *türbes* located in the garden behind the mosque. The tomb of Süleyman the Magnificent is, not surprisingly, the grandest *türbe* ever created by Sinan. Finished in 1566, the structure is an octagon in shape surrounded by a colonnade, and, like

PLAN OF THE SÜLEYMANIYE COMPLEX
The various parts of the *külliye* are arranged about the terrace and in the streets bordering the enclosure: five *medrese,* one of which served as a preparatory school; a *tip medrese* (medical school); a hospital/asylum; an *imaret* or public kitchen; a caravanserai; a *darü'l-hadis* (Koranic college); a *darü'l-kurra* (school for instruction in the various ways to read the Koran); a hammam; and a shopping street. The *darü'l-kurra* is built into the cemetery wall, with its vast, domed, harmoniously proportioned space erected over a small four-column cistern.

The Golden Horn viewed from the Süleymaniye.

THE MAUSOLEUM OF SINAN

Sinan was the greatest architect in the service of Süleyman and two of his successors, Selim II and Murat III. In the course of his long career, Sinan provided Istanbul with twenty mosques and various other monuments. He worked right up to his

death in 1588, at the age of 90. The tomb in which he rests is close to the magnificent masterpiece that he created for Süleyman the Magnificent, whose reign he so brilliantly glorified.

THE WINDOWS OF THE SÜLEYMANIYE

In the 16th century, windows were assembled from pieces of stained glass joined by gesso mullions and mounted in a frame. They were decorated with the motifs most common in the so-called "minor" arts and crafts, especially ceramics and court carpets. Here the motifs are *saz* leaves, arabesques and "four flowers".

some of Sinan's other mausoleums, this one has a double dome. The interior of the cupola, which is supported by columns, has splendid decorations painted in black, gold, and wine-dark red. The walls are entirely clad in Iznik tiles, twice as many of them in this small chamber as in the whole of the enormous mosque. The imposing cenotaph stands like a throne at the center of the room, together with the Sultan's great white turban. The majestic size of this turban clearly indicates the importance of the person who wore it. Süleyman was sultan from 1520, when he ascended the throne at the age of twenty-five, until his death in 1566. His rule, the longest and most illustrious in Ottoman history, was summarized in the mid-17th century by Evliya Çelebi: "In the forty-six years of his reign, he conquered the world and made eighteen monarchs his tributaries. He established order and justice throughout his lands, marched victoriously through seven sectors of the globe, embellished every country vanquished by his arms, and succeeded in all his undertakings." The *türbe* of Roxelana, to the east of her husband's, may be smaller, but its tiles are even more beautiful. The cylindrical base of the cupola, set back somewhat from the building's octagonal cornice, bears an inscription carved in relief like a frieze. The mausoleum dates from 1558, the year of the Sultana's death.

THE SÜLEYMANIYE COMPLEX

Beyond the cemetery, the terrace ends in a triangular area due to the layout of the streets below. It was known in Süleyman's time as the "Wrestling Ground," after the weekly contests held there. To the left of this area, approached from the cemetery, is the *darü'l-hadis*, an unusually built *medrese*, whose twenty-six compartments are arranged in a single, straight row instead of around a courtyard. They face a simple wall, with grilled openings, that encloses the long strip of a garden. The terrace gives us a view of the street below that borders the northern edge of the complex. This old *arasta* – shopping street or bazaar – is still commercially active, though somewhat dilapidated and the subject of plans for restoration. Right across the street are two of the Süleymaniye's five *medrese*. To find the other buildings of the *külliye*, you must retrace your steps to the eastern end of Tiryaki Çarşısı, where the small building at the corner of the esplanade once served as the *mektep* for the children of the Süleymaniye staff. Now renovated, the little school building houses a children's library. Next to the *mektep* are the *medrese* Evvel and Sani, which today contain the celebrated Süleymaniye library, one of the most impotant in Istanbul. On the other side of the street, to the west, is the *imaret* that was converted to a restaurant in 1991. A few steps beyond the Sani *medrese* brings you to the *tip medrese*, once the site of the empire's foremost medical college. All that remains of this building is a row of compartments along the Tiryaki Çarşısı. Turning right off Tiryaki Çarşısı, we move to the western end of the precinct wall to the complex's *imaret*, which once dispensed food to thousands of beneficiaries, both the poor of the quarter and many others directly dependent upon the Süleymaniye. Today the hospital is home to a fundamentalist girls' boarding school. The interior courtyard, with its ancient plane trees, young palms, and pretty marble fountain, is a pleasant, relaxing haven from the roar of the city.

ROXELANA AND SÜLEYMAN
Roxelana is known to the Turks under the name Haseki Hürrem – "the Joyous Favorite." Westerners call her Roxelana, literally "the Russian," because of her presumed origins. At the beginning of his reign, Süleyman fell madly in love with Roxelana and married her. The Italian Bassano, who was a page at Topkapı Sarayı during the period, left this account of the Sultan's passion: "He displays such love and trust that his astonished subjects all say that she has bewitched him, and call her *Cadi* – that is, the Sorceress."

SÜLEYMAN AND SINAN
Sultan Süleyman the Magnificent and his gifted architect, Sinan, were two of the greatest personalities associated with the apogee of Ottoman art in the 16th century. Between the sovereign and the artist there developed a special and mutually rewarding relationship. The architect depended upon the good will of the Sultan for the financing of his ambitious projects. Reciprocally, Süleyman relied entirely upon the genius of Sinan in order to realize his dreams of eternity – to leave the imprint of his power on the works that would survive him.

SINAN'S MAUSOLEUM

At the western end of the Market of the Addicts Street, facing the northern corner of the wall surrounding the Süleymaniye complex, is a domed *sebil* in a small triangular cemetery. This was once the garden surrounding the house in which Sinan lived during the time he worked on Süleyman's mosque. Within the garden the elderly master built his own *türbe*, an open structure composed of an ogival arcade in six sections, supporting a marble roof with a tiny cupola, above a marble sarcophagus surmounted by a large turban similar to the one worn by the deceased in his role as chief architect. The south wall of the garden is inscribed with a long verse composed by the poet Mustafa Sa'i in praise of the great works created by his friend Sinan. Mustafa Sa'i also wrote about Sinan in his *Tezkere-ül Ebniye*, where he compiled a complete list of the numerous achievements of the famous architect.

Constantinop

THE CARAVANSERAI

The next building along is the former caravanserai, which today is closed to the public. This grandly proportioned building included rooms for guests, stables for horses and dromedaries, and a place where travelers could safely leave their baggage. There was also an *imaret*, complete with its own refectory, pantry, bakery, and an olive press, which provided free food. There was an age-old Ottoman custom that all accredited merchants should be given lodging and food free of charge in any hostel within the empire. Evliya Çelebi has left this record of the traditional hospitality practised at the Süleymaniye: "The caravanserai is a splendid establishment in which all travelers receive twice a day a bowl of rice, a dish of groats and some bread, every night a candle, and fodder for each horse, but the welcome is good for only three days." The coherently and thoughtfully planned complex, with its wide range of institutions and services – mosques, hospitals, inns, schools, and a library – inevitably became the very heart of the quarter's religious and social life. Because of the layout and the beauty of the various buildings in the complex, the Süleymaniye remains, even today, unquestionably one of the supreme examples of Islamic architecture.

THE ARCHITECT SINAN AT SÜLEYMAN'S FUNERAL
Süleyman died during the Hungarian campaign and his body was returned to Istanbul for burial.

▲ THE FETHIYE CAMI'I

FETHIYE CAMI'I

FATIH CAMI'I

🏃 Three hours

THE BURMALI CAMI'I
A hundred yards before the Valens Aqueduct, a little beyond the western wall of the Şehzade Cami'i, stands the Burmalı Minare Cami'i, the Mosque of the Spiral Minaret. Founded in 1550 by Emin Nurettin Osman Efendi, the *kadi* (judge) of Egypt, this Muslim place of worship takes its name from the spiral ribs on the brick-built minaret, a traditional form unique in Istanbul although known in Anatolia. Another peculiarity of this edifice is the domeless porch, whose pitched roof is supported by four columns with capitals in the Byzantine Corinthian style.

THE VALENS AQUEDUCT

The Atatürk Bulvarı, running between the Third and Fourth Hills, is spanned by the immense Valens Aqueduct ● 76, which in Turkish is known as *Bozdogan Kemeri*, the "Arcade of the Gray Falcon." Built in 378 during the reign of Emperor Valens, it was part of the vast system supplying water for the New Rome, Constantinople ▲ 356. It has been damaged by several earthquakes, the last in 1967, but restored after each of them.

THE MAIDEN'S COLUMN. Turning left off Macar Kadeşler Caddesi into Kız Taşı Sokağı, you come to a small square in which stands the Kız Taşı, or Maiden's Column. This Roman commemorative column is constructed with a three-step pedestal made of Corinthian marble and a granite column surmounted by a Corinthian capital and, above that, a plinth with eagles. These probably supported a statue of the Emperor Marcian, as a Latin verse on the plinth states that the monument was erected in honor of Marcian (450–457) ● 31. Its Turkish name arises from the broken Nike, or Winged Victory, on the base.

220

THE COMPLEX OF MEHMET II

Higher up, on the right of the main avenue, you turn into
Aslanhane Sokağı, a name that means "Street of the Lion,"
after the menagerie that Mehmet II
installed here. Turning left, halfway
along Aslanhane Sokağı, you
arrive at a vast esplanade laid
out before the *külliye*
founded by Fatih Mehmet,
with a mosque at the
center, an *avlu* in front and
a cemetery alongside. The
rest of the complex stretches
both north and south. Built
between 1463 and 1470 by the
architect Atik Sinan, the Fatih
Cami'i was in its time the largest and most
sumptuous Ottoman *külliye* ever built. The forecourt, the
main entrance, the mirhab, the minarets up to the level of the
şerefe, the southern wall of the cemetery, and the adjoining
gate are no doubt part of the original complex. All else dates
from the reign of Mustafa II, who rebuilt the mosque and
other elements destroyed by the 1766 earthquake. Among
these, the eight *medrese* and the *tabhane* have recently been
restored. Little remains of the public kitchen, and the

caravanserai no
longer exists.

**THE MOSQUE OF
MEHMET THE
CONQUEROR.** In
1766, an
earthquake
demolished the
Fatih Mehmet
Cami'i. Mustafa II
immediately had it rebuilt, but in a Baroque style quite unlike
the original. The new mosque, completed in 1771, is
constructed on the plan devised by Sinan for the Şehzade
Cami'i, the Sultan Ahmet Cami'i, and the Yeni Cami, which
consisted of a central dome flanked by four half-domes.
While the exterior remains agreeably classical, the interior is
weak and over-elaborate. Indeed, the lower walls are revetted
in white tiles of such mediocre quality that they have turned
dark with damp. Still, the mirhab, saved from the old mosque,
is handsome, even if supplemented with gilt-edged Baroque
panels. Its style resembles that of the entrance. Equally
Baroque yet attractive is the elaborate mimbar made of
polychrome marble.

THE TÜRBE GARDEN. The tombs of Fatih Mehmet and his
wife, Gülbahar, the mother of Beyazıt II, were
reconstructed following the earthquake. The interior of
the conqueror's Baroque *türbe* is lavishly decorated.
Outside Fatih Mehmet's *tabhane*, or hospice for
dervishes, stands the *türbe* built in 1817–18 for the
dowager Sultana Nakşidil, the wife of Abdül Hamit I and
mother of Mahmet II. This splendid example of the
Ottoman Baroque style ● *84* contrasts with the classical
austerity of the *külliye*.

**MEHMET II,
THE BUILDER**
By 1453, the capital
of the dying
Byzantine Empire
was little
more than a ghost of
what it had been.
Inside the walls,
vegetation grew in
abandoned quarters,
Roman ruins, and the
dilapidated palaces.
The population,
which had shrunk to
some 40,000 Greeks,
huddled ever-closer
about the Basilica of
Haghia Sophia.
Mehmet II the
Conqueror revitalized
the legendary city.
Within a few years, a
new population, come
from all over the
Ottoman
Empire, took up
residence there,
building mosques,
bazaars, and
caravanserais.

ITINERANT PEDDLER

221

OTTOMAN COINS
Mehmet II initiated the standardization of the Ottoman monetary system. Most coins have only calligraphic inscriptions on both sides, sometimes accompanied by

braided motifs. Coins with portraits are extremely rare. Unlike the gold coins, called *altin*, the silver ones were used mainly in commercial transactions.

THE MOSQUE OF SELIM I

On the right of Fevzi Paşa Caddesi, Yavuz Selim Caddesi brings you to the Sultan Selim Cami'i and an ancient open cistern, the immense Cistern of Aspar, today the site of a municipal market. The Mosque of Selim I, one of the most beautiful buildings in Istanbul, is situated upon a high terrace at the summit of the Fifth Hill, overlooking the Golden Horn. At its completion in 1522, Süleyman the Magnificent dedicated the mosque to his father. The shallow main dome, with its collection of little domes on either side, looks like an enormous crown. The courtyard is one of the most colorful and charming in the city, its space defined by marble and granite columns, arches built of multicolored voussoirs, a very pretty ablution fountain encircled by cypress trees, and magnificent early Iznik tiles decorating the lunettes above windows. The interior furnishings are superb, especially the mirhab, the mimbar, and the Sultan's loge. The border around the ceiling under the loge provides a stunning example of Ottoman painted and gilded woodwork from the 16th century.

THE MAUSOLEUMS.
The cemetery is situated directly behind the mosque. The large octagonal *türbe* capped by a cupola is that of Selim I. The tile panels decorating the porch are

presumed to have come from Iznik, although their color and design do not resemble any other known examples. There is another mausoleum opposite, attributed to Sinan; it houses the remains of four of Süleyman the Magnificent's children who died in infancy. Also standing near the Sultan's tomb is the mausoleum of Abdül Mecit, who died in 1861.

> «VENERATE AND ADORE THE TRUE CONCEPTION
> IN THE PAINTINGS AND IMAGES OF CHRIST. . . .
> IF YOU DO NOT, YOU TAKE IN VAIN THE NAME OF CHRISTIAN.»
> THE LIFE OF SAINT IONNIKIOS

THE THEOTOKOS PAMMAKARISTOS

Leaving the Selimiye Cami'i by Sultan Selim Caddesi, turn right into Manyasizade Caddesi, which leads to the mosque. This was the Byzantine church known as the *Theotokos Pammakaristos* or "Joyous Mother of God", a building splendidly restored in the 1960's by the Byzantine Institute of America. The main body of the church was constructed in the 12th century by two members of the nobility, John Comnenus and his wife Anna Doukaina. At the end of the 13th century, General Michael Doukas Glabas Tarchaniotes, commander of cavalry under Andronicus II Palaeologus (1282–1328), had it reconstructed. Around 1310, a paracclesion (side sanctuary) was added by the general's widow as a chapel for her husband. Following the Conquest, the church served as the Patriarchate of the Greek Orthodox Church from 1456 to 1586. In 1591, Murat III converted the building into an Islamic place of worship, naming it Fethiye Cami'i – the Mosque of the Conquest – to commemorate his victory over the Persians and the annexation of Georgia and Azerbaijan by the Ottoman Empire. However, the conversion had a number of damaging effects. Since the restoration carried out by the Byzantine Institute, the large prayer hall continues to function as a mosque, while the paracclesion, set apart from the nave and with its missing columns restored, has become a museum devoted to the mosaics that survive intact, now cleared and cleaned. Those covering the dome, previously neglected, have now been restored to their original beauty. Although fewer in number, the mosaics in this chapel join those in the Kariye Cami'i as evidence of the brilliance of the last Byzantine renaissance that blazed during the reign of the Palaeologus dynasty.

MOSAICS IN THE PARACCLESION OF THE THEOTOKOS PAMMAKARISTOS
A Christ Pantocrator is depicted on the ceiling, surrounded by the Twelve Apostles of the New Testament. On the conch vault over the apse there is the

Christ Hyperagathos; on the left wall, the Virgin facing St John the Baptist on the right wall. Above each of the latter hover four angels. Elsewhere, on the conches, on the soffits of arches, and on the pilasters figure twenty-seven saints. A long inscription in gold letters on a blue background unfolds between the marble-clad lower wall and the mosaics on the upper wall. It is a threnody written by the poet Philes to commemorate the love that Maria Blachena, the chapel's foundress, bore her deceased husband, General Michael Tarchaniotes.

THE LAND WALLS

The land walls, for the most part, date from the reign of
Emperor Theodosius II (408–450). The initial phase of
construction, which produced one long high wall punctuated
at regular intervals by some hundred bastions or defense
towers, was completed in 413 under the supervision of
Anthemius, Prefect of the Eastern Empire. In 447, an
earthquake destroyed most of this fortified rampart, toppling
fifty-seven towers just when Attila the Hun and his Golden
Horde were advancing upon Constantinople.
Reconstruction began immediately, this time under
Constantine, the new Prefect of the Eastern
Empire, who, aided by all factions of the
Hippodrome, got the new walls built within
two months, reinforcing them with both a
moat and a second, outer wall. These
formidable defenses stopped Attila,
the Scourge of God, who, having
been frustrated in his ambition
to take Constantinople,
turned around and ravaged
the Western Empire.
The Theodosian
system of defense
rested primarily
on the

THE CONQUEROR
Today the only land
walls that survive are
those left intact by
Mehmet II after he
took the city of
Constantinople in
May 1453.

GATE OF CHRIST

MERMER KÜLE

YEDIKÜLE

BELGRAD KAPISI

IMRAHOR CAMI'I

SILIVRI KAPISI

IBRAHIM PAŞA CAMI'I

TOP KAP

«IMAGINE FOUR MILES OF IMMENSE, TRIPLE BATTLEMENTS…»

LORD BYRON

awesome inner rampart, 16 feet thick and 40 feet high. Its 96 towers, most of them square and some 60-70 feet high, were set at intervals of about 180 feet and linked by massive curtain walls. The terraces or *peribolos* between the two fortified lines varied in width from 50 to 65 feet and were raised about 5 feet above the level of the city. The outer rampart, 30 feet thick and 28 feet high, was strengthened with 96 bastions, either square or cresent-shaped, and their positions alternated with the bastions of the inner wall. Completing the system was an outer terrace – the *parateichion* – bordered by a 6-feet-high battlement at the edge of the deep, wide moat, which could be flooded as a further line of defense against attack.

🚶	Seven hours
🚗	Three hours

THE MARBLE TOWER. The Theodosian walls ● *31* were joined to the sea walls along the Marmara by the Marble Tower – MERMER KULE – a small fortification, 42 feet in diameter and 100 feet high, that still dominates the northwest quarter of the old city. Built on a promontory, the bastion is now isolated from the wall by the shore highway. The Marble Tower – named for the revetment on its lower half – may have begun as a beach house for the emperor to use when he went for a trip on the Marmara.

THE GATE OF CHRIST. Moving slightly away from the shore highway is the first of the ancient gates, just beyond the first tower of the inner wall. It is surmounted by the monogram XP crowned in laurel, which accounts for its name: the Gate of Christ. In addition to several small posterns, the Theodosian walls had ten gates, five of them for the public and five reserved for the military. The Gate of Christ counted among the latter, and so it was also known as

THE CASTLE OF SEVEN TOWERS
Along the castle walls facing the water is the Marble Tower, built on a promontory right next to the sea.

THE CASTLE OF SEVEN TOWERS
"At the corner of the city facing Gallipoli, at the edge of the sea, there is, as mentioned earlier, a castle composed of seven huge towers linked into a fortified enclosure by high, strong walls and equipped with much artillery, which castle is called Iadicula."
Nicolas de Nicolay

THE CANNON GATE
For the Byzantines, this was the Gate of St Romanus. On May 29, 1453, when Mehmet II launched the Turks' final assault upon Constantinople, he focused his attack upon the land walls at this point. The sultan sacrificed the first waves of infantry so that their corpses would fill in the moat. Then a great cannon began bombarding the gate with 270-pound cannonballs, which soon broke through the wall. The portal is called Top Kapı ("Cannon Gate"), to commemorate the episode.

the First Military Gate. However, the gates were all essentially alike except that the public ones opened onto bridges across the moat which led to roads going deep into the countryside, while the military gates led only to the outer defenses. Between the Sea of Marmara and the railway line, the great walls are remarkably well preserved. Various inscriptions cite the names of the emperors who, over the centuries, ordered major repairs to be carried out upon the fortifications. Thus, we find John VIII Palaeologus (1425–48) ● *33* mentioned on the first outer bastion; Romanus I Lecapenus (919–944) on the fourth tower of the inner wall; and Leo III (717–741) as well as his son Constantine V (741–775) on the seventh inner tower. Altogether, there are thirty such inscriptions, which cover a period lasting more than a millennium, providing clear proof of the importance the Byzantine emperors attached to the defenses of their capital.

Between the sixth and seventh towers of the inner wall, take the main road outside the walls and cross the bridge over the railway line that cuts through the ramparts at this point. Some distance farther along, you will come to the Yediküle Gate.

THE CASTLE OF SEVEN TOWERS

The Yediküle Kapı is a small Byzantine gateway with an imperial eagle, emblem of the Comnenus dynasty, carved in marble above the arch on the interior. Passing through the gateway, turn right to find the entrance to the Yediküle itself – the Castle of Seven Towers – a curious structure containing both Byzantine and Ottoman features. The whole building projects inward from the Theodosian walls just beyond the railway line. While four of the towers are integrated with the high wall, the other three, built much later by Fatih, stand inside the enclosure, linked together and to the outer defenses by four thick curtain walls, thereby forming a pentagon-shaped enclosure. At the northwest and southwest corners are two of the polygonal bastions of the main Theodosian wall, between which stand the two other towers – actually marble pylons flanking the famous Golden Gate. Two of the towers – particularly the one on the left – served as prisons for foreign diplomats and prisoners of war, and the other towers were depositories for part of the national treasure. A stairway in the so-called Tower of the Ambassadors gives access to the top of the keep and thence to the ramparts along which you can walk as far as the Golden Gate.

This 15th-century engraving shows the sea wall that ran along both shores of the Golden Horn.

THE GOLDEN GATE. This structure originated around 388 as a Roman triumphal arch erected on the route to the Great Palace by Theodosius I, before he began work on his own defense walls. Like all

THE LAND WALLS
"I have travelled through a great deal of Turkey, many another country of Europe and some Asiatic countries, but I have never come across a work of nature or of art that has made such a strong impression on me as the panorama that unfolds on both sides of the Seven Towers to the Golden Horn.**"**
Lord Byron

triumphal arches, the Porta Aurea stood apart. Its classic form – a triple arch composed of a large, central arch flanked by two smaller ones – stood astride the part of the highway that ran along the Marmara coast and then out of Constantinople. A quarter of a century later the Golden Gate would be integrated within the defense system when Theodosius had Constantine's wall rebuilt. The pylon north of the Golden Gate served as a prison, as well as one of the city's principal places for dispatching the condemned. Instruments of torture and death from that period can still be seen there, along with the sinister "well of blood" into which the heads of the executed were tossed for flushing out to sea. Leaving the Castle of Seven Towers, follow Yediküle Caddesi and take Imrahor Ilyras Bey Caddesi.

THE CHURCH OF SAINT JOHN OF STUDIUS

About 500 yards in front of the Yediküle, on the right, is an enormous but dilapidated and roofless building. This is the Imrahor Cami'i, converted from the ancient Ayios Ioannis Prodomos, St John the Forerunner, which is extremely difficult to get into. The foundation dates from the years 454–63, and its related monastery a bit later, both of them under the patronage of the Roman patrician Studius, consul during the reign of Marcian. In the first quarter of the 9th century, the monastery acquired an immense reputation while Theodore the Studite was abbot. An old iron gate leads to the church's walled garden which, in place of the original atrium, spreads before the three-bayed narthex, whose handsome central entrance is composed of four magnificent Corinthian columns *in antis* supporting a sumptuously carved architrave, frieze, and cornice. Also still in place are two of the marble door frames. From the narthex, three portals and two side doors open into the church, a basilican structure ending in an apse and separated from its side aisles by flanking rows of seven columns each. The six surviving columns on the north are verd-antique monoliths with capitals and

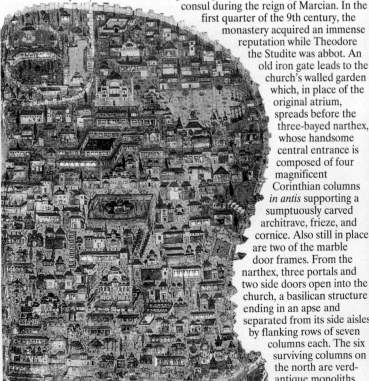

«THE SURROUNDING COUNTRYSIDE
WAS SPANGLED WITH CYPRESSES IN WHOSE SHADE
HUDDLED THOUSANDS OF SEPULCHERS.»

PIERRE LOTI

entablature similar to those in the narthex. The entablatures over the lateral colonnades each supported an upper colonnade upon which rested the timber roof. All of this, along with the main colonnade to the south, was shattered by an earthquake in 1894, which left it in its present ruined state.

TOWARDS THE GATE OF EDIRNE

THE BELGRAD KAPI. Returning to the Yediküle Kapı, walk approximately 600 yards along the walls to the Second Military Gate. This was renamed Belgrad Kapı when Süleyman I reinstalled nearby the artisans he had brought back from Belgrade following his capture of the Balkan city in 1521.

THE SILIVRI KAPI. Along the 680-yard stretch from the Belgrade Gate to the Silver Gate, the line of fortifications is well preserved, including all thirteen of the inner bastions. The Byzantines called the Silver Gate the "Porta ton Pigi" because of its proximity to the pilgrimage site known as the PANANYIA ZOODOCHUS PIGI – "Our Lady of the Life-Giving Spring" – located 500 yards outside the walls. As with all the large gates, the Silivri Kapı is double, opening through both inner and outer walls. It was here that the Byzantines broke through when they recaptured Constantinople from its Latin occupiers in 1261.

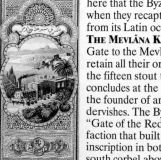

THE MEVLÂNA KAPI. From the Silver Gate to the Mevlâna Gate, the land walls retain all their original elements, including the fifteen stout towers. This stretch concludes at the Mevlâna Kapı, named for the founder of an ancient order of dervishes. The Byzantines called it the "Gate of the Reds," for the Hippodrome faction that built it, according to an inscription in both Greek and Latin on the south corbel above the outer gateway.

CEMETERIES AND WALLS
It was in the first half of the 18th century that a law was promulgated forbidding all further burial within the city. Thereafter a number of cemeteries were developed outside the land walls. Spreading deeper into the countryside, they soon grew to vast dimensions and became known as "fields of the dead." These graveyards were composed of a thronging mass of stelae planted in the midst of sweet, luxuriant vegation. A short distance outside the land walls we find three enormous cemeteries:

Merkez Efendi Merzarlığı, Topkapı Mezarlığı, and Edirnekapı Şehitlığı. But times change, and even the Turks, who once enjoyed picnicking near the tombs, now prefer the country and forests along the upper Bosphorus, near the Black Sea. Meanwhile, the urban sprawl nibbles away at the old fields of the dead, which are left to deteriorate slowly as newly created cemeteries replace them.

229

THE MOSQUE OF TWO HUNDRED WINDOWS
The space inside the Mosque of Princess Mihrimah is magically enhanced by the abundant light pouring in from some two hundred windows, half of them in the huge tympana and around the base of the vast central dome. But the windows are relatively lightly colored, at least by comparison with those in the Süleymaniye or the mosque dedicated to Mihrimah at Üsküdar and Edirne. In the Istanbul mosque, the effect is exquisite, its clarity serving to dramatize the purity of the surrounding space.

TOP KAPI. Along the 900-yard stretch from the Mevlâna Gate to the Cannon Gate, only one of the original fifteen towers has disappeared. However, the ramparts themselves were demolished between the tenth and eleventh towers to make way for Millet Caddesi, punched through in the 1960's. Top Kapı, situated at the summit of the Seventh Hill, takes its name from the mighty cannon aimed at it by the Ottoman forces during the final siege of Constantinople in 1453.

THE MESOTEICHION. The line extending from Top Kapı to Edirne Kapı is about 1,300 yards long, interrupted between the sixth and seventh towers by Vatan Caddesi. This avenue and the Istanbul Metro beneath it follow the course of the old Lycus River. Called the Mesoteichion, meaning "middle of the walls," this part of the fortifications is midway in the defense system between the Sea of Marmara and the Golden Horn. It is also the most vulnerable part of the defenses, since the terrain dips into the Lycus Valley, allowing an enemy to attack from the hills on either side. Thus, in 1453, the Byzantine defenders found themselves caught in the crossfire of the bombardments which finally breached the walls, allowing the Turks to enter the city and leaving these ramparts the most damaged of all.

THE GATE OF THE ASSAULT. Called the Murus Bacchatureus by the Byzantines, the northern portion of the Mesoteichion, between the Lycus and the Edirne Kapı, was pierced by only one gate, the Pyli ton Pempton, or the Fifth Military Gate. Constantine XI transferred his command post here in the final hours of the Turkish siege in May 1453. Even as the walls gave way, he continued to fight valiantly, together with his cousins, Theophilus Palaeologus and Don Francisco of

Toledo, and his faithful companion, John Dalmata. The body of the Emperor is said to have been discovered near the Pempton Gate during the evening of the city's capture and then secretly buried in a church. The Turks would call the gate Hücum Kapı, meaning the Gate of the Assault.

THE MIHRIMAH CAMI'I

Just inside the walls north of Hücum Kapı stands the Mosque of Princess Mihrimah, a major Istanbul landmark that dominates the city's old quarter from atop the Sixth Hill ▲ 265. It is in fact one of the masterpieces of the great Sinan, a foundation dedicated to Süleyman the Magnificent's favorite daughter, who died in 1578.

THE MOSQUE COMPLEX. Constructed between 1562 1565, the *külliye* includes a *medrese* or college, a *mektep* or primary school, a double hammam, the mausoleum of the Grand Vizier Semiz Ali Paşa, Mihrimah's son-in-law, and an *arasta*, or street bazaar, installed in the substructure under the terrace on which the complex was built. We enter through a gate which leads to a flight of stairs that go up to the terrace above. On the right is the *avlu* or

courtyard, enclosed by colonnades and the cells of the *medrese* on three sides and an ablution fountain (*şadırvan*) at the center. The entrance to the mosque is through a porch composed of seven domed bays supported by eight marble and granite columns, a structure that was originally preceded by a "foreporch," probably with a sloping timber roof borne upon twelve columns, traces of which remain on the ground.

THE MOSQUE. Its prominent position reinforces the already imposing nature of the building, with its main dome resting upon a massive cubical structure anchored at the corners by four stout towers buttressing the great arches. The tympana are each pierced by fifteen ogival windows and four round

THE MIHRIMAH CAMI'I
"The plan of the baldachin with a projection of the cupola inscribed. In red, the remains of the supporting structures: the four granite columns and pilasters. Above: Diagonal section of the cupola and its square baldachin, showing the large spherical pendentives."
Augusto Romano Burelli,
La Moschea di Sinan.

ones, all glazed with stained glass. On the interior, the square nave constitutes the central space of the mosque, which is crowned by the vast cupola, 65 feet in diameter and 120 feet high, resting upon a rim base formed by alternating arches and pendentives. On the north and south, the prayer hall opens into triple arcades, each supported by granite columns, while the upper galleries on either side each have three domed bays.

THE EDIRNE GATE. Situated at the point where the main road to Adrianople left the city, the Byzantines' Porta Adrianople became the Turks' EDIRNE KAPI after Adrianople was renamed Edirne ● *308*. Its other name, Porta Polyandriou, or "Cemetery Gate," comes from the presence of a huge necropolis just outside the fortifications. It was through this gate, on top of the Sixth Hill – the highest terrain in the old city – that Mehmet II made his triumphal entrance into Constantinople in the early afternoon of May 29, 1453, a historic moment commemorated by a plaque on the south side of the gateway.

THE KARIYE CAMI'I

MOSAICS IN THE CHRIST PANTOCRATOR CHURCH
The mosaic tondo on the south cupola of the narthex at St Savior-in-Chora is a pendant of the Virgin and Child tondo on the north cupola. These two medalions are each surrounded by twenty-eight figures represented on the ribs of the dome: patriarchs, prophets, leaders of the twelve tribes, and the sixteen kings of Israel.

At the right of the Edirne Kapı, take Fevzi Paşa Caddesi and turn left at the next corner into Vaiz Sokağı. At the third intersection Kariye Cami'i Sokağı appears on the right, leading directly into the square in front of Kariye Cami'i, the former Church of St Savior-in-Chora, situated only a short distance from the Theodosian walls and near the summit of the Sixth Hill.

THE HISTORY OF THE CHURCH. St Savior-in-Chora could very well be translated into "St Savior-in-the-Country," since, as the name implies, the church and its monastery originally stood outside the Constantinian wall. Later, they were integrated into the expanded city enclosed by the Theodosian fortifications. Still, the name stuck, even if used merely in a symbolic sense, reinforced by old inscriptions in the church referring to Christ as the "Country" or "Land of the Living." The actual building dates from between 1077–1081, when it was erected at the behest of Maria Doukas, the mother-in-law

THE DEATH OF THE VIRGIN MOSAIC
Called Koimesis in Greek, the figure appears in the nave of St Savior-in-Chora (Kariye Cami'i). The Virgin, laid out on her bier, is surrounded by the Apostles. At the center, a haloed Christ cradles a babe in swaddling clothes symbolizing the soul of Mary reborn in Paradise.

of Alexis I Comnenus. It probably began as the four-column type much esteemed during this period. At the beginning of the 12th century, Isaac Comnenus, grandson of the foundress and the third son of Alexis I, commissioned a rather elaborate remodeling of the church. Two centuries later, between 1315 and 1321, Theodore Metochites, prime minister and first lord of the treasury during the reign of Andronicus II Palaeologus, undertook to renovate the church yet again, giving it the appearance we know today. This makes the works of art in Kariye Cami'i contemporary with those in the Fethiye Cami'i (Pammakaristos), also produced during the Palaeologian renaissance. St Savior-in-Chora would remain a Christian sanctuary for more than fifty years after the Conquest, until Atik Ali Paşa, Grand Vizier to Beyazıt II, had it converted into a mosque. However, over the centuries, some of the mosaics and frescoes were shaken loose by earthquakes, while the others gradually disappeared under plaster, paint, and grime. Finally, in 1948, Thomas Whittemore and Paul A. Underwood, sponsored by the Byzantine Institute of America and the Dumbarton Oaks Center for Byzantine Studies, launched a major program of restoration.

THE STRUCTURE OF THE CHURCH ● 74.
We enter the sanctuary through an exonarthex followed by a narthex, to find a nave flanked by a paracclesion on the right and a two-story corridor on the left. The central space is capped by a cupola resting upon a tall cylinder, and this superstructure is supported by four enormous pilasters at the corners of the nave. From them spring the arches and the linking pendentives that make the transition from a square base to a circular one for the cylinder and dome. The present dome is Turkish, but the cylinder dates from the reconstruction of 1315 to 1321.

THE DÉCOR OF THE CHURCH. The mosaics and frescoes ● 64 in St Savior are by far the most important works of Byzantine pictorial art known today, in terms of both their beauty and their number. It is fascinating to realize that they are coeval with the frescoes of Giotto in Italy. And while different in certain particulars, they nonetheless appear

THE LAST JUDGMENT FRESCO
In the paracclesion at St Savior-in-Chora, Christ is presented as the Supreme Judge, accompanied by the Virgin Mary, St John the Baptist, and a choir of prophets.

TESSERAE
In this detail from a mosaic, the tesserae are delicate enough to capture the subtle play of light and dark.

THE MARRIAGE AT CANA MOSAIC
This treatment of a scene from the New Testament also reflects everyday life in Byzantium. Vineyards and wine-making were actually the main industry around Constantinople, and the wine was stored in great earthenware jars.

233

CONSTANTINOPLE IN 1422, MAPPED BY CRISTOFORO BUONDELMONTI
In this depiction, executed just a few years before the Conquest, the capital of the Byzantine Empire can be seen completely ringed by its sea and land walls. Only the principal monuments are shown, among them, and easily recognized, the Great Palace, the Basilica of Haghia Sophia, the Hippodrome, the Senate, St John the Studite, the Palace of the Porphyrogenitus, and the many commemorative columns dotted about the city. To the north, on the opposite side of the Golden Horn, stand the walls of Galata, the thriving Genoese concession dominated by its famous tower.

THE GOLDEN GATE
This is a classic Roman triumphal arch, with a large central arcade flanked

by two pylons faced in marble. It was through this gate that the emperors made their triumphal entries into Constantinople following successful campaigns abroad.

to radiate the same sense of living, breathing reality so characteristic of the Early Renaissance. Certainly, they exist in a world well removed from the iconic, static, rigorously stylized painting of the old Byzantine tradition. The movement of the figures, with their graceful gestures, endow many of the scenes represented with an air of lightness and gentle beatitude. The almost painterly vitality of these works is reinforced by clear, luminous colors – blue, green, red, and gold – blended into a harmony of more delicate tones such as gray, mauve, and rose. Finally, the sheer variety of the biblical scenes depicted demonstrates the breadth and power of Byzantine art in this late period.

THE MOSAICS. Iconographically, the mosaics unfold in a very precise order, which can be divided into seven great cycles: the six large Dedicatory panels in the narthex and exonarthex, one of which portrays Theodore Metochites offering his church to Christ; the Ancestry of Christ in the domes of the narthex; the Life of the Blessed Virgin in the first three bays of the narthex; the Infancy of Christ in the lunettes of the exonarthex; the Ministry of Christ on the vaults of the exonarthex and the fourth bay in the narthex; the Portraits of Saints on the arches and pilasters of the narthex; and, finally, the nave panels.

THE MOSAICS. The superb frescoes in the paracclesion, the last commission by Theodore Metochites, probably date from 1320 to 1321. The anonymous author of these masterpieces is

« YOU MADE ME WANDER IN THE LANDS
OF RUMELIA AND DAMASCUS: THEY WILL NOT UNDERSTAND YOU,
THE IGNORAMUSES; THEY WILL ABANDON YOU. . . .»

KARACA OĞLAN

undoubtedly the person who also executed the mosaics in the church. The themes are those generally found in mortuary chapels: Resurrection, Last Judgment, Heaven and Hell, and the Mother of God as Mediator between Earth and Heaven. Below the cornice, between the four tombs, there is a procession of saints and martyrs. The greatest scene of all is the Anastasis – the Resurrection, or the Harrowing of Hell – represented on the conch vault over the apse in the funerary chapel. This extraordinary work is Byzantine art at its very zenith. Indeed, many consider it to be one of the most sublime paintings ever executed. At the center of the grandly spacious composition, Christ triumphant has trampled the gates of Hell beneath his feet, where Satan lies writhing in chains. With his right hand the Savior lifts Adam from his tomb, while with his left he plucks Eve from hers. Behind the First Man comes John the Baptist, David, and Solomon, while Abel stands with another group of the just next to Eve's tomb. The four tombs in the paracclesion occupy deep niches, each of which originally held a sarcophagus with mosaics and frescoes above, fragments of which survive.

THEODORE METOCHITES. The tomb located at the rear of the paracclesion rests under a richly carved and decorated archivolt. Although the inscription has vanished, the sepulcher is probably that of Theodore Metochites: a true Renaissance man, he was a diplomat, high government official, theologian, astronomer, poet, patron of the arts, and major force behind the artistic and intellectual renewal of the Palaeologian era. After Andronicus III seized the throne in 1328, he banished Metochites and other members of the old regime. Late in life, Metochites was permitted to re-enter Constantinople on condition he retire to the St Savior monastery, where he died on May 13, 1331.

THE CAMEL TRAINS
The last emperor to make a triumphal entry into Constantinople through the Golden Gate was Michael VIII Palaeologus (1261–82) on August 15, 1261. Today the Golden Gate is no more than one gate among many others. At the beginning of the century, it was still possible to see fully loaded camel trains passing in single file through certain gates on their way to Edirne. Within Istanbul, they stopped at the *han*, hostelries known to Europeans by the Persian term caravanserai.

THE TEFKUR SARAY
Located on the Sixth Hill, this was one of the residences of the first Byzantine Emperors, and it remain occupied until the end of the Byzantine Empire. Following the Conquest, the palace served a variety of purposes. During the 16th and 17th centuries, it was the imperial menagerie, housing a variety of animals, such as elephants and giraffes, which astonished European travelers. In 1597, Fynes Moryson, described a giraffe thus: "[It was] a wild animal recently imported from Africa, the mother of Monsters. . . . Its fur was red with many black and white spots Even with stretched arms I could barely reach the hind end of its spine, which climbed higher and higher towards the shoulders. Its neck – very thin and of a prodigious length – permitted the beast to extend its head to any part of whatever room it was held in."

THE TEFKUR SARAY

At the end of the Theodosian ramparts, between the inner and outer barriers, stands one of the most remarkable remnants of the Byzantine Empire ● 74. This is the Tefkur Saray, or the Palace of the Sovereign, more popularly called the Palace of the Porphyrogenitus. It is thought to date from the end of the 13th century, and it may have served as an annex to the nearby Blachernae Palace, which was the main imperial residence during the last two centuries of the Byzantine Empire. A huge rectangular building with three stories, it had a vaulted ground floor, which contained a grand hall 55 feet long and with four large arcades opening onto a courtyard preceded by a propyleum. On the next floor up, another vast room, 75 feet long and 32 wide, had six large windows, the last providing access to the rampart's sentry path on top of the defense walls. The top story, which rose above the Theodosian ramparts, was windowed on all sides, with seven openings onto the courtyard. On the south side the wall curiously curves out like an apse, and on the east side there remain traces of a balconied window. Everywhere, but particularly on the couryard façade, the palace displays a geometric décor composed of red brick and white marble, all entirely characteristic of late Byzantine architecture.

THE WALL OF MANUEL I COMNENUS. The Theodosian walls stop abruptly just after the Tefkur Palace, where the defenses are of a later construction, carried out during Manuel I Comnenus' reign in the mid-11th century. The architecture represents a

> «IF YOU SEE BEAUTY YOU STOP. OH MY
> HEART, I CANNOT BEAR YOUR PAIN.»
> ANONYMOUS

significant departure from that of the Theodosian sections. The new barrier, which runs from the Tefkur Saray to the Golden Horn, does not, for the most part, include either an outer wall or a moat; their absence is justified by the greater height and thickness of the wall, as well as by its taller, more massive towers, which were built close together, eight of them square and one round. Structurally, the Manuel wall is composed of a high arcade closed in on its outer face. These defenses contain only one gate, which the Turks call the Eğri Kapı or Crooked Gate, because a *türbe* just outside the gateway causes the narrow road entering the city to bend around it. The remaining stretch of fortification, from the third tower to the retaining wall of the Blachernae terrace, seems to have been constructed still later.

THE BLACHERNAE PALACE

The Blachernae Palace is approached by way of the terrace that once supported the upper part of the building. Its substructures are almost completely intact, and go all the way down to ground level outside the walls. The ruined towers at the outer edge of the terrace are all that remain of the superstructure of the Blachernae Palace, the rest undoubtedly destroyed during the siege of 1453. The fortifications from the north corner of the Blachernae terrace to the Golden Horn consist of two parallel walls joined at either end to form a citadel. The inner wall was built by the Emperor Heraclius (610–641) in 627, apparently replacing the original Theodosian walls in this very vulnerable area where the barbarian Avars had almost succeeded in breaking into the city in 626. The three hexagonal towers are perhaps the finest bastions in the whole system of fortifications. In 813, Leo V (813–820), believing a single wall inadequate, had the outer wall with four towers constructed, though on a less massive scale and to a poorer standard. The "citadel" is entered through the Gate of the Blachernae, situated between the first and second towers of the Heraclian wall. This then brings you to Toplu Dede Sokağı, a winding lane that leads to the ancient Porta Kiliomene, at the west end of the sea wall on the Golden Horn. Here, the land fortifications come to an end, and from there on the sea defenses, when they were still standing, completed the defenses from the Golden Horn to the Sea of Marmara 7 to 8 miles away.

TURKISH WOMEN
Mustafa Kemal, the father of the Turkish Republic, longed to transform his country into a modern, secular state closely modeled on the nations of Europe. Today, while Islamic traditions remain strongly rooted in the countryside, where the veil is frequently worn, the women in the cities have long since abandoned the closed world of the harem and increasingly work outside their homes. However, even in Istanbul, cafés remain the exclusive province of men, and, after a certain hour, women disappear from the streets.

237

▲ THE GOLDEN HORN AND EYÜP

EYÜP · CAFÉ PIERRE LOTI · ZAL MAHMUT PAŞA CAMI'I · EYÜP İSKELESI · AYVANSARAY KAPI · HALIÇ KÖPRÜSÜ

PATRIARCHATE · AYVANSARAY VAPUR İSKELESI · BULGAR KILISESI · GÜL CAMI'I

🚴 Five hours

THE SEA WALLS
It was the Emperor Theophilus (829–942) who built most of the sea walls and had them linked up with the land walls.

FROM THE GALATA BRIDGE
TO THE ATATÜRK BRIDGE

The first half of this journey takes you along the grand avenue – the Ragıp Gümüşpala Caddesi – that runs parallel to the Golden Horn. Standing some 200 yards above the Galata Bridge is an ancient tower dating from the end of the Byzantine period and now recently restored. It is one of the few bastions that survive from the 110 that once formed part of the mighty sea walls erected by the Byzantines on the Golden Horn.

THE MOSQUE OF THE SCALE-MAKERS. Still following the Golden Horn, but now on the left side of the avenue, we come upon three small mosques built just after the Conquest by the craft guilds established in the quarter. The first of them, the Kantarcılar Mescidi, or the Mosque of the Scale-makers, was constructed during the reign of Fatih

«THE LANDSCAPE, THE ENTIRE LENGTH OF THE GOLDEN HORN,
IS CAPTIVATING, ALL THE WAY TO THE LANDINGS
AT HASKÖY AND EYÜP.»

A. T'SERSTEVENS

Mehmet by Sarı Demirci Mevlâna Mehmet Muhittin.
Muhittin appears to have been a member of the guild of
scale-makers, whose still have shops in Kantarcılar Sokağı.

THE MOSQUE OF THE CAULDRON-MAKERS. About 250 yards
farther along is the Kazancılar Cami'i, or the Mosque of the
Cauldron-makers, which is also known as the Üç Mihrablı
Cami'i, the Mosque of the Three Mihrabs. Founded in 1475
by Hoca Hayrettin, the temple was subsequently enlarged by
Fatih Mehmet himself and then again by Hayrettin's
daughter-in-law, each of whom added a mihrab ● *81*,
which accounts for its more
popular Turkish name.

**THE MOSQUE OF THE
LEATHER-WORKERS.**
The third of these
extremely old mosques, the Sağrıcılar Cami'i, or
Mosque of the Leather-workers, is situated
about 150 yards farther along, just
before you come to the Atatürk
Bridge. It is probably the
oldest mosque in
Istanbul, founded
in 1455 by

**THE HARBOR OF
THE GOLDEN HORN**

**A CAIQUE ON
THE GOLDEN HORN**

THE PRISON TOWER
A few remnants of
the sea walls can still
be found along the
upper reaches of the
Golden Horn, usually
surrounded by more
modern structures.
Only two of the walls'
monumental gateways
have survived, but the
ghosts of others linger
in the names of the
sites where they
stood: Aya Kapı and
Cibali Kapı. The huge
defense tower,
standing just beyond
the Galata Bridge,
served as a prison
under both the
Byzantines and the
Ottomans. Indeed,
the Romans called it
"the Prison". Inside
is the tomb of a
Muslim saint, Cafer
Baba, the peaceful
emissary from
Haroun al-Rachid to
Constantinople, who
was nonetheless
imprisoned in the
tower. Found after
the Conquest, his
tomb remains, even
today, a popular
pilgrimage site.

FENER VAPUR
ISKELESI

ATATÜRK
KÖPRÜSÜ

GALATA
KÖPRÜSÜ

Yavuz
Ersinan – who
was Fatih Mehmet's
standard-bearer during the
siege of Constantinople in 1453. Yavuz Ersinan was an
ancestor of Evliya Çelebi, the famous writer and chronicler,
who was born in 1611 in a house next door to Sağrıcılar
Cami'i.

Zeyrek Cami'i

THE MOSQUE OF THE ROSES
In 1453 the feast of St Theodosia, which falls on May 28, was celebrated in the Church of St Theodosia on the very eve of Constantinople's capture by the Turks. According to tradition, the building was still decorated with roses when the first Turkish troops stormed it. When the church was converted into a mosque it was called the Gül Cami'i, meaning the Mosque of the Roses, in memory of this event. Meanwhile, the Greeks call it the Church of the Immortal Rose, and some of them believe that Constantine XI was secretly buried there on the day Constantinople fell to the Turks.

THE CHURCH OF CHRIST PANTOCRATOR

At the end of Atatürk Boulevard, approximately 400 yards from the intersection, stands a church known in Turkish as the Zeyrek Cami'i. This is the ancient Church of the Pantocrator, one of the most famous buildings in Constantinople. In fact, it consisted of two churches with a chapel wedged in between, as well as a large, elaborate, and renowned monastery, which has long since disappeared, except for a few ruins. Around 1120, the Empress Eirene, the wife of John II Comnenus (1118–43), founded the monastery as well as the church to the south and dedicated both to Christ Pantocrator – "Christ the Almighty." After

« THE CAIQUE IS TO ISTANBUL AS THE GONDOLA IS TO VENICE: A RATHER SHORT BOAT, WITH A SHALLOW DRAFT AND A ROWER WHO FACES YOU. »

A. T'SERSTEVENS

her death in 1124, Emperor John II had a second church constructed a few yards away, which was almost identical to the first, and dedicated it to Panayia Eleousa – "Our Lady of Mercy." Next, the Emperor joined the two churches together by building a small chapel of rest between them. This was the place he chose for the burial of the Empress and, in 1143, himself. Three other Byzantine emperors would also be entombed in the chapel: Manuel I Comnenus (1143–80), Manuel II Palaeologus (1391–1425), and John VIII Palaeologus (1425–48), together with his third and final wife, Maria of

Trebizond. She was the last Empress of Byzantium, since the widower Constantine XI did not remarry after he ascended the throne.

FROM THE ATATÜRK BRIDGE TO THE FENER

THE CIBALI GATE. On the other side of Atatürk Boulevard, continue along the Golden Horn through a park laid out on the water's edge. About 450 yards from Atatürk Bridge, on the left, there is one of the two surviving gates from the Byzantine sea walls. This is the Cıbalı Kapı, known in antiquity as the Porta Putea. An inscribed plaque states that Fatih's troops broke through the gateway on May 29, 1453 ● 35, the day that Constantinople finally fell to the Turks.

Here too the Byzantines had taken the full force of the bombardment from the Venetian fleet when the Romans made their assault upon Constantinople in 1203, an attack they renewed successfully in 1204. On the opposite bank, in the Kasımpaşa quarter, we see the Aynalıkavak Kasrı, the Palace of the Arsenal, also known as the Palace of Mirrors. Built during the reign of Ahmet III (1703–30) and renovated by Selim III (1789–1807), the building takes its name from the large Venetian mirrors that decorate the salons, all gifts from the Venetian Republic following the Treaty of Passarowitz, signed in 1718. Today it is a music museum.

THE CHURCH OF ST NICHOLAS. Another 250 yards beyond Cıbalı Kapı there is a Greek church built just inside the sea walls. Dating from 1720, it is dedicated to St Nicholas, the patron saint of sailors. The sanctuary remains open to the faithful, though today there are relatively few.

THE MOSQUE OF THE ROSES. Aya Kapı, the Holy Gate, is the second of the two gateways from the sea walls still standing on the Golden Horn. In the Byzantine era, it was also known as the Gate of St Theodosia, because of the celebrated

A view of the Golden Horn from Pera.

THE GREAT SCHOOL Looming above the Fener Quarter, and clearly visible from a distance, is a large red-brick building. Built in 1881, it is now occupied by a high school serving the Greek community. This was formerly the Megali Scholea, or Grand School, a secular institution of higher education, many of whose graduates went on to fill high positions in the Ottoman Empire. They included some of the most illustrious Feneriotes of the post-Byzantine Empire, from such families as the Palaeologues, Cantacuzenos, Cantemirs, Mavrocordatos, and Ypsilantis.

THE CHURCH OF ST STEPHEN OF THE BULGARS A cast-iron neo-Gothic monument erected in 1871.

church it led to, a Christian place of worship subsequently converted into a mosque. Continue for 50 yards beyond Aya Kapı, then turn left into Kara Sarıklı Sokağı and you arrive at the Gül Cami'i, the ancient Church of St Theodosia, founded in the first half of the 9th century and originally dedicated to St Euphemia. It became known as St Theodosia after the remains of that venerated saint were buried there. The building is in the shape of a Greek cross, with side aisles supporting galleries. The disengaged pillars allow for two-story corner alcoves, but the arches and domes they support date from Ottoman times ● *78*. Following its conversion in the early seventeenth century, the church became known as the Mosque of the Roses in memory of the fact that when the Turkish conquerors stormed the church on May 29, 1453, they found the inside decorated with roses to commemorate the feast day of St Theodosia.

THE CASTLE OF THE PETRION. Past Aya Kapı, about 100 yards farther along, is the Yeni Aya Kapı. However, the "New Gate" was not built in the Byzantine era but in 1582, possibly by the great Sinan ▲ *314*. Another 100 yards farther along is the Sadrazam Ali Paşa Caddesi, which runs next to, but veering away from, the Golden Horn. There was once a gateway here that the Turks called Petri Kapı, which led to a fortified site known as the Castle of Petrion, an enclosure built during Justinian's reign. It played an important role during the Venetian sieges of 1203 and 1204. On May 29, 1453, the stronghold stood fast against the Turkish fleet, and its defenders did not give up until they learned that the capital had been taken. Hearing this, Mehmet II ordered that the houses and churches within the enclave be spared the general pillaging unleashed elsewhere.

THE FENER QUARTER

By the beginning of the 16th century, the Greek merchants and traders of the quarter – the Feneriotes – had amassed substantial fortunes while enjoying the protection of the Sublime Porte, and some of them had even achieved high standing within the Ottoman Empire. An enormously lucrative post traditionally reserved for the Feneriotes was that of *hospodar* – viceroy – to Moldavia and Walachia, Danubian principalities that remained vassal states of the Ottomans until the 19th century.

SMALL TRADES
This itinerant pedlar, near the Blue Mosque, sells his seeds to feed the pigeons. In front of the Mosque of Eyüp a great variety of religious souvenirs are for sale, mainly to tourists: they include amber prayer beads, handkerchiefs, and talismans against the evil eye.

FRIDAY PRAYERS
Before prayers, the Muslim faithful stop at the ablution fountain in the Mosque of Eyüp. On Friday, they listen to an imam who preaches from the top of the mimbar.

A camel train left every year from Eyüp on a pilgrimage to Mecca.

THE GOLDEN HORN
Its Turkish name – Haliç – means simply "Channel." The Golden Horn is a gulf 4 miles long and 870 yards across at its widest point (but its width varies considerably); it has an average depth of 115 feet. Two small rivers feed this gulf, the Alibey and the Kağıthane, formerly nicknamed the "Sweet Waters of Europe." The channel came to be known as the Golden Horn at a time when its banks were places of recreation for the sultans and the great Ottoman families, who lived there in palaces and those charming seaside villas known as *yalı*, all with attractive gardens. Alas, industrialization has made devastating inroads, with workshops and factories built chaotically, spoiling the landscape and polluting the waters. Recently a program of rehabilitation has been undertaken in the hope of restoring the Golden Horn to something of its former glory.

THE GREEK ORTHODOX PATRIARCHATE. Leaving the main, waterside avenue and turning left into Sadrazam Ali Paşa Caddesi, you soon arrive at the Greek Orthodox Patriarchate, transferred here in 1601 after the church it had occupied – the Pammakaristos – was converted into the Fethiye Cami'i. The present Patriarchal Church of St George, which dates from 1720, replaced a much older one of the same name. The ivory-inlaid Patriarchal throne stands in the side aisles on the right. The administrative headquarters of the Greek Orthodox Patriarchate are opposite the church. During the Ottoman period, the Patriarch of Constantinople, although under the suzerainty of the sultan, functioned as the spiritual leader of all orthodox christians within the Empire. Today the Patriarch of Istanbul is the nominal head of the Greek Orthodox Church, but in fact his flock is the Greeks living in the city and on a few islands off the Turkish coast.

THE GATE OF THE LIGHTHOUSE. The street corner just beyond the entrance to the Patriarchate is the site of the famous Porta Phanari, the "Gate of the Lighthouse", which the Turks call the Fener Kapı. Long after the structure disappeared its name survives in that of the Fener Quarter, once famous for its great mansions.

EYÜP İSKELESİ
These boats carry passengers from one bank to the other.

THE MOSQUE OF EYÜP
This is the most frequented and venerated of Istanbul's mosques, thanks to its mausoleum, which contains the bones of Eyüp Ensari, the friend and standard-bearer of the Prophet Mohammed.

THE TOMBS OF THE GRAND VIZIERS
They stand at the head of Cami Kebir Caddesi, leading to the Mosque of Eyüp.

OUR LADY OF THE MONGOLS. High on the hill overlooking the Patriarchate there is a small rose-colored church dedicated to Our Lady of the Mongols. This is the only Byzantine church in the city that has remained continuously under the control of the Greek Orthodox Patriarchate, even during the Ottoman era. Although services continue, the congregation has dwindled considerably. The church is dedicated to the Theotokos Panayiotissa – Mother of God – but is generally known as Mouchliotissa, or Our Lady of the Mongols. Recent investigations indicate that the original church was built as early as the 10th century. Princess Maria, the illegitimate daughter of Michael VIII Palaeologus, ordered its reconstruction around 1282. In 1265, she had married Abagu, the Great Khan of the Mongols, as a result of which she lived at the Mongol court in Persia for about fifteen years. Under her influence, the Khan and his subjects converted to Christianity. Following the assassination of Abagu by his brother, Ahmet, in 1281, Maria found it necessary to return to Constantinople. Shortly afterwards, her father proposed that she be married to another Mongol Khan, but this time she refused, having decided to take up life in a convent. Thus came into being the actual church, to which Maria also added a convent, both dedicated to Theotokos Panayiotissa. The fame of the foundress, as the one-time Queen of the Mongols, meant that the church quickly became known by its more popular name.

THE CHURCH OF ST STEPHEN OF THE BULGARS. Continuing along the shore, you soon come upon the Church of St Stephen of the Bulgars. This sanctuary and the building opposite, the former Exarchate, date from 1871, a time when the Bulgarian Church was declaring its

«Oh my friends, I caused a palace to be erected, and it is I who was the first to bring its beams crashing down.»

KARACA-OĞLAN

independence from the Greek Orthodox Patriarchate. Dedicated to St Stephen, the patron saint of Bulgaria, it is a neo-Gothic building made entirely of cast iron, all of it prefabricated in Vienna and shipped in sections down the Danube and across the Black Sea. In the cemetery of this unusual yet impressive church are buried several local leaders of the Bulgarian Orthodox Church.

THE CHURCH OF ST JOHN THE BAPTIST. A further 250 yards along the Golden Horn brings you to the Greek Church of St John the Baptist. Although a Byzantine sanctuary is thought to have stood here originally, the present building only dates from 1830. The somewhat dilapidated old mansion near the church courtyard is the former Metochion of the Monastery of St Catherine on Mount Sinai. From 1686 until as recently as the 1960's, the Metochion served as the residence of a prelate representing the St Catherine Monastery.

The double portico of the Mosque of Eyüp and the entranceway to its courtyard are both surmounted by cartouches inscribed with calligraphy of verses taken from the Koran.

THE BALAT QUARTER

Some 150 yards or so farther along is the Balat Kapı, the site of one of the former gates in the sea walls. The Turkish name Balat, which also applies to the neighboring quarter, derives from the Greek word *palation,* "palace." Here it also relates to the nearby site of the Blachernae Palace, the last residence of the Byzantine emperors. For centuries Balat was home to an important Jewish community, Greek-speaking Jews and then the more dominant Latin-speaking Sephardim from Spain. Several of the synagogues still in use date from the Byzantine period, though the buildings appear to be late-Ottoman. The most remarkable of the synagogues is the recently restored OKRIDA. Meanwhile, Balat and the neighboring Ayvansaray boast many old Greek and Armenian churches, some founded in the Byzantine era. Beyond the Balat Kapı, on the right, there is a small mosque designed by Sinan. A long, elegantly calligraphed inscription over the entranceway states that it was Ferrah Ağa, the *kethüda* or "steward" to the Grand Vizier Semiz Ali Paşa, who had it built between 1562 and 1563. The mihrab is clad in faience that dates from the period of the Tekfur Saray's construction (11th century). On the east of the mosque stands an old hammam.

A YOUNG BOY IN FESTIVE COSTUME FOR HIS CIRCUMCISION DAY For young Muslim boys, circumcision is comparable to Christian baptism, symbolizing their admission into the community of believers. The day also constitutes a family holiday.

The Mosque of Eyüp viewed from the opposite bank of the Golden Horn.

THE AYVANSARAY QUARTER

THE MOSQUE OF ATIK MUSTAFA PAŞA. The last of the old Byzantine sea gates on the Golden Horn is the Ayvansaray Kapı, approximately 500 yards beyond the Balat Kapı. Another 100 yards before the gate, on the left, is a narrow street leading to the Atik Mustafa Paşa Cami'i, another Byzantine church converted into a mosque at the end of the

15th century, this one by Atik Mustafa Paşa, grand vizier to the sultan Beyazıt II. The apse, on the south side, houses the supposed tomb of Eyüp Ensari, discovered after the Conquest. He was a companion of the Prophet Mohammed, and died during the siege of Constantinople in 670.

THE SACRED SPRING OF THE BLACHERNAE. Turning left into Ayvansaray Sokağı, you come to the *ayazma* of the Blachernae, a "sacred spring" in a little church surrounded by a pretty garden. The church dates from 451, when Empress Pulcheria, the sister of Theodosius II and wife of Marcian, had the sacred spring enclosed in a great church, dedicating it to the Blacherniotissa – Our Lady of Blachernae – who, according to tradition, saved Constantinople from the Avars in 627. The church burned in 1434 and has since been replaced several times, the last time in the 19th century. Returning to the shore – the *iskele* of Ayvansaray – you can then take the ferry as far as Eyüp, about one mile away on the Golden Horn.

THE CEMETERY OF EYÜP
It is only since the end of the last century that Christians have been allowed access to the Mosque of Eyüp. Pierre Loti describes it thus: "A whole world of stelae, tilting, tumbled, shattered by their fall, shapeless heaps, and overgrown with lichens, stained with the color of earth, the color of dried grass, the color of the Byzantine walls, that same ashen brown one sees here all about, save on the blackish cypresses and their bony old frames blanched by time. Almost all of these dead seem to have been long forgotten, since so few of the tombs are maintained, at best only half painted and gilded."

THE EYÜP QUARTER

Eyüp takes its name from Eyüp (Job) Ensari, the companion and standard-bearer of the Prophet Mohammed killed during the first siege of Constantinople (670). Fatih Mehmet, after his own siege of 1453, made the miraculous discovery of the supposed burial place of Eyüp, a site surrounded by hills covered with cypress groves. In less than five years the grateful conqueror had the site endowed with a large *külliye*, including a mosque and a mausoleum for the remains of the disciple. In the Ottoman period, many important people of the empire chose to be interred here, often in splendid *türbe*. Several of the mausoleums are surrounded by large complexes where once all manner of pious activity took place. The structures turn Eyüp into a romantic, open-air museum of Ottoman architecture, especially of funerary monuments ● *79*. Many other Ottomans of more modest means arranged to be buried on the side of the hill above the shrine, thereby making the cemetery the second largest in Turkey, surpassed only by the Karaca Ahmet cemetery above Üsküdar.

AN ORNAMENTAL DETAIL ON A MAUSOLEUM Above, trellis-screened windows of a birdhouse designed like a miniature ablution fountain.

THE MAUSOLEUM OF EYÜP. From the landing stage at Eyüp, follow Eyüp Iskele Caddesi to the intersection with Boyacı Feshane Caddesi, where the classical, octagonal *türbe* of Ferhat Paşa, dating from 1595, is situated. A further 100 yards or so, in Caddesi Kebir Cami'i, is the tomb of the Grand Vizier Sokollu Mehmet Paşa. This severe yet elegant structure, with blue and green stained-glass windows, was designed by Sinan around 1572. On the opposite side of the street is the austere mausoleum of Siyavuş Paşa, another building built by Sinan sometime around 1583. This "street of tombs" leads to the quarter's main square, a place constantly busy with itinerant pedlars selling all kinds of food and religious objects to the hosts of pilgrims who come to visit the *türbe* of Eyüp.

A TALISMAN AGAINST THE EVIL EYE Shops specializing in religious articles also sell talismans against the evil eye, such as this one above made of turquoise stones.

The Mausoleum of Eyüp is hidden away among bushes and trees at the center of cypress gardens. Grass grows wild all around the old tombstones covered with lichens. Until 1926 stones for men had a fez on top and those for women had bouquets of flowers.

SÜTLÜCE
These are old slaughterhouses that the Turkish government plans to convert into a cultural center.

THE MOSQUE OF EYÜP COMPLEX. On the right can be seen the entrance gate to the enclosure around the Mosque of Eyüp. In addition to the mausoleum and the mosque, the *külliye* originally included a *medrese*, a hammam, an *imaret*, a caravanserai, and a covered market, which was constructed in 1458 on the orders of Fatih Mehmet. Thereafter, his successors, beginning with Beyazıt II, would all mark their accession to the throne by coming to Eyüp for the ceremony of having themselves girt in the sword of Osman. At the end of the 18th century, the mosque had fallen into ruin, which prompted Selim III to order its complete reconstruction between 1798 and 1800, except for two minarets replaced earlier by Ahmet III. The mosque is entered through an outer court shaded by enormous old plane trees populated by lame storks and, in spring, gray herons ■ *18*. From the outer courtyard, you enter the inner courtyard, which is bordered on three sides by an unusually imposing colonnade, and it too is shaded by venerable plane trees.

**THE CAFÉ
PIERRE LOTI**
In the evening, as night falls, Pierre Loti liked to smoke a narghile while seated on the terrace of a simple café in Eyüp, overlooking the Golden Horn. The little teahouses around mosques have always been popular with the people of Istanbul. The Café Pierre Loti has old, shady trees, hanging wisteria, and canvas awnings.

THE MOSQUE OF EYÜP. In plan the Eyüp Cami'i – the holiest Muslim shrine in Istanbul – is an octagon inscribed within a rectangle. Even though of recent construction, the mosque is a remarkably attractive one, with its clear, honey-colored stone, its decorations highlighted in gold, its elegant chandeliers suspended from the center of the dome, and its magnificent turquoise carpet covering the floor from wall to wall. (The former Prime Minister Adnan Menderes gave the carpet to the mosque in gratitude for having been saved from an airplane accident.) The blind wall facing the shrine is clad in a patternless mix of tiles from every period, some of which are extremely beautiful. A gate in the wall opens onto the *türbe* of Eyüp Ensari, an octagonal monument three sides of which project into the vestibule. Meanwhile, the vestibule itself is revetted in faience dating in part from the high period of Iznik production. The decoration of the *türbe* is lavish, but mostly in the Turkish Baroque manner.

THE GREAT CEMETERY OF EYÜP ● 250. This enormous cemetery spreads across the hillside overlooking the mosque.

It is one of the most attractive and picturesque sites in all of Istanbul, dotted with thousands of tombs and tombstones scattered among the cypress groves. The oldest stones are beautifully carved and crowned with some kind of representative headdress, often a turban for the men, or a shawl for women, together with a diadem if the deceased had been a princess. The women's tombstones are decorated with floral motifs, usually roses, the number of flowers signifying the number of children borne. Those of men are typically engraved with epitaphs in old Turkish script, some of which have a jocular tone: "Visitor, deny me your prayers, but please do not steal my tombstone."

THE PIERRE LOTI CAFÉ. The path running across the cemetery leads to the small teahouse or café that Pierre Loti frequented during his days as a naval officer living in Eyüp. Several episodes in his novel *Aziyadé* ▲ 354 take place in this ancient cemetery, whose appearance has hardly changed since then. The view from the café is particularly romantic at sunset, when the Golden Horn is flooded with the fading glow of twilight. While smoking his narghile, Loti could see all the way to the source of the Golden Horn, where legend holds that Cereossa gave birth to the child sired by Poseidon, a boy who grew up to be Byzas the Megarian, eponymous founder of Byzantium.

EXCURSIONS UPON THE SWEET WATERS OF EUROPE IN THE 19TH CENTURY

"If, instead of leaving the Golden Horn by its mouth, we turn back into the past across the sea lanes in a city of vessels; if we pass under a floating bridge that closes off the arsenal of the Imperial Navy, then we see the banks of the Golden Horn slowly converging and thus arrive, by following the narrow neck of the gulf, at a small, clear, calm river that runs through the most beautiful meadows. This is the little valley of the Sweet Waters of Europe."

Charles Reynaud

"Disembarking at the Sweet Waters, one experiences that pleasure which always comes with a harmonious ensemble of verdure, shade, and limpid waters spread over a variable terrain. Here the river is squeezed into a channel some one hundred feet wide, whose rocky banks are shaded by rows of beautiful trees. The channel runs through a series of falls that, while shallow, extend completely across the flood. Between the cascades one sees the kiosks dressed in color and picked out in gold."

Castellan

The Muslim cemeteries, or "fields of the dead," are an important part in the life of everyone in Istanbul. They are like immense forests situated on the outskirts of the city, by the land walls, at the top of Üsküdar, around the mosques or sometimes along the streets, and are far from melancholy places. People come to stroll or have picnics, enjoying the peaceful freshnes beneath the shade of the cypress trees. Flowers, milk and perfume a offered to the deceased, demonstrating the intimacy the living feel with death. The Turkish cemeteries are remarkable for their appare disorder: the unkempt vegetation which expresses the vitality of nature, and the sense of abandonment that signifies a gentle resignation to the passage of time.

The tombstones of men and women can be distinguished by their decoration. For the men there is a cylindrical stone topped with a turban, the sophistication of which is in relation to the importance of the deceased. For women a flat stone ends in a crown of flowers or fruit sculpted in relief.

Columns and stelae with epitaphs in ancient Turkish writing.

A small basin is dug in the center of the tombstone to collect the offerings made by friends and family of the deceased.

The dead are celebrated on the second day of the Festival of Delicacies, the *Şeker Bayramı,* which is part of Ramadan. On this occasion cake and candy sellers used to gather at the entrance to the cemetery.

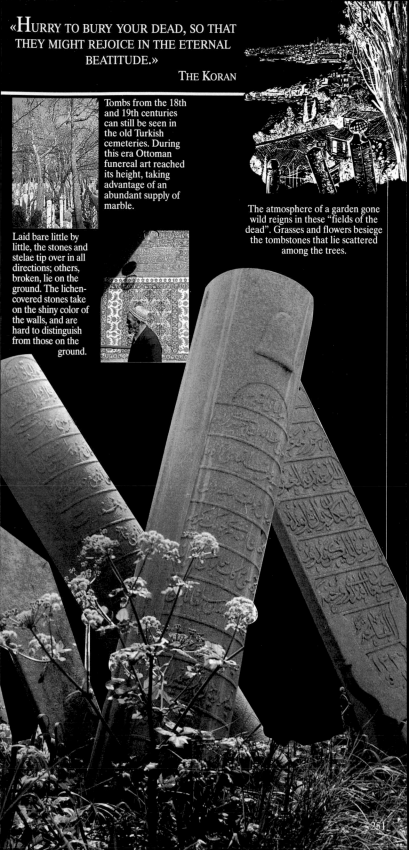

«HURRY TO BURY YOUR DEAD, SO THAT THEY MIGHT REJOICE IN THE ETERNAL BEATITUDE.»

THE KORAN

Tombs from the 18th and 19th centuries can still be seen in the old Turkish cemeteries. During this era Ottoman funereal art reached its height, taking advantage of an abundant supply of marble.

The atmosphere of a garden gone wild reigns in these "fields of the dead". Grasses and flowers besiege the tombstones that lie scattered among the trees.

Laid bare little by little, the stones and stelae tip over in all directions; others, broken, lie on the ground. The lichen-covered stones take on the shiny color of the walls, and are hard to distinguish from those on the ground.

AZAPKAPI CAMİ'İ

GALATA TOWER

GALATASARAY SCHOOL

ÇİÇEK PASAJI

🏃 Half a day

THE GALATA TOWER
High above the modern houses of Galata towers the ancient bastion of the fortified wall which enclosed the Genoese concession. The view from the top, at about 170 feet, is spectacular.

THE GALATA BRIDGE
This watercolor (right) by Hawizy Hvanson, painted in 1908, shows the old wooden bridge before it was rebuilt between 1910 and 1912 with a metal span, which in turn was replaced in 1992.

The two oldest quarters on the north shore of the Golden Horn are Galata and Beyoğlu. Pera, the ancient name of Beyoğlu, means "beyond" or "over there" in Greek. At first it signified the northern side of the Golden Horn; then, in the Byzantine era, the village opposite Constantinople; and, still later, the elegant suburb overlooking Galata.

HISTORY

THE BYZANTINE PERIOD ● 32. Galata, a fortified town in the Greco-Byzantine period and thus older than Constantinople, grew tremendously after the Genoese took control in the 13th century. Beginning in the 11th century, the Byzantine emperors allowed Venice, Genoa, and other city-states to establish trading posts in Constantinople. When the Venetians and their allies, the knights of the Fourth Crusade, took possession of the Byzantine capital in 1204, the Genoese found themselves evicted and forced to make do on the other side of the gulf. They settled in Galata and seized its port. In the last year of the Roman occupation, the Genoese allied themselves with the Byzantines, formalizing the relationship in the Treaty of Nymphaeum, signed at Nicaea on March 12, 1261 by the exiled Michael VIII Palaeologus. By the terms of this agreement, the men from Genoa gained important trading and commercial concessions in the empire. After recovering Constantinople four months later, the Byzantine emperor authorized the Genoese to make maximum use of their concession in Galata, which would soon become an independent city-state under the protection of Genoa. Power rested with an Italian-style *podesta* (governor) appointed annually by the Genoese Senate and aided by a council. When the Ottoman Turks laid siege to Constantinople in 1453 ● *34*, Genoese Galata attempted to secure its own interests by remaining neutral, even though many of its Italian inhabitants decided to fight on

the Greek side. A year later, the sultan integrated the Galata concession into the Ottoman Empire and appointed a *voivode* (mayor) to govern the new possession.

THE OTTOMAN PERIOD. Even after the Conquest, the Genoese retained a degree of independence in Galata, up to the middle of the 17th century, during which time they went on managing their civic affairs through a council known as the "Magnificent Community of Pera." Little by little, however, their power drained away, until by the end of the 19th century it had disappeared entirely.

A CHURCH IN OLD PERA AND A MOSQUE IN GALATA The heavily Europeanized Pera quarter lay next door to Galata, where, following the Conquest, several mosques were constructed. Istanbul long provided the civilized world with a model of religious tolerance.

THE ARSENAL. After the Conquest, Fatih Mehmet had the gigantic Tershane, or Marine Arsenal, constructed on the Golden Horn just above Galata, and the shipyard is still in operation today. Thanks to its infrastructure and its extremely busy port, Galata soon developed into the center of Istanbul's maritime industry, where a host of Italian, Greek, Jewish, and Armenian merchants worked as suppliers to both the ships in port and their multinational crews.
PERA. Within a century after the Conquest, the richest merchants began moving outside the overcrowded, wall-encircled town and taking up residence among the vineyards on the hills above Galata, an area that came to be known as Pera and then Beyoğlu. Here, as well as foreign embassies, they built great mansions surrounded by gardens along what would become the main street of Pera, which in its time was both fashionable and famous.
THE MOSQUE OF THE ARABS. After crossing the Atatürk Bridge from Istanbul, you come to the shipyard on the left and, on the right, the Sokollu Mehmet Paşa Cami'i, which has an exceptionally beautiful Baroque fountain. Going towards the Galata Bridge, it is best to avoid the highway which runs along the shore, and instead follow Tershane Caddesi through the maze of tiny streets that border it. Just beyond the Yanık Kapı Sokağı there is a large building with an imposing campanile, which, on first sight, could be taken for an Italian church. It is, however, the Arap Cami'i, or the Mosque of the Arabs. A vaulted passage beneath the campanile leads to the mosque's main entrance and courtyard.
THE STREET OF THE THURSDAY MARKET. Some 50 yards beyond the Arap Cami'i turn left into Perşembe Pazarı Sokağı, or the Street of the Thursday Market; this runs uphill to the old quarters that the Genoese enclosed within a circuit of defensive walls in 1304. The street is flanked by enormous old buildings with façades of stone and brick laid in alternating courses and with corbeled upper stories thrusting outwards at odd, irregular angles and intervals. The buildings were long thought to have been constructed by the Genoese during the Byzantine era. However, the discovery of the dates 1735–6 inscribed on one of them in Arabic indicates that all the houses in the street were built in the 18th century.

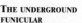

> «Whole clans of Periot families
> move into and occupy space left free by idle consumers
> dressed in European attire.»
>
> Pierre Loti

The old Podestat

Perşembe Pazarı Sokağı concludes in Voyvoda Caddesi, where, on the opposite side of the avenue, in Eski Banka Sokağı (the "Street of the Old Bank"), a flight of stairs takes us down to Galata Kulesi Sokağı.
On the right stands the old Podestat, the Town Hall erected in 1316 to house the podesta dispatched annually from Genoa to govern Galata. Substantially rebuilt in 1939, the building has lost much of its medieval character.

The Caravanserai of St Peter

Take the little street on the left to the top of the stairs; the right side is almost entirely taken up by an old European-style building. This is the *han*, or caravanserai, of St Peter, built in

1771 at the behest of the Count of Saint-Priest for the purpose of establishing "the residence and the bank of the French nation," as he wrote in his will. A plaque on the façade bears the arms of the Bourbon dynasty as well as those of the Count. Another plaque informs us that the French poet André Chénier was born here on October 30, 1762, in a house that pre-dated the present *han*.
San Pietro. Halfway along Galata Kulesi Sokağı, where the street bends to the right, you come to the Roman Catholic Church of Sts Peter and Paul. Better known by its Italian variant, San Pietro, the church was founded at the end of the 15th century by the Dominican order, to which it still belongs. During the Ottoman era, San Pietro came under the protection of

TOBACCO
During the period when İstanbul seemed enveloped in a cloud of romantic smoke from the Orient Express, Turkish cigarettes were all the rage. To protect the legitimacy of Turkish tobacco and assert its distinction relative to foreign imitations then undercutting the product in the marketplace, the Ottoman Office of Tobacco stamped the origin of the contents on every box it sold: "the only authentic Turkish cigarettes."

The entrance to the Tünel in the late 1950's.

The entrance to one of the many commercial arcades in Beyoğlu and the stairs in Eski Banka Sokağı – the "Street of the Old Bank".

DERVISHES
These Whirling Dervishes from the Galata *tekke*, all disciples of the Mevleni Order, perform a dance which symbolizes the planets rotating about the sun and is supposed to induce a state of ecstasy.

France, serving as the parish church for the French community. Later, it administered to the Maltese in Pera. The present structure was erected in 1841 by the Fossati brothers, who restored Haghia Sophia between 1847 and 1849.

THE GALATA TOWER

The Galata Tower rears up at the top of Galata Kulesı Sokağı. This massive, cone-capped structure, built at 115 feet above sea level and rising to a height of 220 feet above its base, overlooks the entire northern side of the Golden Horn. An elevator goes to the penultimate floor, after which you must take the stairs to reach the top, where a restaurant and observation deck 174 feet above ground level provides an unrivaled view over the whole of Istanbul. The Galata Tower is generally thought to have been constructed by the Genoese around 1348 as a great bastion reinforcing the defensive walls designed to protect them in the event of an attack by the Byzantines. After the Conquest, Mehmet Fatih II had its height shortened by 22 feet. The Turks eventually used it to incarcerate prisoners of war. Under Murat III (1574–95), the tower was converted into an observatory, and then, towards the end of the Ottoman period, a lookout for fires, which it remained until the 1960s. After being closed for several years, the old Galata Tower was reopened and became one of Istanbul's major tourist attractions. A plaque near the elevator stop at the summit tells of an extraordinary feat that was performed in the 17th century by Hezarfen Ahmet Çelebi: equipped with wings of his own design, he flew from the top of the Galata Tower all the way across the Bosphorus before landing safely in Üsküdar on the far side.

Modern paintings representing Beyoğlu and the Golden Horn.

THE MONASTERY OF THE WHIRLING DERVISHES

At the upper end of Galip Dede Caddesi, we find a *tekke*, or monastery, of the Mevlevi dervishes on the left next to a charming *sebil*, or fountain, built at the beginning of the 19th century by Halil Efendi. The monastery was established in 1492 by Seyh Muhammad Semai Sultan Divani, a direct descendant of Mevlâna Rumi, the 13th-century saint and mystic poet who founded the Mevlevi Brotherhood, best known in the West as the "Whirling Dervishes." At the bottom of the courtyard we find the *semahane*, the building in which the dervishes performed their dances. Since its restoration in the 1970's, the structure houses the Museum of Literature of the Divan, devoted to the works of mystic poets of the Ottoman era, the most famous of them being Galip Dede. The collection also includes manuscripts and objects once owned by the Whirling Dervishes, who occupied the monastery until the dissolution of their order in 1924. From time to time performances of Mevlevi dances are given here, mainly during the Istanbul Summer Festival.

THE OLD MAIN STREET OF PERA

Galip Dede Caddesi leads to Istiklal Caddesi, which begins immediately on the left, near the terminus of the Tünel, the underground funicular. The tramway service on the former main street of Pera has recently been restored between the Tünel station and Taksim Meydanı, the square at the other end of Istiklal Caddesi. It makes only one midway stop at Galatasaray Square. Save for the tramway, Istiklal Caddesi is closed to all motorized traffic, with the result that a stroll along the avenue is as pleasant as it must have been in former times, when this was still the main street of Pera.

VIEW FROM THE TOP OF THE GALATA TOWER
Galata spreads out at the foot of the old Genoese tower. From the summit of this medieval bastion, one can see old Istanbul from Seraglio Point to the Eminönü quarter, bristling with the minarets of the large mosques: Sultan Ahmet Cami'i, Aya Sofya Cami'i, and Süleymaniye Cami'i.

Turn-of-the-century cabaret beauties.

Istiklal Caddesi can boast a glittering past, dating back to the arrival of the big European embassies, beginning in the 16th century. Each legation, installed within its own little palace and compound, became a kind of separate nation, complete with the ambassador's residence, a church, a post office, and other institutions, all functioning more or less independently of Ottoman authority. The advent of the Turkish Republic in 1923 meant that the embassies moved to the new capital, Ankara, leaving the old ones in Istanbul to become consulates. At the first intersection stands the former Russian Embassy; built in 1837 it was the first building completed in Istanbul by the Fossatis. On the right is the elegant old Swedish Embassy, which probably dates from the late 17th century.

THE PROTESTANT CHURCH

At the next intersection, on the right, is the Kumbaracı Yokuşu, a street that derives its name from the mansion at its upper end once owned and occupied by Kumbaracı Ahmet Paşa. Some 200 yards down this street on the right is the recently restored Crimean Memorial Church, the only large building

of Protestant Christian worship ever built in Istanbul, and one of the most attractive of the city's Western churches. Its principal patron, Lord Stratford of Redcliffe, Britain's influential Ambassador, laid the cornerstone on October 18, 1858, the year the Crimean War ended. Designed by C.E. Street, the architect of the London Law Courts, the Crimean Memorial Church was Istanbul's first neo-Gothic building, the style so esteemed in the West during the Victorian era.

THE CHURCH OF ST MARY DRAPERIS. A little farther along Istiklal Caddesi is the Franciscan Church of St Mary Draperis. In 1453, the Franciscans had built a sanctuary of the same name in Constantinople on a site near the present Sirkeci Station. After the Conquest deprived them of these premises, the monks had to make do with various temporary quarters in Galata, until Clara Bartola Draperis provided a building near today's Customs House. The new Church of St Mary, whose name the Franciscans expanded to include that of their benefactress, was once again displaced in 1660 and then reconstructed several times following fires and an earthquake. The present church dates from 1769.

**NIGHTLIFE
AND THEATER**
Nightclubs have long been a feature of the old European quarter of Pera, now called Beyoğlu. They are especially evident along Cumhuriyet Caddesi, between Taksim Square and the Hilton Hotel. The performances include everything from folk music to all kinds of singers and orchestras, as well as a plenitude of Oriental dancing.

THE PERA PALACE HOTEL

The grand hotel created in 1892 by the Compagnie des Wagons-lits to house Orient Express passengers still exists at 98-100 Mesrutiyet Caddesi in the Tepebaşı quarter. The room occupied by Mustafa Kemal Atatürk (no. 101) has been turned into a museum. But one can also request room no. 103, where Garbo slept, no. 104, which was Mata Hari's room, or no. 304, the accommodation taken by Sarah Bernhardt. Agatha Christie wrote a good part of *Murder on the Orient Express* in no. 411, which has retained an air of mystery ever since. Without having to stay at the hotel, one can still enjoy a cocktail in the elegant Orient Bar and enjoy the magic of this celebrated place.

THE EMBASSIES

Next, on the right, Istiklal Caddesi crosses a steep, narrow lane, Postacılar Sokağı, or the "Street of the Postmen", which leads downhill past, on the left, the former embassies of Holland and France, whose entrances are on Istiklal Caddesi. At the bottom, Postacılar Sokağı opens into a small square flanked by two large European buildings. The one on the left, a 19th-century structure, is the old French Law Court, or Palais de Justice, in which the legal affairs of the European "nations" in Constantinople were processed. The building on the right, the Palazzo di Venezia, served as the embassy of the Serene Republic of Venice from the end of the 16th century to 1797, before becoming the Italian Embassy.

A melodrama at the Pera Theater, some time between 1850 and 1870.

THE FRENCH RESIDENCE

France became the first European nation to establish diplomatic relations with the Ottoman Empire when, in 1535, François I sent an emissary to Süleyman the Magnificent. France was also the

THE ORIENT EXPRESS
On the day in 1883 when the Orient Express was being prepared to leave the Gare de l'Est in Paris for the first time, no one could have imagined that this superb piece of heavy machinery, some 230 feet long, would become a myth capable of enchanting several generations and inspiring works of fiction. Its destination was Istanbul, the "pearl of the Orient." Inside this mother of all the great *trains de luxe* was exquisite wood paneling, fine china, immaculate linens, Lalique crystal, and oceans of champagne.

Galatasaray Lycée and Square.

first to build an embassy in the Grand-Rue de Pera. The 1581 building and its attendant church, Saint-Louis-des-Français, were burned down in 1831 and replaced by the structures there today.

THE CHURCH OF ST ANTHONY. Beyond the second turning on the right, we arrive at the Franciscan Church of St Anthony of Padua; built in 1913 it is a fine example of the Italian neo-Gothic. This Roman Catholic parish was originally served by a much older church dedicated to St Francis, built on the main street in 1725.

GALATASARAY SQUARE

A major intersection halfway along Istiklal Caddesi, Galatasaray Square, like the rest of the quarter, takes its name from the school whose name can be seen on the gateway to the right. Although the buildings only date from 1908, the institution has existed since the late 15th century, when Beyazıt II established it as an extension to the Campaign Hall at Topkapı Sarayı. In 1868 Sultan Abdül Aziz had it reorganized along the lines of French lycées. Since that time the Lycée Galatasaray has educated the political and intellectual élite of Turkey, thus playing an important role in the country's modernization.

THE BRITISH EMBASSY.
The British Embassy is on Hamalbaşı Caddesi, the avenue heading off to the left of the square. The relationship between England and the Sublime Porte began when Elizabeth I and Murat III signed an agreement which allowed English merchants to establish the Levant Company in 1580. Around 1800, Lord Elgin had the first British Embassy

> «UNDER WALLS FRESCOED BY A RUSSIAN ARTIST,
> *LE TOUT-MOSCOU*, ABSURDLY CAPPED IN FEZZES,
> WANDERED AMONG THE PALM TREES.»
>
> PAUL MORAND

THE RUSSIAN RESTAURANT IN THE AYAPAŞA QUARTER IN THE 1940s
This restaurant is situated near the Park Hotel (a modern building which replaced the old hotel of the same name demolished in 1979) and not far from Taksim Square. In the 1940's, it was one of the most famous restaurants in Istanbul, and the whole of the city's artistic and intellectual community went there for borscht and beef stroganoff. This was still the period of Bugattis and the first tramway. Women, obligingly decolletées, tended to imitate Hollywood starlets. Even now, the restaurant continues to evoke the charm and cordiality of yesteryear.

built on this site, but it was destroyed by fire in 1831. Parts of the present building were designed by Sir Charles Barry, one of the architects of the Houses of Parliament in London. W.J. Smith completed it in 1845 along somewhat different lines.
THE PERA PALACE HOTEL. The romantic Pera Palace Hotel, opened in 1876 to serve the passengers on the Orient Express, still exists in Meşrutiyet Caddesi, left of Hamalbaşı Caddesi. Although the whole of the Tepebaşı quarter, once so elegant, has fallen on hard times, the Pera Palace still maintains its original splendor.

THE GALATASARAY MARKETS

The first street on the left, after Galatasaray Square, is Sahne Sokağı, or "Theater Street". Here and in neighboring lanes, is the picturesque Galatasaray Balık Pazar – the local fish market. Its maze of tiny streets is lined with stalls and barrows selling a wide variety of fish, meat, fruit, and vegetables. A short distance along Sahne Sokağı is a gate opening into the famous Çiçek Pasajı, or "Passage of Flowers", whose entrance lies on Istiklal Caddesi. Some twenty years ago Çiçek Pasajı still had a few of its old flower stalls, but the market has since moved to Sahne Sokağı. The L-shaped alleyway passes through a once-elegant apartment block built in 1871 and called the Cité de Pera. For the last fifty years this passage has been taken over by *meyhane*, or beer taverns, which, though formerly notorious for their raffishness, now seem fairly tame. Those nostalgic for the past miss the colorful mob of wandering minstrels, real or phony beggars, sword-swallowers, and other such exotic denizens of Beyoğlu, who have long since been banished from their old haunts.

A street in Pera at the turn of the 20th century.

The Galatasaray
Jesuit College

THE CAFÉS. Meanwhile, the area between Galatasaray Square and Taksim Square remains a popular rendezvous for intellectuals, idlers, and celebrities of Istanbul, who often gather in the early evening at the Café Pub, the Kulis, or the Papyrus, all three of which are located on Istiklal Caddesi.

TAKSIM SQUARE

On the left, at the upper end of Istiklul Caddesi, is the old French Consulate. Constructed in 1719, the building originally served as a hospital for plague victims. Beyond this, we find the octagonal *taksim* (reservoir), from which both the square and the quarter take their name. In 1732 Mahmut I had the reservoir built to collect water from the Belgrade Forest to supply the modern districts on the north bank of the Golden Horn. On the right stands an imposing neo-Byzantine building crowned by a tall tympanum and with a pair of towering campaniles in front. This is the Aya Trianda, the Greek Orthodox Church of the Holy Trinity, which dates from 1882. The group of sculptures standing on the western edge of the square are of Atatürk and other nationalist heroes. On the east side of the square is the glass-walled Atatürk Cultural Center, which is also the home of the Istanbul Opera. The Center is also the main venue for most performances of music, theater, and dance, including the events of the Summer Festival.

THE HARBIYE QUARTER

Cumhuriyet Caddesi, on the north side of Taksim Square, leads into the more modern quarters of the city: Harbiye, Maçka, Şişli, and Nişantaşı. Harbiye boasts not only two important museums but also the Sports and Exhibition Palace (Spor ve Sergi Sarayı) and the Istanbul Concert Hall, both used for performances during the Istanbul Summer Festival. The first, and larger, of the museums is the Askerı Müzesi, or Military Museum, in whose remarkable collection of objects can be found the whole of Turkey's martial history. Here too the famous Mektar Band gives concerts of Ottoman military music. At 25 Halaskargazi Caddesi there is a small museum devoted to Mustafa Kemal Atatürk, the father of modern Turkey, who lived in this house from 1918 to 1919 during the last days of the old Pera, just prior to his departure for Anatolia, where he would organize the nationalist movement ● *44*.

Sidebar

TAKSIM SQUARE
A painting by Sabri Bekel from 1948. He studied at the Fine Arts Academy in Belgrade, returning to Turkey in 1935.

THE MAIN STREET OF PERA
At the turn of the 20th century, Istiklal Caddesi was the most modern avenue in Istanbul; some of its elegance can be seen in this little, five-story neo-classical building.

The façade of a 19th-century building in Beyoğlu.

MONUMENT TO THE WAR OF INDEPENDENCE
This monument commemorating the heroes of the War of Independence, which liberated Turkey from the occupying armies, stands in the center of Taksim Square.

ATIK VALIDE KÜLLIYE PRINCES' ISLANDS İSKELE CAMİ'İ ÜSKÜDAR İSKELESİ ŞEMSI AHMET PAŞA CAMİ'İ

🔆 One day

ÜSKÜDAR
This is the Asian quarter of Istanbul and, as such, it retains a certain oriental feel. Amongst the maze of narrow streets there are picturesque old wooden houses, but also some great Ottoman buildings, among them several mosques designed by Sinan ● *314*. There is also the immense Karacaahmet Cemetery, with many fine examples of Ottoman funerary art.

HISTORY

Üsküdar, the largest and most historic of Istanbul's Anatolian suburbs, is situated on the Asian shore of the lower Bosphorus, directly opposite the Constantinople peninsula. The town or quarter was known in antiquity as Chrysopolis – "City of Gold" – and was founded at about the same time as Byzantium. Given its proximity to Constantinople, Chrysopolis inevitably had much the same history as the capital itself. However, the community could not be so well defended and thus suffered the disasters of several invasions and occupations, while Constantinople remained protected by its great walls until the sack by the Crusaders in 1204 and the Turkish siege of 1453 ● *32*. Finally, in the mid-14th century, Chrysopolis – by then known as Scutari – succumbed to the Turks and was never recovered by the Byzantines. During the long Ottoman era that followed some of the great men and women of the realm endowed Üsküdar with splendid mosque complexes and other pious foundations, all of which

KIZ KULESI

THE ÜSKÜDAR ISKELESI.

Ferries leave from both Eminönü and Kabataş on the European shore of the lower Bosphorus. The great square by the ferry landing pier (*iskelesi*) in Üsküdar is known as Hakimiyeti Milliye Meydanı, the former destination of Anatolian commercial routes. It was also the mustering place for the Sürre-i-Hümayun, the "Sacred Caravan" that departed for Mecca and Medina every year with its long train of pilgrims and its sacred white camels bearing gifts from the sultan to the Şerif of Mecca.

From Eminönü or Kabataş, on the European shore, ferries cross the lower Bosphorus to the port of Üsküdar. In antiquity, this was the port of Chalcedonia, today's Kadıköy, though a bit farther south on the Sea of Marmara. Like the villages of the Bosphorus, Üsküdar preserves its fishing industry, with tiny vessels working alongside the big oil tankers. At lunchtime, local people throng the quays to buy fish sandwiches.

MIHRIMAH SULTAN CAMI'I

The square has a majestic Baroque fountain in the center, and is dominated by a graceful *külliye* at its northern end built upon a high terrace close to the shore. This imperial mosque complex, which the Turks call the Iskele Cami'i ("Mosque of the Landing"), was built by the great Sinan between 1547 and 1548 for Sultana Mihrimah, the daughter of Süleyman the Magnificent and the wife of the Grand Vizier Rüstem Paşa ▲ *231*. This was the first of two *külliye* that Sinan built for Princess Mihrimah, the second one being the imperial complex already seen on the other side of the Bosphorus, at the top of Istanbul's Sixth Hill. The mosque was given its imposing raised position because it had previously been flooded by the sea. It has a double portico with a belvedere which shelters a charming ablution fountain. The interior, however, is disappointing, as the central dome is supported by three instead of the usual two or four half-domes, giving it a somewhat awkward and truncated appearance.

THE ELEMENTS OF THE COMPLEX. The *külliye* of Mihrimah Sultan included an *imaret*, a *medrese*, and a *mektep*, but only the last two survive. The former *medrese*, or college, to the north of the mosque, is a rectangular building and now used as a clinic.

ÇAMLICA
From the top of Çamlıca Hill, northeast of Üsküdar, there is a splendid view of the Bosphorus below. On the opposite European shore stands the Palace of Dolmabahçe clad in glistening white marble.

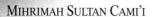

A small birdhouse under the entablature of the Mihrimah Sultan Cami'i.

KIZ KULESI
This symbol of the Bosphorus appears on boxes of candy and Turkish delight.

THE MOSQUE OF PRINCESS MIHRIMAH, AS DEPICTED BY AHMET ZIYA AKBULUT
At the foot of the stairs leading down from the terrace of the Mihrimah Sultan Cami'i there is an elegant Baroque fountain, constructed in 1726 and dedicated to Ahmet III. Théophile Gautier described it thus: "Bordered all about in arabesques, foliage, and flowers, colorful Turkish inscriptions relief-carved in marble, surmounted by one of those charming, deeply overhung roofs, whose Top-Hané fountain modern *good taste* has seen fit to remove, a fountain graciously occupies the center of the little quay-like square to which the main street of Scutari leads."

The old *mektep*, or primary school, stands behind the mosque on such steeply rising ground that its supporting arches are revealed. The building is now used as a children's library. Passing the fountain and entering Hakimiyeti Milliye Caddesi – Üsküdar's busy main street, where on weekends a number of antique dealers set up shop in a small street bazaar– you come to a new supermarket housed in an old but recently restored hammam on the corner of Büyük Haman Sokağı. The sign identifies it as Sinan Hamam Çarşısı a bold attempt at claiming the baths as the work of Sinan, the great architect who worked for Süleyman the Magnificent. Although no sure evidence supports this attribution, the structure certainly dates from Sinan's era, which was the 16th century. Farther along on the same side of the street is the 15th-century Nişancı Kara Davut Paşa Cami'i, a religious building preceded by a forecourt and garden. Inside the mosque, the prayer hall is a long, narrow room divided into three sections by arches, with each section having a dome, a design that is unique in Istanbul.

YENI VALIDE CAMI'I

Across the street and opening into Hakimiyeti Milliye
Meydanı is the large mosque complex known as the Yeni
Valide Cami'i, or the "New Mosque of the Dowager Sultana,"
built between 1708 and 1710 for Ahmet III ● *39* and
dedicated to his mother, the Valide Sultan Gülnûş
Ümmetullah. At the corner is her open *türbe*, which looks like
a large aviary, and next to it a large *sebil*, or public fountain.
The mosque itself, whose plan adheres to the octagon-within-
a-square theme, is one of the last to be built in the classical
Ottoman style. The *mektep* of the *külliye* ● *79* is over the main
gate, and outside this gateway stands the *imaret* (public
kitchen), at one corner of which is a Baroque fountain added
at a later date ● *66*.

ŞEMSI PAŞA CAMI'I. Returning to the shore of the Bosphorus,
by Şemsipaşa Caddesi, west of Hakimiyeti
Millieye Meydanı, you come to the
Şemsi Ahmet Paşa Cami'i, which
Evilya Çelebi described as "a small
pearl of a mosque on the lip
of the sea." Sinan built it in
1580 for Şemsi Ahmet
Paşa, a famous
Vizier descended
from the dynasty
of Selçuks who
reigned over
Anatolia
before the
Ottomans
● *33*. The Şemsi Ahmet Paşa Cami'i
is sober in style, with a prayer hall crowned by a cupola
supported upon a pair of flanking conch vaults. The Vizier's
türbe is separated from the mosque by nothing more than a
green grille. The *medrese* takes up two sides of the forecourt,
leaving the fourth side to be formed by a wall with windows
opening directly upon the quay along the Bosphorus.

LEANDER'S TOWER

South of the quay is a fortified islet off the Asian shore at the
mouth of the Bosphorus. This is Kiz
Kulesı, or "Maiden's Tower," so named
after the legend of the sultan's daughter
who was locked in a tower to protect her
from a prophetess' prediction that she
would die from a snake bite. The bastion
is known in English as Leander's Tower.
According to the Byzantine chronicler
Nicetas Choniates, Manuel I Comnenus
was the first to fortify the islet, in the
mid-12th century, using it to anchor one
end of the great chain that was stretched across the
Bosphorus in time of siege. Since then the islet has been used
as the site of a lighthouse, a semaphore station, a quarantine
post, a customs control point, and now an inspection station
for the Turkish Navy. The present quaint structure dates from
the late 18th century.

LEANDER'S TOWER
The name comes
from the mistaken
belief that Leander
died at this point in
the strait during his
swim to join his love,
the priestess Hero.
Today the scene of
the tragic legend is
situated near Abydus
in the Dardanelles.
Its Turkish name, Kiz
Kulesı, was inspired
by another tale, albeit
one that is also
associated with all the
castles and towers
along the Anatolian
coast. According to
this popular myth, a
prophetess warned a
king that his
daughter, a princess
of great beauty, would
die of a snake bite.
The king immediately
had a small tower
erected far offshore
and there hid his
daughter in order to
save her from the
sinister prediction.
However, his enemies
sent the princess a
basket of fruit in
which a reptile had
been hidden, and the
child perished just as
it had been foretold.

267

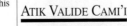

RUM MEHMET PAŞA CAMI'I

On the hill behind Şemsi Paşa Cami'i we see Rum Mehmet Paşa Cami'i, the oldest mosque in Üsküdar, dating from 1471. Perched on a hill behind the Şemsi Ahmet Paşa Cami'i, the mosque appears Byzantine on the exterior. The high cylindrical drum of the dome, the exterior cornice following the curve of the round-headed windows and the square base broken by the great dome arches suggest a Byzantine influence. This is perhaps connected with the fact that Mehmet Paşa was Greek (Rum means European, hence the name), a renegade, who, following the Conquest of 1453, became one of the viziers to Fatih Mehmet, serving between 1467 and 1470. In the interior, the prayer hall is vaulted by the usual central cupola, here borne upon smooth pendentives and one half-dome to the east, with side chambers that are completely cut off from the nave. Behind the mosque is Rum Mehmet Paşa's *türbe*.

AYAZMA CAMI'I

Leaving the mosque precinct by the back gate and following the winding Eşretsaat Sokağı outside, while keeping to the right, you come to a Baroque mosque of the same name. Built 1760–1 by Mustafa III and dedicated to his mother, the Ayazma Cami'i – "Mosque of the Sacred Fountain" –is one of the more successful of the Ottomans' Baroque mosques, particularly the exterior. A handsome entrance opens onto a courtyard from which a pretty flight of semi-circular steps leads up to the mosque porch. On the left is a large cistern, and beyond that an elaborate two-story colonnade providing access to the imperial loge. The upper structure is also decorated with little domes and turrets.

Numerous windows allow light into the interior, which, however, is of little interest beyond the gray-marble gallery supported by a colonnade running the length of the entrance wall.

ATIK VALIDE CAMI'I

The most important Ottoman monument in Üsküdar is the Atîk Valide Cami'i, which stands in a dominant position in the hills above the lower town. This great mosque complex was built by Sinan in 1583 for the Valide Sultan Nur Banu, wife of Selim II and mother of Murat III. This is the most splendid and extensive of all of Sinan's constructions in Istanbul with the sole exception of the Süleymaniye.

THE MOSQUE COURTYARD. You enter the precincts through an alley beside a graveyard and find one of the most beautiful of all the mosque *avlu* in the city, a grandly proportioned cloister with domed porticoes supported on marble columns. In the center the *şadırvan*, or ablution fountain, is shaded by ancient plane trees and cypresses. The mosque is entered by way of an elaborate double porch; the outer one has a penthouse roof, while the inner is domed and has attractive tiled inscriptions over the windows. The facade, above the windows, is sheathed in tiles decorated with calligraphic motifs.

THE MOSQUE. The prayer hall is a rectangular room with a central dome supported by a hexagonal arrangement of pillars and columns. The side aisles on the north and south are composed of domed bays. Along three sides of the nave run galleries, under which the wooden ceilings retain their rich painted decorations, all quite typical of the period: floral and arabesque designs in black, red, and gold. The mihrab is in a square, projecting apse entirely clad in the best Iznik tiles ▲ *292*. The window frames are also worthy of attention, made of deep-red marble mosaic, and their shutters are richly inlaid with mother-of-pearl. The mihrab and mimbar are pale, carved marble.

THE KÜLLIYE. The complex of the Atîk Valide Cami'i consists of a *medrese*, or college, a hospital, a hammam, and a public kitchen, which included several refectories meant for the *medrese*'s students and faculty, as well as patients in the hospital. Even today the kitchens serve meals to the poor of Üsküdar. All the buildings survive, most of them in a good state of preservation. The *medrese*, situated at a lower level than the mosque, is reached by a staircase in the western wall of the courtyard. The courtyard of the *medrese* is almost as pretty as that of the mosque itself. It is oddly irregular, having five domed bays to the south but only three to the north. The *dershane* is in the center of the west side in the axis of the mosque, though at an obtuse angle to it; the lecture hall projects over the street below, which passes under it through an archway. At the next corner beyond the *medrese* stands the huge hospital, which is also irregular in plan. The remaining buildings of the complex are today either part of a prison or in a poor state of repair.

The beaches of Sedef Odasi, famous for their relatively clear waters, are increasingly popular among those who love to swim in the sea. On the shore and around the central square modern construction has made some inroads but the government takes care not to sell land except at a prohibitive price. One can only hope that the islands will long remain like rare pearls, even while, not far away, the yalı along the Bosphorus are left to decay and collapse, just as the Beyoğlu quarter is violated by wide modern boulevards.

BÜYÜK ADA
The island of Büyük Ada is covered

with dwarf pines and has sandy beaches. Beautiful gardens surround the town, which is situated on the northern coast. The port is an excellent anchorage.

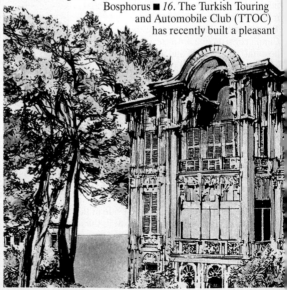

ÇINILI CAMI

The street east of Atîk Valide Cami'i leads, after about a mile, to the Çinili Cami – the "Tiled Mosque" – which is surrounded by a garden filled with flowers and trees. This small complex was built in 1640 for the Valide Sultan Kösem, wife of Ahmet I and the mother of the Sultans Murat IV and Ibrahim the Mad.

THE MOSQUE. Constructed by the architect Koca Kasım in 1640, the mosque is small and simple, just a square prayer

room vaulted by a circular dome. It takes its name from the Iznik tiles ▲ *292* that cover both the façade and the interior. Even if from a period later than the Iznik's golden age of craftmanship, the faiences – pale blue and turquoise on a white background – are quite superb. The conical roof of the mimbar is decorated with tiles of white marble picked out in gold, red, and green. The mosque's Baroque porch is a later

addition, as is the minaret. Here the *şerefe*, or balcony, from which the muezzin calls the faithful to prayer, has a corbel of folded-back acanthus leaves, apparently unique in Ottoman architecture. Within the precinct there is *şadırvan* with a huge witch's cap for a roof, as well as a tiny, triangular-shaped *medrese* sloping headlong downhill. Just outside the precinct stands the *mektep* of the *külliye*, and the hammam can be found a short way along the main street beyond the mosque.

THE GREAT MOUNTAIN OF PINES

A popular excursion from Üsküdar leads to Büyük Çamlıca – the "Great Mountain of Pines" – which is 875 feet above sea level, the highest point in the immediate vicinity of the Bosphorus ■ *16*. The Turkish Touring and Automobile Club (TTOC) has recently built a pleasant

> « THOSE CRYSTAL STREAMS OF PARADISE
> FLOW. THE NAME OF GOD REPEATING,
> THE NIGHTINGALES OF ISLAM THERE
> SING, THE NAME OF GOD REPEATING.» YUNUS EMRE

café and a teahouse on the summit, from which there are stunning views over the lower Bosphorus and the imperial city between the Golden Horn and the Sea of Marmara ● *274*. The scene clearly explains the phrase "city ringed about by a diadem of water," used by Procopius, the chronicler at the court of Justinian and Theodora, to describe the sight that greets those who journey to the hilltop.

THE PRINCES' ISLANDS

Ferries leave from both Eminönü and Üsküdar for the Princes' Islands (Adalar in Turkish), an archipelago off the Asian coast in the southwest of the Sea of Marmara some 20 miles from Istanbul. For those on a tight schedule, a more rapid service is available on motorboats that make frequent trips to and from the port of Kabataş. Arriving at the islands in summer, one cannot avoid being struck by the contrast

between the noisy bustle of a fashionable seaside resort and the surviving remains of a bygone era. The group consists of nine islands, four of them fairly large, listed here with their Greek names in brackets: Kınalı (Proti), Burgaz (Antigone), Heybeli (Chalki), and Büyük Ada (Prinkipo). In Byzantine times, Prinkipo, the largest and most populated island, gave its name to the entire group.

HISTORY. In the Byzantine era, the islands were also called Panadanisia, meaning the "Priests' Isles," because of the monasteries built there. Those on Kınalı Ada and Burgaz Ada are now in ruins, but Heybeli Ada has a monastery on every hilltop. Holy Trinity was founded in 850 and then rebuilt in 1844 by the Patriarch Germain IV, who transformed it into a seminary.

MOVING ABOUT ON THE ISLANDS
Carriages drawn by ponies or donkeys, and bicycles are the only means of transportation on the islands, where cars have been outlawed since 1928 except for ambulances and fire engines.

OTTOMAN HOUSES
The Princes' Islands have preserved several of the old wooden Ottoman houses, which require constant upkeep.

GARDENS
Large houses are surrounded by gardens flowering with magnolia, lilac, mimosa, honeysuckle, and jasmine. One can buy necklaces of jasmine from little street stalls. Under the boughs of pine trees grow arbutus, lentisks, myrtle, and rock roses, which fill the air with their scent in spring.

271

Panaghia Camariotissa, to the east, was founded in the 14th century by John V Palaeologus. In 1942, after being used as an orphanage for a long time, it became the Turkish Naval College. Another peculiarity of the Princes' Islands is the concentration, in a small area, of the country's entire ethnic and religious diversity. Greeks, Armenians, and Jews of Spanish origin – whose ancestors fled persecution by Queen Isabella the Catholic – all converge upon the islands once summer arrives. Princes' Islands take their name from one of the more sinister practices of the Byzantine Empire, for it was here that each new monarch relegated fallen patriarchs and princes plotting against him, the better to reinforce his accession to power. The prisoners, with their wives and children, were even blinded or otherwise mutilated to take away their will to return to Constantinople. The Turks also speak of the *kızıl adalar* – the "red islands" – because the nine small land masses were once famous for the wealth generated from the local copper mines, which made them vulnerable to repeated lootings, such as by Crusaders bound for the Holy Land, Genoese pirates, and all manner of sea rovers. However, only an informed visitor would discern the traces of this past, especially when distracted by the spectacle of the Belle Epoque relived before their very eyes.

THE YALI. Today, the Princes' Islands derive much of their charm from the old wooden houses, the numerous examples of which testify to the prosperity the islands in the 19th century. Fortunately, their façades are protected by law, and any renovation must be in keeping with the original plans. However, unless it is a recognized historic monument, a house can easily fall apart. But even now, the old yalı evoke the light-hearted, carefree

THE WOODEN PALACES OF BÜYÜK ADA
The former mansion of Izzet Paşa, chief of police under Abdül Hamit II (1876–1909), is one of the most beautiful yalı on Büyük Ada, located at 55 Çankı Caddesi. One of its celebrated guests was Leon Trotsky during the first years of his exile, from 1929 to 1933. Also well worth a visit is the palace of the papal nuncio outside the city. The future Pope John XXIII lived there during his long tenure as the pope's emissary to Greek and Islamic Turkey from 1933 to 1944.

spirit of the Belle Epoque.

THE ANADOLU CLUB.
Mustafa Kemal
Atatürk, the "father of
modern Turkey," took
over the Anadolu Club,
founded in the last
century at Büyük Ada by
the English, and made it a
resort for his cabinet as well
as for himself. Even today,
every Turkish deputy becomes
a lifetime member of this very
exclusive club, with its
luxurious salons and gaming
room – the only one on the island.

Its park is studded with statues of more or less antique
origin and below it has a private beach. The Hotel Splendid,
opposite, is also a place favored by the country's old ruling
élite and well-off, who appreciate the refined and somewhat
old-fashioned atmosphere of the paneled salon. However,
for all its propriety, the hotel can boast that Edward VIII
and Mrs. Simpson have stayed there.

THE MONASTERIES OF BÜYÜK ADA

A sanctum of orthodox Catholicism until the fall of
Byzantium, Büyük Ada continues to be very much the home
of monasteries. The Monastery of Jesus Christ, built in 1597,
stands among the pines on top of the Hill of Jesus. The
island's convent, which served as a place of retreat for several
Byzantine princesses, houses the tomb of
the Empress Eirene (1066–1123). The
Franciscan mission from Ancona and the
Eastern Orthodox rites observed in San
Pacifico, an ecumenical Christian church
where Armenians also worship, attract
regular attendance during the summer
months, even in this Islamic land.

THE MONASTERY OF AYOS YORGIOS. The
Monastery of St George on Ayios
Yorgios, constructed in the 10th century
high on the hill of the same name, still attracts many pilgrims.
The bushes along the road to the monastery are bedecked
with little strips of white cloth, symbols of the prayers
addressed to St George, who, according to the faithful, has
the power to make young people fall in love. The steep and
uneven path winds its way through the pine forest that grows
across some two-thirds of the island. On several occasions the
government has attempted to improve the surface of the path,
in order to encourage tourism, but just as often devotees of St
George remove the paving stones to preserve the penitential
way. Although the path is in almost constant use, it becomes
most crowded on April 23, the saint's feast day, when
thousands of pilgrims, of all persuasions, climb the hill to
attend the first mass at dawn. Afterwards most of them retire
to the terrace of a local restaurant to celebrate the day and
enjoy the local wine, which the monks of Ayios Yorgios have
been making for centuries.

WOODEN MANSIONS
These dwellings were
constructed in the
18th and 19th
centuries by the
merchants of
Istanbul. They usually
have two and
sometimes three
stories as well as fairly
large rooms and
salons. Balconies
extend from the
façades and look out
over the bay or the
nearby woods.

Motor yachts and
large sailing ships
worthy of the most
famous ports in the
Mediterranean are
anchored in deep
water. During
summer, little coastal
vessels make regular
trips between the large
island of Büyük Ada
and the most
inhabited of the
Princes' Islands:
Kınalı, Burgaz, and
Heybeli.

▲ THE BOSPHORUS

"Loud was the lightsome
tumult of the shore,
Oft music changed, but
never ceased her tone.
And timely echo'd back
the measured oar,
And rippling waters made
a pleasant moan."
Lord Byron

One day

BELGRADE FOREST

EĞRIKEMER

MECIDIYE CAMI'I

ÇIRAĞAN SARAYI

DOLMABAHÇE SARAYI

ALIBEY SUYU

KAĞITHANE SUYU

GALATA TOWER

GALATA KÖPRÜSÜ

ATATÜRK KÖPRÜSÜ

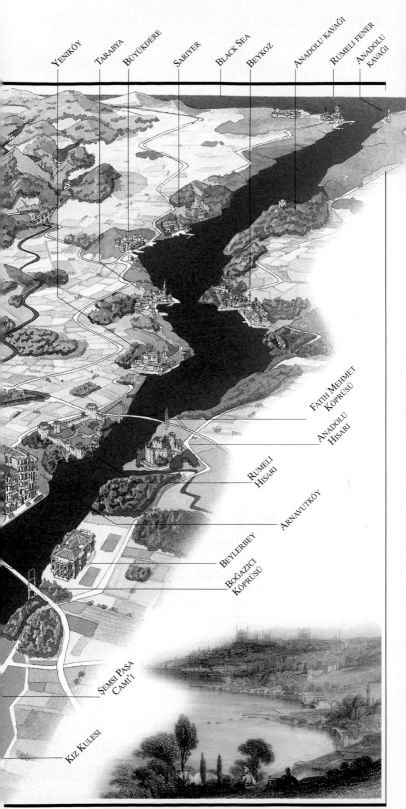

YENİKÖY

TARABYA

BÜYÜKDERE

SARIYER

BLACK SEA

BEYKOZ

ANADOLU KAVAĞI

RUMELİ FENER

ANADOLU KAVAĞI

FATİH MEHMET KÖPRÜSÜ

ANADOLU HİSARI

RUMELİ HİSARI

ARNAVUTKÖY

BEYLERBEY

BOĞAZICI KÖPRÜSÜ

ŞEMSİ PAŞA CAMİ'İ

KIZ KULESİ

THE EUROPEAN SHORE

EMINÖNÜ. Ferries sail from Eminönü for the villages along both shores of the Bosphorus, or Boğazıçı in Turkish, meaning "strait". The villages along the Bosphorus, some of which date back to the period of the ancient city of Byzantium, have in the past fifty years been, for the most part, amalgamated into the urban sprawl of Istanbul. Nevertheless, they still retain a village-like quality, particularly on the upper Bosphorus, where many of the men continue to earn their living as fishermen. Any description of the Bosphorus involves the names Rumeli and Anadolu, for these are used in referring to the opposing continental shores of the strait, the first to the European side and the second to the Anatolian or Asian side. The Bosphorus is usually serene, though even on the calmest of days one can feel its power as the mass of water surges between the continents. It is beautiful at any time, day or night and in all seasons, but particularly under a full moon, which rises out of the hills on the Asian side and casts a silver path across the strait to the European shore, a phenomenon that the Turks call *mehtap*. The first full moon in autumn usually marks the beginning of the season for the Bosphorus fishermen, for it is then that great schools of *lüfer*, a small bluefish, make their way down the strait. The fishermen use a rowboat called a *sandal*, derived from the Venetian word *sandalo*. Most of the vessels are now equipped with outboard motors, and they all have a bright lamp which is used to shine down into the water to attract the fish. As the Bosphorus ferry heads up along the European shore it passes the docks at Galata ▲ 252–6, after which can be seen a collection of monuments in Tophane, a village which surrounds the old marine arsenal of the same name.

DOLMABAHÇE SARAYI
Lamartine, during a visit to Istanbul in 1833, had this to say about Dolmabahçe: "It could be a palace of amphibians, for however slight the wind on the Bosphorus, it stirs up waves that sheet the windows and fling their foam into the ground-floor apartments. Even the steps leading into the palace tread water. Grillework gates open onto the sea from both the courtyard and the gardens. Here there are sheds for the caiques and baths for the sultans, who can swim in the sea sheltered by the slatted shutters of their salon."

DOLMABAHÇE CAMI'I. Designed by Nikoğos Balyan, grandson of Kirkor Balyan, the Dolmabahçe Mosque was completed in 1853. A year later, Nikoğos added the cut-stone clock tower to the north. The tower is 88 feet tall, making it one of the most prominent landmarks on the European shore of the lower Bosphorus.

DOLMABAHÇE SARAYI. The Dolmabahçe palace is by far the largest and grandest of the imperial Ottoman residences on the Bosphorus. In Byzantine times the site of Dolmabahçe, which means "filled-in garden," was an inlet on the strait. Fatih Mehmet II had the little harbor filled in and a garden laid out ● *50*. In 1842, Abdül Mecit decided to construct a huge new palace on the site, giving the task to the architect Karabet Balyan and his son Nikoğos, who completed the work in 1853. The main entrance to Dolmabahçe Sarayı is through the gardens at its southern end. The palace faces the Bosphorus, which reflects the entire length of its 814-feet gleaming white marble façade. The quay itself is about 650 yards long. Inside, the palace consists mainly of a great hall flanked by two main wings containing the state rooms and royal apartments, with the *selamık* on the south side and the harem on the north. The complex also includes quarters for the staff who lived in, bringing the total number of rooms to 285, among them 43 salons and 6 hammams.

In the 18th century, Princess Hatice had a summer palace built at Beşiktaş, from designs by the painter Melling.

BEŞIKTAŞ ISKELE. About 300 yards beyond Dolmabahçe Sarayı the ferry stops at the Beşiktaş Iskele. In the park behind this landing stands a statue of the famous Ottoman Admiral Hayrettin Paşa, known in the West as Barbarossa. The Admiral's *türbe*, or tomb, is opposite the sculpture.

DENIZ MÜZESI. South of the Beşiktaş Iskele we come to the Deniz Müzesi or Naval Museum. The most famous item in the collection is a chart of the Atlantic coast of North America drawn in the 16th century by Piri Reis, the great Ottoman navigator. The museum houses a collection of *pazar* caiques, the beautiful rowing barges that ferried the sultans to and from their palaces and yalı on the Bosphorus and the Golden Horn.

The white-marble seafront façade of Dolmabahçe is bordered by a 650-yard-long quay.

▲ THE DOLMABAHÇE PALACE

Cupola from the great
Muayede reception hall

The design of the Dolmabahçe
palace is an amalgamation of two
styles – half-occidental, half-oriental –
a singular and baroque mix of classical
orders with ornamentation evocative of the far off Indies. The
285 rooms and the 46 salons are in keeping with the overall mix
of styles. The extravagant decorations include mural paintings
by Russian and Italian artists, enormous candelabra in
Bohemian or Baccarat crystal, and the sumptuous furniture.

THE RED SALON
Divan and armchairs are
upholstered in red silk,
matching the drapes. On
the table is a red Bohemian
crystal chandelier.

**BACCARAT CRYSTAL
CHANDELIER AND
FURNITURE IN THE ROCOCO
STYLE**

**PALACE ENTRANCE
PORTAL, GARDEN
SIDE**
The entrance is
flanked by two curved
wings which give
access to the upper
level. The door is
framed with Greek
columns, and topped
by an extremely
ornate balustrade.

VASES FROM THE DOLMABAHÇE PALACE
Going through the rooms one notices numerous vases: Chinese vases, painted vases made in the Yıldız porcelain factory (left and center) and Sèvre vases (right).

THE GREAT STAIRS OF HONOR
The balusters that support the banister are made of crystal incrusted with gold. There are marble columns on both sides of the landing, which is lit by a large glass dome.

MAYBEN OR COURT ROOM The roof is enhanced with gilding and decorated with paintings of flowers. At the four corners hang pendant candelabra and consoles crowned with large mirrors.

A yalı in Yeniköy.

NAVIGATION ON THE BOSPHORUS
High-speed tankers on the Bosphorus constitute a major threat to the houses and palaces along the waterfront. During the last twenty years, a dozen "classified" yalı have been destroyed by such shipping. The powerful waves and wake they generate eventually damage both the quays and the foundations of the palatial old dwellings.

YENIKÖY
This is one of the Bosphorus villages least touched by urbanization. Here, many of the beautiful 19th-century Ottoman houses were influenced by Art Nouveau. The repair and maintenance of these seaside villas are demanding tasks, even when undertaken by specialists. The Greek Church of St George in Yeniköy shelters not only the tombs of three patriarchs but also an ancient icon of the Blessed Virgin.

ÇIRAĞAN SARAYI ● *84.* Some 550 yards beyond the Beşiktaş Iskele the ferry passes Çırağan Palace, recently rebuilt as a casino attached to the new Çırağan Hotel. Abdül Asiz commissioned the palace, which Sarkis Balyran designed and then completed in 1874. In 1910, Çırağan was destroyed by fire, which left only the smoke-blackened shell of the façade standing by the Bosphorus until the recent reconstruction of the building.

YILDIZ PARK ● *50.* A short distance beyond Çırağan Sarayı on the shore highway is the entrance to Yıldız Park, a place originally known as the "Gardens of Çırağan," after the various pavilions of Yıldız Sarayı. On the right of the entrance there is also a mosque built by the Sultan Abdül Mecit in 1848. A few yards beyond the entrance to the park, a steep but short lane leads up to the charming little complex of Yahya Efendi, who was one of Istanbul's most celebrated Muslim saints. He was born in Trebizond on the same day as Süleyman the Magnificent, also at Trebizond, and Yahya's mother even served as wet nurse to the future sultan. When Süleyman succeeded to the throne in 1520, Yahya Efendi accompanied him and became one of the most

renowned divines of his age. The little *külliye*, built by the great Sinan shortly before Yahya Efendi's death in 1570, is a popular shrine attracting a constant stream of pilgrims.

ORTAKÖY. The next ferry stop is Ortaköy, or the "Middle Village." In recent years Ortaköy has become an arts-and-crafts center. In addition to its many recently restored old houses, Ortaköy boasts an abundance of restaurants and cafés ◆ *378* around the ferry slip, where in summer craftsmen and secondhand booksellers set up their stalls. On the promontory beyond the *iskele* or landing is the charming Mecidiye Cami'i, a mosque built in 1854 for Abdül Mecit by Nikoğos Balyan. On either side of the main street, in what still remains a fishing village, stand three monuments that deserve notice: a synagogue built at the beginning of the 20th century; a 19th-century Greek Orthodox church; and a hammam ● *58* built in 1570 by Sinan for Hürsev Kethüda, head steward to the Grand Vizier Sokollu Mehmet Paşa.

> «AFTER DOLMABAHÇE THERE BEGINS
> AN UNBROKEN STRING OF PALACES, MANSIONS, AND GARDENS.
> ALL SLUMBER BESIDE THE SEA IN ORDER TO BREATH
> THE FRESHNESS OF THE AIR.» LAMARTINE

THE BOSPHORUS BRIDGE. Just beyond Ortaköy the ferry passes under Boğaziçi Köprüsü, the Bosphorus Bridge. Its graceful span arcs across to the hills south of the village of Beylerbey on the Asian shore. Opened on October 27, 1973, the Boğaziçi Köprüsü is the sixth longest suspension bridge in the world, measuring 3,524 feet from tower to tower and 210 feet above the water at its mid-point.

ARNAVUTKÖY. This "Albanian Village" has one of the most colorful landing stages on the Bosphorus, with a row of pretty yalı along the shore south of the *iskele*. The streets of the equally picturesque inner village are lined with old wooden houses festooned with vines, a scene straight out of Ottoman times.

BEBEK BAY. Rounding Akıntı Burnu, the ferry enters the calm waters of Bebek Bay, a very beautiful inlet on the Bosphorus. The hillside above still retains its original woods, mainly umbrella pines and tall cypresses ■ *26*. Just before reaching the *iskele*, the ferry passes the former Egyptian Embassy, a splendid example of Art Nouveau architecture constructed in 1912 by Raimondo d'Aronco. Situated just beyond the landing stage there is a charming little mosque which was built in 1913 by the Turkish architect Kemalettin Bey.

THE UNIVERSITY OF THE BOSPHORUS. A few hundred yards beyond the *iskele* the shore road passes the lower entrance to the Boğaziçi Universitesi. The university campus occupies a hilltop site between Bebek and Rumeli Hisarı, the next village to the north. This Turkish university was founded in 1971, taking over the buildings and grounds of the former ROBERT COLLEGE, which, during the 108 years of its existence, numbered among its faculty and graduates many important and influential figures, including several people who played leading roles in the cultural and political life of Turkey.

RUMELI HISARI AND ANADOLU HISARI. On either side of the strait there are two Ottoman fortresses, Rumeli Hisarı and Anadolu Hisarı – the Fortresses of Europe and Asia – both surrounded by charming old villages. After the Conquest in 1453 ● *34* the two fortresses were no longer of any military importance. Anadolu Hisarı gradually fell into ruins, but Rumeli Hisarı survived and was used to hold prisoners of war, as well as ambassadors from unfriendly powers. Since 1953 this "Fortress of Europe" has become a museum and is open to the public; on summer evenings it is also used for theatrical performances during the Istanbul Festival.

TARABYA
During the last two centuries of the Ottoman Empire, Tarabya was a favorite rendezvous of the Greek upper middle classes from the Fener and Pera quarters. They were attracted by the beauty of the place, and by the cultured and sophisticated society at the summer embassies of the European powers.

GUILLOTINE OR SASH WINDOWS IN THE TURKISH BAROQUE STYLE

The Sadberk Hanim Museum.

YILDIZ PARK
Here, both the Malta Köşkü, or Pavilion, and the Pembe Köşkü have been restored and transformed into elegant cafés.

THE FATIH MEHMET BRIDGE. The ferry now passes under the Sultan Mehmet Fatih Köprüsü, the new bridge over the Bosphorus. It is 33 feet longer than the bridge between Ortaköy and Beylerbey, and spans the strait between the hills above the two fortresses. Fatih Köprüsü opened in 1988, exactly 2,500 years after Mandrocles built his bridge of boats for Darius across this same stretch of the Bosphorus.

EMIRĞAN. The next village on the European shore is Emirğan. The village square is pleasantly shaded by plane trees and beneath them people gather to drink tea, which is particularly delicious because of the quality of the local water. Beside the square on its southern side is a Baroque mosque, constructed between 1781 to 1782 by Abdül Hamit I. Above the village are the famous tulip gardens of Emirğan, well worth a visit in spring. The Turkish Touring and Automobile Club has restored a number of Ottoman kiosks in the gardens, among them the Beyaz Köşk, or White Pavilion, which has been converted into a concert hall. The others now serve as cafés.

ISTINIYE. After Emirğan, still on the European side, is Istiniye, which has a deeply indented bay that up until 1990 contained a floating dock. Istiniye is still an active fishing port, and the local fishermen sell their daily catch at a colorful market along the quay.

YENIKÖY. The Byzantines called this village Neapolis – New Town – which is what the Turkish name means as well, despite the great antiquity of the village. There are more churches in Yeniköy than in any other village on the Bosphorus, three of them Greek Orthodox, one Armenian Catholic, and another Roman Catholic. Yeniköy is famous for its row of terraced houses by the water's edge. At the northern end of the village there is a stone-built mansion that was once used as the summer embassy of Austria-Hungary, and today is still Austria's summer consulate. Beyond that lies Kalender, a hamlet named after the order of mendicant dervishes who had a *tekke*, or monastery, there. A bit farther along is a huge wooden yalı ● 88 that serves as Germany's summer embassy .

Fishing port and trawler at Ortaköy.

At Arnavutköy, a number of bars, including the Café Siné, feature concerts by young musicians.

TARABYA. The next village on the European shore is Tarabya, long celebrated for the beauty of its crescent bay. During the 18th and 19th centuries, Tarabya was a favorite resort of prominent Greeks from the Fener, as well as the affluent of Pera. Originally named Therapia, meaning "cure," by the Greek Patriarch Atticus, the village now bears the Turkish version of the same name and for the same reason – the beneficial climate.

BÜYÜKDERE. The next ferry stop brings us to Büyükdere, which means "Great Valley." The Byzantines called the village Kalos Agros or "Beautiful Meadow." It was here that the knights of the First Crusade camped in 1096, before they crossed the Bosphorus on their long arduous march across Asia Minor to recover the Holy Land for Christianity.

THE SADBERK HANIM MUSEUM. In its splendidly restored yalı, this museum houses a rich collection of antiquities, ranging from the Bronze Age ● 28 up to the Greco-Roman era ● 30, along with Ottoman arts, crafts, and costumes, all beautifully displayed. The museum is dedicated to the memory of Sadberk Hanim, the late wife of Vehbi Koç, a leading Turkish industrialist.

KILYOS. Roads lead from both Büyükdere and Sariyer through the Belgrade Forest ◆ 356 to Kilyos, a fishing village on the Black Sea which has a sandy beach, hotels, pensione, and restaurants. The road from Büyükdere passes through one of the arches of Egrikemer, the "Bent Aqueduct" ● 76, built by Mahmut I and completed in 1732.

SARIYER. This is the largest village on the European shore of the upper Bosphorus, and the principal fishing port on the strait. The port and the fish market around it are delightful, particularly when the fishermen of Sariyer return after voyages that take them not only to the upper Bosphorus and the Black Sea but also to the Marmara, the Dardanelles ▲ 322, and the Aegean. Some of their catch is served in restaurants around the port, with tables set out on the quay in good weather.

RUMELI KAVAĞI. The last ferry stop on the European shore is Rumeli Kavağı. From there most ferries cross the strait to Anadolu Kavağı, the last *iskele* on the Asian side. There are numerous seafood restaurants all about the landings in both villages, which are popular places to have lunch during a journey along the Bosphorus.

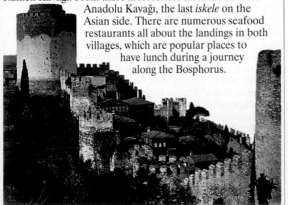

YALI AT BEBEK
Since the 18th century Bebek has been a residential village where rich Istanbuli built summer houses, such as the superb Yılanlı Yalı, now restored. Today, there is also an attractive marina.

THE VILLAGE OF RUMELI HISARI
Nestling in the green countryside, the houses of this little village rise in tiers on the hillside, with cobblestone lanes that descend towards the Bosphorus.

RUMELI HISARI
In 1452, Mehmet II prepared to besiege Constantinople by constructing a fortress at Rumeli Hisarı. It took less than four months to build, thanks to 3,000 laborers and master masons assigned to the task. Around the turn of the 20th century, wooden houses were built within the walls of the ruined fortress. They disappeared when the site was restored in 1953.

THE UPPER BOSPHORUS

The only way to explore the Bosphorus beyond the last ferry stop is by boat, for the shore roads do not extend much farther beyond the last two villages. An excursion by boat along the upper Bosphorus can be exhilarating, for both shores are wild, rugged, desolate and quite beautiful. At several places there are sandy beaches hidden away in secluded coves. Gray herons ■ 18 haunt the cliffs, black cormorants dive into the limpid water, flights of shearwaters, *kirlangiç* in Turkish, skim along the surface in mid-channel, and schools of dolphins can occasionally be seen in the strait, which is considered a good omen by sailors.

GARIPÇE. Three nautical miles beyond Rumeli Kavağı we pass a very craggy promontory on the European shore named Garipçe, meaning "strange," or "curious," probably because of its very contorted features. The Blue Rocks were also called Cyanean, or the Symplegades, and Gillius identified them as a striking feature at the mouth of the Bosphorus on the European side, 100 yards offshore at Rumeli Feneri.

RUMELI FENERI. Called the "Lighthouse of Europe," this huge rock still has the remains of a fort built in 1769 by a Greek military engineer in the Ottoman army. There was a similar fortress on the Asian side – a Byzantine toll station known as the "Lighthouse of Asia" – but this has not survived, probably worn away by the pounding waves of the Black Sea, which the Greeks called "Hospitable" only to placate it.

THE ASIAN SHORE

ANADOLU KAVAĞI. Travelling down the Asian shore of the Bosphorus you will come to the most prominent monument of the upper Bosphorus, a great fortress whose ruins are on the heights north of Anadolu Kavağı, a name which means "poplars of Anatolia." This fortified site is also commonly known as the "Genoese Castle," even though it was probably built by the Byzantines as a toll gate and merely taken over by the city-state of Genoa in the 14th century. The loss of revenue from the collection of tolls, on both sides of the strait, may well have been a contributing factor in the decline of the Byzantine Empire. The fortress encloses an area twice as great as that of Rumeli Hisarı, and though mainly a ruin, it is still impressive. It is from here that the ferry begins its return journey back down the Bosphorus.

THE HILL OF JOSHUA. Opposite Sariyer we pass the Yuşa Tepesi – Hill of Joshua – the second highest peak on the Bosphorus, reaching a height of 660 feet above sea level. On the summit is a shrine to a Muslim saint named Yuşa Baba, whose grave, marked by green pillars at the head and feet, is 40 feet long. His tomb, which Europeans call the "Giant's Grave," was known in antiquity as the "Bed of Hercules."

AN AERIAL VIEW OF RUMELI KAVAĞI AND ITS MOSQUE

The balconies which extended from the façades of old Turkish houses were held up by wrought-iron corbels or brackets.

> « THE CHANNEL, ALONG ITS ENTIRE LENGTH . . . LOOKS
> THE SAME AT EVERY POINT; IT IS BORDERED BY PALACES,
> KIOSKS, COUNTRY HOUSES, AND VILLAGES. »
>
> CASTELLAN

SELVI BURNU. Opposite Büyükdere is a long shallow bay with a rugged and forbidding shoreline. At Selvi Burnu – "Poplar Point" – the coast turns east to the valley of Tokat Deresi. It was here Fatih built a villa, as did Süleyman. Gillius described the place as a "royal villa shaded by woods of various trees, especially planes," before going on to mention the landing stairs, "by which the King, crossing the shallow shore of the sea, disembarks into his gardens," hence the modern name of the site, Hünkar Iskelesi, or the "Emperor's Landing Place." The present little palace ● 84 was built in the mid-19th century for Abdül Mecit by Sarkis Balyan, a brother of Nikoğos Balyan. It is still shaded by a lovely grove of plane trees, but it is now used as a hospital.

BEYKOZ. The ferry stops at Beykoz, the largest fishing village on the Asian shore of the Bosphorus above Üsküdar. At weekends during the summer its seafood restaurants and small cafés are packed with visitors from the city. The principal monument in Beykoz is a beautiful street fountain ● 66 in the village square. Ishak Ağa, a customs inspector, had it designed and installed in 1746.

ŞILE AND INCIR KÖYÜ. A road leads from Beykoz to the picturesque village of Şile on the Black Sea, where there is a splendid sandy beach, with hotels and restaurants. Since antiquity the women of this village have woven a particularly light and silken cotton called *şile bezi*. Much of the cloth is exported. The French-built lighthouse just east of the village is now a registered historic monument. The Kumbaba Motel, which is on the beach east of Şile, occupies the site of ancient Calpe, a number of ruins of which have been uncovered by archeologists. South of Beykoz at Incir Köyü, or "Figtree Village," is the charming valley of Sultaniye Deresi, where Beyazıt II had extensive gardens laid out.

PAŞABAHÇE. A little farther on is Paşabahçe – the Paşa's Garden ● 50 – so called because of the palace and garden established here by Hezarpara Ahmet Paşa, who was grand vizier under Murat IV. Its renowned glass works produce the finest

A WALK THROUGH THE LAST CENTURY
During the summer, the wooded hillsides of the Bosphorus were beautifully fresh and cool. They became a favorite resort for young women, who arrived from the city in carriages. For their picnics, they wore light yaşmaks and muslin veils, showing only their eyes.

THE BAY AT BEYKOZ
Beykoz is an important village in the former Bay of Amycos. In this view we can see the beautiful yalı of Mehmet Ali Paşa, viceroy of Egypt. The valley beyond Beykoz is one of the most beautiful on the Bosphorus.

285

THE BOSPHORUS AT PAŞABAHÇE
In this watercolor, by Hoca Ali Riza, from the beginning of this century, the wooden yalı is painted in a traditional color – rose-red. Yet nothing could be more modern than the numerous bay windows, all large enough to permit the rooms within to be viewed from the garden. The garden surrounding the yalı is planted with pines, plane trees, and climbers, such as wisteria and sweetly fragrant honeysuckle.

glassware in Turkey. Paşabahçe also has a large *rakı* factory with a cascading fountain not of fresh water but of *rakı*, a Turkish alcoholic drink derived from aniseed.

ÇUBUKLU. The ferry stops next at Çubuklu, which means "with a cane" (in Turkish *çubuk*). Evliya Çelebi, writing in the mid-16th century, tells an amusing story about it: "Beyazıt II, having brought his son Selim, the future Selim I, from Trebizond to Constantinople, gave him in this place, in a fit of anger, eight strokes with a cane, which eight strokes were

prophetic of the years of his reign. At the same time, he said to him, 'Boy, don't be angry, these eight strokes shall fructify during the eight years of your reign.' Selim stuck the dry cane into the ground, praying to heaven that it might strike root and bear fruit. The Şeyh Kara Beyazıt and Beyazıt himself said, 'Amen,' after which the cane began to grow and even now bears cornels, five of which weigh a drachma." On a hilltop between Çubuklu and Kanlıca, the next village along the Bosphorus is the former palace of the Khedives, the viceroys of Egypt. Its distinctive tower makes it one of the most distinctive landmarks on this stretch of the strait. It was built in c. 1900 by Abbas Hilmi Paşa, the last Khedive. The western façade, overlooking the Bosphorus, is semi-circular, with a marble-columned porch and a semi-circular hall within. The upper floor, especially the tower room and a loggia on the roof, commands some of the finest views of the Bosphorus. The Turkish Touring and Automobile Club has recently restored and redecorated the palace to its original Art Nouveau splendor. The structure now serves as a deluxe hotel and restaurant ◆ *377*.

KANLICA. The village of Kanlıca has long been famous for its delicious yogurt, which is served in restaurants around the *iskele* and the little square behind it. The mosque at the rear of the square was built by Sinan between 1559 and 1560 for İskender Paşa, a grand vizier under Süleyman the Magnificent. The mosque is of the simplest type, with a wooden porch and a prayer room covered by a flat ceiling.

Yalı of Sefik Bey at Kanıca.

AMCAZADE HÜSEYİN PAŞA KÖPRÜLÜ YALI. Between Kanlıca and Anadolu Hisarı, the next ferry stop, we pass once again under Fatih Köprüsü, the bridge spanning the upper Bosphorus. Just along here, on the Asian shore, you can see the oldest of all the surviving yalı on the Bosphorus, a rose-red wooden ruin suspended over the water on rotting stilts and corbels. The yalı, which is being restored, was

Yalı of Rutiye Sultan.

built in 1698 by Amcazade Hüseyin Paşa Köprülü, grand

vizier to Mustafa II. The Peace of Carlowitz was signed here on January 26, 1699, which concluded one of the several wars between Tsarist Russia and the Ottoman Empire.

THE FORTRESS OF ASIA. The old fortress of Anadolu Hisarı lies just downstream from the *iskele* of the same name. Beyazıt I had the site fortified in 1394 as a base from which to keep Constantinople under siege. This lasted until 1402, when Tamerlane defeated the Turks at the Battle of Ankara, thereby granting the Byzantines a reprieve until 1453. A relatively small fortress, Anadolu Hisarı comprises a donjon or keep encircled by stout walls with barbican outworks, now partly demolished, and three bastions. According to the French scholar Gabriel, only the keep and its walls date from the reign of Beyazıt I. The barbican wall and the three bastions would have been added by Fatih Mehmet ● *34* when he built the fortress of Rumeli Hisarı on the opposite shore, in order to control the Bosphorus and thus strangle Constantinople. The village itself is very picturesque, with old wooden houses clustered around the castle on its promontory, where the Bosphorus is joined by a little river known as Göksu – the "Heavenly Stream".

THE PALACE OF KÜÇÜKSU. This pretty little rococo building ● *84* on the Bosphorus was built for Abdül Mecit 1856–7 by Nikoğos Balyan. The sultans used the palace as a pied-à-terre when they visited the Sweet Waters of Asia. Later, under the Turkish Republic, it was used as a presidential residence and also as a guest house for visiting dignitaries. Restored in the 1970's, it is now a museum. Beside the palace to its south stands the Küçüksu Çesmesi, an exceptionally beautiful Baroque fountain, built for Selim III in 1806. A 32-line calligraphic chronogram inscribed on the fountain gives the Sultan's name and the date of construction. The text is by the poet Hatif, who refers to the *çeşme* as a "soul-caressing fountain . . . a fragile beauty in the meadow."

The Ostrorog yalı at Küçüksu.

THE LITTLE PALACE OF KÜÇÜKSU
The palace's marble façade is reflected in the waters of the strait. The beautifully maintained garden around the palace is planted with rare trees, magnolias, and pines. The terraces behind the residence spread over the side of the hill.

The yalı of Sadullah Paşa.

THE YALI OF KÜÇÜKSU. South of the *iskele* at Küçüksu are two of the oldest of the surviving yalı on the Bosphorus. The one next to the beach at Küçüksu is the Kıbrıslı (or Cypriot) Mustafa Emin Paşa Yalısı, built originally c. 1760 but expanded and redecorated later on. It is still inhabited by the descendants of Mustafa Emin Paşa. A little further downstream we see the Ostrorog Yalısı, a very handsome wooden mansion painted rust-red. This dates from c. 1790, when it became the residence of the Counts Ostrorog, Polish aristocrats ennobled by the King of France, who enlisted in the Ottoman service in the late 18th century.

KANDILLI. The ferry stops next at Kandilli, adjacent to the promontory opposite Bebek Bay. The waters at Kandilli are known as the Devil's Current, the strongest on the Asian side of the strait, with a speed of over 5 knots when the prevailing wind blows from the north. The deepest point in the Bosphorus is some 300 yards off the Kandilli promontory, where the water reaches a depth of 360 feet.

VANIKÖY. Next is Vaniköy, opposite Arnavutköy. On the hilltop above this village we see the tower and telescope dome of the Istanbul Rasatname, a meteorological station and astronomical observatory. The Rasatname preserves the instruments used by the great mid-16th-century Turkish astronomer Takiuddin.

THE KULELI NAVAL STATION. The ferry continues on to Çengelköy, some 1,600 yards down the strait. About halfway between Vaniköy and Çengelköy we pass the Kuleli Military College, a large building flanked by cone-capped towers. The original training school and barracks were built in c. 1800 by Selim III, as part of his attempted reform of the Ottoman armed forces. The present structure dates from 1860 when an extensive rebuilding program, ordered by Abdül Mecit, was completed. The original building was used as a military hospital from 1855 to 1856, during the Crimean War. This was one of two hospitals in Istanbul directed by Florence Nightingale, the other being in the much larger Selimiye Barracks in Üsküdar.

ÇENGELKÖY. According to Evliya Çelebi, the name of this village, which means "Village of Hooks," probably came from the ships' anchors discovered there after the Conquest. Despite the rather sinister tag, the village is a pretty one, with a number of waterfront restaurants offering a view of the Bosphorus and the skyline of old Istanbul. Downstream from the *iskele* we see the Sadullah Paşa Yalısı, a handsome seaside mansion dating from c. 1790.

BEYLERBEY. The next ferry stop is at Beylerbey, where, near the port, we see the Imperial Beylerbey Cami'i ● *84*. An inscription gives the date of construction as 1778 and the architect as Mehmet Tahir Ağa. The mosque is an attractive example of the Ottoman Baroque, with a dome sectioned by its prominent structural ribs into an octagon, a mihrab set into a deep apse, and a profusion of decorative tiles dating from the 16th to the 18th century. The mimbar and the *Kuran kürsü* (the lectern for reading the Koran) are particularly fine, elegantly fashioned of ivory-inlaid wood.

BEYLERBEY PALACE. Beyond the village we come to Beylerbey Sarayı, the far end of which is almost underneath the Bosphorus Bridge. The name of the village and the palace – Beylerbey – means provincial governor, in memory of Mehmet Paşa, who administered Rumeli in the reign of Murat III. Mehmet Paşa built a *konak* (mansion) here in the last quarter of the 16th century. Sarkis Balyan constructed the present sarayı between 1861 and 1865 for Abdül Aziz. For the exterior the architect adopted European neo-classicism, but left the interior to be completed in the traditional Ottoman manner.

KUZGUNCUK. Passing under the lower Bosphorus bridge, the ferry then stops at Kuzguncuk, a lovely village that has retained its character despite the proximity of a rapidly expanding Üsküdar. The next call is at Üsküdar, after which the ferry crosses the strait to the terminus on the shore of Eminönü on the Golden Horn, which was the start of this journey along the Bosphorus.

THE PALACE OF BEYLERBEY
This palace was used both as a summer lodge and as a residence for visiting royalty, the first of whom was the Empress Eugénie of France. The anti-reformist and overthrown Abdül Hamit II was confined at Beylerbey after his return from exile in Thessalonica, and he died here in 1918. The palace was splendidly restored in the 1970's and converted into a museum.

THE VILLAGE AND BAY OF BEYLERBEY
Here, as in all the Bosphorus villages, the most agreeable place is the quay at the port where both fishermen and tourists find shade and comfort at the little bowered cafés.

NORTHWEST TURKEY

🚶 Half a day

THE RAMPARTS
Even though partially ruined, Iznik's ancient defense walls remain an imposing presence, surrounding almost the whole of the city. An earlier wall, Hellenistic in origin, was replaced by the Emperor Gallienus following the sack of the town by the Goths in 256. Claudius II Gothicus completed the project in 268–9, which is known from inscriptions still visible on the Yenişehir and Lefke Gates. Other inscriptions cite major programs of reconstruction

IZNIK LAKE

ROMAN AMPHITHEATER

ISTANBUL KAPIS

carried out during the reign of Michael III in 858, after one of the many earthquakes that periodically devastated Nicaea. The last restoration came during the reign of John III Vatatzes (1222–54), who added an outer fortification and increased the height of the inner walls and their towers.

HISTORY

The walls enclosing Nicaea were constructed during the Hellenistic era, at the time of the wars that broke out following the death of Alexander the Great in 323 BC. Despite the fortifications, the first city, Antigonia, fell in c. 300 BC to Lysimachus, who renamed it Nicaea in memory of his first wife. The city served as the capital of the kingdom of Nicomedia and then of Bithynia from the 3rd century to the 1st century BC. Still later, Pompey made Nicaea the capital of the Roman province of Bithynium, and it would play a similar role during the Byzantine Empire. Diocletian resided there for a while, as did both Constantine the Great and Justinian. In the Middle Ages,

MURAT I HAMAMI   YENIŞEHIR KAPISI   HAGHIA SOPHIA   HACI ÖZBEK CAMI'I   IZNIK MUSEUM   CHURCH OF KOIMOISIS   YEŞIL CAMI   LEFKE KAPISI

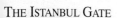

Atatürk Caddesi

Caddesi

Nicaea was conquered in turn by Goths, Arabs, Persians, Selçuks, Crusaders, Byzantines, Ottomans, Mongols, and again by Ottomans in 1331. After this last conquest, Nicaea entered a new era altogether, a period named after the Sultan Orhan Gazi. From the 15th to the 17th century, the city enjoyed great fame for the magnificent faience tiles produced by its workshops.

THE ISTANBUL GATE

You enter the town through an opening in the walls beside the Istanbul Kapısı, one of the four main gateways in the defense system. Like the other entranceways, this is a double gate because the city was surrounded by two concentric walls, each guarded by more than a hundred towers. Between the two gates there is a triumphal arch, constructed to commemorate

AN OTTOMAN CARAVANSERAI IN THE 17TH CENTURY The dining room reserved for travelers opened onto the central courtyard.

293

a visit by the Emperor Hadrian in AD 123. The lintels of the innermost gate are surmounted by ancient theatrical masks, taken from Nicaea's Roman theater. A little farther along, on the left, is the hammam built for Murat I (1359–89), which makes it one of the oldest of all the surviving Ottoman baths.

THE FORMER BASILICA OF HAGHIA SOPHIA

AYASOFYA
4. YÜZYILDA İNŞA EDİLMİŞ BİR BAZILİKADIR. M.S. 787. YILINDA II. İZNIK KONSÜLÜ BURADA TOPLANMIŞTIR. 1331 YILINDA CAMİ OLARAK AÇILMIŞTIR.

IT IS A KIND OF BASILICA WHICH WAS BUILT IN THE 4th CENTURY. THE SECOND IZNIK'S COUNSIL MET HERE IN 787 AD. IT WAS OPENED AS A MOSQUE IN 1331.

In the town center, at the southeast corner of the intersection where Atatürk Caddesi and Kiliçaslan Caddesi meet, are the ruins of the ancient Basilica of Haghia Sophia, Iznik's most important Byzantine monument ● 74 after its great ramparts. Converted into a mosque by Orhan Gazi in 1331, the building suffered extensive damage during the 15th and 16th centuries. It was probably restored by the great architect Sinan ● 314, but was subsequently allowed to disintegrate slowly over the centuries. Parts of the structure, principally the apse, the pair of domed side chapels flanking it, and the lateral walls, have since been renovated. A glass covering protects the nave's mosaic pavement. All that survives of the frescoes is a Deisis under an arch on the north side of the nave. In the apse, there is a *synanthron*, a semicircular tier of seats for the clergy.

HACI ÖZBEK CAMI'I

YEŞIL CAMI
The entrance to the Green Mosque is through a three-bay porch. The small, ribbed dome over the central bay porch is supported by an octagonal drum resting upon a band of Turkish triangles. The prayer hall, capped by a large cupola, is preceded by an antechamber, a sort of narthex with three bays whose arches spring from two massive columns. The principal dome, measuring 36 feet in diameter, and which at its crown is 57 feet above the floor, rests upon a circle of Turkish triangles very similar to those in the Hacı Ozbek Cami'i. The brick minaret is clad in a geometric pattern of red, black, and, most of all, blue-green tiles.

Iznik's most important Ottoman monuments are situated in the eastern part of the city, which you can reach by walking along Kılıçaslan Caddesi in the direction of the Lefke Kapı. After some 380 yards you come to Hacı Özbek Cami'i, which was constructed in 1333 and so is the oldest Ottoman mosque in existence. The brick dome is covered with terra-cotta tiles curved to fit the spherical surface, a typical feature of early Ottoman mosques. The Hacı Özbek Cami'i is unusual in that it is too small to have a minaret. The original three-bay porch was removed when the road was widened in 1959. The vestibule that replaced it mars the external appearance of the structure. Fortunately, the interior has scarcely been altered, save for the galleries and a few minor renovations made in 1959. Hacı Özbek Cami'i is a single-unit type of mosque, with a 25-feet square room, covered by a hemispherical dome which is supported on a belt of Turkish triangles.

THE GREEN MOSQUE ★

Farther still, on the left in Müze Sokağı, is the Yeşil Cami – the Green Mosque, so called for the color of the glazed brick that originally sheathed the minaret. This revetment has subsequently been replaced by tiles of a much inferior quality from Kütaya, the capital of Phrygia. Commissioned by the Grand Vizier Çandarlı Kara Halil Hayrettin Paşa, the Green Mosque was built between 1378 and 1392 by Hacı ben Musa.

THE IZNIK MUSEUM
The *imaret* of Nilüfer Hatun now houses the Iznik Museum, whose archeological and ethnographical collections include objects from the Hellenistic, Roman, Byzantine, Selçuk, and Ottoman periods. One section of particular interest is devoted to the famous Iznik kilns, which have recently been excavated.

THE IMARET OF NILÜFER HATUN

Continuing along Müze Sokağı, you arrive at the *imaret* of Nilüfer Hatun, built in 1388 by Murat I, who dedicated it to his mother Nilüfer Hatun, wife of Orhan Gazi. The *imaret* is constructed of stone courses alternating with four courses of brick. Square tiles cover both vaults and domes. The building is fronted by a five-bay porch open at either end and topped by a small cupola over the central bay. A large dome resting on a band of Turkish triangles crowns the main room within. On either side there are large shallow-domed rooms, each with a generous *ocak*, or hearth, which could be used as a kitchen or a dormitory. Before the principal room another chamber of comparable size, divided into two lateral sections by a great arch, served as a small mosque.

THE LEFKE KAPISI. This gate has a triumphal arch between its inner and outer gates, also constructed to mark Hadrian's visit in 123. Two panels of ancient reliefs have been built into the façade of the outer gate. They show Roman centurions in battle against tribesmen, perhaps the Goths who were defeated by Claudius II Gothicus.

A small ceramic lamp (Iznik Museum).

THE CHURCH OF THE KOIMOISIS

Returning along Kılıçaslan Caddesi, you will see the ruins of a Byzantine church at the end of the fourth block of houses on the right. This is the Koimoisis, or Assumption of the Virgin, dating from the 7th or 8th century. Unfortunately only a few sections of wall and a bit of the mosaic pavement survive. The church served as an imperial chapel for the first Byzantine Emperor from Nicaea, Theodore I Lascaris, who was buried here in 1222. The chapel was damaged during the Greco-Turkish wars of 1913.

A GREEK SARCOPHAGUS IN THE IZNIK MUSEUM

THE AYAZMA

East of the Koimoisis we come to the remnants of a sacred Byzantine fountain or spring – an *ayazma* – which may have been the baptistery for the

295

▲ Iznik

From the 15th to the 17th century, Iznik faience became well known and was used to decorate palaces, mosques, tombs, and other sumptuous buildings of the Ottoman Empire. The tiles made in the city of Iznik constituted a major

contribution to Islamic art during the Golden Age of Ottoman culture. The Iznik workshops reached the peak of their craftsmanship towards the end of the 16th century, a period in which the great architect Sinan used their products for the embellishment of all his important buildings. After 1620, the quality of the faience went into rapid decline, and the ceramicists seem to have lost their skill. The kilns were kept in operation until the middle of the 18th century, but they would never again match their past achievements.

imperial chapel. One of the stones still bears a low relief depicting the Jewish *menorah*, the eight-branched candelabrum used in Jewish worship, together with an inscription in Hebrew, which suggests that an ancient synagogue once stood in the vicinity. Certainly, Nicaea had a substantial Jewish community during the late Roman and early Byzantine eras.

THE ROMAN AMPHITHEATER

Some distance farther along Yakup Sokağı, cross Atatürk Caddesi and continue for another 300 yards or so, until you come to Nicaea's Roman amphitheater. The excavations now under way have revealed parts of the stage building and its side exits, as well as the proscenium, orchestra, *cavea*, and *diazoma*. It seems that, in its heyday, this vast theater could accommodate around 15,000 spectators. The remains of a 13th-century Byzantine church and a large burial ground have also been found above the *cavea*. The excavation of the stage area revealed many ancient architectural and sculptural remains, including a relief depicting Roman charioteers in action. Archeologists have also uncovered on the site large quantities of pottery from the Roman, Byzantine, Selçuk, and Ottoman periods. The theater was commissioned by Pliny the Younger during his tenure as the Roman governor of Bithynium from AD 111 to 113.

IZNIK LAKE

Kılıçaslan Caddesi leads westward, all the way to the Göl Kapı – the "Lake Gate" – which opens on to the waterfront, lined with restaurants and attractive picnic sites. Indeed, there could not be a more agreeable place in which to conclude a visit to Iznik, since there is a magnificent view from here of the Bithynian countryside that surrounds the lake as well as the massive ramparts, which are a reminder of the old and once-powerful city of Nicaea.

▲ BURSA

MURAT I CAMI'I   ESKI KAPLICA   MURADIYE   SURVIVING RAMPARTS   ULU CAMI

✻ One day

**BURSA,
THE TURKISH CITY**
Until the beginning of
the 15th century
Bursa was the capital
of the Ottoman
Empire ● *36*, which
was then expanding
rapidly. When the
central government
moved to Edirne,
Bursa continued to
hold pride of place

as the former capital
and the burial site
of Osman Gazi and
the first five sultans.
Their imperial
mosques, mausoleums, and
religious foundations
continue to adorn the
venerable city, which
the Turks call Yeşil
Bursa – "Bursa the
Green."

HISTORY

Bursa, or *Prusa* in Greek, was founded by Prusias I in 183 BC.
The letters of Pliny the Elder confirm that the city was a
prosperous one with a number of impressive public buildings.
Its most prominent feature was the citadel, and remnants of
its defensive walls can be seen on the acropolis, which the
Turks call Hisar. Otherwise, nothing remains of ancient Prusa
apart from a few exhibits in the Archeological Museum. All
evidence of the Greek city disappeared after it was captured
in 1326 by Orhan Gazi ● *36*, the first
sultan of the Ottoman Turks, and the
son and successor of Osman Gazi, the
eponymous founder of the imperial
Osmanli line.

THE OLD MARKET QUARTER

ULU CAMI. At the center of Bursa, in
Cumhuriyet Meydanı, take Atatürk
Caddesi, which leads westward towards
Ulu Cami (the "Great Mosque"). The mosque is situated in
the old market quarter at the base of the citadel hill. Ulu
Cami was built between 1396 and 1399 by Beyazıt I
(1389–1403), known to the Turks as Yıldırım, "Lightning,"
because of the speed with which he moved his armies back
and forth between campaigns in Europe and Asia. The Sultan
financed the construction of Bursa's Ulu Cami with the loot
from his victory at the Battle of Nicopolis on September 24,
1396. It is the most ambitious of all the great mosques
constructed in Anatolia during the two centuries prior to the
Turkish Conquest of Constantinople. The exterior of Ulu

298

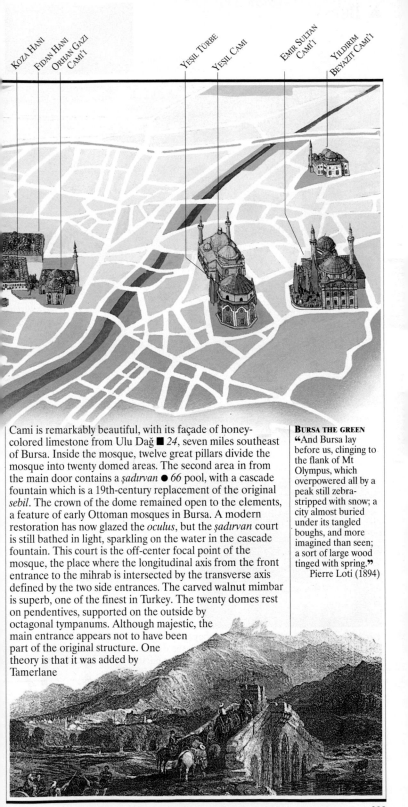

KOZA HANI | FIDAN HANI | ORHAN GAZI CAMI'I — YEŞIL TÜRBE | YEŞIL CAMI — EMIR SULTAN CAMI'I | YILDIRIM BEYAZIT CAMI'I

Cami is remarkably beautiful, with its façade of honey-colored limestone from Ulu Dağ ■ *24*, seven miles southeast of Bursa. Inside the mosque, twelve great pillars divide the mosque into twenty domed areas. The second area in from the main door contains a *şadırvan* ● *66* pool, with a cascade fountain which is a 19th-century replacement of the original *sebil*. The crown of the dome remained open to the elements, a feature of early Ottoman mosques in Bursa. A modern restoration has now glazed the *oculus*, but the *şadırvan* court is still bathed in light, sparkling on the water in the cascade fountain. This court is the off-center focal point of the mosque, the place where the longitudinal axis from the front entrance to the mihrab is intersected by the transverse axis defined by the two side entrances. The carved walnut mimbar is superb, one of the finest in Turkey. The twenty domes rest on pendentives, supported on the outside by octagonal tympanums. Although majestic, the main entrance appears not to have been part of the original structure. One theory is that it was added by Tamerlane

BURSA THE GREEN
"And Bursa lay before us, clinging to the flank of Mt Olympus, which overpowered all by a peak still zebra-striped with snow; a city almost buried under its tangled boughs, and more imagined than seen; a sort of large wood tinged with spring."
  Pierre Loti (1894)

A view of Bursa
from the hillside.

BASHIBAZOUKS
Part-time soldiers, or
Ziebek, near Bursa in
the 19th century.

THE BAZAAR In
Bursa, as in Istanbul,
the heart of the
covered market is the
bedestan, formerly
reserved for valuable
merchandise. It was
rebuilt during the
reign of Beyazıt I.
North of the *bedestan*
is the horse bazaar,
an open market built
in Mehmet I's reign.

Above, an aerial view
of the Ulu Cami.

during his occupation of Bursa from 1402 to 1403.

ORHAN GAZI CAMI'I. Retrace your steps a short distance back
along Atatürk Caddesi, and you come to the oldest of Bursa's
imperial mosques, the Orhan Gazi Cami'i built in 1339. It
has twice been destroyed, first by the Karamanid Türkoman
tribe in the interregnum that followed
the battle of Ankara in 1402, and then by
an earthquake in 1855; it was repaired
after both catastrophes, presumably with
some changes in structure. The essential
plan of the mosque is the same as the
original, which was the first example of a
mosque formed like an upside-down "T".
The five-bay porch is supported on the
façade by six pillars, with a slender
column separating the two arches at
either end; the three central bays are
domed and those at the ends cross-
vaulted and flat-topped. You pass through a domed
antechamber to reach the central hall, a rectangle with a
deep arch on the north that creates a
square base on the upper level for the
hemispherical dome. In the south, the
main prayer hall is raised up on three
steps from the central chamber.
Because the design is rectangular
at both lower and upper levels,
the dome is ellipsoidal rather
than spherical, with a niche in
its southern wall containing
the mihrab. The central space is
flanked by two other rectangular

«A SIMPLE ROUND ORIFICE, FROM DEEP WITHIN THE CHILL POOL, BROUGHT FORTH A SURGE OF QUIVERING WATER, THE SILENT BIRTH OF A SPRING INTO WHICH I LONG PEERED. . . .»

ANDRÉ GIDE

rooms, with back-to-back arches on the north and south forming a square base at a higher level for the hemispherical domes. The height of the domes over the central hall and the three rooms varies, as does the system of transition from the square base to the circular or elliptical cornice. On the exterior, however, all the cupolas rest upon octagonal drums.

THE COVERED MARKET. The principal market of Bursa lies behind the two mosques. The entire area was gutted by fire in 1955, but since then most of the quarter has been restored to its original appearance. Something of the former oriental atmosphere has unfortunately been lost in the process of restoration, but one is still able to experience the sense of what it must have been like in an old Ottoman market town.

THE CARAVANSERAI. Within the market complex are four caravanserai and two hammams. The Koza, or "Silk Cocoon," Hanı was built in 1490 by Beyazıt II to accommodate the silk trade, a function it still performs. At the center of its porticoed courtyard is an octagonal şadırvan surmounted by a *mescit* (a small mosque), a feature derived from the imperial Selçuk caravanserai of the 13th century. The two baths are the Sengul Hammam and the Bey Hamamı, both part of the *külliye* of Orhan Gazi Cami'i.

HAMMAMS ● *58*
"The sonority of the word contains all the sensuality of a purification rite. Haloed in mist that softens the harshness of reality, ghostly silhouettes wander from room to room with the demeanor of penitents, then kneel at the base of marble fountains to rest near those horns of plenty atrickle with scalding water. Under beams of light issuing from occuli set into the cupolas or the spectral glimmer of

AROUND THE CITADEL

West of the Ulu Cami, Atatürk Caddesi divides into two avenues, one running around the hill and the other climbing steeply along the ramparts of the citadel, or Hisar. These are the massive remnants of the citadel's ancient defensive wall, constructed in the Hellenistic era and then rebuilt in both the Byzantine and Ottoman periods. This is all that remains above ground of the Greek city of Prusa. At the top of the acropolis are the tombs of Osman and Orhan Gazi. Osman Gazi died in the nearby town of Soğut in 1324, but his body was reinterred here following the capture of Prusa two years later, in what had originally been the baptistery of the Byzantine Church of St Prophitis Elias, which was converted into a mosque. When Orhan Gazi died in 1359, he was buried in the former nave of St Prophitis Elias.Today all that remains of the original church are a few fragments of mosaic pavement around the catafalque of Orhan Gazi, whose wife Nilüfer Hatun is also buried beside him.

neon tubes, bodies are kneaded, joints crack, thighs slap against wet marble, and spirits give up to long hours of moist languor."

E.P.

OSMAN GAZI
Founder of the Osmanli dynasty.

A traditional wooden house with overhanging upper stories and a little painted shop on the ground floor.

TRADITIONAL OTTOMAN HOUSES ● *86,* ▲ *297.* Behind the citadel, in the picturesque back streets of Bursa, a few old, wooden Ottoman houses still survive, although they are fast disappearing.

THE MURADIYE

BURSA, THE CAPITAL OF A PROVINCE
The city of Bursa is renowned for its fruit trees, agricultural products, olive oil, wine, honey, tobacco, and cotton. Since antiquity,

The Muradiye was built between 1424 and 1426 by Murat II (1421–51), father of Mehmet the Conqueror. This was the last imperial mosque complex to be constructed in Bursa. Besides the mosque itself, it included a *medrese*, an *imaret*, the *türbe* of the founder, and many other tombs, some built in later times.

THE MOSQUE AND MEDRESE OF MURAT II. Like the Orhan Gazi Cami'i, the Muradiye Cami'i was built following a cross-axial upside-down "T" plan ● *78*, with a five-bay porch, and it too has a pair of *zaviye* (shelters for pilgrims or dervishes) flanking its main chamber. The *medrese* is the most beautiful in Bursa. The courtyard forms a perfect square with five *hücres* (studies for students) each on the east and west sides, larger rooms in the corners, and a pair of rooms on either side of the entranceway. The little *dershane* (lecture hall) opposite the entrance has brilliant tile decoration. The *medrese* serves as a dispensary, its courtyard converted into a pretty garden with a fountain at its center. Little now remains of the *imaret* that once served food to the students and the staff of the complex.

Bursa's prosperity has depended on the production of silk-worm cocoons. Until the 20th century, the Ottoman government supplied peasants with mulberry seedlings free of charge.

THE MAUSOLEUMS. The *türbe* of Murat II stands in the garden beside his mosque and *medrese*, surrounded by a dozen other tombs. The great warrior died in Edirne on February 3, 1451 and was brought back to be interred in his *külliye*, the last Ottoman sultan to be buried in the old capital of Bursa. His tomb has a simple grandeur about it, with his earth-filled marble catafalque standing alone under the open oculus of the dome; its octagonal drum is supported by four pillars and four columns with Byzantine capitals from

«... BURY ME DIRECTLY IN THE GROUND.
MAY THE RAIN, SIGN OF THE BENEDICTION OF GOD,
FALL UPON ME. . . .»

SULTAN MURAT II

which rise eight ogival arches. Murat's tomb was left open to the elements according to the terms of his last will and testament. The next *türbe* to the west is that of Prince Mustafa, the eldest son of Süleyman the Magnificent ● *36*. Mustafa was heir apparent until he was executed in 1551 by Süleyman, who had been persuaded by Roxelana that his son was plotting to usurp the throne. Thereby Roxelana's son, Selim "the Sot," succeeded to the throne when Süleyman died in 1566, and with his reign began the long decline of the Ottoman Empire. The next *türbe* to the southwest contains the graves of two sons of Fatih, Princes Mustafa and Cem. Mustafa was killed in action in 1474 at the age of 25, and Fatih brought his body to Bursa for burial next to his grandfather Murat. Cem died in 1495 in Italy, having spent fourteen years in exile after being defeated by his brother Beyazıt II in a war of succession. The deceased Prince was not brought back to Bursa for burial until 1499, for even after his death he continued to be the subject of negotiations between Beyazıt and the European powers that had held him captive. Evilya Çelebi, in his *Seyahatname*, spins a fable about the body's return to Bursa: "The remains of Cem, and the possessions of the departed, among which figured a magic cup (which refilled itself whenever it was taken in hand by a drinker), a white parrot,

A SILK FACTORY IN 1900
"We expected to find one of those sad interiors dominated by machines. We entered a room, populated by young people, handsome and happy. On the right, Greek and Armenian girls, their huge eyes glued to us. On the left, Turkish women, their yaşmak slightly lowered, their noses sharp, a bit long, the mouth delicate, timid but graceful, modest."
Comtesse de Gasparin, 1867

▲ BURSA

An unglazed
ceramic jug and
a bronze candlestick
from the 18th century.

and thousands of splendid works, were entrusted to Saïd
Çelebi and Haydar Çelebi for delivery to the Sultan. Just as
his grave was being dug, there came such a clap of thunder
followed by such confusion in the funerary chapel that
everyone present took flight, and no one could cross the
threshhold for the next six days. When the Sultan learned of
these events, he ordered that the body of Cem be interred
near his grandfather. . . ."

THE HÜDAVENDIGAR COMPLEX

The oldest of Bursa's three other mosque complexes is the
Hüdavendigar *külliye*. Hüdavendigar was
the pompous imperial title assumed by
Murat I (1359–89), the only sultan who
ever styled himself "Creator of the
World." The *külliye*, built by Murat I
between 1365 and 1385, is situated in the
pleasant suburb of Çekirǧe, in the heights
west of the city. The Hüdavendigar *külliye*
is less a complex of the familiar type than
a two-story building with a mosque-cum-
hospice on the ground floor and a *medrese*
above. The mosque is fronted by a five-bay porch with a
gallery of five bays above, now walled in, the two floors
connected by a pair of stairways flanking the vestibule. The
interior of the ground floor comprises four *eyvans* around a
central fountain court, as well as six other rooms. The two-
story central hall is a square surmounted by a dome 36 feet in
diameter and 72 feet high, with an oculus at the apex of its
crown. A flight of steps leads up from there to the prayer hall,
a rectangular room covered by a barrel vault, with the
mihrab placed inside a niche at the back of the building.
The *medrese*, or college, on the second floor has a large
room between the staircases, eight studies for
students on either

THE MURADIYE KONAK
The grandest of
Bursa's old Ottoman
mansions, the
Muradiye Konak,
stands in the square in
front of the Mosque
of Murat II. Built in
the early 18th century,
the *konak* has been
restored and is now
open to the public,
with some of its
rooms furnished as
they were in
Ottoman times.

side of the central hall and the prayer hall, as well as a small room above the mihrab. The Hüdavendigar is an extraordinary building, and nothing like it would ever again be built by the Ottomans. Murat I is buried in a *türbe* in front of his complex.

THE THERMAL BATHS

Bursa has been famous for its thermal baths ● *58* since Roman times, and the oldest of its bathing establishments, the ESKI KAPLICA, stands at the foot of the Çekirğe hill, a short distance below the Hüdavendigar. According to tradition,

these baths were first built by Justinian and Theodora. They were constructed in their present form during Murat I's reign, but the ancient columns and capitals incorporated into the building indicate that the original structure dates back to late Roman or early Byzantine times. Returning toward the city center, you see in the fields below the road the Yeni Kaplıca, built in the 1550's by Rüstem Paşa.

THE KÜLTÜR PARKI. Next on the left is the Kültür Parki, where the people of Bursa come in the summer to enjoy themselves at outdoor cafés and an amusement park. Within the park is the ARCHEOLOGICAL MUSEUM, which exhibits antiquities found in Bursa and the surrounding region, including a number of funerary stelae from the late Roman and early Byzantine eras.

YEŞIL CAMI

Yeşil Cami ● *78* – the Green Mosque – was commissioned by Mehmet I in 1412, the year before he became sultan. Designed by the architect Haci Ivaz Paşa, the mosque was not finished when Mehmet died in 1421. Although work continued for another three years, the building was never completed, and lacks its entrance portico. Nevertheless, Yeşil Cami is the most beautiful of the imperial mosques in Bursa, both in the harmony of its design and the opulence of its interior decoration. The plan is yet another variation of the upside-down T, or

PANORAMA
The postcard above, from the beginning of the century, gives an idea of the beautiful countryside around Bursa. Seen here is a mosque with its cemetery in the foreground.

A HOLIDAY RESORT
Since the beginning of the 20th century, Bursa has become an important holiday and tourist resort, where visitors can enjoy the hot springs. This 16th-century miniature depicts the steam room in a hammam.

A MINIATURE FROM THE 17TH CENTURY
This dancer, painted by the miniaturist Levni, wears an elegant costume made of silk from Bursa.

cross-axial *eyvan* type. Beyond the vestibule you pass through a small barrel-vaulted *eyvan* into the central court, in the middle of which is a *şadırvan* pool. On the left and right there are side *eyvans* raised above the central court by a single step, while the main *eyvan* – the prayer hall – is raised by four steps. Each of the side *eyvans* is flanked by a pair of rooms of comparable size. The dome over the central court, slightly higher than the one over the prayer hall, is surmounted by a lantern, replacing the original open oculus. From the central court you can see the beautifully tiled imperial loge, and to either side of it the screened balconies reserved for the royal family. This is the most beautiful mosque interior in Bursa, with the magnificent mihrab framed in the great arch of the prayer hall, and the still water of the *şadırvan* pool mirroring the colors of the stained-glass windows in the kiblah wall.

YEŞIL TÜRBE ★

Yeşil Türbe, the "Green Tomb", the mausoleum of Mehmet I, stands at the top of the hill across the street from the mosque. Originally its exterior walls were revetted in the turquoise tiles from which the *türbe* and the mosque took their names, but these were destroyed by the 1855 earthquake and replaced by Kütahya tiles. The interior decoration of the *türbe* rivals that of the mosque, particularly the finely carved doors, the tile revetment of the walls, the beautifully decorated mihrab, and the Sultan's sarcophagus, with its epitaph in golden calligraphy on a blue ground.

THE MUSEUM OF TURKISH AND ISLAMIC ART. The *külliye* of Mehmet I also included a *medrese*, an *imaret*, and a hammam, but of these only the *imaret* has survived. It now houses the Museum of Turkish and Islamic Art, whose collections include Ottoman weapons, kitchen utensils, jewelry, calligraphy, and antique books in Arabic and Osmanli script.

THE COMPLEX AND MOSQUE OF BEYAZIT I

The fourth of Bursa's imperial mosque complexes is that of Beyazıt I, located on a hilltop site northeast of Yeşil Cami and reached by Yeşil Caddesi. The complex was begun in 1390 and completed in 1395. It suffered severe damage in the 1855 earthquake ■ 16, since which it has been restored twice, in 1878 and in 1948. Nevertheless, the *külliye* appears to have retained most of its original character. When finished, the complex consisted of the mosque with its dervish hospice, along with two *medreses*, a hospital, a palace, and the *türbe* of the founder. Today all that remains are the mosque, the *türbe*, and one of the *medreses*, which now serves as a dispensary.

THE MOSQUE OF BEYAZIT I. The mosque is entered through a five-bay porch and then a domed vestibule, which leads into the large central prayer hall. The interior plan is of the familiar reversed-T or cross-axial *evyan* type, with pairs of *zaviye* – hospices for pilgrims or dervishes – flanking each of the side *eyvans*. The three rooms are raised three steps higher than the central hall. All are domed, with the cupola of the main space being only slightly higher than that of the central court, while those of the side *eyvans* are considerably lower.

The two minarets were destroyed by earthquakes, one of them in 1855 and the other in 1949, and they have never been rebuilt. The exterior of the mosque is particularly handsome, with its impressive portico of five arches and its shining façade of marble and cut stone.

THE YEŞIL TÜRBE
The "Green Tomb" takes its name from the green faience with which its façades are decorated (above left).

THE ULU DAĞ
NATIONAL PARK ★

The best time to visit Bursa is in spring, when the broad plain below Ulu Dağ turns a verdant green and the hillsides are bright with wild flowers and blossoming trees. And of course no visit to Bursa is complete without an ascent of the Great Mountain, which in winter becomes a popular ski resort. One approach is to take the cable car that starts from the hillside east of town, not far from Yeşil Cami; another is to drive or take a taxi up the mountain road that ascends from Çekirğe. This leads to the Ulu Dağ massif and from there it is a three-hour walk to the summit, 8,343 feet above sea level, by far the highest peak in northwestern Anatolia. In the resort village there are numerous hotels and restaurants, and thermal facilities remain open throughout the year. The mountain is now part of the Ulu Dağ National Park, more than 27,000 acres of woodland, which includes olive groves and clumps of bay, chestnut, elm, oak, plane, beech, pine, juniper, and aspen trees ■ *24*. A sizeable bird population nests here, and this includes a number of rare species ■ *18*. The summit offers an unforgettable view over the whole of Bythnia. On a clear day you can see the domes and minarets of Istanbul sparkling on the northern horizon.

In the vast garden of the Muradiye there are several mausoleums of the princes of the Ottoman dynasty as well as for Sultan Murat himself.

A mountain stream in the Ulu Dağ National Park.

TUNCA

BEYAZIT II
CAMİ'İ

🔏   One day

THE CITADEL QUARTER
The old quarter of
Kale İç spreads out
west of the Semiz Ali
Paşa bazaar. Its name
means "inside the
citadel" and comes
from the Byzantine
era when the
ramparts of the
citadel did indeed
surround it. The
streets of the quarter,

which extends to
Saraçlar Caddesi to
the west and to Salat
Paşa Caddesi to the
south, form a regular
grid-pattern square.
To the southwest
flows the Tunca, near
which the remains of
the ancient Byzantine
defense walls can still
be seen.

HISTORY

Edirne, ancient Hadrianopolis, is situated near the confluence
of the rivers Meriç and Tunca, known in antiquity as Hebrus
and Tonsus. The original settlement on this site was a Thracian
market town founded in the 7th century BC. It bore the name
Odrysia, for the Odryses, the Thracian tribe then in control of
the region. The Odryses would be supplanted by the Orestes, a
Hellenic tribe from Epirus, who established themselves nearby
and called their city Orestia. In AD 125, the Roman Emperor
Hadrian joined the two cities under the common name
Hadrianopolis, which in Greek became Adrianopolis and thus
in English Adrianople. Diocletian (284–305) made
Hadrianopolis the capital of one of the four provinces of
Thrace. When Constantine the Great
transferred his capital to
Constantinople in 330,
Adrianople developed rapidly
and grew into the most
prosperous as well as the
most populous city in
Thrace. And so it would
remain to the end of the
Byzantine era. During the
following five and a half
centuries Adrianople was fought
over and captured in turn by the
Byzantines, Avars, Bulgars, Romans, and Turks, finally
succumbing to Murat I in 1361, after which it would be called
Edirne ● *33*. Edirne became the capital of the expanding
Ottoman Empire, a position it held until a few months after the
Conquest of Constantinople. Nonetheless, Edirne remained
prominent long after Istanbul replaced it as the principal seat
of government. Indeed, several of the sultans and their grand
viziers looked upon the city as their second home, continuing to
adorn it with splendid buildings. Its status did not begin to dim
until the Ottoman Empire itself fell into decline. During the

ÜÇ ŞEREFELİ CAMİ'İ

RÜSTEM PAŞA HANI
ESKİ CAMİ

SELİMİYE CAMİ'İ

19th century Edirne suffered terribly at the hands of various invading armies: the Russians in 1829 and 1878, the Bulgars in 1913, and the Greeks between 1919 and 1923, after which the Treaty of Lausanne granted it to Turkey in 1923. Today Edirne is a lively market town, made glorious by its numerous imperial Ottoman monuments.

THE ESKI CAMI

The Eski Cami, or "Old Mosque," was begun by the Emir Süleyman Çelebi, son of Beyazıt I, shortly after his father's defeat at the Battle of Ankara in 1402. Construction then ceased while Süleyman fought a war of succession with his brothers Musa Çelebi and Mehmet Çelebi. After Musa defeated Süleyman in 1411, he himself suffered defeat at the hands of his only surviving brother. As Mehmet I, the victor ordered Eski Cami to be completed, which the dedicatory inscription on the mosque confirms. This also cites Ömer ibn Ibrahim as master mason and Hacı Alaettin of Konya as architect. Damaged by a fire in 1749 and an earthquake in 1752 ■ *16*, the Old Mosque was restored during the reign of Mahmut I and then again as recently as 1932 and 1944. The interior is a perfect 162 feet on each side, divided into nine equal sections covered by nine domes supported on the inside by four massive pillars.

RÜSTEM PAŞA'S CARAVANSERAI

Southwest of the Eski Cami is the bazaar quarter, which boasts three old Ottoman buildings of great interest, the

THE SULTANIYE
Edirne can count more than fifty historic monuments, including Ottoman mosques, *medrese*, hammams, fountains, and bridges, as well as the scattered remains of Roman and Byzantine walls and an ancient synagogue.

THE FOUNTAIN OF HACI ADIL BEY

**MINARETS OF THE
ÜÇ ŞEREFELI CAMI'I**
The first Ottoman
mosque to have four
minarets. Those on
the east are decorated
with lozenges, while
on the southwest the
three-balcony minaret
is embellished with
zigzagging geometric
patterns. The most
original of all is the
minaret on the
northwest, with its
distinctive spiral form.

first of which is the caravanserai of Rüstem Paşa – the
Rüstem Paşa Hanı – constructed by the great Sinan between
1560 and 1561. Built for travelers, the building is now being
converted into an exhibition center.

THE COVERED MARKET. Just beside Eski Cami we see the
bedesten built by Mehmet I as a source of income for the
mosque. In Edirne, the *bedesten* became more than a market;
it functioned as the heart of the city's commercial life,
providing secure storage and a safe display area for merchants
dealing in valuable goods and commodities, such as gold,
jewelry, armor, brocade, and fine carpets.
Only major trade centers like Istanbul,
Edirne, and Bursa would have such a
facility.

THE SEMIZ ALI PAŞA ARASTA. An old
Ottoman street-market flanks the west
side of Saraçlar Caddesi, the first main
street west of Eski Cami. This is the
Semiz Ali Paşa Arasta, built by Sinan in
1568 to 1569, four years after the death
of the Grand Vizier whose name it bears.
The *arasta* is a long (320 yards) and
narrow structure with 126 vaulted shops on either side.

THE MOSQUE OF THREE BALCONIES

A water tower.

The Üç Şerefeli Cami'i – the Mosque of Three
Balconies – stands to the right of the *arasta*, in
a little street that crosses Hükümet Caddesi.
The Üç Şerefeli is an imperial mosque, built
by Murat II between 1437 and 1447 to be the
most monumental building in the Ottoman
Empire, which it remained until the conquest
of Constantinople. Architectural
historians view it as a turning point
in the history of Ottoman
architecture, as it was the first
central dome to have a
diameter of 79 feet, which was
only surpassed by the mosques
of Süleyman and Selim in the
16th century ● 78. Like
the Eski Cami, the
Mosque of Three
Balconies was restored by
Mahmut I after it was badly

damaged by fire and an earthquake in the mid-18th century. The mosque takes its name from the fact that there are three (üç) balconies (şerefe) on one of its four minarets, at the southeast corner. This minaret is 222 feet high, and at the time of construction it was the tallest in the Ottoman Empire. The diameter of its dome was not surpassed until Fatih Cami'i in Istanbul was built. The dome is supported on the north and south by the exterior walls, and on the east and west by two huge hexagonal pillars, 19 feet in diameter, which obstruct the view of the mihrab and mimbar from the side areas.

THE RÜSTEM PAŞA KERVANSARAYI
Divided into two sections, each with its own plan and function, the caravanserai accommodated the merchants of Edirne and travelers. The former were housed in the Büyük Han (Big Caravanserai) and the latter in the Küçük Han (Small Caravanserai). The whole has been recently restored and transformed into a deluxe hotel called the Rüstem Paşa Kervansarayi. The renovation won the Agha Khan Prize for Architecture in 1980.

THE SELIMIYE IMPERIAL COMPLEX

The culmination of classical Ottoman architecture came with the Selimiye Cami'i● 80, which stands only a few hundred yards away down Mimar Sinan Caddesi, named after the great architect who built this magnificent mosque complex. Sinan built the Selimiye for Selim II during the years 1569 to 1575, completing it when he was at least 79 years old, and to the end of his life he regarded the mosque as the masterpiece of his career, surpassing even the Süleymaniye in grandeur. The Selimiye dominates Edirne from its prominent position on the east side of town, built on a platform called Kavak Meydanı, where Beyazıt I had built a palace in the last quarter of the 14th century. The mosque and its *avlu*, or forecourt, which are both identical rectangles, each 196 feet wide and 144 feet long, are situated toward the northern end of this platform.

Grape-gathering in the village of Soufli near Edirne.

Fontaine dans la cour de Sultan Selim

Intérieur de Sultan Selim

Intérieur de Sultan Selim

THE COBBLERS' ARCADE. The west side of the precinct is occupied by the Kavaflar Arasta, which used to contain 124 shops once used by the guild of shoemakers, with a *dar-ül kura* projecting from the middle of its outer side. The arcade has been severely damaged by fire. These buildings seem to have been added by the architect Davut Ağa, on commission from Murat III, but the *külliye* contains few elements comparable with the grandeur of Selimiye, the greatest Ottoman mosque ever built.

THE PRAYER HALL IN THE SELIMIYE CAMI'I
The dome, with its crown at 143 feet above the floor, is supported by eight elegant pillars, two of which flank the main entrance, while two others frame the mihrab set in the recess of a vaulted apse. The tribune of the muezzin stands at the center of the prayer hall, directly under the keystone of the dome. It consists of a marble platform supported by rectangular pillars and surmounting a patio with a pretty fountain at the center, an arrangement which is unique in Ottoman architecture.

Detail of a minaret in the Selimiye Cami'i.

THE EXTERIOR. The Selimiye dome is ringed by eight buttresses topped with turrets and framed by its four slender minarets, which at 232 feet are the tallest in the Islamic world. The buttresses are the projections of the eight octagonal piers that provide the main internal support for the great dome, which is flanked at the corners by semicircular exedrae, with a rectangular apse on the south containing the mihrab.

THE INTERIOR. The dome of the Selimiye is 143 feet from floor to crown, whereas that of Haghia Sophia is 182 feet high. However, the important thing is not whether Sinan could build a dome higher and wider than that constructed by Justinian's architects, but that in developing classical Ottoman architecture to its logical conclusion, he could design and

construct a building that compares in grandeur with Haghia Sophia. Two of the Selimiye's huge dome pillars flank the main entrance from the *avlu* and two others flank the mihrab. Meanwhile, the lower walls of the mihrab apse are revetted in beautiful Iznik tiles above which there is a calligraphic inscription with flowing white letters on a blue background. At the southwest corner of the prayer hall, the imperial loge partly rests upon the arcade of a portico linked to the east gallery. The loge is particularly splendid, with its decoration of superb Iznik tiles. The mihrab of the imperial loge is also beautiful, with two wooden shutters opening on to a view over Edirne and the surrounding countryside.

THE MUSEUMS. The Selimiye *medrese* now serves as the Archeological Museum, while the *dar-ül hadis* (college for the study of the Koran) houses the Museum of Turkish and Islamic Works. The ethnographic collection includes Turkish embroideries, kilims, antique armaments, Ottoman coins, and beautiful Thracian folk costumes. In the archeological collection there is ancient jewelry, pottery, ceramics, coins, architectural fragments, and sculpture. The *dar-ül hadis* contains inscriptions from demolished Ottoman monuments, kitchen utensils, glass, tiles, and embroideries, as well as hand-written Korans and various objects that once belonged to a local monastery of Mevlevi dervishes.

THE MOSQUE OF MURAT II

The Muradiye Cami'i stands on a hill to the northeast of Edirne, and is best approached along Mimar Sinan Caddesi. Murat II had the building constructed in 1435 as a *zaviye*, or hostel, for Mevlevi dervishes, whose founder, Celalettin Rumi, appeared to the Sultan in a dream and requested that he build such a facility for his brotherhood. Later Murat converted the *zaviye* into a mosque and rehoused the dervishes in a separate *tekke*, or monastery, in the garden. The mosque is of the cross-*eyvan* or upside-down-T variety, comprising a five-bayed porch, a minaret, and four interior units. The largest unit is the one just inside the entrance, its dome resting on Turkish triangles and culminating in a lantern which is on top of the originally open oculus. The main *eyvan*, or room, is richly decorated with ceramic tiles and frescoes, especially the mihrab.

THE MOSQUE OF SELIM II

DECORATIVE CALLIGRAPHY IN ESKI CAMI
Calligraphy plays a major role in the decoration of mosques. Allah could not be represented other than by his name, as here.

SURRENDER OF EDIRNE TO TSAR FERDINAND OF BULGARIA
The Bulgarians' capture of the Turkish fort at Edirne occurred during the Balkan War of 1912–13. It cost many lives on both sides.

▲ SINAN, IMPERIAL ARCHITECT

Sinan's real name is not known, but it is known that he was born into a Turkish-speaking Christian family in the village Aghrianos (today called Agurnas) in Cappadocia, in the final years of the 15th century. During Selim I's reign (1512–1520) he was enrolled by imperial agents as a *devşirme* in the sultan's service. From the beginning of Süleyman I's reign (1520–1566) he joined the Janissaries and participated in the Belgrade (1521), Rhodes (1522), Hungary (1526), Vienna (1529), Baghdad (1534), Corfu (1537), and Moldavia (1538) campaigns, after which he was named imperial architect. For half a century until his death in 1588 he exercised an unlimited power over Ottoman architecture.

THE SYMBOLISM OF THE CUPOLA
Plan, section, and perspective in a simultaneous projection of the cupola and the minarets. The cupola symbolizes unity and the minarets the power of the spoken word. During Sinan's time, it was common to draw the floor plan and project the sections in two dimensions. In this drawing P. Carnelutti used the process to represent the cupola of the mosque and its position in relation to the space that it covers.

MIHRIMAH MOSQUE, ISTANBUL (1562–5)
Sinan constructed this mosque with 200 windows:

"God is the light of the heavens and the earth" (Koran, *Sourate* XXI).

RÜSTEM PAŞA CAMI'I (1561–62)
View from the prayer room decorated with Iznik ceramics.

THE CUPOLA OF THE SELIMIYE MOSQUE IN EDIRNE
The size, height, and elegant architecture of this magnificent cupola seem to signify the unity of the empire under Sultan Selim II – a unity that is further emphasized by the four cardinal points symbolized in the four minarets.

THE SELIMIYE OF EDIRNE (1569–75)
The prayer room and gallery, situated in the center of the mosque.

SÜLEYMANIYE
The architects present a model of the mosque. *Sûrnâme*, 1582.

"Architects of any importance in Christian countries consider themselves far superior to Muslims, because until now the latter haven't accomplished anything comparable to the cupola of Sainte Sophia. Thanks to the All Powerful and the favour of the sultan, I have succeeded in building a cupola for Sultan Selim's mosque that surpasse[s] that of Sainte Sophia, one that is four zira (alders) in diameter, and six in height."

Sinan,
Autobiography

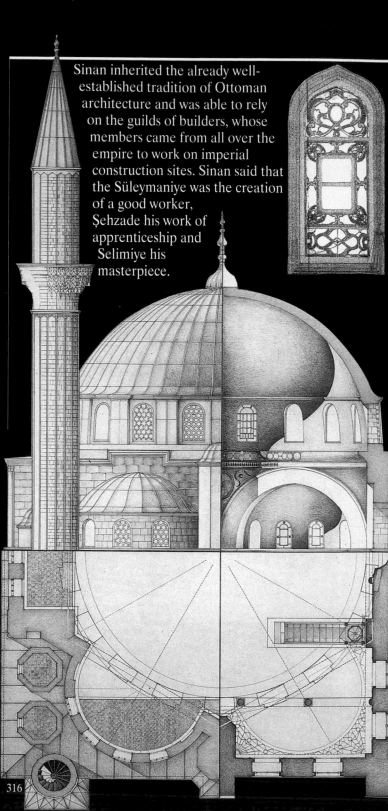

Sinan inherited the already well-established tradition of Ottoman architecture and was able to rely on the guilds of builders, whose members came from all over the empire to work on imperial construction sites. Sinan said that the Süleymaniye was the creation of a good worker, Şehzade his work of apprenticeship and Selimiye his masterpiece.

The gypsum stained glass played an important decorative role in the architecture. The most remarkable examples are the tinted stained glass of the mirhab wall of the Süleymaniye, the Mihrimah stained glass, and that of the Rüstem Paşa. Opposite, the stained glass of the Piyale Paşa mosque and of the *türbe* of Süleyman in Istanbul.

PLAN, SECTION, AND FAÇADE OF SOKOLLU MOSQUE BY ROBERTO PETRUZZI
Color plays an important part in this mosque. It is used to distinguish different sections, and to highlight symbolic functions, masking pendentives, and softening the planes of the free-standing walls.

The entrance and the mihrab of the mosque are oriented in the direction of Mecca. The cornices highlighted with white and the oblique arches accentuate the liveliness and originality of the hexagonal baldaquin.

MIMBAR The marble pulpit of the Edirne Selimiye is very airy. It is decorated with geometric patterns; interlacings of hexagons, stars, and circles that are of selçuk inspiration.

Without abandoning the rectangular prayer room, the architect tests all of the spaces with square-plan cupolas like those at Selimiye (above).

At least 477 buildings are attributed to Sinan, including 107 mosques (*cami*), 52 small mosques (*mescit*), 45 *türbe*, 74 *medrese*, 56 hammams, 38 palaces, and 31 caravanserais (*han*). Of these, 204 survive today, most of them in Istanbul and Edirne.

▲ SINAN, IMPERIAL ARCHITECT

Whereas many other monuments were the work of a group of architects, those commissioned by the imperial family and great dignitaries were seen to be the personal creations of Sinan and they demonstrate his genius. He invented numerous variations on the basic task of covering a rectangular area with a dome. Haghia Sophia represented the standard to be surpassed, and Sinan's desire to improve on previous sucesses led him to create variations on half-domes (two at the Süleyman mosque, four at Şehzade's), galleries (the mosque at Kılıç Ali Paşa), and tympani (the Mihrimah).

Sinan's inventiveness is evident in his attempts to mount a dome on a hexagonal (Sokollu mosque) or octagonal plan (Rüstem Paşa mosque), and in the judicious layouts of the schools (Şemsi Paşa mosque in Üsküdar, and Sal Mahmut Paşa's in Eyüp). Sinan also distinguished himself with his search for new forms (the Rüstem Paşa *medrese*) and with a certain decorative exuberance (Süleyman and Selim II *türbes*), as well as with his special effects on façades (Süleyman mosque).

SÜLEYMANIYE
Ablution fountain in marble in the central courtyard (*avlu*) at the mosque portico.

SELIMIYE
The muezzin *mahfili*, or gallery for the singers, is placed directly beneath the key of the cupola, and marks the center. Beneath the gallery a small fountain complements the one in the courtyard.

LONGITUDINAL SECTION OF THE SELIMIYE COMPLEX
This section shows the interior space, and outlines in blue the arches and the cupola that rests on eight pillars. For the first time Sinan introduces an arcade with alternating large and small arches on pairs of columns. The weight of the cupola is absorbed by eight buttresses which create the exterior rhythm of the façade, designed around pairs of windows. The four minarets, one measuring 232 feet in height, are positioned at the four corners of the mosque. The two minarets close to the courtyard (*avlu*) have triple spiral staircases, and each one leads to a balcony or *şerefe*. Drawing by Pietro Carnelutti, in Burelli's *The Mosque of Sinan*.

▲ EDIRNE

Bass drum and clarinet set
the pace for contenders in the
Kirkpinar wrestling match.

THE KÜLLIYE OF BEYAZIT II

The River Tunca divides into two branches,
the first of which is spanned by a stone
bridge constructed during the reign of
Süleyman the Magnificent which leads to
Sarayıcı Island. Leaving the island by the
Fatih Mehmet Bridge, you cross the second
branch of the Tunca, where, on the opposite
bank, a highway runs along the river and
towards the *külliye* of Beyazıt II. This is the
most extensive and elaborate of the
imperial mosque complexes in Edirne,
designed and built for the sultan by the
architect Hayrettin between 1484 and
1488.The religious foundations line the vast
outer courtyard, where the horses and
camels of the caravans that stopped at the
caravanserai were once tethered. Along the
east side of the courtyard are the *imaret* and
the food store. Both served the needs of
travelers, while also supplying food for the patients and staff
of the hospital, the various buildings of which are on the west
side of the courtyard. Just beside the mosque is the domed
structure that served as the hospital proper, with the asylum
for the insane (*timarhane*) adjoining it and the medical school
(*tip medrese*) set back at the end.

THE SÜLEYMAN BRIDGE
Built in 1554 by
Süleyman, the bridge
leads to Tunca Island,
the site of the famous
but long-gone Edirne
Sarayı, a palace
begun by Murat II
in 1450 and finished
by Fatih Mehmet.
Unfortunately, the
structure went up
in flames in 1878
during the Russian
occupation and
not a trace of it
remains.

THE MOSQUE OF MURAT I. The oldest of Edirne's imperial
mosques stands to the southwest of the Beyazıt II complex.
Once attributed to Beyazıt I and dated to the period of his
reign, this mosque is now believed to date from Murat I
Hüdavendigar's reign, probably built soon after his capture of
Hadrianopolis in 1361. It was undoubtedly built upon the
ruins of a Greek church, since the foundations and the lower
courses are obviously of Byzantine construction. This is the
oldest mosque in Turkey's European region, and though badly
in need of repair, it is still serving the faithful of Edirne.

THE KIRKPINAR WRESTLING MATCHES.

Back on Sarayıçı Island, you will see the site of the mid-June Kirkpinar ("Forty Springs") wrestling matches. Although held annually only since the beginning of the Republic, the festival goes back to the mid-14th century, when the Ottomans first penetrated Thrace under Süleyman Paşa, the son of Orhan Gazi. The matches commemorate those organized by the leader among his forty favorite companions, for their amusement in camp between campaigns. As heroes died in battle each supposedly gave rise to a spring, hence the name. Today, the festival

attracts at least 100,000 spectators. Some 800 contestants, well oiled and clad only in leather pants, advance slowly, clap their hands with extended arms, and finally make body contact, each one striving to pin down his adversary in less than thirty minutes. The contest lasts for three days and then the victor receives a Golden Belt. Meanwhile, the public enjoys other aspects of the festival – children's competitions, horse races, and the election of Miss Edirne.

PAINTING BY L-F. CASSAT (1756–1827)
The captain attends a wrestling match.

OIL WRESTLING
Ottoman soldiers used to smear themselves with grease and wrestle with one another before departing on a military campaign. The tradition of wrestling survives, and the annual champion is acclaimed throughout Turkey.

SEDDÜLBAHIR KILITBAHIR ÇANAKKALE

One day

TROY KUMKALE

The Dardanelles strait, which the Turks call Çanakkale Boğazı, is approximately 38 miles long. Its width varies from just under 1 mile to 5 miles, and it is widest where it joins the Sea of Marmara. The most important port on the European coast is Gelibou, and on the Asian, Çanakkale.

The entrance to the strait is flanked by white cliffs and the western point is crowned by a lighthouse. The coast of the Gelibolu, or Gallipoli, peninsula is quite steep. On the Asian bank, are cultivated fields fed by rivers and valleys covered with forest.

LAPSEKI

At the entrance to the Marmara, the ports of Gelibolu and Lâpseki face one another across the tips of two continents, Europe and Asia. Lâpseki is descended from ancient Lampsacus, a town founded in 654 BC by Ionians from Milos and Phocea ● 28, who settled on this fertile strait. However, modern Lâpseki retains not one trace of its antique past. During the Greco-Roman era, the port, together with Abydos near Cape Nagara, controlled all maritime commerce on the Hellespont, where the Dardanelles join the Sea of Marmara. Lampsacus was well known for its wine, which the inhabitants believed to have been blessed by the gods. After his banishment from Athens in 450 BC, for impiety and "Medeism" (pro-Persian sympathies), the great philosopher Anaxagorus, the teacher of Pericles, came to end his days at Lampsacus, where he founded a school of philosophy.

A VIEW OF THE PORT OF GELIBOLU

GELIBOLU

EUROPEAN BANK

ASIAN BANK

A PIRATE SHIP
IN THE DARDANELLES
Painting by
L. Garneray
(1783–1857)

At the death of
Anaxagorus, in 428 BC, the
local population built an
altar in his memory,
dedicated to the Spirit and
to Truth.

GELIBOLU

Gelibolu, known to Westerners as Gallipoli, was the Greeks'
Callipolis – the "Beautiful City." In antiquity it was less
important than Lampsacus, but this position was reversed
during the Byzantine era, when it became the stronghold of
the Hellespont. Justinian fortified the site, and it
was further strengthened by Emperor
Philippicus Bardanes (711–713), since
by controlling the Hellespont the
Byzantines could secure the
western maritime approaches to
Constantinople. It was here that
Frederick Barbarossa led his
army from Europe to Asia in
1190 during the Third
Crusade.
GELIBOLU CASTLE. The
principal monument in
Gelibolu is its Byzantine castle,
the ruins of which form part of
the inner harbor. As Callipolis
Castle, it constituted the key to the
maritime route giving access to
Constantinople. In 1303, the site was
occupied by the Grand Army of Catalonia,

HERO AND LEANDER
The crossing between
Sestus and Abydus is
the site of the
romantic legend of
Hero and Leander.
Leander, a youth of
Abydus, fell in love
with Hero, a priestess
of Aphrodite in
Sestus, and each night
he swam the
Hellespont to see her,
guided by a lamp that
she placed on the
European shore. But
one night the lamp
was extinguished in a
gale, and Leander
lost his way, and
drowned in the
Hellespont. When his
body was washed
ashore in Sestus
Hero threw herself
into the water in
despair and was also
drowned.

ΚΑΛΛΙΠΟΛΙΣ ·

An auction of the water tanks from a shipwrecked yacht.

THE FORTRESSES ON THE DARDANELLES, AN ENGRAVING OF 1711
When Mehmet II mounted the throne in 1451, he began to prepare for the Conquest by constructing forts on the Dardanelles, in order to isolate Constantinople from the West: the Kale-i-Sultaniye on the Asian side (near Çanakkale) and Kilitbahir on the European side (near Eceabat). A century later, during the war between Venice and the Ottoman Empire, the Turks built two more fortresses, at the Aegean end of the strait: Kumkale and Seddülbahir.

which was composed of mercenaries raised by Andronicus II to help the Byzantines fight against the Turks. However, the Catalans, under the command of Roger de Flor, seized the fortress, from which they proceeded to launch raids across Thrace. For seven years they withstood repeated attempts from the Byzantines and their Genoese allies to drive them out, before giving up the castle in 1310 and moving south to conquer Athens. Then, in 1354, came Süleyman Paşa, who in his turn seized the fortified site, which allowed the Ottomans to gain a foothold in Europe. Even so, the Byzantines managed, on rare occasions and only briefly, to retake the territory.

THE GELIBOLU CEMETERY. After the Conquest of 1453, the Ottoman navy made Gelibolu one of their bases, staying there between campaigns in the Mediterranean. Often the ships' captains returned, after a life of adventure, to end their days at Gelibolu. In the old cemeteries outside the city there are several *türbe* of ships' captains. The most famous of these is the tomb of the navigator Piri Reis (1465–1554) whose *Katibe Bahriye* (*Book of the Sea*) was the first treatise on navigation ever written by a Turk. His statue still looks out over the sea, while a small museum in the town commemorates his career. Apart from several other tombs of local celebrities, the most interesting funeral monument is a small open-air mosque, or *namazgah*, dating from 1407. Built of marble blocks and panels taken from an ancient structure, the mausoleum is unique with a mihrab flanked by a pair of mimbars. Gelibolu also boasts an important *bedesten*, although it is more modest than the covered markets of Istanbul, Bursa, and Edirne, with six domes in two rows of three each, all supported by paired columns.

THE EUROPEAN SHORE OF THE DARDANELLES

About eight miles beyond Gelibolu the road follows the European coast of the Dardanelles near the little cove known as Ince Limani, the "Port of the Pearl," at the confluence of the Dardanelles and the Cumali Çayı, which the Greeks called Aegospotami, the "River of the Goat."

SESTUS AND ABYDUS. Eleven miles further, you come to a bay, the site of ancient Sestus, at the beginning of the narrows opposite Cape Nagara, the site of ancient Abydus. Both were Greek colonies founded in the 7th century BC, Sestus by Aeolians from the northern Aegean coast of Asia Minor and Abydus by Ionians from Miletus. As the main crossing point of the strait, Sestus and Abydus were the two most important cities on the Hellespont in Classical times. The armies of Alexander the Great traversed the Hellespont in 334 BC on their way to conquer Asia. Meanwhile, Alexander himself crossed at the Aegean end in order to make a pilgrimage to Troy.

ECEABAT. Following the European coast of the Dardanelles for a further four miles you come to Eceabat, where there is a ferry service across the strait to Çanakkale. Eceabat, which was known to the Greeks as Madytos, was founded in the 7th century BC by Greeks from the Aeolian coast of Asia Minor.

THE PREFECTURE AND COURTHOUSE IN GALLIPOLI

GREEK SCULPTURE IN THE ÇANAKKALE MUSEUM (LEFT)

THE KILITBAHIR FORTRESS
The Turks built new forts in the second half of the 18th century, during the war between the Ottomans and the Russians. The fortresses from the 14th and 15th centuries, such as Kilitbahir, were modernized as well as re-equipped, and later played a decisive role during World War One.

THE GOEBEN AND THE BRESLAU
When the Russian fleet threatened Istanbul, Germany, Turkey's ally, sent two powerful battleships, the *Goeben* and the *Breslau*, which entered the Dardanelles on August 10, 1914.

THE TRIPLE ALLIANCE
The Alliance leaders – Wilhelm II (Germany), Franz Joseph (Austria), and President Giolitti (Italy) – are depicted in this emblem with their Ottoman ally, Sultan Mehmet V.

KILITBAHIR AND KALE-I-SULTANIYE. Three miles from Eceabat is Kilitbahir, the "bolt" that locks or unlocks the passage to the sea. The Ottoman fortress here, with its two stout towers linked by a curtain wall, was, together with that of the Kale-i-Sultaniye on the opposite bank, one of the key features in the plan of action prepared by Mehmet II for the final capture of Constantinople in 1453. The two fortifications would also play an important role during World War I, when the English and French attempted to force a passage through the Dardanelles, a major line of defense for inland Turkey.

THE GALLIPOLI CAMPAIGN

When World War One broke out, in July 1914, Ottoman Turkey hesitated to join the conflict. However, Germany, with which Turkey maintained extremely close ties, wasted no time in taking action. On the evening of August 10, the *Goeben*, a German warship feared for its speed and fire power, entered the Dardanelles and, together with the *Breslau*, blocked all access to the strait. On October 29, it bombarded Odessa, forcing Russia to issue an ultimatum and Turkey to choose a side, that of the Central Powers. On November 13 Sultan Mehmet V called for a Jihad, a holy war against the enemies of Islam. Rallied by three men – Mustafa Kemal, Enver Paşa, and the German General Liman von Sanders – a mixed band of soldiers, underequipped and raggedly uniformed, quickly assembled themselves into an army of liberation. Although at the price of heavy casualties, this ill-prepared Turkish army would force the Allies to pull back. In February 1915 ships from the Franco-British naval forces began bombarding the fortresses on either side of the strait. When these held firm against all attack, the Allies decided to send an armada to shell the

Gallipoli peninsula in preparation for a troop landing. But in a single day, March 18, mines set afloat by the Turkish ship *Nusret* sank three of the sixteen battleships, put four others out of action, and killed 2,750 British and French sailors. The Allies gave up on this naval tactic and, through some inexplicable strategic error, recalled their vessels and did not launch the long-anticipated land offensive until later, leaving the Turkish troops time to recover their strength and their leaders time to reorganize the defense. A first contingent of 8,000 Allied soldiers landed at the foot of the promontory at Cape Helles on April 25. In the eight months between this date and January 9, 1916, the day the Allied expeditionary force evacuated the peninsula, more than 110,000 men died in the effort to take possession of the narrow maritime corridor – just a few square miles – separating the Aegean Sea and the Sea of Marmara: 34,000 British and Commonwealth soldiers, including many troops from Australia and New Zealand; 9,000 French soldiers; 500 Senegalese infantrymen (who were killed during an attack on Kumkale); and 66,000 Turks.

MEMORIAL TO THE BATTLE OF GALLIPOLI. The battlefield at Gallipoli can be reached by driving along the coastal highway, north of Eceabat, to Anzac Cove, the site of numerous cemeteries and memorials. Kabatepe also has the Atatürk War Museum. You can also take the road that, beginning at Kilitbahir, descends along the coast and then veers inland before climbing the hills through a pine forest as far as Alçıltepe, the Greeks' Kritia. The main road then turns left and leads back out to Cape Helles at the end of the peninsula, where the British and Commonwealth Memorial is situated as well as the Turkish monument known as the Mehmetcik Aniti, not far from the French War Memorial. The Turkish memorial at Cape Helles overlooks Morto Bay, another Allied landing site.

SEDDÜLBAHIR AND KUMKALE. Viewing the bay from the top of the promontory, you can see on the right the ruins of the

The Ottoman government purchased the German battleships sent to Istanbul. The Admiral in charge of the *Goeben*, renamed *Yavuz*, became a *paşa* and took to wearing a fez. On October 29, 1915, he sailed off to bombard Odessa, which resulted in an ultimatum being issued by Russia and Turkey's entry into the war.

MUSTAFA KEMAL PAŞA
The Dardanelles campaign made Mustafa Kemal Atatürk famous among his compatriots.

THE TURKISH FLEET ATTACKING THE SHIPS OF THE RUSSIAN NAVY Russia declared war on the Ottoman Empire on November 2, 1914, dragging the country into World War One.

▲ THE DARDANELLES

The Ottoman Empire in 1913 as represented on a promotional label.

LANDING AT SEDDÜLBAHIR
To seize the fort at Seddülbahir, the Allied forces adopted a strategy reminiscent of the famous Trojan horse. The British transport ship *River Clyde*, loaded with troops, ploughed into the beach and ran aground. Great ports fitted into the hull broke open, permitting the soldiers to pour down a pair of ramps, all the while covered by fire from cannons on the foredeck. With this tactic they managed to take the Turks by surprise.

A MEMORIAL IN THE TURKISH CEMETERY AT ÇANAKKALE.

Ottoman fortress of Seddülbahir, one of the two castles in the outer line of Turkish defense in the Dardanelles, with Kumkale on the opposite coast. Both were constructed in 1659 by Mehmet Köprülü Paşa, Grand Vizier to Mehmet IV, and rebuilt between 1773 and 1775 by Baron François de Tott, a Hungarian military engineer in the service of Abdül Hamit I.

THE SITE OF ELÆUS. The promontory on the left of the bay is known as Eski Hisarlık, meaning "old fortress." The name comes from the scattered ruins of ancient Elæus, the westernmost city of the Thracian Chersonese, the remains of which lay strewn all about until the Gallipoli campaign entirely destroyed them. Founded in the 6th century BC by colonists from Athens, Elæus sided with their native homeland throughout the Peloponnesian War. Heinrich Schliemann, the famous German archeologist who discovered Troy, studied the site and excavated a mound identified as the tomb of Protesilas, the uncle of Jason, a Thessalian King, who was the first Achaean victim of the Trojan War.

Homer mentions it in Book II of the *Iliad*, where he also lists the various contingents in Agamemnon's army at the siege of Troy. Herodotus and Thucydides also cite the tomb, which, in antiquity, sheltered an oracle frequently visited by Greek sailors crossing the Hellespont. Alexander the Great himself offered a sacrifice there before crossing the Strait on his way to invade Asia. His biographer, Arrien, assures us that he "performed this ceremony in the hope of knowing better fortune than Protesilas had." From there he landed at Elæus. Alexander, writes Arrien, made the crossing by "taking the helm of the flagship and, midway, cut the throat of a bull as an offering to Poseidon. Then, he poured into the sea wine

> «HEAVY FIGHTING HAS BEEN GOING ON IN THE DARDANELLES...
> THE SITUATION IS OBVIOUSLY VERY CRITICAL. SHOULD THE
> DARDANELLES FALL, THE WORLD WAR WILL HAVE BEEN
> DECIDED AGAINST US.» ADMIRAL VON TIRPITZ

from a golden cup to gain the favor of the Nereids." On the Asian side Alexander landed on the same beach where, long before, Agamemnon had assembled his army, and then went on a pilgrimage to Troy. Lord Byron, inspired by the story of Hero and Leander, swam the Hellespont on May 3, 1810.

ÇANAKKALE

To reach Çanakkale, on the Asian side of the strait, take a ferry at Eceabat. For the last two centuries this lively city has been the principal port on the Dardanelles. During the early Ottoman era the city was known by the name of the fortress – Kale-i-Sultaniye – which is still visible south of the quay. A great many Greeks, Armenians, and Jews once lived there, whereas today's population is almost exclusively Turkish. Since the 18th century the city has been famous for its earthenware potteries, which in Turkish are known as *Çanak*.

THE MUSEUM OF ÇANAKKALE. The fortress of Kale-i-Sultaniye, renamed Çimenlik Kale, is still used by the Turkish Army, which makes it inaccessible to the public, save for the inner courtyard, where you can find the Military Museum devoted almost entirely to memorabilia of the Gallipoli campaign. The foremost exhibit is the famous mine ship *Nusret*. The Archeological Museum of Çanakkale is situated on the outskirts of town, near the national highway heading for Izmir. It houses a collection of archeological pieces unearthed during excavations at several sites in the Troad, the region extending south of the Dardanelles along the Aegean Coast. The museum also owns remarkable vases, clay statuettes, and obsidian jewelry from the collection of the archeologist Frank Calvert who was the first to direct Heinrich Schliemann to the site of Troy. Moreover, a room is reserved for the bronze utensils, terracotta pottery, and jewelry unearthed on the site of the tumulus of Dardanus, an antique cemetery located south of Çanakkale and excavated in 1974. Dated from the 4th to the 1st centuries BC, they are relics from the city of Dardanus, whose eponymous founder gave his name to the Dardanelles strait.

ÇANAKKALE ŞEHİTLERİ
ABİDESİ

THE CEMETERIES IN ANZAC COVE
Several military cemeteries, British, French, and Turkish, situated not far from the battle scene at Gallipoli, bear witness to the heavy casualties sustained by all sides.

In 1915, *The Times* of London published this photograph of "a Turkish sniper cunningly camouflaged thanks to the branches that mask him."

BEAR TAMERS ON THE ROAD TO TROY
Wandering gypsies used to perform with tame bears.

▲ The Dardanelles, March 18, 1915

At the beginning of World War One, the Allies planned the Dardanelles operation in the hope of opening the strait, to enable the Allied fleet to resupply hard-pressed Russia with arms and munitions. The British Admiralty decided to launch a naval attack. In February 1915, an Anglo-French fleet of 90 vessels and 22,000 seamen assembled off the island of Mondros. From February 19 until March 17, the Allied ships bombarded the Turkish forts and swept the sea for mines. The main naval attack took place on March 18. At 9 a.m. a squadron of English battleships gathered at the entrance to the narrows and fired at long range upon the Turkish positions, particularly those at Çanakkale. At noon, the French squadron commanded by Admiral Guépratte entered the action and sailed into the first section of the strait. It was relieved thirteen hours later by an English flotilla.

BRITISH VICE-ADMIRAL DE ROBECK
On March 16 de Robeck became commander of the Allied fleet, taking over from Vice-Admiral Carden, who had prepared the plan of attack.

REAR-ADMIRAL GUÉPRATTE
Commander of the French squadron.

12 NOON. Of the eighteen vessels in the line, three, including the *Bouvet*, were sunk by floating mines; three other ships, the *Inflexible*, the *Gaulois*, and the *Suffren*, were seriously damaged.

Admiral de Robeck launched the attack upon the Straits. The French squadron – *Suffren, Bouvet, Charlemagne,* and *Gaulois* – had the perilous honor of leading the engagement. Meanwhile, the most modern of the Allied vessels – HMS *Queen Elizabeth, Inflexible, Agamemnon,* and *Lord Nelson* – bombarded the Çanakkale forts at long range. On the front line, *Suffren, Charlemagne, Bouvet,* and *Gaulois* fired on the Turkish strongholds from a range of 7,000 to 8,000 yards. By noon all forces were engaged in the battle.

The *Suffren*, a 3,000-ton battleship launched in 1899, from which Admiral Guépratte directed his part of the operation.

▲ THE DARDANELLES, MARCH 18, 1915

In the foreground, one of the *Gaulois'* large guns and beyond it the silhouette of the *Charlemagne*.

Throughout the afternoon the exchange of fire never ceased between the Allied fleet and the Turkish defenses. At the end of the day the Allies had suffered heavy casualties. Of the sixteen battleships sent into action, six were lost. The attack by sea had failed. Only by a combined action of troops on land and ships at sea could the Allies hope to force the strait open. There was a new landing on April 25, 1915. The main thrust was aimed at Gaba-Tépé, but a strong current carried the vessels farther north. Australian and New Zealand forces began the assault upon the hills but the Turkish officer, Mustafa Kemal, at the head of his troops, stopped the Allied advance for a second time.

The *Inflexible* ran aground on the beach at Tenedos. After the crew abandoned ship, the *Ocean* arrived for the rescue only to meet the same fate as the *Inflexible*.

HMS *Irresistible*, after relieving the French at the front, struck a mine and began to sink. The crew was picked up by HMS *Agamemnon*. Adrift, the *Irresistible* went down before the white cliffs of the Asian coast.

11 A.M. On the front line, Britain's HMS *Queen Elizabeth* (below), *Lord Nelson*, *Inflexible*, and *Agamemnon* opened fire on the forts along both European and Asian coasts. The *Suffren*, under Admiral Guépratte, the *Bouvet*, the *Charlemagne*, and the *Gaulois* closed in to neutralize the defenses.

12 NOON. The duel intensified. The *Inflexible* caught fire; the *Agamemnon*, the *Bouvet*, and the *Gaulois* were hit. Admiral Guépratte stoped the *Suffren* in order to concentrate his fire on Kilit Bahır.

4 P.M.
The Turkish fire lessened. Admiral Guépratte decided to take advantage of the lull to force the strait open. Admiral de Robeck ordered him to pull back and accept relief from six English battleships.

5 P.M.
During these maneuvers, the *Bouvet* struck a mine and foundered. The *Gaulois*, hit at the waterline, was saved by her commander, who ran the ship aground on the beach at Tenedos.

7.30 P.M. Admiral de Robeck gave the order to withdraw. Of the eighteen ships which entered the battle, three battleships had been lost and four put out of action.

When Heinrich Schliemann discovered Hısarlık in 1868, he wrote: "The site fully agrees with the description that Homer gives of Ilium. The hill appears destined by nature to support a great city. No other place in the region is comparable to this one." The city

is entered by the East Gate in the walls erected about Troy VI. Here we see the remnants of two towers, Mycenaean houses, and the Temple of Athena. Farther along stand the *megarons* of Troy I and II, where

Schliemann unearthed "Priam's Treasure." The Roman theater and the *bouleuterion* are situated outside the defense walls.

TROY

From Çanakkale you can reach the site of Troy (Truva in Turkish) by taking highway E87 in the direction of Izmir. After Güzelyak, the road no longer runs along the strait but turns inland, climbing the mountain through a forest of pine and oak as far as Intepe. At this point the view over the Trojan plain is panoramic and splendid. Thereafter the road descends towards Dürek Su, Homer's Simois, and then comes to the hamlet of Gökçay, where the exit for Hısarlık leads to ancient Troy. At the entrance to the archeological site stands a huge replica of the famous "Trojan horse."

HISTORY OF EXCAVATIONS

FRANK CALVERT'S DISCOVERY. There is very little doubt today that Hısarlık is indeed the site of Homer's Troy. Frank Calvert, the American and British Consul at Çanakkale in the second half of the 19th century, made an early contribution towards proving this. This diplomat owned a farm in Troad, which happens also to be the location of the Hısarlık mound, a place long associated with the site of Ilium, which specialists assumed to have been the flourishing Hellenistic and Roman city built upon the ruins of Troy. Convinced that an ancient city had once existed there, Calvert began to excavate the site in 1865.

SCHLIEMANN'S EXCAVATIONS. However, solid proof that Hısarlık was the site of ancient Troy did not come until Heinrich Schliemann, a German who had made a fortune in the United States, began to dig in 1870, following this initiative with three further excavations from 1871 to 1873. Employing an average of 150 workmen daily, he cut right through the mound in a great north-south trench some 130 feet wide. As he made the cut, Schliemann noticed that the excavated earth was stratified in layers, which he correctly assumed represented a succession of settlements on the same site. Calling the lowermost stratum Troy , Schliemann thought he could discern seven distinct layers, of which he believed Troy II to be the Homeric city because of the wealth of jewelry and gold objects found there, a hoard that he called "Priam's Treasure." In 1883, Schliemann resumed digging, this time with the assistance of Wilhelm Dörpfeld, a young German archeologist. Eight years later the two men made an important discovery in the southern sector of the tumulus, at the level later called Troy VIIa, where they unearthed a palatial structure known as a *megaron*. It was so similar to the royal halls discovered at Mycenae and Tiryns that

Schliemann was forced to change his mind about the dating of the various strata. Finally, he decided that the sixth layer from the bottom was the Homeric city for which he was searching. This view is still generally held, though the numbering of the layers has been changed. After Schliemann's death in 1896, Dörpfeld took charge of the operation and, between 1893 1894, laid bare the massive fortifications of Troy VII.

THE TWENTIETH-CENTURY EXCAVATIONS. After a long delay, new excavations got underway in 1932, when a team of archeologists from the University of Cincinnati went to work at the Troy site under the direction of Carl W. Blegen. Blegen's group continued digging until 1938, but World War Two ended their project and delayed the publication of their findings until 1950. By this time, researchers had revealed

forty-six strata in all. They had also exposed the city's ring of defense walls, including several massive towers and two monumental gateways. This evidence confirmed Schliemann's hypothesis whereby Troy VIIa would have been the city of King Priam, destroyed around 1200 BC about the same time that Mycenae, Pylos,

and other Greek fortress cities met the same fate. The strata of Troy IV to V have been assigned to the Early Bronze Age lasting from 300 to 1800 BC (all dates are approximate); Troy VI to the Middle and Late Bronze Ages, that is 1800–1300 BC; and the various sublevels of Troy VII to the 1300–1100 BC period. In 1990, the University of Cincinnati launched a new program of excavation and research at the site, in collaboration with German and Turkish archeologists.

THE TROY MUSEUM
"Priam's Treasure," discovered at Troy II by Schliemann, comprised gold objects and jewelry that the archeologist sent to Berlin, where they disappeared during World War Two. Therefore, the artifacts exhibited at the Troy Museum in Turkey are the fruit of subsequent excavations. Many receptacles were found, among them *pithoi*, terracotta jars, and both vases and goblets made of glass, all with double handles. Other than utensils, the excavated articles include primarily arms, jewelry, and tools, fashioned of gold, silver, or bronze.

THE TROJAN HORSE
The main sources of information on the Trojan War are the *Iliad* and the *Odyssey*, the epic poems attributed to Homer. After Paris abducted Helen, Ulysses and other former suitors rallied behind Menelaus, her husband, whose honor they swore to avenge. For six years the Achaeans, under the command of Agamemnon, laid siege to Troy, during which time the great warriors of both sides confronted one

another: Ajax, Achilles, Nestor, and Ulysses in the Greek camp, and Aeneas and Hector on the Trojan side. Ulysses conceived the idea of taking the city by ruse. This involved building a colossal wooden horse inside which a contigent of soldiers would be hidden.. Believing the horse an offering to the gods, the Trojans allowed it to enter the city.

THE SITE OF TROY

THE PALACE OF PRIAM.
Archeologists now locate the main gateway into Troy on the south side of the city. This Southern Gate gave access to the citadel from the lower plain, and just inside it stands the most impressive of the dwelling places unearthed at Troy.

This is the Pillar House, which by Mycenaean standards is a building of heroic proportions. It probably occupies the same site as Homer's Palace of Priam, while the Southern Gate would seem to stand on the exact site of the Skaian Gates, with the Great Tower of Ilium right beside it. Following the destruction of Troy VIIa, the site appears to have been only sparsely inhabited for about four centuries – the Dark Ages of the ancient Greek world – until Aeolian colonists arrived from Tenedos or Lesbos in c. 700 BC. Now came into being what Blegen identifies as Troy VIII, while Troy IX would be the *Ilium Novum* of the Hellenistic and Roman eras, venerated by the Classical world as the heir to Homeric Troy.

THE TEMPLE OF ATHENA. The most important monument from Ilium is the Temple of Athena, the ruins of which have been found in the northeast sector of the Hısarlık mound. Alexander the Great swore to reconstruct the sanctuary. In 323 BC, Lysimachus, Alexander's successor, honored the old promise and had a new, Doric temple built, architectural fragments of which were unearthed by Schliemann in the northwest sector of the excavation.

THE ROMAN ADDITIONS. After Troy was severely damaged during the first war waged by Mithridates the Great against Rome, the Romans, under Augustus, rebuilt the city. They also raised the peak of the tumulus in order to expand the sacred enclosure of the temple dedicated to Athena, reconstructing it with many elements from the older building. Other buildings dating from the period are the *odeum*, the theater, and the *bouleuterion*, all situated in the southeast.

PRACTICAL INFORMATION

BY AIR
◆ Many European and American international airlines have flights to Istanbul, direct or with one stopover. From London Heathrow, British Airways and Turkish Airlines operate a regular service. There are no direct flights from the US so change at London, Paris or Brussels. There are charter flights from several cities in Europe and the US at lower prices for round trips.

GETTING TO THE CITY
◆ **BY TAXI**
The city center is 14 miles from the airport by the expressway (Çevreyolu) or the more scenic coast road(Sahilyolu).
◆ **BY BUS**
The white Havas buses travel every 30 min. from 8am to 11pm to Beyoğlu via Aksaray. It is also possible to transfer from the airport by minibus, normally by paying a supplement when buying your ticket.

BY TRAIN
◆ The Orient Express is the most glamorous (and expensive) way to travel across Europe to Istanbul. It departs from London's Victoria Station (071-928-6000). More practical but less luxurious are the daily services from various European countries, but you may have to change trains and the journey will take at least a day and a half.
BY BUS
◆ Turkish lines (e.g. Bosfor Turizm, Ulusoy,

Main road
Secondary road
Motorway
Railway
Ferry
Borders

Airports
Lakes
Urban centers

BLACK SEA

Bosphorus

Kilyos

ISTANBUL

Princes
Islands

KOCAELI

Yalova

Orhangazi

Motorway E5, to Ankara

Iznik

Mudanya

Yenişehir

Karacabey

BURSA

▲ Mount Ulu Dağ

Varan) and private operators operate regular services from many places in Europe. The day of departure varies according to where you start. Travel is usually comfortable and moderately priced. Always book in advance.

BY AUTOMOBILE
◆ The shortest route from the UK is to a northern channel port then through Germany, Austria, former Yugoslavia, and Bulgaria. Check on the political situation in the countries crossed before leaving. An N.B.A transit visa is required for Bulgaria.
◆ Via Greece: take a car ferry from an Italian port (Brindisi, Ancona or Bari) to Igoumenitsa, then drive via Thessalonika. Allow for 2 to 3 days' traveling.

BY BOAT
◆ Ships operate from numerous places (e.g. Venice, the Greek islands, Cyprus) but services can be erratic and expensive. Contact Turkish Maritime Lines (Turkiye Denizcilik Isletmeleri, Rihtim Caddesi, Karaköy tel.(1) 144-0207 or 149-7178) who sail from Venice to Izmir every Saturday evening (April to October), arriving Tuesday am (return trip Wednesday –Saturday).

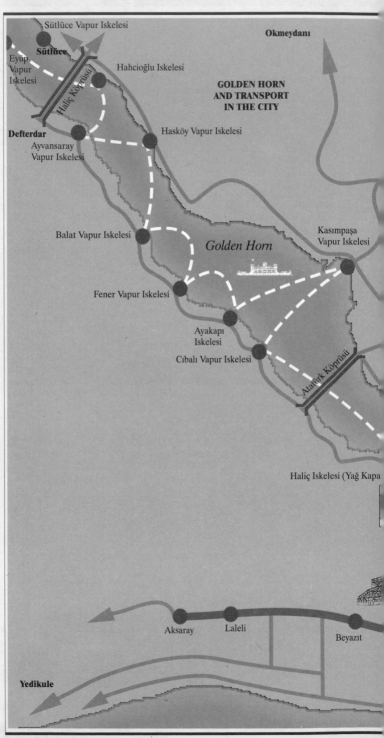

Sütlüce Vapur Iskelesi

Okmeydanı

Eyüp
Vapur
Iskelesi

Sütlüce

Hahcioğlu Iskelesi

**GOLDEN HORN
AND TRANSPORT
IN THE CITY**

Defterdar

Haliç Köprüsü

Hasköy Vapur Iskelesi

Ayvansaray
Vapur Iskelesi

Balat Vapur Iskelesi

Golden Horn

Kasımpaşa
Vapur Iskelesi

Fener Vapur Iskelesi

Ayakapı
Iskelesi

Cıbalı Vapur Iskelesi

Atatürk Köprüsü

Haliç Iskelesi (Yağ Kapa

Aksaray   Laleli

Beyazıt

Yedikule

Main streets
Funicular
Trams
Ferries
Bridges
Halts and embarcation points

Pangalti

Tesvikiye

Dolapdere

Taksim

Galatasaray

Kabataş

Tünel

Towards ferry docks for Bosphorus

Ferry to Üsküdar

Ferry to Princes' Islands

l docks

posite)

Sirkeci

Sultanahmet

Sea of Marmara

main roads
secondary roads

Kilyos

BOSPHORUS FERRY DOCKS

Rumeli Fener

Black Sea

Garipçe

Forest of Belgrade

The Bosphorus

Avrupa (Europe)

Rumeli Kavağı

Anadolu Kavağı

Sariyer

Asya (Asia)

Büyükdere

Tarabya

Beykoz

Yeniköy

Incir Köyü

Istinye

Pasabahçe

Emirğan

Çubuklu

Kanlica

Fatih Mehmet Köprüsü
(*Fatih Mehmet Bridge*)

Rumeli Hisarı

Anadolu Hisarı

Bebek

Küçüksu

Arnavutköy

Kandilli

Vaniköy

Ortaköy

Çengelköy

Beşiktaş

Boğazici Köprüsü (*Bosphorus bridge*)

Beylerbey

Kuzguncuk

Üsküdar

N.B. Iskelesi (ferry dock)
The timetables in the waiting room at each ferry dock are printed in black for the ports on the European bank and in red for those on the Asian bank.

ISTANBUL DOCKS

Galata Köprüsü

A   B   C

D   E   F   G   H   I   J

DOCKS (ISKELESI)	DESTINATION
A - Haydarpaşa Isk	Haydarpaşa station
B - Deniz Otobüsü Isk	Karaköy to Bostanci
C - Kabataş Isk	Princes' Islands, Armutlu and Mudanya
D - Haliç Isk	Golden Horn
E - Boğaz Hatti	The Bosphorus
F - Üsküdar Isk	Üsküdar
G - Kadiköy Isk	Kadiköy
H - Araba Vapuru Isk	The Harem
I - Adalar Isk	Princes' Islands
J - Sarayburnu Isk	Black Sea

TURABİ BABA SOKAĞI 131

Blue plaques are used for street names which have only recently been introduced in Istanbul, and so are unfamiliar. Local people and taxi drivers therefore tend to find their way in relation to quarters, mosques and major intersections.

Getting about Istanbul is not easy. The medieval streets were not designed for cars, let alone buses. However, the major urban developments of the 20th century have made it possible to widen some avenues and open up others. The building of a subway system, under discussion for a long time, began in 1992 but the engineers have met many problems with the city's steep terrain, its underground waterworks, its numerous ruins and inevitably the cost. Turkish ingenuity has to some extent compensated for this difficulty: old tram lines have been reopened and the bus system, in spite of its imperfections, is extensively used. Cabs, both communal and individual ones, are numerous as are the boats sailing the Bosphorus and Golden Horn. Walking is still the best way of discovering the city.

TAXIS
Yellow in color and all equipped with a meter. Pickup costs about 6000 TL from 6 am to midnight and 25% more thereafter. The ride itself is about 5500 TL a mile.

BUSES
Buses are red, blue or orange. One ticket (about 6000 TL) covers all journeys. Buy them in kiosks at the main bus-stops. The sign on the front of the bus indicates the terminus. Buses –often crammed – do not always pull up between main stops.

This sign indicates a bus-stop. Beware: the stops are quite a long distance from one another.

Two crossed anchors is the sign of the Maritime Bank which runs the public lines.

The Bosphorus and the Golden Horn are crossed by craft of every size and there are rush hours even for boats. Some private lines operate like the communal cabs: boats do not leave until there are enough passengers on board.

TRAMS

The old Istiklal Caddesi tram line has been renovated, and resumed service in 1991. With a bus ticket you can travel from Taksim to Tünel via Galatasaray. Departures are every quarter of an hour. At Tünel a funicular built in 1877 takes you down to Karaköy, leaving every 5 to 10 minutes until 10 pm.

PRINCES' ISLANDS

On Büyük Ada the only means of transport is a horse-drawn carriage (*fayton*), bicycle, donkey, or on foot. The only vehicles allowed are those of the police, fire service, or ambulances. The carriage terminal is run by a cooperative which fixes the prices for each ride under an agreement with the municipality. It is about 220,000 TL for the grand tour and 165,000 TL for a short one.

DOLMUŞ

These old American vehicles from the 1950's and 1960's are used as communal taxis.

They are more practical than buses, but have a limited number of seats. They only leave when they are full (*dolmuş* actually means "full") and pull up on request. The starting point and terminus are fixed (to find out the route ask the regulars). These vehicles cover almost all the main arteries in the city using a fixed route. Although a little dearer than buses for short distances, they are faster and cheaper than cabs. If you are lost the driver or passengers will go to great lengths to help you.

Turkey gets more modern with each day, as does infrastructure for welcoming tourists. Communications and payment facilities are now as good as in any large European city. You will be pleasantly surprised by the prices, especially those in restaurants, but do not take advantage of this too ostentatiously so as to avoid offending the Turks you are dealing with, because their average salary is very low.

The local currency is the Turkish pound (*Türk lirasi*, TL). Its subdivision, the *kurus*, disappeared long ago. There is no point in changing your money before leaving home: it will take too much time and the rates are unfavorable. Exchange bureaux in Turkey are open day and night and can be found at all the border crossings. Because of fluctuations in the exchange rate for the Turkish pound, it is best to change money only as and when required. Do not worry about the state of the notes: new ones are rarely issued so notes are often worn down to the watermark.

BANKS AND EXCHANGES
Many banks and automatic cash dispensers will accept the international VISA card. You can change your traveler's checks by showing a passport at banks with the sign *Kambiyo* and at post offices. Banks are usually open from 8.30am–12 noon and 1.30pm–5pm. except on Saturdays and Sundays. Hotels will exchange money, but commission can sometimes be excessive. Exchange bureaux at the main tourist sights are open at weekends. However, the simplest way is to use your own currency: it can be legally exchanged in post offices, hotels and shops.

COST OF A TELEPHONE CALL

İSTANBUL	3 MIN	+3 MIN
İSTANBUL	350 TL	350 TL
	À 380 TL	TO 380 TL
İSTANBUL	**1 MIN**	**+1 MIN**
BURSA (24)	1400 TL	Same/min.
EDIRNE (181)	1400 TL	Same/min.
İSTANBUL	**3 MIN**	**+3 MIN**
EUROPE	10 000 TL	1 378 TL
USA	20 000 TL	1 378 TL
JAPAN	20 000 TL	1 524 TL

TELEPHONE
Telephone booths operate with tokens (bought in post offices) or sometimes with telephone cards. Telephone tokens (*telefon jetonu*) come in three sizes: small (*küçük*) worth one unit; medium (*orta*) worth five units and large (*büyük*) worth ten units. Similarly cards (*telekart*) may be bought for thirty (*otuz*), sixty (*altmis*) or one hundred (*yüz*) units.

For international calls dial 99, then the number of the country (e.g. US = 1; UK = 44; Australia = 61),then the area code, and finally the local number.

TOWN CODES
Istanbul = 1 (but if the personal number begins with 1 replace this with 2); Ankara = 4; Bursa = 24; Izmir = 51.

TOURIST POLICE
They wear a blue uniform and are available to help you at some of the main tourist sights.

POST OFFICE
Turkish post offices can be recognized by the yellow and black emblem of the PTT (*posta, telefon, telegraf*). Apart from the main office at Sirkeci, the most important offices (at Taksim, Aksaray, Galatasaray, and the Grand Bazaar) open from 8am Monday through Saturday and from 9am to 7pm on Sunday. Most are equipped with fax machines.

You can buy stamps (*pul*) at the post offices and at shops selling postcards.Check on current postal rates since these change around every six months.

345

"The taste for coffee was so widespread in Constantinople that the imams complained about the mosques being empty whilst the coffee houses were always full" (*Alexander Dumas, Dictionnaire de cuisine*). Living in Istanbul means knowing how to take your time. Practise *keyif*, hours of peaceful reverie into which you drift while smoking a narghile and sipping a *rakı* or tea. As you slowly walk about savor the excellent *börek* (cheese-flavored flaky pastries), or the *pide* (a kind of pizza with different garnishes). Taste the fresh fish in sandwiches or small fried portions, prepared by the fishermen themselves. For refreshment buy a *ayran* (yoghurt drink) or cherry juice (*vişne suyu*) from a street vendor.

NEWSPAPER KIOSKS

Here you can buy telephone tokens, maps of Istanbul, bus tickets and of course the local and sometimes the international press. The main Turkish daily newspapers are: *Sabah* (Morning), *Hürriyet* (Freedom), *Milliyet* (The Nation), and *Cumhuriyet* (The Republic). You may find English-language newspapers in some of the major hotels.

TEA

Tea from the Black Sea is the national drink and is taken at any hour of the day. In offices *çaycı* (tea-makers) do the rounds. But it is in the *çay-evi* and the *nargileci*, mainly frequented by men, that you are most likely to drink it. In the *çay-bahçesi* (tea gardens), where there is an area reserved for women (*aile salonu*), it is prepared in samovars which contain well brewed tea in the top part and hot water in the lower, so you can have a choice of light (*açik*) or dark (*koyu*) tea.

TURKISH COFFEE

Nowadays not much coffee is drunk in Turkey because it is so expensive. *Turk kahvesi* is prepared in small copper pots (*cezve*). Order it according to taste: *sade* (no sugar), *orta* (quite sweet), and *şekerli* (very sweet). Do not drink to the bottom of the cup, because the grounds are very fine.

NARGHILECI

The *narghileci* used to be the main places for socializing in Istanbul, but they have almost all disappeared. You can still smoke a narghile in the area around the Grand Bazaar or the Rüstem Paşa Mosque. Do not be discouraged if the tobacco goes out on your first attempt or if your head starts to swim. Smoking the narghile is an art acquired only by experience.

As you walk around Istanbul you are bound to be accosted by well-dressed young men who speak English perfectly. After striking up a friendly conversation they will suggest you take a cup of tea or coffee at their "uncle's" or "cousin's" carpet shop. These "touts" are highly esteemed in Turkish society because their profession is very lucrative.

STREET VENDORS
There are many of them, such as this seller of *simit* (small bread rings). Others offer pastries from stalls or trays, fruits or cucumbers in summer and chestnuts in winter.

RAKI
Rakı is for the Turks what pastis is for the French: an aniseed-flavored spirit which accompanies every conversation.

A state monopoly, like tobacco and matches, alcohol is sold by a company called *Tekel*.

THE FISH MARKETS
From anchovies caught in the Black Sea to groupers from the Mediterranean, the colorful stalls at Eminönü, Beşiktaş or Galatasaray offer a variety of merchandise artistically arranged to attract the attention of the passers-by.

The *kebapçı* is a well-known figure in Istanbul streets. He prepares the *döner*, a roast made up of layers of lamb, cooked on a vertical spit and dexterously sliced to fill generous-sized sandwiches.

Tea (Çay)	Glass of rakı	Turkish bath (hammam)	Kebab	Museum	Cabaret (dinner & belly dancing)	Meal	Hotel
3,000 to 50,000	15,000 to 25,000	90,000 to 100,000	15,000 to 25,000	25,000	300,000 to 500,000	35,000 to 420,000	98,000 to 2,100,000

FESTIVALS AND EVENTS

	JANUARY	FEBRUARY	MARCH	APRIL	MAY	JUINE	JULY	AUGUST	SEPTEMBER	OCTOBER	NOVEMBER	DÉCEMBER
• **RAMADAN**	●	●										
• **ŞEKER BAYRAMI** (SUGAR FESTIVAL ENDING RAMADAN)			●									
• **KURBAN BAYRAMI** (FESTIVAL OF SACRIFICE)					●							
• **TULIP FESTIVAL IN EMIRĞAN** (ISTANBUL)				●								
• **FOLKLORE AND MUSIC FESTIVAL** (BURSA)							●					
• **FESTIVAL OF TROY** (ÇANAKKALE)								●				
• **NEW YEAR**	●											
• **CHILDRENS' DAY AND FESTIVAL OF NATIONAL SOVEREIGNTY**				●								
• **FESTIVAL OF YOUTH AND COMMEMORATION OF ATATÜRK**					●							
• **VICTORY FESTIVAL** (VICTORY OF TURKS OVER GREEKS IN 1922)								●				
• **FESTIVAL OF THE REPUBLIC**										●		

	1994	1995
• **START OF RAMADAN** (RAMAZAN)	Feb 12	Jan 1
• **ŞEKER BAYRAMI** (SUGAR FESTIVAL)	Mar 14	Mar 3
• **KURBAN BAYRAMI** (FESTIVAL OF SACRIFICE)	May 21	May 10

RAINFALL (ins) AND DAYS OF RAIN

SUNSHINE AND AVERAGE TEMPERATURES

GOLD

CARPETS

JEANS

FABRICS

SOUVENIRS

LEATHER/SKIN

ANTIQUES

COPPER

SILVER

c MOSQUES

🏠 HAMMAMS

‡ FOUNTAINS

🍵 TEA GARDENS

🍴 RESTAURANTS

📞✉ POST OFFICE

🏧 BANKS

⊕ EXCHANGE

🚻 TOILETS

FIRST DAY. In the Soğuk Çeşme Sokağı old Ottoman houses have been restored and converted into hotels and restaurants by the Touring and Automobile Club of Turkey. You can spend the night in one and take breakfast in the gardens between the "houses of Haghia Sophia" (*Aya Sofya Evleri*).
10 AM. Go along the street as far as the fountain of Ahmet III to visit the Haghia Sophia museum ▲140.
12 NOON. When you leave turn left and pass through the Bab-i Hümayün (the "Gate of Felicity") which used to mark the entrance to Topkapı Sarayı ▲ 150. Visiting the whole of this magnificent site and its numerous collections will take at least two hours. If you are doing the tour in two stages, have

lunch at about 1pm inside the palace at the Konyah Restaurant. It is at the rear of the fourth courtyard in the Abdül Mecit pavilion looking out on to the Bosphorus.
3 PM. Next go to the Sultan Ahmet Cami'i ▲ 175, also known as the Blue Mosque. There is no shortage of cafés in this quarter if you want to rest for a few moments.

THE GRAND BAZAAR
The largest covered market in the world and one of the main tourist centers in Istanbul – but not always the cheapest place to shop.

4 PM. Opposite the mosque is At Meydanı ▲ 177, a square which is built on the site where the Hippodrome once stood; this used to be the hub of Byzantine life, where the "Blue" and the "Green" factions competed against each other in horse races. Go on up the Divan Yolu. Stop at the Çorlulu Pasajı where you can experience the pleasures of the narghile.
6 PM. From here take the Divan Yolu to the Grand Bazaar, Kapalı Çarsı ▲ 186 where you will have half an hour to make your purchases before it closes. Or, if you prefer, go to the Şark Kahvesi, an attractive café in the heart of the market.
7 PM. To relax, go to a hammam: either Çemberlitaş opposite the "banded stone" column on the Divan Yolu, or Cağaloğlu in the quarter of the same name. Afterwards, dine in one of the many excellent fish restaurants in the Kumkapı district ◆ 370 near the Sea of Marmara.

SULTAN AHMET CAMI'I, THE BLUE MOSQUE
Built between 1609 and 1616 this mosque, with its six distinctive minarets, is most famous for its faience tiles, with 21,043 different designs.

SECOND DAY. From your hotel head for Sirkeci station along the Alemdar Caddesi. On your way you will pass the "Sublime Porte" ▲ *134*. Go straight on to the spice bazaar. Have breakfast on the first floor of the Güllüoğlu pâtisserie (which was formerly a warehouse) overlooking the bazaar.

An aerial view of Haghia Sophia and the Blue Mosque.

10 AM. Now go to the Eminönü dock to take a ferry heading for Üsküdar ▲ *264*. The trip takes 25 minutes. In this suburb on the Asian shore are the stelae of the largest Ottoman cemetery in Istanbul.

12 NOON. Lunch in one of the small, popular restaurants (*lokanta*) near the docks (*iskele*) of Üsküdar.

1 PM. Take a boat to Beşiktaş to visit the palace of Dolmabahçe ▲ *278* which closes at 4pm.

4 PM. From here take a cab to Taksim square ▲ *262*. The Gezi pâtisserie above the Gümüşsuyu Caddesi will not deceive you with its false Viennese café appearance but its chocolates are genuinely delicious and will satisfy the sweetest tooth. Opposite the confectionery is a *dolmuş* (communal taxi) stop which serves Teşfikiye, one of the chic suburbs of Istanbul. There you will see a much more westernized aspect of Istanbul, with boutiques and shops selling imported luxury goods. Window-shopping is a must.

Fruit juices – cherry (*visne*), peach (*seftali*), apricot (*kayisi*) or lemonade (*limonata*) – are the favorite local refreshments.

6 PM. Return to Taksim. Have a relaxing apéritif in the bar on the top floor of the Etap Marmara hotel while enjoying its panoramic view. Then go along the Istiklal Caddesi to Çiçek Pasajı ▲ *261*. Go round the British Embassy on the left and head for Tepebaşı. As you pass look at the caryatids of the Londra Hoteli looking out over the Golden Horn.

8 PM. You could dine in the splendid restaurant of the Pera Palace Hotel ◆ *373* not far from there, or you could try the succulent meze of the Yorgos Restaurant in the first street on the left as you leave the Pera Palace.

10 PM. If you still have some energy go back to the Istiklal Caddesi, past the Galatasaray college and continue to the Kuloğlu Sokağı. Go down it. Just at the corner on your left hidden away in a basement is a small bar decorated with cinema posters called the Papyrus. It is open till 1 am.

12 MIDNIGHT. For those who wish to make a night of it there is one final destination: Hayal, a bar situated in the Çukurlu Çeşme Sokağı which is very popular with the young people of Istanbul. The décor is quite bare and stark but it regularly features jazz and rock concerts. Visiting the other night spots in the area is not advised, however, because honesty is not always a feature of their dealings with tourists.

DOLMABAHÇE SARAYI
Baroque, rococo and Empire styles mingle both inside and outside the palace.

8 AM. If you are staying in one of the districts in the center of Istanbul cross the Golden Horn ▲ *238* by the new Galata Bridge ▲ *129*. The old bridge with its fish restaurants and *narghileci* at water level burned down in 1992. In the first avenue on the left you will see the entrance of the Tünel ▲ *255*, a funicular built by the French in 1875 and originally drawn by horses. When you leave the Tünel take the first street on the right; immediately on your left is a former *tekke,* or dervish monastery, which has been converted into the Museum of Literature. Here you can see beautiful old Korans, as well as the costumes ● *52* and musical instruments

● *54* used by the Mevlevi dervishes during their ceremonies. Dance performances are held here regularly: contact the custodian or the Tourist Office for dates. The Count of Bonneval – an adventurous French officer who entered the service of the Turks and changed his name to Ahmet Paşa when he became a Muslim – lies buried in the middle of the gardens of a charming

Since the secular reforms of Mustafa Kemal Atatürk the dancing dervishes have retained the traditions of their Sufi order solely for the public. You can watch one of their ceremonies: with cyclical songs accompanied by percussion and flutes (*ney*) the participants imitate the movement of the stars as they whirl around in ecstasy. Mevlâna Celaludin Rumi, the order's founder, is buried in Konya.

Ottoman cemetery (ask the custodian to show you where his tomb is situated).

10 AM. Return to the funicular. On your right enter the Tünel Geçidi (the Tünel passage) where antique-dealers have their shops and look out in particular for Mustafa Kayabek at no.

10/12. He sells old *dolmans* (patterned silk Ottoman robes), pictures, furniture and postcards. You come out on to the Istiklal Caddesi ▲ *258*, the "Avenue of Independence," which is lined with apartment blocks, in the rococo and Victorian styles, churches and alleys as well as former European embassies demoted by Atatürk to consulates. Before arriving at the junction of Galatasaray ▲ *261* do not miss the Danişman Pasajı, the button-sellers' passage. Continue on to the famous Turco-French college of Galatasaray where the élite of the country have been educated for a century. At the entrance there is

The Istiklal Caddesi ("Avenue of Independence") has not changed much since the 1930's when this photograph was taken. There are still just as many shops and the trams, withdrawn at the start of the 1950's, resumed service in 1991.

«THE HILLS OF GALATA, OF PERA [...] GLIDE
BELOW MY FEET TO THE SEA, STREWN WITH TOWNS
OF MANY DIFFERENT COLOURS.»

LAMARTINE

a museum which details the history of this institution. Opposite, a fish market sells almost everything that can be caught along the coastline of Turkey. Not far from there in the Aslı Han passage, which is below street level, is a book market where you can find both Turkish and foreign books. This is where the *entel* ("intellectuals") of the district come to browse.

12 NOON. Leave by the Çiçek Pasajı where there are numerous restaurants offering that classic Near Eastern dish, meze. Nearby, at the end of the Olivo cul-de-sac, is the famous Rejans Restaurant ♦ *373*, one of Istanbul's legendary eating places, which was opened by White Russians in the 1920's.

2 PM. Go up the avenue to Taksim square and take a *dolmuş* (communal taxi) ♦ *343* in the Inönü Caddesi (better known as Gümüşsuyu) in the direction of Beşiktaş ▲ *277*. Walk around this unspoiled quarter, bedecked with the black and white colors of its football team, the Beşiktaşlı. Their great rivals are the Galatasaraylı team whose rallying cry is *Cim bom bom*.

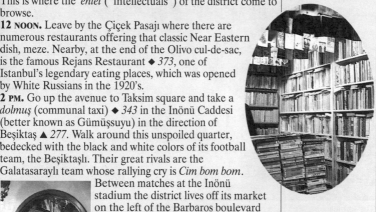

Christian institutes, now closed, provided the booksellers with much of their stock.

Between matches at the Inönü stadium the district lives off its market on the left of the Barbaros boulevard behind the mosque of Koca Sinan Paşa. **4 PM.** Walk along the coast of the Bosphorus as far as the Çirağan Palace ▲ *280*. Before reaching it you will pass below a bridge linking the palace to the huge Yıldız park, named after the beautiful favorite of Sultan Abdül Mecit I. One of his successors, Abdül Hamid II, built a complex of pavilions and residences on top of the hill, which was reached by a broad carriageway. You can visit the Swiss chalet where Mustafa Kemal used to have a modest office. Important visiting dignitaries, such as General de Gaulle and the Empress Farah Dibah, were officially received here. The Çadir Köşkü has an outstanding view over a mass of greenery ■ *26* all the way down to the Bosphorus. Take a well-deserved rest here and enjoy the scenery over a refreshing cup of coffee or a cherry juice (*vişne suyu*).

6 PM. On your way back head for the Boğazçi Köprüsü ▲ *274*, the Bosphorus Bridge, at the foot of which nestles the Ortaköy quarter, where you can still find a number of traditional wooden houses. This has recently become a fashionable part of the city because of its bars which stay open till late at night. The young people of Istanbul come to hear local rock groups or popular singers. If you choose to dine here you will be spoiled for choice, as there are countless restaurants. If you do decide to have a late night, remember that you will have to get a taxi back to your hotel because there are no buses after 11pm.

Westernization of the country has relegated many traditional costumes and objects to antique shops.

Not far from the pavilions of Yıldız and Ortaköy is the Bosphorus Bridge, or Boğazçi Köprüsü, opened in 1973 on the occasion of the 50th anniversary of the Republic.

The former Séraskiérat, or Ministry of War, is now occupied by the university of Beyazıt.

The Frenchman Pierre Loti (1850–93) wrote about the fascination of Istanbul for Europeans. He lived here on several occasions, initially settling like all Europeans of the time in the Pera district ▲ 257. However, he was soon more attracted by the ambience of the mosques and the smaller, secret areas of old "Stamboul", where he could absorb a more authentic oriental atmosphere. If you wish to do the same this itinerary will take a very full half of a day.

8 AM. Leave the Beyazıt Meydanı, formerly Séraskiérat Square ▲ 202, "full of lights, people, music and costumes". The writer "only needs to cross this place to penetrate more deeply into the heart of the old city, into the exquisite and as yet unspoiled districts of the Suléimanieh and Sultan-Sélim. The darkness of the gloomy little streets alternates with lights and crowds. In the cafés there is music: sad violins wailing out melodies to melt the soul; the sour, plaintive note of traditional tunes played on bagpipes by country men, and Asiatics dancing hand in hand in long lines."

The ablutions fountain (şadırvan) of the Mosque of Süleyman the Magnificent, built by the great architect Sinan ▲ 314.

Going up the Bozdoğan Kemeri Caddesi you will see some old, rather dilapidated Ottoman houses as well as workshops. Then you come out into the courtyard of the Mosque of Süleyman the Magnificent (Süleymaniye Cami'i) ▲ 200, where Loti liked to wander among the craftsmen. "Each in his open stall, the patient illuminators, brush in hand, bent forward amid their little flasks of gilt and silver. Almost all of them look old, men from another era, you might say. With their thin fingers, agile and accurate, they trace out impeccable symbols onto paperboard, leaning their turbanned heads over their work". The calligraphers ▲ 206 are no longer there, but the mosque and Süleyman's tomb, with its diamond-encrusted cupola, are worth at least an hour of your time.

10 AM. Take a taxi to the Mosque of Mehmet the Conqueror, Fatih Mehmet Cami'i ▲ 221. "In front of this venerable mosque, which was once a Byzantine church, the small well-shaded square is unchanged, it still has the same air of intimacy, so enclosed that one almost feels it is indiscreet to appear there. Modest cafés surround it, once decorated with nothing but inscriptions from the

«THE DISTANCES OF STAMBOUL BEHIND US, SEEN THROUGH
THE BREAKS IN THE WALL, LOOK EXACTLY LIKE
A DEAD CITY UNDER THE HEAVY WINTER SKY.»

PIERRE LOTI

Koran; it is crammed with wooden couches with backs covered with strikingly colored carpets from Asia for the hookah smokers to sit on". Discretion is required in this very religious district. During certain festivals, such as Kurban bayram and Seker bayram, the cloak of the Prophet, which is kept in the Topkapı museum, is displayed in the mosque for veneration by the faithful.

Take another taxi and ask the driver to drive you to Edirne Kapı ▲ 232, originally the "Adrianople Gate," with its broken arch (a 10 to 15 minute journey) where the ancient walls of Byzantium stand. "All along these solitary grey walls which unfurl their line of crenelated bastions as far as the eye can see, there is one cemetery after another. Into the farthest distance stretch groves of cypress, with their almost black funereal foliage [...] It is a world of slabs and pillars, tilted, fallen and broken in their falling, now without form and covered with lichen." Nowadays the Savaklar Caddesi, a wide avenue built in the 1960's, has replaced the old dirt road which once separated the walls from the cemetery, where rests the beautiful Aziyadé, who was so dear to Pierre Loti's heart.

12 NOON. When you leave this precinct take a *dolmuş* ◆ *343* in the direction of Eminönü district (the journey will take about 20 minutes). Behind the spice market ▲*132* is "this square with its ancient plane trees dominated on one side by the Mosque of Valideh, with its tall, gray bulk, minarets and Arabic serrations. On the other side are arbors of vines, small cafés and barbers' shops."

Today, you will still find a few cafés but also corn chandlers, pet-sellers and men selling leeches which are still used in traditional medicine. Your visit here can be prolonged by a stop at the famous Pandeli Restaurant ◆ *364* decorated with blue ceramic tiles, which was the former guardhouse for the spice bazaar.

Julien Viaud, *alias* Pierre Loti, revealed the charms of the Ottoman capital to other Europeans.

The silhouettes of inscribed Ottoman funeral stelae abound in Istanbul cemeteries ▲ *250*.

Near the Edirne Kapı cemetery the old road runs beside the ancient walls of Byzantium, which are now being restored.

◆ AN EXCURSION TO THE BELGRADE FOREST

CABECI   GÜZELCEKEMER   ALIBEY BARAJI   MAĞLOVA   KOVUKKEMER (EĞRIKEMER)

TOWARDS ISTANBUL

TOWARDS FATIH MEHMET BRIDGE

To cope with the threat of sieges the Byzantines constructed a remarkable water-supply system. Each inhabitant of the city had his own cistern for collecting rainwater and the emperors also built a network for distributing springwater, which was further developed by the sultans, as can be seen from the many aqueducts and dams (*bent*) built in the Belgrade Forest.

MAĞLOVA AQUEDUCT, KNOWN AS "JUSTINIAN'S"

Nowadays this structure, accessible by road from Büyükdere or Kemerburgaz, has become a center for walks and country picnics. When the public fountains supplied by their networks dried up the city-dwellers came to collect water from this spring, considered to be the best in town.

There are two water catchment systems within the forest. The first, built between 1554 and 1584 by Sinan, partially follows the Roman and Byzantine layouts. It has 32 miles of pipes and more than 30 aqueducts, supplying around 600 fountains and hammams in Istanbul. The rise in the population on the other bank of the Golden Horn around Galata led to the installation from 1730 onwards of a second system connected to the distribution reservoir, known as *taksim* in Turkish, situated at the entrance to the square of the same name. In a car you can, in one day, visit the main features of this network which are marked by road signs with an orange arrow. Leaving Taksim head for the Bosphorus which you follow as far as Büyükdere. From there take the road on the left to Bahçeköy in the Belgrade Forest. About half a mile before the village you will see the Bahçeköy aqueduct, or Mahmut I Kemeri, completed in 1732 during the reign of Mahmut I. It is 450 yards long and 90 feet high and takes water from the three *bent* (dams) upstream to the reservoirs of Şişli and Beyoğlu.

THE NETWORK OF MAHMUT I. The first dam, northeast of Bahçeköy, is the Topuzlubent. Completed in 1750, its sloping wall buttressed against the water predates the arched dams which were not built in Europe until the 19th century. Continue to the end of the road, passing through Bahçeköy, before proceeding on foot to the Mahmut II Bendi, constructed in 1739 by Mahmut II. This 100-yards long structure, which ends in a cutwater, is completely faced with white marble. Opposite it is the huge Valide Bendi built in 1796 by Mihrisah, Sultan Selim III's mother. Return to the road to Büyükdere. At the Mahmut II Kemeri the road forks towards Kemerburgaz. Before reaching this village you can see the Kirazlıbent ("the cherry dam") built by Mahmut II on the ruins of the old system. From Kemerburgaz you

356

KEMERBURGAZ   UZUNKEMER   PAŞAKEMERI   KIRAZLIBENT   BUYÜKBENT   AYVAD BENDI   OSMANBENDI (KARANLIKBENT)   MAHMUTKEMER   BAHÇEKÖYKEMERI   MAHMUT II BENDI   VALIDE BENDI

TOPUZLUBENT

TOWARDS BÜYÜKDERE

TOWARDS PINAR
AND YENIKÖY

... can visit two of the most impressive buildings in the network, the Kovukkemer and the Uzunkemer.

SINAN'S WORKS. A mile from the village is the long aqueduct (Uzunkemer) started by Sinan in 1563 and completed in 1564. It is over 780 yards long and 85 feet high, with a double row of arches, broad and narrow, buttresses and the rounded channel running through the arches. The Kovukkemer, also known as Eğrikemer, or the "Bent Dam", spans the Kağithane river. This monumental work, 450 yards long and 110 feet high, comprises three series of arches. Sinan is responsible for the form in which we see it today.

THE DARK DAM. Upstream from the Egrikemer is the Karanlıkbent ("the Dark Dam") built by Osman II (1618–22). It is a straight wall some 6 yards thick, 8 yards high and 70 yards long, and its massive appearance is reinforced by the thrusting buttresses and the double parapet which is used as a seat by those wishing to gaze at the water reflecting the surrounding trees. From here, following forest tracks suitable for vehicles for part of the way, you eventually come to the Ayvad Bendi with its causeway of white Marmara marble. The absence of buttresses lends very clean lines to this dam. The two balconies supported by brackets are there solely as amenities.

THE COUNTRYSIDE. These constructions carry the two branches of the system towards a reservoir from which the water is taken to the aqueduct of Mağlova. Visit this before returning to Istanbul. Situated in the heart of the countryside 3 miles southwest of Kemerburgaz it can be reached only by following a low-grade dirt track. However it is the most imposing of all with its two levels pierced in the middle by four great arches. It is 120 feet high and 284 yards long, and is reflected in the artificial lake during times of heavy rainfall. During periods of drought it dominates a desert-like valley. Before arriving in the old city the waters are directed over another monumental aqueduct, the Güzelcekemer ("Beautiful Aqueduct"). However you will need to be very dedicated and have a detailed map if you wish to reach this one.

In the typical Ottoman style of combining the practical and the aesthetic, the top of the buttresses of the Topuzlubent is designed as a pavilion, with the small corner pillars serving as tent poles, and a viewing platform on top. In the middle facing the water is a marble plaque with an inscription in praise of Mahmut I (1730–54) who commissioned the building.

The Güzelcekemer or Çebeçiköy aqueduct, built by Sinan 1563–4, is 45 feet high and has two series of arches running the length of its 185 yards.

357

In Istanbul, the lively and noisy street life is like a permanent theatrical performance which cannot fail to fascinate children.

THE FISH MARKET. Near to the new Galata Bridge ▲ 129 crowds of people with fishing lines – sometimes using only a short piece of iron wire as a rod – share the shore with the professional fishermen, who can be seen preparing fried-fish sandwiches on their large fishing boats. From the shops, stalls and pedlars near the bridge you can buy just about anything, from products that can change lead into silver to little wheels for cutting glass, and each and every sale is conducted with animated conversations and gestures. The tribe of itinerant vendors – boys often little taller than the pile of bread rolls they are hawking, or shoe-shiners and water-carriers – adds to the vivid color and liveliness of this area.

THE SPICE BAZAAR. On the way to the spice bazaar you pass the Beyazıt Mosque ▲ 200 which resounds to the flapping of the flocks of pigeons that live there, sensibly close to the grain-sellers. In the flower market behind, puppies, rabbits and birds bustle about inside

The hawkers at Karaköy get almost all their catches from the Sea of Marmara.

If we are to believe Théophile Gautier the pigeons of the Beyazıt Cami'i are descendants of two ring doves bought by Sultan Beyazıt from a poor woman and then offered to the mosque.

In the flower market a rabbit tells your fortune by pulling a card from a box whose compartments are full of predictions.

The old boats from Sirkeci Iskelesi which connect with the Princes' Islands hark back to another era, just like the coaches of Büyük Ada.

their cages amid the roses and petunias. In the bazaar itself the powerful smells from the large bags of brightly colored spices are almost overwhelming.

PRINCES' ISLANDS. Even on the old boats sailing out to the Princes' Islands ▲ 271, crammed full at the weekend, entire families from Istanbul take up the refrain of the streets and join together in ear-splitting song. At Büyük Ada take your children to eat in one of the restaurants on the edge of the water before riding in a horse-drawn coach into the inner regions of the island, where children can play about in the quiet of the woods.

USEFUL ADDRESSES

⚡ VIEW
🅲 CITY CENTER
⊡•• ISOLATED
Ⓜ LUXURY RESTAURANT
◑ TYPICAL RESTAURANT
○ BUDGET RESTAURANT
🏛 LUXURY HOTEL
🏠 TYPICAL HOTEL
⌂ BUDGET HOTEL
🅿 PARKING
🚗 SUPERVISED GARAGE
📺 TELEVISION
🏠 QUIET
⌖ SWIMMING POOL
💳 CREDIT CARDS
🧍 REDUCTION FOR CHILDREN
🚫 NO ANIMALS
♫ MUSIC
🎺 LIVE BAND

◆ CHOOSING A RESTAURANT

♦ less than 70,000 TL
♦♦ 70,000–140,000 TL
♦♦♦ more than 140,000 TL

Restaurant	VIEW	GARDEN /TERRACE	AIR-CONDITIONING	CAR PARK	CREDIT CARDS	SPECIALTIES	P...
EMINÖNÜ							
ODA RESTAURANT					L	♦♦	
PANDELI					N	♦♦	
SIRKECI							
SEPETÇILER KASRI					I	♦♦♦	
SULTANAHMET							
ALTIN KUPA					N	♦♦	
CAFÉ MEDUSA					L	♦♦	
ÇAMLIK RESTAURANT					N	♦	
KONAK PUB					N	♦	
KONYALI					N	♦	
SARNIÇ					NI	♦♦♦	
SULTAN RESTAURANT					NI	♦♦	
SULTANAHMET							
YEŞIL EV RESTAURANT					N	♦♦♦	
AKSARAY							
GAZIANTEPLI CAVUŞOĞLU					L	♦	
GÜNES KEBAP SALONU					L	♦	
GÜNEÇ SARAY RESTAURANT					L	♦	
RESTAURANT OF THE HOTEL FUAR					N	♦♦♦	
SAIT RESTAURANT					L	♦♦	
BEYAZIT							
SUBASI RESTAURANT					N	♦♦	
KUMKAPI							
CEMAL BALIK RESTAURANT					F	♦♦♦	
YENGEÇ					F	♦♦	
YOSUN					F	♦♦	
LÂLELI							
HACI BOZAN OĞULLARI					L	♦	
ORIENT HOUSE					N	♦♦♦	
ÖZLÂLE RESTAURANT					L	♦	
GOLDEN HORN							
SAHIL RESTAURANT					N	♦	
URFAM RESTAURANT					L	♦	
BEYOĞLU							
4 SEASONS					I	♦♦♦	
ÇIÇEK PASAJI					L	♦♦	
HACI ABDULLAH					N	♦♦	
HACI BABA RESTAURANT					N	♦♦	
ISTANBUL SÜPER RESTAURANT					N	♦	
REJANS					I	♦♦	
RESTAURANT OF THE GALATA TOWER					N	♦♦♦	
RESTAURANT OF THE PERA PALACE					I	♦♦	
YAKUP 2					L	♦♦	
TAKSIM							
BORSA RESTAURANT					N	♦♦	

	VIEW	GARDEN/TERRACE	AIR-CONDITIONING	CAR PARK	CREDIT CARDS	SPECIALTIES	PRICE
...ASERO STEAK RESTAURANT			■		■	I	♦♦
... LOKANTASI			■			I	♦♦
...E CHINA RESTAURANT)							
...BELI RESTAURANT						L	♦
...AMINGO RESTAURANT			■			NI	♦♦
...NORAMA RESTAURANT	■					NI	♦♦♦
...RK RESTAURANT		■				N	♦
...OL RESTAURANT		■	■			I	♦♦♦
...NDEZ-VOUS RESTAURANT		■	■			I	♦♦
...STAURANT OF THE DIVAN HOTEL			■			N	♦♦♦
...STAURANT ROSA			■		■	I	♦♦
...ISS PUB RESTAURANT			■			I	♦♦♦
...VA PUB-RESTAURANT		■				NI	♦♦
...KÜDAR							
...NAAT			■			N	♦
...NCES' ISLANDS							
...APTAN RESTAURANT	■		■			-	♦♦♦
...RÜK ÂLI RESTAURANT		■				-	♦♦
...SIAN SHORE OF BOSPHORUS							
...BORAN RESTAURANT		■				L	♦♦
...ĞAZIÇI		■				F	♦♦♦
...MLICA CAFÉ-RESTAURANT			■			N	♦♦♦
...DIV RESTAURANT		■	■			N	♦♦♦
...AVAK DOĞANAY RESTAURANT		■				F	♦♦
...SUN RESTAURANT		■		■		F	♦♦
...UROPEAN SHORE OF BOSPHORUS							
...YAZ PARK RESTAURANT		■				F	♦
...ASSERIE OF THE CIRAĞAN PALACE						I	♦♦♦
...FTNAL			■			N	♦♦
...ENIZ PARK GAZINOSU		■				F	♦♦
...E BAR						N	♦♦♦
...LICITAS			■			L	♦♦
...LIZ RESTAURANT			■			F	♦♦♦
...AN RESTAURANT			■			F	♦♦
...ANEDAN						N	♦♦
...ALET 2			■			F	♦♦♦
...ENI BEBEK			■			F	♦♦♦
...LDIZLAR RESTAURANT			■			L	♦♦♦
...URSA							
...ACI BEY			■			L	♦
...KENDER KEBABÇI				■		L	♦
...EHIR LOKANTASI						N	♦
...EZEN RESTAURANT		■				L	♦
...ZNIK							
...ALIKÇI RESTAURANT	■		■			-	♦♦
...RIKÇATAL			■			-	♦♦

...cal ...ational	I : international F : fish

◆ CHOOSING A HOTEL

◆ less than 450,000 TL
◆◆ 450,000–900,000 TL
◆◆◆ more than 900,000 TL

Hotel	GARDEN/TERRACE	TV IN ROOM	AIR-CONDITIONING	QUIET	VIEW	CONFERENCES/SEMINARS	QUALITY OF SERVICE	RESTAURANT	24-HOUR ROOM	NUMBER	PRICE
SIRKECI											
Askoç										114	◆
Eris										44	
SULTANAHMET											
Pierre Loti										34	◆
Pirlanta										30	
Sunshine										28	◆
Vezirhan										9	
SULTANAHMET											
Alzer										21	◆
Amber										54	◆
Ayasofya										21	◆
Ayasofya Pensione										61	◆
Barut's Guesthouse										23	
Hali										35	
Hippodrome										14	◆
INTERNATIONAL YOUTH											
Hostel Istanbul										35	◆
Küçük Ayasofya										15	◆
Topkapı Hostel										8	◆
Yeşil Ev										20	◆◆
AKSARAY											
Fuar										61	◆◆
Imga										25	◆
Pelikan										29	◆◆
BEYAZIT											
Benler										94	◆
Cantur										45	◆
Inter										30	◆
Marmara										60	
Padova										15	
President										204	◆◆
Selenay										53	◆◆
Selman										20	◆
KUMKAPI											
Kumkapı										40	◆
Paradise										37	◆◆
LÂLELI											
Astor										114	◆◆
Bazaar										36	◆
Klas										126	◆◆
Midi										29	◆
Oran										100	◆◆
Prestige										111	◆◆

	GARDEN/TERRACE	TV IN ROOM	AIR-CONDITIONING	QUIET	VIEW	CONFERENCES/SEMINARS	QUALITY OF SERVICE	RESTAURANT	24-HOUR ROOM SERVICE	NUMBER OF ROOMS	PRICE
AMADA										427	♦♦♦
ESTERIA										54	♦♦
KSEL										81	♦♦
ATIH											
ARIYE										24	♦♦♦
EYOĞLU											
ERA PALACE										145	♦♦♦
CHMOND										101	♦♦♦
E MARMARA										390	♦♦♦
AKSIM											
RUPA										20	♦
LSON										114	♦♦♦
VAN										180	♦♦♦
RESIN										75	♦♦
OLDEN AGE										121	♦♦♦
ILTON										498	♦♦♦
ERVANSARAY										62	♦♦♦
AMARTINE										60	♦♦♦
ODGE										41	♦♦
VA										71	♦♦♦
HERATON										427	♦♦♦
TAR										26	♦
STA										61	♦♦
SKÜDAR											
MEK										19	♦
RINCES' ISLANDS											
RINCESS											♦♦♦
PLENDID PALACE											♦♦♦
ÖRÜK ALI											♦
SIAN SHORE OF BOSPHORUS											
IDIV										13	♦♦♦
UROPEAN SHORE OF BOSPHORUS											
EBEK										47	♦♦
ÜYÜK TARABYA										286	♦♦♦
IRAĞAN PALACE										324	♦♦♦
UAT PAŞA										51	♦♦♦
URSA											
ELIK PALAS										173	♦♦♦
IKMEN										50	♦
ILMEN										102	♦♦♦
DIRNE											
ALTA											♦
ENER											♦

EMINÖNÜ

CULTURE

RÜSTEMPAŞA MOSQUE
Hasırcılar Cad. n° 90
Unkapanı, Eminönü.
Currently being restored.

RESTAURANTS

ODA RESTAURANT
Zindankapı Değirmen
Sok. n° 15 Eminönü
(bank of Golden Horn,
left of Galata)
Tel. 5 20 15 30
Open 8am–midnight
Closed Sun.
Difficult to find. Fine dining area with parquet flooring and green bamboo furniture. View over Golden Horn. Menus with assortment of Turkish specialties including grills.
67,000 TL
◐ ⊡ ⋇ P

PANDELI
Egyptian market.
Tel. 5 27 39 09
Open 11.30am–4pm
Closed Sun.
101,000 TL
⊡

SIRKECI

RESTAURANTS

SEPETÇILER KASRI
Kennedy Cad.
Saray Burnu
Tel. 5 11 45 03
Open 11–12.30am.
Site classed as historical monument. Incredible view over Bosphorus in the Septeçiler pavilion. High-class international cuisine.
Specialty: filet mignon.
146,000 TL
◐ ⊡ ⋇

ACCOMMODATION

ASKOÇ
Istasyon Arka Sok. n°
15
Tel. 5 11 80 89
Fax 5 11 70 53.
Luxury hotel but this is not obvious from the unattractive façade. View over Bosphorus from some rooms. Noisy (close to station).
675,180 TL
⌂ Ⓒ ⋇ ▭ 🚗
⊡

ERIS
Istasyon Arkası
Sok. n° 9
Tel. 5 27 89 50
Fax 5 11 59 06.
Very clean hotel, close to the Topkapı with fine view out on to Asian shoreline. Note that prices reduce the longer you stay. Reckon on 33,000 TL for breakfast
214,000 TL–281,000 TL
⌂ Ⓒ ⋇ 🚗

SULTANAHMET

CULTURE

ARCHEOLOGICAL MUSEUM
Sarayıcı Osman Hamdi
Yokusü
Tel. 5 20 77 40
Open 9.30am–4.30pm
Closed Mon.
Not far from Topkapı. Contains very rich collection of antiquities. Well worth a visit.

MUSEUM OF ORIENTAL ANTIQUITIES, TURKISH CERAMICS
In the Archeological
Museum
Tel. 5 20 77 40
Open 9.30am–5pm.
Closed Mon.
Objects d'arts from Middle Eastern civilizations. (Babylon, Mesopotamia, Assyria, Phrygia, ancient Egypt, ancient Arabia and the Hittites).

CHURCH OF DIVINE PEACE
Court of the Janissaries
to right of Topkapı.
Being restored.

Authorization necessar
for visits.

LIBRARY OF KÖPRÜLÜ KÜTÜPHANESI
Divan Yolu n° 29.
No visits allowed.

CISTERN OF YEREBATAN SARAYI
Yerebatan Cad. n° 13
Tel. 5 22 12 59
Open 9am–5pm.
West of Haghia Sophia Byzantine cistern of 6t century supplying water to Byzantines and Ottomans. Columns in Byzantine style support a fine stone vault.

HAMMAM CAĞALOĞLU
Cağaloğlu Cad.
Prof. Kazim Gürkan
Cad. n° 34
Tel. 5 22 24 24
Open 7am–10pm.
For women
open 8am–8pm.
Very old baths established by Mahmut I at start of

3th century. Coffee
vailable and bar.

**AMMAM
EMBERLITAŞ**
erzirhan Cad. n° 8
emberlitaş
el. 5 22 79 74
pen 6am–midnight.
lassified historical
onument.

AREM OF TOPKAPI
opkapı Sarayı
pen 10am–5pm.
losed Tues.
ppointments to visit
ust be made in
dvance. Groups only.

INILI KÖSKÜ
el. 5 20 77 40
Open 9.30am–5pm.
ri. only.
n the garden of the
rcheological Museum.

TOPKAPI SARAYI
ehind Haghia Sophia
el. 5 12 04 80
Open 9am–5pm.
losed Tues.
Magnificent palace of
he Ottoman sultans of
5th to 19th centuries.
Chinese porcelain,
rocades and
mbroideries, famous
ewels and miniatures.

**TÜRBE OF ABDÜL
HAMIT**
Hamidiye Sok.
Under restoration.

TÜRBE OF MAHMUT II
Divan Yolu n° 82
Çemberlitaş
Open 9.30am–4.30pm.
Closed Mon. and Tues.

**NURUOSMANIYE
MOSQUE**
Nuruosmaniye Cad.
Kapalıçarşı Girişi,
Cağaloğlu.
*At entrance to Grand
Bazaar, 18th-century
mosque inspired by
Baroque architecture .*

RÜSTEMPAŞA MOSQUE
Hasırcılar Cad. n° 90
Unkapani, Eminönü.
Being restored.

YENI CAMI'I
Eminönü Meydanı
(opposite Galata
bridge).

**ZEYNEP SULTAN
MOSQUE**
Alemdar Cad.

RESTAURANTS

ALTIN KUPA
Yerebatan Cad. n° 6

Tel. 5 19 47 70
Open 8am–midnight.
*Pleasant terrace
overlooking Haghia
Sophia. Specialty:
fresh vegetables au
gratin.*
67,000 TL
◐ ▭

CAFÉ MEDUSA
Yerabatan Cad.,
Muhteremefendi Sok.
n° 19
Tel. 5 11 41 16
Open 7.30am–midnight.
*In a small four-story
house; pretty paneled
restaurant, pleasant
atmosphere, for
sampling a large choice
of Turkish cuisine at
reasonable prices
Specialty: diliç medusa.*
67,000 TL
◐

ÇAMLIK RESTAURANT
Divan Yolu Cad. n° 15
Tel. 5 16 84 16
Open 11.30am–
midnight.
*Self-service. Alcohol
served with meals.
Good value for money.
Specialty: Meatballs in
cream cheese.*
44,000 TL
○

KONAK PUB
Divan Yolu Cad. n° 66–8
Tel. 5 26 89 33
Open 8am–midnight.
*Conspicuous and eye-
catching neon sign
compensated for by
pleasant atmosphere
and reception.
Specialty: Various
pastries.*
44,000 TL
◐ ▭

KONYALI
Topkapı Sarayı
Tel. 5 13 96 97
Open 9.30am–5pm.
Closed Tues.
*Essential stop after
hours of sightseeing.
Sunny terrace and fine
view. Prices sometimes
high and waiters rather
aggressive.
Specialty: kebab
koyade.*
67,000 TL
◐ ▭ ⌁ ⊗

SARNIÇ
Soğukçeşme Sok.
Tel. 5 12 42 91
Open 12–3pm,
8pm–midnight.
Closed Mon.
Old restored cistern.
202,000 TL
▭

KÜÇÜK AYASOFYA HOTEL
AYASOFYA PENSIONES
ALZER HOTEL

AT MEYD.

KÜÇÜK AYASOFYA CAD.

AKSA S.

**SULTAN
RESTAURANT**
Divan Yolu Cad. n° 2
Tel. 5 26 63 47
Open 6am–midnight.
*Close by Haghia
Sophia. Very quiet.
International and
Turkish cuisine. Small
portions.
Specialty: any kind of
meat.*
146,000 TL

ACCOMMODATION

PIERRE LOTI
Piyerloti Cad. n° 5
Çemberlitaş
Tel. 5 18 57 00
Fax 5 16 18 86.
*In main artery of
Istanbul, modern luxury
hotel to international
standards. Service
impeccable. Breakfast
included. Only
criticism: rather noisy.*
675,000–956,000 TL

PIRLANTA
Divan Yolu Cad.
Tel. 5 27 70 85
*Warm welcome. Very
centrally located with
reasonable prices.
Rooms rather spartan.*

*Breakfast costs extra
70,000–112,000 TL*

SUNSHINE
Alayköşkü Cad. n° 1
Cağaloğlu
Tel. 5 13 26 73
Fax 5 27 42 66.
*Clean new hotel near
Haghia Sophia.
Pleasant rooms and
reasonable prices.
Breakfast included. Pity
there is no air-
conditioning.*
675,000 TL

VEZIRHAN
Alemdar Cad. n° 5
Tel. 5 11 24 14
Fax 5 11 17 85.
*Comfortable new hotel
located close to
entrance to Topkapı.
Breakfast included.
Good value for money.*
338,000–450,000 TL

BARS

SULTAN PUB
Divan Cad. n° 2
Tel. 5 26 63 47

Open 7pm–4am.
*Atmosphere
reminiscent of English
pub. Many kinds of
cocktails (about
55,000 TL).*

SULTANAHMET
CULTURE

**MUSEUM OF TURKISH
AND ISLAMIC ART**
Ibrahim Paşa Sarayı,
Sultanahmet Meydanı
(near Hippodrome)
Tel. 5 18 18 05
Open 10am–5pm.
Closed Mon.

MUSEUM OF MOSAICS
Seyitmacan Sok. Arasta
Çarşisi (to left of Blue
Mosque)
Tel. 5 18 12 05
Open 9.30am–5pm.
Closed Tues.
*Displays mosaics
recently discovered in
the Great Palace of
Byzantium.*

**MUSEUM OF CARPETS
AND KILIMS**
Sultanahmet Cami'i'

Sultanahmet
Tel. 5 18 13 80
Open 9am–5pm.
Closed Mon.
*Excellent collection of
Turkish carpets and
kilims.*

TANZIMAT MUSEUM
Gülhane Parkı
Sultanahmet
Tel. 5 12 63 84
Open 8.30am–5pm.
Closed Mon.
*Small museum
recounting the 1839
reforms.*

HAMMAM HASEKI
Kabasakal Sok. (just
opposite Haghia
Sophia)
Open 9.30am–5pm.
Closed Tues.

**HAGHIA SOPHIA
BASILICA**
Ayasofya Meydanı
Tel. 5 22 17 50
Open 9.30am–5pm.
Closed Mon.

KÜÇÜK AYA SOFYA
Küçükayasofya
Mahallesi
Open 10.30am–5.30pm

HIPPODROME HOTEL
HALI HOTEL
YEŞIL EV RESTAURANT
YEŞIL EV HOTEL
TOPKAPI HOTEL
BARUT'S GUEST HOUSE

BLUE MOSQUE
Sultanahmet Parkı.

FIRUZ AĞA MOSQUE
Divan Yolu n° 5.

SOKOLLU MEHMET PAŞA MOSQUE
Şehit Mehmet Paşa Sok.

RESTAURANTS

YEŞIL EV RESTAURANT
Kabasakal Cad. n° 5
Tel. 5 17 67 80
Open 12–3pm.
7–!0.30pm.
*Splendid garden.
Lunch there in summer
among the fountains
and trees. Very good
international and
Turkish cuisine. A little
expensive. Also a hotel.
Specialty: meats in
various sauces.
270,000 TL*
🏨 📺

ACCOMMODATION

ALZER
At Meydanı n° 72
Tel. 5 16 62 62
Fax 5 16 00 00.
*Choose a room
overlooking the
Hippodrome with TV
and mini-bar. Breakfast
included.
536,000–900,000 TL*
🏨 📺 ✳ 💱 🚗 📺

AMBER
Yusuf Aşkin Sok. n° 28
Küçük Ayasofya
Tel. 5 18 48 01
Fax 5 18 81 19.
*Brand new hotel in a
poor area of
Sultanahmet, near the
sea. Saunas, hammam
and bar.
675,000–956,000 TL*
🏨 📺 ✳ 💱 📺

♦ YEŞIL EV HOTEL ♦

This old Ottoman house has
been tastefully redecorated. It is
right by Haghia Sophia,
Topkapı Sarayı and
the Blue Mosque.

AYASOFYA
Küçükayasofya Cd.
Demirci Reşit Sok. n° 28
Tel. 5 16 94 46
Fax 5 13 76 22.
*In a19th-century
Ottoman house.
Comfortable rooms with
shower and telephone.
Breakfast included.
Rather expensive.
506,000–788,000 TL*
🏨 📺 ✳ 📺

AYASOFYA PENSIONES
Soğukçeşme Sokaği
(closed to traffic)
Tel. 5 13 36 60
Fax 5 13 36 69.
*Nine houses built in the
18th century make up
this fine and unusual
hotel. Charming 19th-
century décor. Very
quiet. Breakfast
included.
1,013,000–1,125,000TL*
🏨 📺 🛏 💱 ✳ 📺

BARUT'S GUESTHOUSE
Ishakpaşa Cad. n° 8
Tel. 5 17 68 41
Fax 5 16 29 44.
*Simple but spacious
rooms with private
bathrooms. View over
Bosphorus from dining
room on top floor.
Breakfast included.
281,000–360,000 TL*
🛏 📺 🛏 💱 ✳ 📺

HALI
Klodfarer Cad. n° 20
Çemberlitaş
Tel. 5 16 21 70
Fax 5 16 21 72.
*Some rooms overlook
the Blue Mosque. Very
large bathrooms. TV on
request. Breakfast
included.
450,000–731,000 TL*
🏨 📺 ✳ 📺

HIPPODROME
Mimar Mehmet Ağa
Cad. n° 17
Tel. 5 17 68 89
Fax 5 16 02 68.
*In old Ottoman house
(no lift). Sparsely
decorated rooms, no
air-conditioning. In
summer breakfast
served on roof. Rather
expensive.
450,000–619,000 TL*
🏨 📺 ✳ 📺

INTERNATIONAL YOUTH HOSTEL ISTANBUL
Caferiye Sok. n° 6
Tel. 5 13 61 50

BENLER HOTEL · INTER HOTEL · ALTIN KUPA · ORIENT HOUSE DINNER-SPECTACLE · PRESIDENT HOTEL · PADOVA HOTEL

ATATÜRK KÖPRÜSÜ · ATATÜRK BULVARI · SCHZADEBAS CAD · FUAT PAŞA CAD · ORDU CAD · YENIÇERILER CAD.

Fax 5 12 76 28.
Youth hostel with pleasant décor. Dormitories and toilet facilities. Cafeteria. Breakfast up to 55,000 TL.
146,000–169,000 TL
⌂ C ✣

KÜÇÜK AYASOFYA
Şehit Mehmet Paşa Sok. n° 25 Küçük Aya-Sofya
Tel. 5 16 19 88
Fax 5 16 83 56.
Typical Ottoman building in centre of Sultanahmet. Warm welcome. Green paneling in rooms. Breakfast included.
338,000–731,000 TL
🏨 C ⌂ ⊡ ⅍ ✣ ▱

TOPKAPI HOSTEL
Cankurtaran Mah. Ishak Paşa Cad. Kutlugün Sok. n° 1
Tel. 5 17 65 58.
Good address for this category. Double rooms with shower. Breakfast extra.
90,000–112,000 TL
⌂ C ⌂ ✣ ▱

YEŞIL EV
Kabasakal Cad. n° 5
Tel. 5 17 67 85
Fax 5 17 67 80.
Splendid hotel hiding away in large park. Has retained period furnishings. Luxury, peace, in rural setting. Prior booking essential (only 24 rooms). A very special address.
1,406,625 TL
🏨 C ⌂ ⅍ ▱ ✣ 🚗 ▱

BARS

ÇALIK
Iskele Meydanı n° 12
Yenikapı
Tel. 5 27 09 25
Open 8pm–12.30am.
Well-known bar, located in old Istanbul. Cheapest of the bars putting on standard show (belly dancers, etc.).

AKSARAY
RESTAURANTS

GAZIANTEPLI CAVUŞOĞLU
Şair Fitnat Sokaği 4 / 1 Ordu Cad. Laleli
Tel. 5 18 76 65
Open 12 noon–11pm
Located within striking distance of several middle-range hotels. Convivial atmosphere. Food a bit stodgy. Specialty: kebab in gravy.
33,000 TL
O

GÜNEÇ KEBAP SALONU
Inkilâp Cad. n° 12
Tel. 5 86 58 57
Open 11am–11pm.
Near the large hotels in Laleli. Good restaurant. Ample well-presented dishes. Clientèle mainly Turkish. Specialties: mixed kebab (3 types of lamb).
33,000 TL
O

GÜNEY SARAY RESTAURANT
Atatürk Bulvarı n° 126
Tel. 5 19 30 34
Open noon–midnight.
Near aqueduct of Valens, on lively boulevard. Pretty European décor with paneling. Very clean. Good solid food. Specialty: karisik kebab.
44,000 TL
O

PATISSERIE ŞÜTIŞ
Namık Kemal Cad. n° 14
Tel. 5 29 50 60
Open 6am–midnight.
Essential address for those with a sweet tooth. Great variety of desserts at good prices. Real Turkish delight.

RESTAURANT OF THE HOTEL FUAR
Hotel Fuar
Namık Kemal Cad.
Tel. 5 89 14 40
Open 12 noon–3pm. 7pm–11pm.
Very large choice of international dishes. Meats in savory sauces. Reasonable prices for high-quality cuisine. Specialties: filet Fuar, cordon bleu.
214,000 TL
⏍ ▱

SAIT RESTAURANT
Mustafa Kemal Paşa Bulvarı n° 86
Tel. 5 18 55 45
Open 8am–11pm.
Very popular restaurant halfway between fast-food and quality restaurant. Excellent kebab with yogurt. Specialty: grilled lamb.
67,000 TL
O

ACCOMMODATION

FUAR
Namık Kemal Cad.
Tel. 5 89 14 40
Fax 5 88 60 48
Décor a bit flashy but high class. Courteous welcome and pleasant view over Bosphorus. Breakfast included.
563,000–1,013,000 TL
🏨 ⊡ ▱ 🚗 ▱

IMGA
M. Kemal Paşa Cad. n° 41
Tel. 5 87 62 82
Fax 5 89 97 55.
Well-respected hotel offering all essential services with – unusually – a garage. However, expensive and noisy. Breakfast included.
450,000–731,000 TL
🏨 C ▱ ✣ 🚗 ▱

PELIKAN
Küçük Langa Cad.
Tel. 5 29 55 13
Fax 5 88 10 56.
Rather small rooms with showers. Breakfast included. Garage.
1,069,000 TL
🏨 ▱ ✣ 🚗 ▱

BEYAZIT
CULTURE

MUSEUM OF CALLIGRAPHY
Eski Beyazıt Kitaplığı
Tel. 5 27 58 51.

Open every day except Mon.
Only museum of its kind in the world. The Ottomans rate calligraphy very highly as an art form.

MUSEUM OF THE PRESS
Divan Yolu n° 84
Çemberlitaş
Tel. 5 13 84 58
Open 10am–12 noon, 1.30–6.30pm
Closed Sun.

BEYAZIT MOSQUE
Hürriyet Meydanı
Built in 1505, one of the oldest mosques in Istanbul. Fine inner courtyard with pillars. Note the Sultan's gallery decorated with precious marbles.

SÜLEYMAN THE MAGNIFICENT MOSQUE AND PRECINCT
Süleymaniye Cad.
Sinan's masterpiece commissioned by Süleyman.

ŞEHZADE MOSQUE
Şehzadebaşı
Built in 1544 by Sinan in memory of the prince-heir Mehmet, the son of Süleyman.

RESTAURANTS

SUBASI RESTAURANT
Tavuk Pazari Sok.
Kürkçüler Kapısı n° 58/A
Çemberlitaş

Tel. 5 12 78 44
Open 11am–4pm.
6pm–4am.
Closed Sun.
Right next to the Grand Bazaar. Very tasty food but limited choice. Specialty: stuffed aubergines.
101,000 TL
◑ 🔲

ACCOMMODATION

BENLER
Ordu Cad., Ağaçeşme Sok. n° 11
Tel. 5 17 08 51
Fax 5 17 08 55.
The rooms on the top floor overlook the Bosphorus. Classic comfort. Rather abrupt reception. Breakfast included.
394,000 TL
🏠 🇨 �no 🔲

CANTUR
Balipaşa Yokuşu n° 71
Kumkapı
Tel. 5 16 13 76
Fax 5 17 18 67.
Good quality hotel. Very fine terrace overlooking Bosphorus. Good prices. Breakfast included.
450,000–641,000 TL
🏠 🇨 🔲

INTER
Mithatpaşa Cad.
Büyük Haydar Efendi Sok.
Tel. 5 18 35 35
Fax 5 18 35 38.
Standard comfort hotel.

Breakfast with buffet served on terrace.
540,000 TL
🏠 🔲 ✗ 🚗 🔲

MARMARA
Beyazıt Meydanı
Ordu Cad. 23
Tel. 5 16 78 83.
Very cheap and central location. Acceptable comfort but noisy. Not to be confused with the hotel "The Marmara" in Taksim. Breakfast extra.
158,000 TL
🏠 🇨 ✗

PADOVA
Çarşıkapı, Asma Kandil Sok. n° 9
Tel. 5 16 11 20
Fax 5 18 49 68.
Rooms small but clean with shower and telephone. Good value. Restaurant on the terrace. Breakfast included.
338,000–450,000 TL
🏠 ✗ 🔲

PRESIDENT
Tiyatro Cad. n° 25
Tel. 5 16 69 80
Fax 5 16 69 99.
Elegant hotel in the heart of old Istanbul. Roof pool with view over the Bosphorus. Very fine traditional restaurant with screens and wrought-iron chandeliers.
1,519,000 TL
🏛 🇨 ⚗ 🔲 🛏 ✗ 🚗 🔲

SELENAY
Soğanağa Mah.
Tavşantaş Sok. n° 12

Tel. 6 38 00 45
Fax 5 16 73 21.
Average hotel with rather dark rooms. Good view out to sea and Princes' Islands. Restaurant, bar and discotheque. Breakfast included.
562,000–675,000 TL
🏠 🇨 🔲 ✗ 🚗 🔲

SELMAN
Soğanağa Mah.
Tavşantaş Sok. n° 2
Tel. 5 17 03 52
Fax 5 16 13 08.
Perfectly decent rooms with shower and telephone. Warm welcome. Cafeteria on roof. Breakfast included. Recommended.
281,000–338,000 TL
🏠 🇨 🚗 🔲

NIGHT LIFE

ORIENT HOUSE
Tiyatro Cad. n° 27
Tel. 5 71 61 63
Open 8pm–2am.
Best show in Istanbul (belly dancers, parade of traditional costumes). Very entertaining.
450,000 TL per drink.
🎵

THE PUB
Hotel President
Tiyatro Cad. n° 25
Tel. 5 16 69 80
Open 11am–2am
"Only English pub in Istanbul", says the publicity. Elaborate décor. Lots of tourists.
🍽

KUMKAPI

RESTAURANTS

CEMAL BALIK RESTAURANT
Capari Sok. n° 27
Tel. 5 17 22 78
Open 10.30am–2am.
Recommended by the Turks but still undiscovered by tourists (unusual in Kumkapı). Specialty: red mullet.
146,000 TL
◑ 🔲

YENGEÇ
Telli Odalar Sok. n° 6
Tel. 5 16 32 27
Open every day 11am–midnight.
In the heart of Kumkapı. Terrace overlooks

pedestrianized area where musicians play. Warm welcome. Very filling menu for 202,000 TL Prices negotiable. Specialty: blue fish. *112,000 TL*

YOSUN RESTAURANT
Üstat Sok. n° 13
Tel. 5 17 59 05
Open every day 10am–midnight.
Best way of discovering Kumkapı, a district of fish restaurants. Excellent reception. Expensive for the quality and quantity actually served. Specialty: seasoned fish with mushrooms.
124,000 TL

ACCOMMODATION

KUMKAPI
Çifte Gelinler Cad. n° 16
Tel. 5 16 01 31
Fax 5 16 20 71.
Adequate hotel, located in fishing district with many restaurants. Good value for money. Breakfast included.
394,000–428,000 TL

PARADISE
Tiyatro Cad. n° 114
Tel. 5 16 73 23
Fax 5 17 47 94.
Recently built hotel with pleasant rooms overlooking the Bosphorus or Kumkapı. Could be cleaner. Splendid views from bar terrace.
405,000–619,000 TL

LÂLELI

CULTURE

LÂLELI MOSQUE
Ordu Cad. (near Ramada hotel).
Being restored.

RESTAURANTS

HACI BOZAN OĞULLARI
Ordu Cad. n° 214
Tel. 5 28 51 61
Open 6am–midnight.
Quiet atmosphere on main artery, Ordu Caddesi. Very good Turkish cuisine.

Excellent kebab with aubergine. First-class service. Specialty: lamb.
44,000 TL

ORIENT HOUSE
Tiyatro Cad. n° 27
(beside Hotel President)
Tel. 5 17 61 63
Open 8pm–midnight.
Attractive lounge with decorated arches. Good dinner amid many plants. Traditional orchestra and show. Well worth the expense. Specialties: Ottoman-style boiled beef, chicken kebabs.
563,000 TL

ÖZLÂLE RESTAURANT
Fethibey Cad., Zeynep Kamil Sok. n° 64
Tel. 5 11 47 75
Open 11am–12.30am.
Very pretty with lots of paneling. Food adequate. Rather syrupy westernized background music. First-class service. Specialty: calf's liver
55,000 TL

ACCOMMODATION

ASTOR
Lâleli Cad. n° 12
Tel. 5 18 64 70
Fax 5 18 64 80.
In this double hotel with sauna, hammam, and massages, prices are very modest given the

comfort and quality. Breakfast included. Recommended.
450,000–563,000 TL

BAZAAR
Ordu Cad. n° 245
Tel. 5 18 77 00
Fax 5 18 77 04.
Not far from historic centre of Istanbul. Very simple quiet rooms. Breakfast included.
450,000–563,000 TL

KLAS
Harikzedeler Sok. n° 48
Tel. 5 11 78 74
Fax 5 12 33 54.
Hotel with hammam, sauna and air-conditioning. TV in some rooms. Breakfast included.
743,000 TL

MIDI
Zeynep Kamil Sok. n° 52-54
Tel. 5 12 54 83.
Simple rooms with showers and toilets. Breakfast included. Excellent value.
248,000–281,000 TL

ORAN
Harikzedeler Cad. n° 36-42
Tel. 5 13 82 00
Fax 5 13 82 05.
Very comfortable and spacious rooms. Air-conditioned, bath,

telephone, terrace. Breakfast included. Pleasant pool.
450,000–731,000 TL

PRESTIGE
Koska Cad. n° 8
Tel. 5 18 82 80
Fax 5 18 82 90.
Luxurious and well located. Outstanding décor. All the comforts of a high-class hotel: air conditioned, mini-bar, satellite TV. Breakfast included.
731,000–1,013,000 TL

RAMADA
Ordu Cad. n° 226
Tel. 5 13 93 00
Fax 5 12 63 90.
One of the most luxurious hotels. Apart from its ideal location, its décor of marble and paneling is tasteful and attractive.
1,564,000 TL

RESTERIA
Lâleli Cad. n° 43
Tel. 5 18 78 78
Fax 5 18 78 82.
Very new and modern hotel in the Laleli caddesi. Spacious rooms and quality of service fully justify the price. Breakfast included.
675,000–900,000 TL

YÜKSEL
Mesih Paşa Cad. n° 79-81
Tel. 5 18 79 38
Fax 5 18 79 40.
Pleasant interior and quite large rooms. Breakfast included Street noise might sometimes be annoying.
563,000 TL

NIGHT LIFE

ASUDE
Ordu Cad. n° 315
Tel. 5 18 61 28
Open day and night.
Beautiful, below Ordu Caddesi with bar, restaurant, discotheque. Rather lacking in atmosphere. Cocktails
394,000 TL

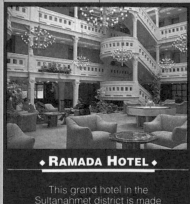

◆ RAMADA HOTEL ◆

This grand hotel in the Sultanahmet district is made up of four small blocks.

FATIH

CULTURE

FETHIYE CAMI'I
Fethiye Cad.
Open 9.30am–4pm.
Closed Tues.

MUSEUM OF CARICATURES
Saraçhane
Tel. 5 13 60 61
Open 10am–5pm.

KARIYE CAMI'I
Kariye Cami'i Sok. n° 28
Edirnekapı
Tel. 5 23 30 09
Open 9.30am–5pm.
Closed Tues.
This 11th century Byzantine church, the most important one after Haghia Sophia, contains a remarkable museum of Byzantine art. Superb murals, frescoes and mosaics.

TEKFUR PALACE
Between Edirnekapı and Eğrikapı, along the ramparts heading towards the Kariye museum.
Visits only with special authorization.

BASILICA OF POLYEUCTOS
Saraçhane Parkı
Open permanently.

GREEK ORTHODOX CHURCH OF SAINT GEORGE
Sadrazam Alipaşa Cad.
Open 7am–5pm.

ORTHODOX CHURCH OF SAINT NICHOLAS
Abdülezel Paşa Cad.
Ring for admittance.

CHURCH OF ST JOHN THE BAPTIST
Kamış Sokağı
Closed.

CHURCH OF ST JOHN OF STUDION
Samatya Cad.
Open 8am–6pm.

CHURCH OF ST MARY OF THE MONGOLS
Sancaktar Yokuşu Sok.
Ring for admittance.

MEDRESE LIBRARY
Feyzullah Efendi College
Feyzullah Efendi Sok.
Open 9am–5pm.

CHURCH OF PANTOCRATOR (ZEYREK MOSQUE)
Vefa.
Old Byzantine church converted into a mosque.

AMCAZADE HÜSEYIN PAŞA MOSQUE
Kardisher Cad.
Being restored.

ATIK MUSTAFA PAŞA MOSQUE
Ayvansaray Cad. Fatih.

GÜL CAMI'I – MOSQUE OF THE ROSES
Vakıf Mektebi Sok.
Open 12 noon–2pm.

FATIH MOSQUE
Shambol Cad.
Open 10am–7.30pm.

KARA AHMET PAŞA MOSQUE
Millet Cad.

YEDIKULE KAPISI
Yedikule Cad.
Tel. 5 85 89 33
Open 10am–5pm.
Closed Mon.

ACCOMMODATION

KARIYE
Kariye Cami'i Sok. n° 18
Edirnekapı
Tel. 5 34 84 14
Fax 5 21 66 31.
This typically Ottoman house of green wood contains the Kariye museum. Large rooms of very stylized design overlook a verdant garden. Breakfast on request.
1,013,000–1,238,000 TL
🏠 🛏 🖶 ☼ ⬜ 🚫 📷

GOLDEN HORN

CULTURE

CHURCH OF ST STEPHEN OF THE BULGARS
Balat Vapur Iskelesi Cad.
Balat.
Being restored.

FENERIOTE MANSIONS
Vapur Iskelesi Cad.
Fener
Open permanently.
Architectural curiosity.

EYÜP MOSQUE
Eyüp.
Sacred site where the sultans were crowned.

AYNALI KAVAK PALACE
Kasımpaşa
Tel. 2 50 40 94
Open 9am–5pm.
Closed Mon. and Tues.
Recently restored 18th-century palace, with attractive colored glass ornamentation.

EYÜP SANCTUARY
Defterdar Cad.
Open 10am–5pm
Closed Tues.

RESTAURANTS

SAHIL RESTAURANT
Karabaş Mah.

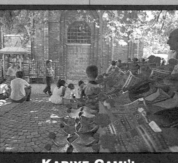

♦ KARIYE CAMI'I ♦

The entrance to this museum of Byzantine art is decorated with an attractive frieze of peacocks.

Dermirhisar Cad. n° 49
Sahil Yolu, Balat
Tel. 5 25 61 85
Open 9am–10.30pm.
On the shore of the Golden Horn near Byzantine remains. Very good food. Specialties: sas kavurma (veal à la turque).
450,000 TL
◐ ☼

URFAM RESTAURANT
Balıkçılar Çarşısı,
Ayan Sok. n° 63
Balat
Tel. 5 23 57 04
Open 9am–9pm.
One of the few cheap restaurants in the picturesque district of Hizircauus, close to the banks of the Golden Horn. Turkish atmosphere guaranteed. Good cooking, not too much oil. Specialty: lamb kebabs.
450,000 TL
○

BARS

PIERRE LOTI CAFÉ
On the slopes overlooking the Eyüp sanctuary. Leave the mosque and a well-signed path on the right will take you to the café.
Open 10am–10pm.
Favorite café of the French writer. Superb view out over the Golden Horn, with small tables under flowery arbor.
☼

BEYOĞLU

CULTURE

ADAM MICKIEWIÇ MUSEUM
Serdar Ömer Cad. Tatli Badem Sok. n° 29
Tarlabaşı
Tel. 2 53 66 98
Open 9.30am–5pm.
Closed Mon.

MUSEUM OF OTTOMAN LITERATURE
(Galata Mevlevihanesi)
Galipdede Cad. n° 15
Tünel
Tel. 2 45 41 41
Open 9.30am–5pm.
Closed Mon.

MILITARY MUSEUM
Valikonaği Cad.

Harbiye
Tel. 2 47 24 97
Open 9am–5pm.
Closed Mon.and Tues.
*Large collection of
weapons from the early
invaders to the
Ottomans.*

SPANISH CHAPEL
Tomtom Kaptan Sok.
n° 37.
Being restored.

**CHURCH OF AYA
TRIADA**
Meselik Cad. n° 11
Open 8–9am.

CHURCH OF ST PETER
Galata Kulesi Cad.
n° 44a
Open 7–8am.

**CHURCH OF SANTA
MARIA DRAPERIS**
Istiklal Cad. n° 443
Open 9am–6.30pm.

**HAMMAM
GALATASARAY**
Turnaci Başı Sok. n° 24
Galatasaray
Tel. 2 49 43 42
Open 8am–8pm.
Men only.

HAMMAM TARIHI AĞA
Turnaci Başı Sok. n° 66
Kuloğlu Mahallesi
Tel. 2 49 50 27
Open 9.30am–6pm
for women,
6pm–9am for men.
Men only on Sun.
*Founded in 1454 by the
Ottoman Sultan Mehmet
Fatih*

**THE TEKKE OF THE
SINGING DERVISHES**
Sahkulu Bostani Cad.
Open 9 .30am–5pm.
Closed Mon.

RÜSTEM PAŞA HAN
Kardeşim Sok.
Open 8.30am–6.30pm.
Closed Sunday.
Caravanserai.

BEDESTEN
Tersane Cad.
Open 8am–5pm.
Closed Sat.,Sun.and
holidays.

HOUSE OF FRANCE
Tomtom Kaptan Sok.
n° 20.

ARAP MOSQUE
Hoca Hanım Sok.

AZAPKAPI MOSQUE
Tersane Cad.

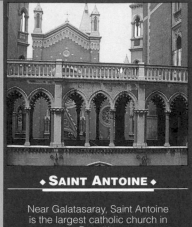

◆ SAINT ANTOINE ◆

Near Galatasaray, Saint Antoine
is the largest catholic church in
Beyoğlu.

Open 8am–9pm.

DOLMABAHÇE MOSQUE
Dolmabahçe Cad.
(beside Dolmabahçe
Palace).

**ALI PAŞA
KILIC MOSQUE**
Necatibey Cad.

VENETIAN PALACE
Italian Embassy
21 Tomtom Kaptan
Sok.n° 21
Open 9am–7pm.
Closed Sat.,Sun. and
holidays.

TOWER OF GALATA
Galata Kulesi
Tel. 2 41 11 60
Open 9am–6pm.
*14th-century Genoese
tower.*

RESTAURANTS

4 SEASONS
Istiklal Cad. 509
Tünel
Tel. 2 45 89 41
Open noon–3pm,
6pm–10pm.
169,000 TL

ÇIÇEK PASAJI
Istiklal Cad.
Galatasaray
Open 11.30am–1am.
67,000 TL

HACI ABDULLAH
Sakizağaci Cad. n° 19
Beyoğlu
Tel. 2 44 85 61
Open 11 .30am–10pm.
Located in a street at

right angles to the
streetcar line to Istiklal.
*Very pleasant interior
design. Food excellent
(remarkable stewed
fruit). Reasonable
prices.*
67,000 TL

**HACI BABA
RESTAURANT**
Taksim Istiklal
Cad. n° 49
(near French
consulate)
Tel. 2 44 18 86
Open noon–11pm.
*Universally praised
restaurant.Very well
presented dishes.
Impressive choice of
desserts. Pleasant
terrace. Specialties:
mantarci sote, tandir
kebab.*
101,000 TL

**ISTANBUL SÜPER
RESTAURANT**
Bekâr Sok. n° 3
Tel. 2 43 06 50
Open 9.30am–3pm,
and 5pm–2am.
*90,000 TL menu has six
specialties from
traditional Turkish
cuisine. Simple and
cheap.*
67,000 TL

REJANS
Emir Nevruz Sok. n° 17
Galatasaray
Tel. 2 44 16 10
Open noon–3pm.
7pm–11pm.

Closed Sun.
112,000 TL

**RESTAURANT OF THE
GALATA TOWER**
Galata Tower, 8th floor,
Karaköy
Open noon–3pm,
8pm–midnight.
*85-ft-high restaurant
with superb views.
There is a 200,000 TL
menu with various
options. Show in
evenings (135,000 TL
extra). Specialty: grills.*
169,000 TL

**RESTAURANT OF THE
PERA PALACE**
Hotel Pera Palace,
Meşrutiyet
Cad. n° 98-100
Tepebasi
Tel. 2 51 45 60
Open noon–3pm,
7–11.30pm.
*Undoubtedly the most
beautiful restaurant in
Istanbul. Fantastic
period décor with
sumptuous
ornamentation and
engravings. Very
reasonable prices.
Orchestra. Not be
missed.*
146,000 TL

YAKUP 2
Asmalımescit Cad. n°
35-37
Galatasaray
Tel. 2 49 29 25
Open noon–midnight.
Closed Sun.
*Not far from Pera
Palace hotel. Warm
rustic mood. Renowned
for succulent gratins.
Specialty: beef-
mushroom gratin.*
90,000 TL

ACCOMMODATION

PERA PALACE
Meşrutiyet Cad. n° 98-
100
Tepebaşı
Tel. 2 51 45 60
Fax 2 51 40 89.
*This spendid hotel,
opened in 1892 to
welcome passengers
from the Orient Express,
has accommodated
many famous guests,
from Garbo to Tito. It
inspired Agatha
Christie, who wrote
"Death on the Orient*

**Express" there. A
monument.**
,025,000 TL
🛏 🇨 ⛷ 🔲 ⚡
🚗 🖵

RICHMOND
tiklal Cad. n° 45-47
el. 2 52 54 60
ax 2 52 97 07.
*his hotel is very quiet
s the street is closed
o traffic. Some rooms
verlook the Bosphorus.
Breakfast included.*
,688,000 TL
🛏 🇨 🏠 ⛷ 🔲 🖵

THE MARMARA
aksim Meydanı
el. 2 51 46 96
ax 2 44 05 09.
*his large 18-floor hotel
dominates the modern
own of Beyoğlu.
Comfortable rooms,
hammam, sauna, pool,
casino, patesserie.*
,476,000 TL
🛏 🇨 ⛷ 🔲 🍴 ⚡
🚗 🖵

NIGHT LIFE

**GALATA TOWER
DISCOTHEQUE**
th floor,Galata Tower,
el. 1 45 11 60.
*Visit it for its view of
stanbul by night.
Fixed price show
plus disco*
450,000TL
⛷ 🎵 🔲

TAKSIM

RESTAURANTS

BORSA RESTAURANT
Halaskargazi Cad.
Osmanbey
el. 2 32 42 00
Open 11am–11pm.
*Right next to Taksim
square. Turkish fast-
food. Quality average.
Specialties: fried
chicken, kebab
sandwich.*
12,000 TL
◐

**BRASERO STEAK
RESTAURANT**
Cumhuriyet Cad. n° 149
Tel. 2 32 72 16
Open 12.30pm–
midnight.
*For lovers of meat
American style.Large
choice of steaks, any
weight. Specialty:
barbecued meat.*
79,000 TL
◑ 🖵

◆ ISTANBUL ILLUMINATED ◆

From the restaurant-cabaret in the
tower you can see the old town lit up,
dominated by the Süleymaniye
`with its four minarets.

**ÇIN LOKANTASI (THE
CHINA RESTAURANT)**
Lamartin Cad. n° 17/1
Tel. 2 50 62 63
Open noon–3pm
7pm–10.30pm.
Closed Sun.
*Definitely the best
Chinese restaurant
in Istanbul. Turkish
dishes can be ordered
as well. The dining
room is a bit old-
fashioned but there is a
warm welcome.
Recommended.
Specialties: chicken
with almonds, beef with
green peppers.*
112,0000 TL
◑ 🖵

FILIBELI RESTAURANT
Lamartin Cad. n° 30/A
Tel. 2 50 66 57
Open noon–9.30pm.
Closed Sun.
*Equidistant from most
large hotels in Taksim.
Owner is a Spaniard.
Food is adequate for
the price. Specialty:
kofte (meatballs).*
33,000 TL
○

**FLAMINGO
RESTAURANT**
Recceppaşa Cad. 15/C
Tel. 2 50 63 22
Open 10am–2am.
*A real surprise: the
setting is superb, the
cooking excellent and
service perfect. An
orchestra plays French
music. Nowhere else
offers such value for*

money. Specialty: steak.
112,000 TL
◐ 🖵

**PANORAMA
RESTAURANT**
The Marmara Hotel,
19th floor
Taksim Meydanı
Tel. 2 51 46 96
Open 7.30pm–11.30pm.
*Unique view of Istanbul.
The city at your feet as
you dine superbly.
Pianist every evening. A
luxury restaurant at
affordable prices.
Specialties: fillet of
steak with three
peppers.*
428,000 TL
◐ 🖵 ⛷ 🅿

PARK RESTAURANT
Sağlik Sok. n° 27
Tel. 2 45 38 73
Open 12pm–12am.
Closed Sun.
*Just behind "The
Marmara" hotel. Very
pleasant terrace
looking out on to small
quiet street. Food
perfect; unique
atmosphere.
Recommended.
Specialty: manti
(raviolis).*
56,000 TL
◐ 🖵

POOL RESTAURANT
Hilton Hotel
Cumhuriyet Cad.
Harbiye
Tel. 2 31 46 50
Open noon–5pm.
Enjoy the pool and the

*Hilton grounds with
views over the
Bosphorus. Good
restaurant but service
mediocre. Specialty:
döner kebab.*
281,000TL
◐ 🖵 ⛷ 🅿

**RENDEZ-VOUS
RESTAURANT**
Lamartin Cad. n° 7
Tel. 2 55 33 62
Open noon–12.30am.
*Perfect welcome in
richly decorated room.
Dishes meticulously
presented and fairly
ample portions.
Specialties: blue fish,
fillets.*
112,000 TL
◐ 🖵

**RESTAURANT OF THE
DIVAN HOTEL**
Cumhuriyet Cad. n° 2
Harbiye
Tel. 2 31 41 00
Open 11am–midnight
Closed Sun.
*Colonial atmosphere in
this beautiful restaurant
considered to be one of
Istanbul's best.
Orchestra every
evening. Specialty:
kebab in yogurt.*
349,000 TL
◐ 🖵 🅿

RESTAURANT ROSA
Cumhuriyet Cad. n°
131/1
Harbiye
Tel. 2 41 28 27
Open noon–11pm.
*Just next to the Hilton.
Very well known. Pizzas
are among the best in
town although a little
expensive. Specialty:
pizza rosa.*
68,000 TL
◐ 🖵

**SWISS PUB
RESTAURANT**
Cumhuriyet Cad. n° 14
Harbiye
Tel. 2 47 30 35
Open 12.30pm–
midnight.
*Dine out in arbors
looking on to Taksim
square. International
and Turkish specialties.
Very reasonable prices.
Specialties: kebab in
yogurt, Swiss special.*
202,000 TL
◐ 🖵 ⛷

**YUVA PUB-
RESTAURANT**
Recceppaşa Cad. n° 3/1

◆ USEFUL ADDRESSES

Tel. 2 56 16 66
Open 11am–11.30pm.
Closed Sun.
*Restaurant frequented
by Turkish executives.
Highly recommended.
Pleasant arbor in
courtyard. Specialty:
ıslım kebab (charcoal
grilled lamb)*
90,000 TL

ACCOMMODATION

AVRUPA
Topçu Cad. n° 32
Tel. 2 50 94 20.
*Simple but clean rooms.
No Visa cards.Breakfast
included. Good value.*
394,000 TL

DILSON
Sıraselviler Cad. n° 49
Tel. 2 52 96 00
Fax 2 49 70 77.
*Standard top-class
facilities (air
conditioned, TV,
mini-bar) and
comfort. Rather
expensive.
Prices higher in
April and May
than in high summer.
Breakfast included.*
1,125,000 TL

DIVAN
Cumhuriyet Cad. n° 2
Tel. 2 31 41 00
Fax 2 48 85 27.
*Comfort is a priority:
very spacious rooms
double glazing, doors
locked by magnetic
cards, marble
bathrooms, satellite TV.*
2,025,000 TL

ERESIN
Topçu Cad. n° 34
Tel. 2 56 04 88
Fax 2 53 22 47.
*Bright rooms with air-
conditioning, mini-bar,
and satellite TV. Large
conference room in
basement.
Breakfast included.*
1,125,000 TL

GOLDEN AGE
Topçu Cad. n° 22
Tel. 2 54 49 06
Fax 2 55 13 68.
*Hotel offers videos,
hammam, jacuzzi, and
even a barber.
Breakfast included.
Service sometimes*

over-the-top.
1,125,000 TL

HILTON
Cumhuriyet Cad. n° 2
Harbiye
Tel. 2 31 46 50
Fax 2 40 41 65.
*Hotel complex with 498
rooms, 4 restaurants,
shops, 5 tennis and
squash courts, casino,
etc. Breakfast extra.*

2,453,000 TL

KERVANSARAY
Şehit Muhtar Cad. n° 61
Tel. 2 35 50 00
Fax 2 53 43 78.
*Fine 4-star hotel, new
and clean, in center of
Beyoğlu. Particular care
devoted to décor and
comfort (satellite TV,
hair drier, laundry).*
1,407,000 TL

LAMARTINE
Lamartin Cad. n° 25
Tel. 2 54 62 70
Fax 2 56 27 76.
*All-marble hall. Rooms
decorated simply but
comfortably. Good room
service. Breakfast
included.*
1,125,000 TL

LODGE
Meşrutiyet Cad.
n° 201-203
Tel. 2 44 58 44
Fax 2 43 65 00.
*Good rooms with
telephone, TV and bath.
View over Bosphorus
from hotel restaurant.
Breakfast included.*
563,000 TL

RIVA
Aydede Cad. n° 8
Tel. 2 56 44 20
Fax 2 56 20 33.
*Pleasant rooms with
satellite TV. Breakfast
included. Good prices
compared with
everything else in
Taksim.*
956,000 TL

SHERATON
Taksim Park.
Tel. 2 31 21 21
Fax 2 31 21 80.
*This hotel benefits from
the relative calm of
Taksim Square.
Spacious rooms, bars,
restaurants, pool,
casino. Pleasant stay
guaranteed.*
2,172,000 TL

STAR
Sağlik Sok. n° 11

Tel. 2 45 00 50
Fax 2 51 78 22.
*Rather kitsch place
but very comfortable.
Quite large rooms (with
showers) at good
prices. Breakfast
included. Bar.*
360,000 TL

USTA
Topçu Cad. n° 19
Tel. 2 35 10 00
Fax 2 54 75 95.
*Comfortable rooms with
shower, air-
conditioning, satellite
TV. Breakfast included.
Garage located right
opposite hotel.*
506,000 TL

NIGHT LIFE

CLUB 33
Cumhuriyet Cad. n° 18
Tel. 2 47 59 22
Open 10.30pm–3am.
*Well-known
discotheque but
clientèle a bit
disreputable. Rather
expensive and very
touristy.*

CHMOND HOTEL   **ISTANBUL SÜPER RESTAURANT**   GOLDEN AGE, RIVA, LAMARTINE, USTA, AVRUPA, ERESIN   **SWISS PUB RESTAURANT**   DILSON HOTEL, MARMARA   **PARK RESTAURANT**   STAR HOTEL

CUMHURIYET MEYD. — ISTIKLAL CAD. — TAKSIM — MECLIS-I MEBUSAN CAD.

HACI BABA RESTAURANT, YUVA-PUB, FLAMINGO, RENDEZ-VOUS, ÇIN LO KANTASI, FILIBELI

DESPINA MIN YERI
Açikyol Sok. n° 6
Tel. 2 43 33 57
Open 12pm–12.30am.
Pleasant inn frequented by both Turkish and tourist clientèle.

DISCO 2000
Sheraton Hotel
Taksim Square
Tel. 2 48 90 00
Open 10pm–4am.
International disco.

KERVANSARAY
Cumhuriyet Cad. n° 30
(not far from Hilton)
Tel. 2 47 16 30
Open 8pm–12.30am.
Adults will feel out of place. Two belly-dance shows per evening.

ÜSKÜDAR

CULTURE

FLORENCE NIGHTINGALE MUSEUM
Selimiye Kişla Cad.
Selimiye
Tel. 3 43 73 10.

ATIKVALIDE MOSQUE
Valide Imaret Sok.
Üsküdar.

ÇINILI MOSQUE
Valide Imaret Sok.

MIHRIMAH MOSQUE
Üsküdar.
Built 1547 by Mimar

Sinan. Mausoleum behind mosque and fountain in front.

SEMSI AHMET PAŞA MOSQUE
Sahil Yolu Cad.

YENIVALIDE MOSQUE
Hakimiyeti Milliye Cad.

RESTAURANTS

KANAAT
Selmanipak Cad. n° 25
Tel. 3 33 37 91
Open
10.30am–10.30pm.
56,000 TL

ACCOMMODATION

EMEK
Ahmediye, Gündoğumu
Cad. n° 7
Tel. 3 34 34 29.
Acceptable hotel within

◆ THE GALATA TOWER ◆

Over the centuries the tower has been the symbol of the European side of Istanbul.

its category. Rooms quite big and bathrooms adequate. Breakfast will cost extra.
112,000 TL

PRINCES' ISLANDS

RESTAURANTS

KAPTAN RESTAURANT
Liman Çıkmazı Sok.
n° 11A
Büyükada
Tel. 3 82 34 16
Open 10am–midnight.
On promenade of main island near ferry dock. Superb view. Warm welcome. Specialty: turbot.
157,000 TL

YÖRÜK ALI RESTAURANT
Leave main village of Büyükada, take coast road following the coaches (on right). After first headland, next to beach.
Tel. 3 82 74 54
Open 10am–midnight.
Difficult to find, in middle of bathing resort. Worth seeing because of impressive colors of décor. Food adequate. Clean and cheap. Specialties: sole, chicken.
112,0000 TL

ACCOMMODATION

PRINCESS
Iskele Meydanı n° 2
Büyükada
Tel. 3 82 16 28
Fax 3 82 19 49
Closed Oct. to May.
All the services of a luxury hotel: restaurant, pool, bar, discotheque, casino, playroom. In the

375

ATIK VALIDE KÜLLIYE — PRINCES' ISLANDS — İSKELE CAMİ'İ — EMEK HOTEL — ÜSKÜDAR İSKELESİ

HALK CAD.

HAKİMİYET İ MİLLİYE CAD.

YENİ DÜNYA

---

magical setting of the Princes' Islands.
1,238,000 TL

🏛 🏠 📞 ⛷ 🔲 🛏
✂ 🖼

SPLENDID PALACE
Nisan Cad. n° 71
Büyükada
Tel. 3 82 69 50
Fax 3 82 67 75
Closed Oct. to May.
This majestic white building, crowned by two cupolas, has all the charm of an old building and the comfort of a modern hotel. Good pool and pleasant view.
1,013,000 TL

🏛 🏠 📞 ⛷ 🛏 ✂
🖼

YÖRÜK ALI
Yörük Ali Turistik
Tesisleri
Tel. 3 82 73 94
Closed from Sept. to May.
Modest rooms in bungalows set out in a garden beside the sea, each with kitchen area.

Access to the hotel's private beach.
450,000 TL

🏠 📞 🔲 ✂ 🖼

ASIAN SHORE OF THE BOSPHORUS
CULTURE

BEYLERBEYI PALACE
Abdullah Ağa Cad.
Beylerbey
Tel. 3 21 93 20
Open 9.30am–4pm.
Closed Mon. and Tues.
Summer palace of the sultan Abdülaziz dating from 1865.

KÜÇÜKSU PALACE
Küçüksu
Tel. 35 23 03
Open 9am–4.30pm.
Closed Mon. and Thurs.
Small palace in rococco style on Asian shore.

RESTAURANTS

ALBORAN RESTAURANT
Hisar Cad. n° 5 A/1

Kanlıca
Tel. 3 32 03 78
Open noon–midnight.
Well-run restaurant in Kanlıca, which is known as the Turkish capital of yogurt. Friendly owner and well presented food. Specialties: roast lamb, Cantonese rice.
101,000 TL

🌑 🖼

BOĞAZIÇI
Fevzi Paşa Cad. n° 3/1
Beykoz
Tel. 3 23 54 37
Open 9am–midnight.
In Beykoz, charming little town on Asian shore of the Bosphorus. Slightly faded interior but good terrace and fresh fish.
146,000 TL

🌑 🖼 ⛷

ÇAMLICA CAFÉ-RESTAURANT
Sefa Tepesi
Çamlıca
Tel. 3 29 81 91
Open 9am–midnight.
146,000 TL

🖼 ⛷

HIDIV RESTAURANT
Hidiv Kasrı
Çubuklu, small village on Bosphorus
Tel. 3 31 26 51
Open 8am–midnight.
Superb restaurant classed as historic monument. Hidden away in splendid grounds. Unique setting. Also hotel. Specialty: steak in mushroom sauce.
146,000 TL

🍷 🖼 ⛷ 🅿

KAVAK DOĞANAY RESTAURANT
Yalı Cad. n° 13
Anadolu Kavağı
Tel. 3 20 20 36
Open 9am–midnight.
Best sign on the Anadolu Kavağı promenade. Discreet service. All kinds of fish. Specialty: hot shrimps.
90,000 TL

🌑 🖼 ⛷

YOSUN RESTAURANT
İskele Meydanı n° 1
Anadolu Kavağı
Tel. 3 20 21 48
Open noon–midnight.
Right next to dock for the village, one of the pearls on the Asian shore of the

376

ŞEMSI AMHET PAŞA CAMİİ

ATATÜRK MUSEUM

Halaskargazi Cad. n° 250 Şişli
Tel. 2 40 63 19
Open 10am–noon, 2pm–4.30pm.
Closed Sun., Thurs. and holidays.
*House where Atatürk lived before war of independence.
His own furniture, photos and*

RUMELI HISARI MUSEUM

Between Emirgan and Bebek
(Bosphorus)

Tel. 2 61 42 98
Open noon–4pm.
Closed Mon. and Tues.
Works by Turkish and foreign artists, exhibition of folklore-inspired works, some ceramics.

looking out over Bosphorus.

DOLMABAHÇE PALACE

Dolmabahçe Meydanı
Tel. 2 58 55 44
Open 9am–3pm.
Closed Mon., Thurs.

Dating from 1853, houses fine collection of paintings and 36 chandeliers of great value.

IHLAMUR PALACE

Ihlamur
Beşiktaş
Tel. 2 61 29 91
Open 9.30am–5pm.
Imperial palace set in beautiful garden.

MASLAK PALACE

Maslak
Tel. 2 76 10 22
Open 9.30am–5pm.
Small hunting pavilion of the sultan.

YILDIZ PALACE

Çiragan Cad.
Yıldız Parkı, Ortaköy
Tel. 2 60 80 60
Open 9am–6pm.
Being restored. Former residence of the sultans. Grounds and outbuildings of palace cover 40 acres. Almost 10,000 people lived in this complex of pavilions.

SINAN PAŞA MOSQUE

Beşiktaş Cad.
(opposite Marine Museum).

ŞBAĞİ CAD.

DOĞANCILAR CAD.

*Bosphorus. Very large, bright and clean room.
Specialties: stuffed mussels, prawns.
112,000 TL*

ACCOMMODATION

HIDIV

Çubuklu (on way out of village, take road to right)
Tel. 3 31 26 51
Fax 3 22 34 34.
*In large grounds the magnificent palace of the last khediv of Egypt welcomes you in a splendid period setting.
Wondrous outlandish decoration.
1,609,000 TL*

EUROPEAN SHORE OF THE BOSPHORUS

CULTURE

ASIYAN MUSEUM

Asiyan Yokuşu
Bebek
Tel. 2 63 69 86
Open 9.30am–noon
1–7pm.
Closed Mon., Thurs. and holidays.
In the house of Tevfik Fikret, famous Turkish poet of 19th century.

other belongings are on show.

MARINE MUSEUM (DENIZ MÜZESI)

Cezayir Cad.
Tel. 2 61 00 40
Open 9.30am–5pm.
Closed Mon. and Tues.

ISTANBUL MUSEUM OF PAINTING AND SCULPTURE

Ground floor of Dolmabahçe Palace
Beşiktaş

Tel. 2 63 53 05
Open 9.30am–5pm.
Closed Mon.
The sultan Mehmet the Conqueror built this fortress in 1452.

SADBERK HANIM MUSEUM

Piyasa Cad. n° 25-29
Büyükdere
Tel. 2 42 38 13
Open 10am–5.30pm.
Closed Wed.
Collection of Turkish works of art in old Turkish house

RESTAURANTS

BEYAZ PARK RESTAURANT

Çayir Başi Cad. n° 74
Sariyer
Tel. 2 42 65 51
Open noon to 5pm
7pm–2am.
*Set menu at 202,000TL with various kinds of fish and crustaceans.
Pleasant spot.
Specialty: smoked fish.
67,000–180,000TL*

BRASSERIE OF THE ÇIRAGAN PALACE

Çiragan Cad. n° 84

◆ BURGAZ ISLANDS ◆

This is one of the Princes' Islands.

Beşiktaş
Tel. 2 58 33 77
Open noon–3pm
7pm–10.30pm.
On the shores of the Bosphorus in the grand setting of a restored former palace. Sumptuous and varied buffet permits gourmets to sample specialties at reasonable price.
304,000 TL
⓾ ▭ ⩴ ⌘ P

ÇIFTNAL
Yenimahalle, Ihlamur
Yolu n° 6
Beşiktaş
Tel. 2 61 31 29
Open noon–midnight
112,000 TL
▭

DENIZ PARK GAZINOSU
Daire Sok. n° 9
Yeniköy
Tel. 2 62 04 15
Open noon–11pm.
Closed in Feb.
Floating restaurant, difficult to find but definitely best in Yeniköy. Terrace with unbeatable view over Bosphorus. Specialties: squid, shrimps.
101,000 TL
◑ ⩴

ECE BAR
Kamacı Sok. n° 10
Arnavutköy
Tel. 2 65 96 01
Open noon–midnight.
Closed Sun.
214,000 TL
▭

FELICITAS
Cevdet Paşa Cad. n° 343
Bebek
Tel. 2 63 14 39
Open 1noon to 5pm
6pm–2am.
Bar-restaurant run by German woman Restaurant offers two 66,000 TL menus comprising meats and salads. Average price
146,000 TL
◯ ▭ P

FILIZ RESTAURANT
Port of Tarabya
Tel. 2 62 01 52
Open 7am–midnight.
Best-known restaurant in Tarabya. Fine wooden house on marina. Excellent fish. Good by any standards. Specialties: fillets, squid, shrimp.
146,000TL
⓾ ▭ ⩴

HAN RESTAURANT
Yahya Kemal Cad. n° 10
Rumelihisarı
Tel. 2 65 29 68
Open noon–midnight.
Right next to Rumeli Hisarı fortified castle of Mehmet II. Very good light meals. Renowned for the huge tree in the middle of the restaurant! Specialties: fish balls, soups.
90,000 TL
⓾ ▭ ⩴

HANEDAN
Motor Iskelesi Yanı
Beşiktaş
Tel. 2 61 49 82
Open noon–11pm.
112,000 TL
▭ ⩴

PALET 2
Yeniköy Cad. n° 80
Tarabya
Tel. 2 62 70 70
Open noon–midnight.
Famous floating restaurant. Pleasant atmosphere.Good choice of alcoholic drinks, which is rare. Specialties: lüfer (blue fish), turbot.
146,000 TL
⓾ ▭ ⩴

YENI BEBEK
Cevdet Paşa Cad. n° 123
Bebek
Tel. 2 63 34 47
Open 11am–midnight.
First-class service. Recommended for its turbot. Specialties: turbot, lüfer (blue fish).
214,000 TL
◑ ▭ ⩴

YILDIZLAR RESTAURANT
Kefeliköy Cad. n° 62-64
Tarabya
Tel. 2 62 33 98
Open noon–midnight.
Turks celebrate marriages of their offspring here. Fine Ottoman fountain and splendid view over port. Spacious room. Specialties: turbot, lüfer (blue fish).
146,000 TL
◑ ▭ ⩴

ACCOMMODATION

BEBEK
Cevdet Paşa Cad. n° 113–115
Bebek
Tel. 2 63 30 00
Fax 2 63 26 36.
Average comfort and simple décor but rooms are big. Choose it for view over Bosphorus and picturesque setting of fishing village. Breakfast included.
563,000–788,000 TL
🏠 ⌂ ⩴ ☐ ⌘ 🚗 ▭

BÜYÜK TARABYA
Kefeliköy Cad.
Tarabya
Tel. 2 62 10 00
Located in one of the most pleasant villages on the European shore, a high quality hotel most of whose rooms have a magnificent view over the Bosphorus. Breakfast included.
1,159,000 TL
🏠 ⩴ ☐ ⌂ ⌘ ▭

ÇIRAGAN PALACE
Çiragan Cad. n° 84
Beşiktaş
Tel. 2 58 33 77
Fax 2 59 66 87.
Former sultan's palace, totally restored. Now the most luxurious hotel in Istanbul. Has been used in the past by presidents, notably Mitterrand and Bush. Superb garden overlooking Bosphorus.
3,038,000 TL
🏛 ⌂ ⌸ ⩴ ☐ ⌂ ⌘ 🚗 ▭

FUAT PAŞA
Çayırbaşı Cad. n° 238
Büyükdere
Tel. 2 42 98 60
Fax 2 42 95 89.
Hotel in a fine 18th-century Ottoman house, all pink and green. A large internal courtyard is reached

MLICA: CAFÉ
AMLICA

BEYLERBEYI

BEBEK: BEBEK HOTEL
YENI BEBEK

RUMELI HISARI: HAN

BUYUKDERE:
FUAT PASA HOTEL
SARIYER: BEYAZ
PARK RESTAURANT

TARABYA: PALET 2,
YILDIZLAR

KANLICA:
ALBORAN

ÇUBUKLU: HÔTEL
RESTAURANT KHEDIVE

BEYKOZ:
BOGAZIÇI

ANADOLU KAVAGI:
YOSUN RESTAURANT

and has advantage of being a long way from the road.
☼

by an imposing staircase. Rooms overlooking the yard are quieter.
1,125,000 TL
🏠 📺 ☼ 📷 🚗
📺

BARS

BAR OF THE HOTEL BEBEK
Cevdet Paşa Cad.
n° 113-115
Bebek
Tel. 1 63 30 00
Open 10am–10pm.
A Proustian atmosphere pervades this extraordinarily relaxing place.Its terrace overlooks the marina

---

◆ **BÜYÜKADA** ◆
This is a very busy holiday resort in summer.

Open 11am–8.30pm.
79,000 TL
📺

ISKENDER KEBABÇI
Atatürk Cad. n° 60
Tel. 21 10 76
Open 11am–5pm.
As name indicates, specialty is iskender kebab.
56,000 TL

ŞEHIR LOKANTASI
Inebey Cad. n° 85
Tel. 22 62 03
Open 7am–9pm.
Closed Sunday
45,000 TL

SEZEN RESTAURANT
Hamamlar Cad. n° 37
Çekirge
Tel. 36 91 56
Open 11am–midnight.
45,000 TL

ACCOMMODATION

ÇELIK PALACE
Çekirge Cad. n° 79
Tel. 35 35 00
Fax 36 19 10.
In western suburb of Çekirge, very high

quality hotel. Breakfast costs 338,000 TL extra.
1,069,000 TL

🏠 🖳 🛋 🖵

DIKMEN
Maksem Cad. 78
Tel. 24 18 40
Fax 24 18 44.
In town center. Shower costs 78,000 TL extra and breakfast 27,000 TL extra.
450,0000 TL

🏠 🖳 🚗

DILMEN
1 Murat Cad. n° 20
Çekirge
Tel. 36 61 14
Fax 35 25 68.
In western suburb of Çekirge. Extra 124,000 TL for room with view over valley. Breakfast included.
990,000 TL

🏠 🖳 🚗 🖵

ACCOMMODATION

BALTA
Talatpaşa Asfaltı n° 97

Tel. 18 15 52 10
Fax 18 15 35 29.
259,000 TL

🏠 🖳 ⚡ 🚫 🚗

YENER
Demirciler Cad. n° 1
Kesan
Tel. 18 44 36 60
Fax 18 44 57 55.
Breakfast included but 28,000 TL extra for TV.
247,000 TL

🏠 🖳 🚫 🚗

RESTAURANTS

BALIKÇI RESTAURANT
Göl Kıyısı
Tel. 25 27 11 52.
Fish restaurant.
112,000 TL

◑ ⚡

KIRIKÇATAL RESTAURANT
Göl Kıyısı
Tel. 25 27 15 76.
Near lake in a quiet isolated spot. Good fish restaurant.
90,000 TL

◑ ⚡

◆ ULU CAMI ◆

The fountain in the great mosque at Bursa.

APPENDICES

BIBLIOGRAPHY

ESSENTIAL
♦ READING ♦

♦ FREELY (J.): *Istanbul (Blue Guide)*, London and New York, 1987.
♦ HAUSSIG (H.W.): *Byzantine Civilization* (trans. J. Hussey), London, 1971.
♦ KINROSS (J.B. Lord): *The Ottoman Centuries, the Rise and Fall of the Turkish Empire*, London, 1977.
♦ NORWICH (J.J.): *Byzantium, the Early Centuries*, London 1988 *Byzantium, the Apogee*, London, 1991.
♦ SUMNER-BOYD (H.) and FREELY (J.): *Strolling through Istanbul, a Guide to the City*, Istanbul, 1973.

♦ GENERAL ♦

♦ AMICIS (E. de): *Constantinople* (trans. C. Tilton), London, 1878.
♦ BUTLER (R.): *City Breaks in Istanbul*, London, 1991.
♦ CRAWFORD (F. MARION) *Constantinople*, New York, 1895.
♦ DWIGHT (H.G.): *Constantinople Old and New*, New York, 1915.
♦ EKREM, (Selma), *Turkey Old and New*, New York, 1967
♦ FREELY (J.): *The Companion Guide to Turkey*, London, 1979.
♦ HÖFER (H.): *Istanbul (City Insight Guides)*, Istanbul, 1991.
♦ JACOBS (D.): *Constantinople, City on the Golden Horn*, New York, 1969.
♦ KELLY (L.): *Istanbul, a Traveller's Companion*, London, 1987.
♦ LEWIS (J.F.): *Illustrations of Constantinople*, London, 1835–6.
♦ MACLAGAN (M.): *The City of Constantinople*, London, 1968.
♦ PARDOE (J.): *The Beauties of the Bosphorus*, London, 1861.
♦ PENZER (N.M.): *The Harem*, London, 1965.
♦ RICE (D. Talbot): *Constantinople; Byzantium; Istanbul*, London, 1965.
♦ YOUNG (G.): *Constantinople*, London, 1926.

BYZANTINE
♦ HISTORY ♦

♦ ANNA COMNENA: *The Alexiad* (trans. E.R.A. Sewter), London, 1969.
♦ BARKER (J.W.): *Justinian and the Later Roman Empire*, Madison, Wis.,1960.
♦ BROWNING (R.): *The Byzantine Empire*, London, 1980; *Justinian and Theodora*, London, 1971.
♦ DE CLARI (R.): *The Conquest of Constantinople* (trans. E.H. McNeal), New York, 1936.
♦ DIEHL (C.): *Byzantine Empresses* (trans H. Bell and T. de Kerpely), London, 1964.
♦ FINLAY (G.): *A History of the Byzantine Empire*, London, 1854.
♦ GRABAR (A.): *Byzantium, from the Death of Theodosius To the Rise of Islam* London, 1967.
♦ HUSSEY (J.) (ed): *The Byzantine Empire (Cambridge Medieval History, Volume IV)*, Cambridge, 1966–7; *The Byzantine World*, London, 1957.
♦ JENKINS (R.): *Byzantium, the Imperial Centuries*, London, 1966.
♦ JONES (A.H.M.): *Constantine and the Conversion of Europe*, New York, 1962.
♦ MICHAEL PSELLUS: *Fourteen Byzantine Rulers (Chronographia)*, (trans. E.R.A. Sewter), Harmondsworth, 1966.
♦ OSTROGORSKY (G.): *History of the Byzantine State* (trans. J. Hussey), Oxford, 1956.
♦ PROCOPIUS: *The Secret History* (trans. R. Atwater), Ann Arbor, 1967.
♦ RUNCIMAN (S.): *The Fall of Constantinople*, Cambridge, 1969.
♦ URE (P.N.): *Justinian and his Age*, Harmondsworth, 1951.
♦ VASILIEV (A.A.): *History of the Byzantine Empire* (trans. S. Ragozin), Madison, Wis., 1928, and Oxford, 1952; *Justin the First. An Introduction to the Epoch of Justinian the Great*, Cambridge, Mass., 1950.
♦ VILLEHARDOUIN (G. de): *The Conquest of Constantinople* (trans. F. Marzials), London, 1908.

OTTOMAN
♦ HISTORY ♦

♦ ALDERSON (A.D.): *The Structure of the Ottoman Dynasty*, Oxford, 1956.
♦ BABINGER (F.): *Mehemed the Conqueror and his Time* (trans. R. Mannheim), Princeton, 1978.
♦ EVLIYA ÇELEBI EFFENDI: *Narrative of Travels in Europe, Asia and Africa* (trans. J. von Hammer-Purgstall), London, 1834.
♦ HORNBY, Lady: *Constantinople during the Crimean War*, London, 1863.
♦ INALÇIK (H.): *The Ottoman Empire, The Classical Age, 1300–1600* (trans. N. Itzkowitz and C. Imber), London, 1973.
♦ KRITOVOULOS (M.): *History of Mehmed the Conqueror* (trans. C.T. Riggs), Princeton, 1954.
♦ SHAW (S.J.): *Between Old and New, the Ottoman Empire under Selim III*, Cambridge, Mass., 1971.
♦ SHAW (S.S. and E.K.): *History of the Ottoman Empire and Modern Turkey*, Cambridge, Mass., 1976–77.
♦ WITTEK (P.): *The Rise of the Ottoman Empire*, London, 1938.

BYZANTINE
ARCHITECTURE
♦ AND ART ♦

♦ GRABAR (A.): *From Theodosius to Islam*, London, 1966.
♦ HAMILTON (J.A.): *Byzantine Architecture and Decoration*, London and New York, 1934.
♦ KINROSS (J.B. Lord.): *Hagia Sophia*, London, 1973.
♦ KRAUTHEIMER (R.): *Early Christian and Byzantine Architecture*, Harmondsworth, 1965.
♦ LEACROFT (H.): *The Buildings of Byzantium*, London, 1977.
♦ LETHABY (C.) and SWAINSON (H.): *Santa Sophia Constantinople: A Study of Byzantine Building*, London, 1894.
♦ MAINSTONE (R.J.): *Hagia Sophia: Architecture, Structure and Liturgy of Justinian's Great Church*, London, 1988.
♦ MANGO (C.): *Byzantine Architecture*, London, 1979.
♦ MATHEWS (T.F.): *The Byzantine Churches of Istanbul*, Pennsylvania State University, 1976.
♦ MILLINGEN (A. van): *Byzantine Constantinople: the Walls of the City*, London, 1899; *Byzantine Churches in Constantinople, their History and Architecture*, London, 1912.
♦ RICE (D. Talbot): *The Art of Byzantium*, London, 1959; *The Great Palace of the Byzantine Emperors*, Oxford, 1947–58.
♦ WITTEMORE (T.): *The Mosaics of Haghia Sophia at Istanbul*, Oxford, 1933–52.

OTTOMAN
ARCHITECTURE
♦ AND ART ♦

♦ CAGMAN (T.) and TANINIDI (Z.): *The Topkapı Saray Museum: The Albums and Illustrated Manuscripts* (trans. J.M. Rogers), London, 1986
♦ ÇIĞ (K.): *Treasury: Guide, Topkapı Palace Museum*, Istanbul, 1966.
♦ ETTINGHAUSEN (R.): *Turkey: Ancient Miniatures*, UNESCO, 1954.
♦ FREELY (J.) AND BURRELL (A.R.): *Sinan: Architect of Suleyman the Magnificent and the Ottoman Golden Age*, London, 1992.
♦ GOODWIN (G.): *A History of Ottoman Architecture*, London, 1971.
♦ GOODWIN (G.): *Sinan*, London, 1993.
♦ KOSEOGLU (C.): *The Topkapı Saray Museum: The Treasury* (trans. J.M. Rogers), London, 1987.
♦ STRATTON (Arthur), *Sinan*, New York, 1972
♦ VOGT-GÖKNIL (U.): *Living Architecture: Ottoman*, London, 1966.

RELIGION
♦ CHRISTIAN ♦

♦ HUSSEY (J.): *The Orthodox Church in the Byzantine Empire*, London, 1986.
♦ STANLEY (A.P.): *The Eastern Church*, London, 1861.

RELIGION
♦ ISLAM ♦

♦ ARBERRY (A.J.): *The Koran Interpreted*, Oxford, 1964.
♦ GUILLAUME (A.): *Islam*, Harmondsworth, 1956.

◆ LITERATURE ◆

BLANCH (L.): *Pavilions of the Heart*, London, 1974.

BYRON (Lord): *Letters and Journals, Vol I, 'In My Hot Youth'*, London, 1973.

CARLISLE (Earl of): *Diary in Turkish and Greek Waters*, London, 1854.

CHANDER (R.): *Travels in Asia Minor*, London, 1776.

COLTON (W.): *A Visit to Constantinople and Athens*, New York, 1836.

DOLLOWAY (J.): *Constantinople, Ancient and Modern*, London, 1797.

ELIOT (T.): *Diary of an Idle Woman in Constantinople*, London, 1893.

GRAVES (R.): *Count Belisarius*, London, 1955.

HAYES (B.): *Midnight Express*, London, 1977.

HOBHOUSE (J.C.): *A Journey through Albania ... to Constantinople during the years 1809 and 1810*, London, 1813.

LOTI (P.): *Constantinople (Aziyadé)* (trans. M. Lowrie), London, 1927

MACAULAY (R.): *The Towers of Trevizond*, London, 1956.

MONTAGU (Lady Mary Wortley): *Letters*, London, 1763 (many later editions).

◆ TRADITIONS ◆

◆ ATAZOY (Nurhan) and RABY (Julian), Petsopoulos (Yanni) (ed.) *Iznik, the Pottery of Ottoman Turkey*, London, 1989.

◆ BALPINER (Beluis) and PETSOLPOULOS (Yanni), *100 Kilims, Masterpieces from Anatolia*, London, 1991.

◆ BEKTAS (C.): *Living in Turkey*, London, 1992.

◆ DWIGHT (H.G.): *Constantinople, Settings and Traits*, London, 1927.

◆ GARNETT (L.M.J.): *Turkish Life in Town and Country*, London, 1904.

◆ HUBBARD (G.E.): *The Day of the Crescent: Glimpses of Old Turkey*, Cambridge, 1920.

◆ HULL (A.) and BARNARD (N.): *Living with Kilims*, London, 1988.

◆ LEWIS (R.): *Everyday Life in Ottoman Turkey*, London, 1971.

◆ ORGA (I.): *Portrait of a Turkish Family*, London, 1950.

◆ PARDOE (J.): *The City of the Sultan and Domestic Manners of the Turks in 1836* London, 1838.

◆ PEARS (E.): *Forty Years in Constantinople* London, 1916.

◆ PETSOPOULOS (Yanni), *Kilims*, Fribourg, 1979; *Tulips, Arabesques and Turbans*, London, 1982

◆ SPRY (W.J.J.): *Life on the Bosphorus*, London, 1895.

◆ COOKING ◆

◆ EDMONDS (A.G.) (ed.): *Cooking in Turkey*, Istanbul, 1986.

◆ HALACI (N.): *Nevin Halaci's Turkish Cookbook*, London, 1989.

◆ HAROUTUNIAN (A. der): *A Turkish Cookbook*, London, 1987.

◆ YAYINLARJ (A.): *The Turkish Kitchen*, Istanbul, 1988.

◆ YAYINLARJ (M.): *The FamousTurkish Cookery*, Istanbul, 1988.

We would like to thank the following publishers or copyright-holders for permission to reproduce the quotations on pages 97–120.

◆ ARTHUR STRATTON, *Sinan*, 1972. US Charles Scribner's & Sons.

◆ W.B.YEATS, *"Sailing to Byzantium"* from *Collected Poems*. UK Everyman's Library. US Macmillan Publishing Co.

◆ LORD KINROSS, INTRODUCTION TO *Turkey*, ed. Robert Mantran, 1959. UK and US Thames & Hudson.

◆ MICHEL BUTOR, *The Spirit of Mediterranean Places*, 1986, translated by Lydia Davis. UK and US Marlboro Press.

◆ ROSE MACAULAY, *The Towers of Trebizond*, 1956. US Carroll & Graf Publishers.

◆ LATIFE TEKIN, *From the Garbage Hills*, 1993. UK and US Marion Boyars Publishers.

◆ VIRGINIA WOOLF, *Orlando*, 1928. UKHogarth Press. US Harcourt, Brace & Co.

◆ CHARLIE CHAPLIN, *My Autobiography*, 1964. UK & US Bodley Head.

◆ SELMA EKREM, *Turkey Old and New*, 1967. UK and US Charles Scribner's & Sons.

◆ GRAHAM GREENE, *Stamboul Train*, 1932. UK Heinemann. US Viking.

◆ List of illustrations

atih district. Photo
idem.
73 Süleymaniye
Cami'i at night. Photo
Ara Güler.
75 Galata Tower,
postcard. EDM coll.
77 Burgaz Ada
(island). Photo H.
Özözlü.
79 Büyük Ada
(island). Photo idem.
80 Fountain of Ulu
Cami, Bursa. Photo Ara
Güler.

Maps of itineraries
Pierre-Xavier Grézaud,
assisted by Jean-
François Binet, Philippe
Pradel and Samuel
Tranlé.

D. T. P. Maps
Samuel Tranlé
Jean-Michel Belmer.

Diagrams
Emmanuel Calami: 340-
343, 345, 347

Illustrators
François Brosse: Back
cover, 73 to 88.
Kaya Dinçer: 276, 277,
280, 281, 282, 284, 286,
288, 289.
Maurice Pommier: 341,
343, 344, 346, 347, 359
to 380.
Norbert Boussot: 46-48,
108, 184, 186, 220, 248,
251, 256, 260, 264, 270,
271, 272, 276, 327, 328,
336, 354.
Philippe Marchand:
110, 240, 267, 269.
Dimitri Botkine: 52, 61.

Abbreviations :
Coll.: Collection.

We have not been able
to trace the heirs or
publishers of certain
documents. An account
is being held open for
them at our offices.

◆ Glossary

◆ A ◆

AĞA: school teacher, lord, honorary title in the Turkish army.
ARASTA: covered street with shops; shopping mall.
AVLU: large square or courtyard in front of mosque.
AYAZMA: sacred fountain.

◆ B ◆

BAYRAM: festival.
BEDESTEN: structure in the middle of covered bazaar where objects of value are displayed and sold.
BENT: dam; water in reservoir.
BEY: governor of town or district (*beylicat*).
BEYLERBEY: "bey of beys", governor-general of province.

◆ C ◆

CAIQUE: small sail-boat with oars used on Bosphorus and Golden Horn till turn of century.
CAMEKAN: reception area and cloakroom (apodyterium) of a hammam.
CAMI: mosque with mimbar.
ÇARSI: market, bazaar.
ÇELEBI: Turkish gentleman.
ÇEŞME: fountain.
CUMHURIYET: Republic.

◆ D ◆

DARÜL'HADIS: Koranic college.
DARÜ'S SIFA: Ottoman hospital.
DERSHANE: amphitheater, lecture room in *medrese*.
DERVISH: member of religious brotherhood (Kalender, Mevlevi etc.).
DEVŞIRME: Christian child offered in tribute by family for enrolling in service of sultan.
DIVAN: Imperial Ottoman council; by extension, the Ottoman government generally.

◆ E ◆

EYVAN: vaulted or domed areas positioned round central chamber of mosque.

◆ F ◆

FIRMAN: edict of the sultan.

◆ G ◆

GRAND VIZIER: sort of prime minister of the Ottoman Empire.

◆ H ◆

HADIM: eunuch.
HALI: carpet with knot stitches.
HAMMAM: Turkish baths.
HAN: caravanserai, inn for merchants and their caravans.
HARARET: hot-water and steam-bathing room (*caldarium*) in hammam.
HAREM: section reserved for women in Ottoman houses and palaces.
HASEKI: the sultan's favorite.
HÉGIRE: Islamic calender with year 1 corresponding to 622 in Christian calender.
HISAR: Ottoman fortress.
HÜBTE: sermon given on Fridays in large mosques.
HÜNKA KASRI: lodge or gallery reserved for sultan in imperial mosque.
HÜCRE: student's study room in *medrese*.

◆ I ◆

IMAM: leader of prayers attached to a mosque.
IMARET: institution where meals are served free to the poor.

◆ J ◆

JANISSARY: member of the élite guard force serving the sultan.

◆ K ◆

KADIN: legitimate spouse of the sultan.
KALENDER: mendicant order of the wandering dervishes.
KAPI: gate.
KEMER: aqueduct.
KETHÜDA: steward, manager.
KIBLAH: at the rear of the prayer chamber in a mosque, the wall pointing perpendicularly towards Mecca.
KILIM: woven carpet.
KILISE: church.
KONAK: private Ottoman town house.
KÖPRU: bridge.
KÖŞK: Turkish summer-house or pavilion.
KÖY: village, hamlet.
KULE: tower.
KÜLLIYE: socio-religious precinct in a mosque comprising various public-utility establishments.
KURAN KÜRSÜ: pulpit where Koran is read.

◆ L ◆

LÂLE DEVRI: the age of the Tulips, reign of Ahmet III.

◆ M ◆

MEDRESE: establishment in a *külliye* which provides higher education.
MEKTEP: primary school.
MESCIT: small mosque without mimbar.
MEVLEVI: brotherhood of the wandering dervishes.
MIHRAB: in a mosque, a recess in the wall of the Kiblah.
MIMAR: architect.
MIMARBASI: chief architect.
MIMBAR: pulpit where the preacher stands during Friday sermon.
MINARET: tower from which the muezzin calls the people to prayer.
MUEZZIN: official in a mosque whose role is to call the faithful to prayer.

◆ N ◆

NARGHILE: pipe with long tube connected to flask where the smoke cools in contact with scented water; the tobacco burns in a small bowl above the water.

◆ O ◆

ODA: public or private room, chamber.
OSMANLI: Ottoman dynasty founded by Osman (13th century) which held power till 1923.

◆ P ◆

PAŞA: title given to high officials, governors and generals in Turkey.

◆ S ◆

ŞADIRVAN: ablutions fountain usually located in the courtyard of a mosque.
SARAY: Ottoman palace, harem.
SARNIÇ: water tank.
SEBIL: public fountain
SELAMLIK: area reserved for men in Ottoman houses and palaces.
ŞEREFE: balcony of a minaret.
SEHZADE: prince, son of sultan.
SOFA: raised platform ceremonial rostrum.
SOĞUKLUK: intermediate temperature bathing room (*tepidarium*) in hammam.
SUBLIME PORTE: entrance to the palace of the Grand Vizier; by extension, the Ottoman government in general.
SULTAN: sovereign of the Ottoman empire.
SULTANA: wife or daughter of sultan.
SUTERAZI: Turkish water tower.
SÜTUN: column.

◆ T ◆

TABHANE: hospice for wandering dervishes.
TEKKE: dervish monasteries.
TUĞRA: calligraphic signature of sultans attached to all official documents.
TÜRBE: Ottoman mausoleum.

◆ U ◆

ULU CAMI: Great Mosque, also called the mosque of Friday.

◆ V ◆

VALIDE SULTANE: sultan's mother, mother of reigning sultan.

◆ Y ◆

YALI: private town-house made of wood and built on edge of water.

◆ Z ◆

ZAVIYE: religious establishment to accommodate pilgrims and dervishes.

◆ Useful phrases ◆

WHAT TIME?: saat açta?

DO YOU SPEAK ENGLISH? : gilizce konusuyor usunuzi

ENJOY YOUR MEAL: afiyet sun

EXCUSE ME: özür dilerim

GOODBYE: iyi günler

GOOD EVENING: iyi akşamlar

GOOD HEALTH: şerefinize

GOODNIGHT: iyi geceler

HELLO (MORNINGS): ünaydin

HELLO: merhaba

HOW MUCH?: kaç?

HOW?: nasıl?

HOW ARE YOU?: asılsınız?

I'M LOOKING FOR: anyorum

I DON'T UNDERSTAND: nlamıyorum

I MUST GO: gitmeliyim

IS IT FAR?: uzak mi?

IS THERE? var mi?

NO: hayır

O.K.: tamam, peki

PLEASE REPEAT THAT: lütfen tekrar eder misiniz?

PLEASE: lütfen

PLEASED TO MEET YOU: nos bulduk

THERE IS: var

THERE IS NOT: yok

THINK NOTHING OF IT: rica ederim, birsey degil

THANKS: teşekkür ederim

THANKS A LOT: teşekkürler

WELCOME: hos geldiniz

WHEN? ne zaman?

WHERE..FROM?: nereden?

WHERE IS IT?: nerede?

WHERE..TO?: nereye?

WHICH? WHAT?: ne?

WHICH ONE?: hangi?

WHY? niçin, neden?

YES: evet

◆ Buying ◆

I WANT TO BUY THIS: bunu almak istiyorum

HOW MUCH IS THAT?: bu ne kadar?bu kaç lira?

TOO EXPENSIVE: çok pahali

CAN YOU LOWER THE PRICE?: fiyatı indirebilir misiniz?

HAVE YOU GOT SOMETHING CHEAPER?: daha ucuz bir şey yok mu?

I'LL TAKE THIS: bunu alıyorum

◆ Counting ◆

ONE: bir

TWO: iki

THREE: üç

FOUR: dört

FIVE: bes

SIX: alti

SEVEN: yedi

EIGHT: sekiz

NINE: doküz

TEN: on

ELEVEN: on bir

TWENTY: yirmi

THIRTY: otuz

FORTY: kirk

FIFTY: elli

SIXTY: altmiş

SEVENTY: yetmiş

EIGHTY: seksen

NINETY: doksan

HUNDRED: yüz

HUNDRED AND ONE: yüz bir

TWO HUNDRED: iki yüz

THOUSAND: bin

TWO THOUSAND: iki bin

◆ Times ◆

HALF: buçuk

HOUR: saat

NOON: öğle, güney

MIDNIGHT: gece yansi

MINUTE: dakika, müsvedde

QUARTER: çeyrek

WHAT TIME IS IT?: saat kaç?

SEVEN O'CLOCK: saat yedi

HALF PAST SEVEN: saat yedi buçuk

QUARTER PAST SEVEN: saat yedi çeyrek geçiyor

QUARTER TO SEVEN: saat yedi çeyrek var

◆ Days ◆

DAY: gün

MORNING: sabah

MIDDAY: öglede

AFTERNOON: ögleden sonra

EVENING: aksam

NIGHT: gece

MONDAY: pazartesi

TUESDAY: sali

WEDNESDAY: çarsamba

THURSDAY: persembe

FRIDAY: cuma

SATURDAY: cumartesi

SUNDAY: pazar

◆ Months ◆

MONTH: ay

JANUARY: ocak

FEBRUARY: subat

MARCH: mart

APRIL: nisan

MAY: mayis

JUNE: haziran

JULY: temmuz

AUGUST: agostos

SEPTEMBER: eylül

OCTOBER: ekim

NOVEMBER: kasim

DECEMBER: aralik

◆ A ◆

ACCEPT (TO): kabbul etmek

ACCIDENT: kaza

AIRPORT: havaalani

AIRPLANE: uçak

AIRLINES: hatlan

ALCOHOLIC DRINK: içki

ANCIENT MONUMENTS: eski eseler

ANTIQUARY: antikaci

APARTMENT: daire

APPETIZER: meze

AQUEDUCT: kemer

ARCHITECTURE: mimarî, mimarlik

ARRIVAL (TRAIN): varis

ART: sanat

AUTUMN: sonbahar

AVENUE: caddesi

◆ B ◆

BAD: kötü

BAKER: ekmekçi (dükkâni)

BANK: banka

BARGAINING (HAGGLING): pazarlik

BEAUTIFUL: güzel

BED: yatak

BILL: hesap, fatura

BLACK: siyah

BLOCK (OF APARTMENTS): apartman

BLUE: mavi

BOAT: gemi

Book: kitap

BOOKSHOP: kitabevi

BREAKFAST: kahvaltı

BUFFET: büfe

Bus: otobüs

BUS-STOP: durak

BUSY: mesgul

BUTCHER: kasap (dükkâni)

BUTTER: tereyag

BUY (TO): almak

◆ C ◆

CAKE: pasta

CANCEL (TO): iptal etmek

CAR: araba

CARPET: halı

CHANGE (coins): bozuk para

CHANGE (TO) (FOREIGN CURRENCY): bozdurmak

CHEAP: ucuz

CHECK: çek

CHEESE: peynir

CHESTNUT (brown): kahve rengi

CIGARETTE: sigara

CINNAMON: tarçın

CITY CENTER: sehir merkezi

CLOSED: kapali

COFFEE: kahve

COFFEE POT: cevze

COLD: soğuk

COLOR: renk

COOL: taze

COPPER: bakır

CRAFTSMEN: zanaat

CUSTOMS: gümrük

◆ D ◆

DARK (COLOUR): koyu

DATE: tarih

DEPARTURE (TRAINS): kalkis

DESSERT:tatli

DIFFICULT: zor

DINNER: aksam yemegi

DOCTOR: doktor

DOCK: iskele

DO, MAKE (TO): etmek, yapmak

DOOR: kapı

DOUBLE ROOM: iki oda

DRESSMAKER: terzi

DRIED FRUIT: kuru yemis

DRINK (TO): içmek

DRINK (NOUN): içecek

◆ E ◆

EAT (TO): yemek

EGG: yumurta

EMPLOYEE: memur

ENTER (TO): girmek

ENTRANCE: giriş

EXCHANGE BUREAU: kambiyo

EXPENSIVE: pahali

◆ F ◆

FAR: uzak

FASHIONABLE: moda olan gözde, çok tutulan

FERRY: vapur

FESTIVAL: beyram

FIG: incir

FINE: iyi

FLOWER: çiçek

FOOD: besin, yiyecek

FOREST: orman

FORK: çatal

FOUNTAIN: çeşme

FREE (NO CHARGE): ücretsiz, bedava

FREEWAY: otoban

FRITTER: kizarmis

FRONTIER: peynir

FRUIT: meyva

FRUIT JUICE: meyva suyu

FURNITURE: mobilya

◆ G ◆

GARAGE: garaj

GARDEN: bahçe

GASOLINE (PUMP): benzin (istasyonu)

GIRL: genç kşz

GO (TO): gitmek

GOLD: altın

GOOD: iyi

GREEN: yeşil

GROCER: bakkal (dükkâni)

GUEST: misafir, davetli

GUIDE: rehber, kılavuz

◆ H ◆

HALF: yarim

HANDKERCHIEF: mendil

HAVE (TO): sahip olmak, -i, var olmak

HEAR (TO): işitmek

HERE: burası, buraya, burada

HONEY: bal

HOSPITAL: hastane

HOT: sıcak

HOTEL: otel

HUNGRY (BE): acımak

◆ I ◆

ICE CUBES: buz

IDENTITY CARD: nüfus kağidi

ILL: hasta

INTERPRETER: tercüman

INVITE (TO): davet etmek

IVORY: fildişi

◆ USEFUL PHRASES

◆ J ◆

JADE: yeşim taşı
JAM: reçel
JASMINE: yasemin
JEWEL: mücevher

◆ K ◆

KEY: anahtar
KNIFE: bıçak

◆ L ◆

LAKE: göl
LAMB: kuzu
LARGE: büyük
LEATHER: deri
LETTER: mektup
LIGHT: isik
LIGHT (COLOUR): açık
LIGHTER: çakmak
LIVE (IN) (TO): oturmak
LOBSTER: istakoz
LONG: uzun
LOOK FOR (TO): aramak
LUGGAGE: bagaj
LUNCH: öğle yemeği

◆ M ◆

MADAM: bayan
MARBLE: mermer
MARKET: çarsı, pazar yeri
MASSAGE: uvuşturma
MATCH: kibrit
MEATBALL: köfte
MEDICINE: ilaç
MENU: menü, yemek listesi
MILK: süt
 (COFFEE WITH MILK: sütlü kahve)

MINIATURE: minyatür
MISTER: beyefendi
MISUNDERSTANDING: anlasmazık
MONUMENT: anit
MOSQUE: cami, mescit
MOUNTAIN: dağ
MUSEUM: müze

◆ N ◆

NAME (FIRST): isim, ad
NECESSARY: lazim
NEIGHBORHOOD: çevrede, etrafta, civarda
NEW: yeni
NEWSPAPER: gazete
NO: hayır
NOW: simdi, su anda

◆ O ◆

OCCUPIED: meşgul
OLD: eski
OLIVE: zeytin
ONION: sogan
ORANGE (COLOUR): turuncu
ORANGE JUICE: portakal suyu
ORCHESTRA: orkestra
OTTOMAN: osmanlı

◆ P ◆

PAYMENT: ödeme
PENCIL: kalem
PIECE: parça
PLATE: tabak
POSSIBLE: mümkün
POST OFFICE: postanen (büro)
PRESCRIPTION: reçete

◆ Q ◆

QUARTER: mahalle, semt
QUESTION (TO ASK A): soru (sormak)

◆ R ◆

RAMADAN: ramatan
RENTAL: kiralama, kira
ROOM: oda
ROOM WITH BATH: banyolu oda
ROUND TRIP: gidiş dönüş

◆ S ◆

SAY (TO): demek, söylemek
SEASON: mevsim
SEA: deniz
SEND (TO): göndermek
SHOP: magaza, dükkân
SHOWER: duş
SILVER: gümüs
SMOKE (TO): içmek
SPICES: baharat
SPOON: kaşik
SQUARE: meydan
STAMP: pul
STREET: sokak
STATION (railway): istasyon
STOP: durmak
SUMMER: yaz
SURNAME: soğadi

◆ T ◆

TALK TO (TO): -le görusmek
TAXI: taksi
TEA: çay

TELEPHONE: telefon
TOBACCONIST: tütüncü (dükkâni)
TODAY: bugün
TICKET: bilet
TIRED: yorgun
TOMORROW: yarin
TOOTHPASTE: diş macunu
TOURIST OFFICE: turizm bürosu
TRAIN: tren
TURKISH BATHS: hammarr

◆ U ◆

UNDERSTAND (TO): anlamak
URGENT: acele

◆ V ◆

VACANT: boş
VACCINE: asi

◆ W ◆

WAITER: garson
WATER: su
 (GLASS OF WATER: bardak su)
WATER PIPE: narghile
WHITE: beyaz
WICKET: gise
WINTER: kiş
WOMAN: kadin
WORK (OF ART): sanat eseri

◆ Y ◆

YEAR: yil, sene
YELLOW: sari
YES: evet
YESTERDAY: dün
YOUNG: genç

INDEX